THE DICTIONARY OF SPORTING CHAMPIONS

THE DICTIONARY OF SPORTING CHAMPIONS

2nd edition

IAN MORRISON

British Library Cataloguing in Publication Data
Morrison, Ian, 1947 –
   The dictionary of sporting champions. – 2nd ed.
   1. Sports, Encyclopaedias
   I. Title
   796'.03'21

   ISBN 0-7235-1224-8

CONTENTS

ABBREVIATIONS

ARG	Argentina	HOL	Holland	POL	Poland
AUS	Australia	HUN	Hungary	POR	Portugal
AUT	Austria	INA	Indonesia	PR	Puerto Rico
BAH	Bahamas	IND	India	RHO	Rhodesia
BAR	Barbados	IRE	Ireland	ROM	Romania
BEL	Belgium	IRN	Iran	SAF	South Africa
BER	Bermuda	ISR	Israel	SCO	Scotland
BOL	Bolivia	ITA	Italy	SIN	Singapore
BRA	Brazil	JAM	Jamaica	SKO	South Korea
BUL	Bulgaria	JAP	Japan	SPA	Spain
CAN	Canada	KEN	Kenya	SRI	Sri Lanka
CHI	Chile	LIE	Liechtenstein	SUR	Surinam
CHN	China	LUX	Luxembourg	SWE	Sweden
COL	Colombia	MAL	Malaya/Malaysia	SWI	Switzerland
CUB	Cuba	MEX	Mexico	TAN	Tanzania
DEN	Denmark	MTA	Malta	TCH	Czechoslovakia
DOM	Dominican Republic	NI	N. Ireland	THA	Thailand
EGY	Egypt	NIC	Nicaragua	TRI	Trinidad & Tobago
ENG	England	NIG	Nigeria	TUN	Tunisia
ETH	Ethiopia	NKO	North Korea	TUR	Turkey
FIN	Finland	NOR	Norway	UGA	Uganda
FRA	France	NZ	New Zealand	URU	Uruguay
FRG	West Germany	PAK	Pakistan	USA	United States
GB	Great Britain	PAN	Panama	USSR	Soviet Union
GDR	East Germany	PAR	Paraguay	VEN	Venezuela
GER	Germany	PER	Peru	VI	Virgin Islands
GHA	Ghana	PHI	Philippines	WAL	Wales
GRE	Greece	PNG	Papua New Guinea	YUG	Yugoslavia
				ZIM	Zimbabwe

American Football evolved from the English games of Association Football and Rugby in the latter part of the 19th century. It became popular in the colleges and the Intercollegiate Football Association was formed in 1876. The first professional game took place in 1895 but it was not until the formation of the American Professional Football Association in 1920 that it became an organised sport along similar lines to the present-day American Football League.

NATIONAL FOOTBALL LEAGUE CHAMPIONS
From 1921-32 there was just one league.

1921 Chicago Staleys
1922 Canton Bulldogs (Ohio)
1923 Canton Bulldogs (Ohio)
1924 Cleveland Bulldogs
1925 Chicago Cardinals
1926 Frankford Yellow Jackets
1927 New York Giants
1928 Providence Steamroller
1929 Green Bay Packers
1930 Green Bay Packers
1931 Green Bay Packers
1932 Chicago Bears

From 1933-49 the NFL was divided into Eastern and Western Divisions with the two winners playing off for the NFL Championship.

	Eastern Division	Western Division	Championship
1933	New York Giants	Chicago Bears	Bears 23 Giants 21
1934	New York Giants	Chicago Bears	Giants 30 Bears 13
1935	New York Giants	Detroit	Detroit 26 Giants 7
1936	Boston	Green Bay Packers	Green Bay 21 Boston 6
1937	Washington	Chicago Bears	Washington 28 Bears 21
1938	New York Giants	Green Bay Packers	Giants 23 Green Bay 17
1939	New York Giants	Green Bay Packers	Green Bay 27 Giants 0
1940	Washington	Chicago Bears	Bears 73 Washington 0
1941	New York Giants	Chicago Bears	Bears 37 Giants 9
1942	Washington	Chicago Bears	Washington 14 Bears 6
1943	Washington	Chicago Bears	Bears 41 Washington 21
1944	New York Giants	Green Bay Packers	Green Bay 14 Giants 7
1945	Washington	Cleveland	Cleveland 15 Washington 14
1946	New York Giants	Chicago Bears	Bears 24 Giants 14
1947	Philadelphia	Chicago Cardinals	Cardinals 28 Philadelphia 21
1948	Philadelphia	Chicago Cardinals	Philadelphia 7 Cardinals 0
1949	Philadelphia	Los Angeles	Philadelphia 14 Los Angeles 0

From 1950-52 the two divisions were known as the American and National Conferences.

	American Conference	National Conference	Championship
1950	Cleveland	Los Angeles	Cleveland 30 Los Angeles 28
1951	Cleveland	Los Angeles	Los Angeles 24 Cleveland 17
1952	Cleveland	Detroit	Detroit 17 Cleveland 7

	Eastern Conference	Western Conference	Championship
1953	Cleveland	Detroit	Detroit 17 Cleveland 16
1954	Cleveland	Detroit	Cleveland 56 Detroit 10
1955	Cleveland	Los Angeles	Cleveland 38 Los Angeles 14
1956	New York Giants	Chicago Bears	Giants 47 Bears 7
1957	Cleveland	Detroit	Detroit 59 Cleveland 14
1958	New York Giants	Baltimore	Baltimore 23 Giants 17
1959	New York Giants	Baltimore	Baltimore 31 Giants 16

The AFL was formed in 1960 with an Eastern and Western Division while the NFL still had its Eastern and Western Conferences. Both the AFL and NFL had end-of-season Championships.

AFL Championship	NFL Championship
1960 Houston 24 Los Angeles Chargers 16	Philadelphia 17 Green Bay Packers 13
1961 Houston 10 San Diego 3	Green Bay Packers 37 Giants 0
1962 Dallas Texans 20 Houston 17	Green Bay Packers 16 Giants 7
1963 San Diego 51 Boston 10	Chicago 14 Giants 10
1964 Buffalo 20 San Diego 7	Cleveland 27 Baltimore 0
1965 Buffalo 23 San Diego 0	Green Bay Packers 23 Cleveland 12
1966 Kansas City 31 Buffalo 7	Green Bay Packers 34 Dallas 27

(The Super Bowl was inaugurated in 1966 with the AFL and NFL Champions playing each other – full Super Bowl results appear on following page)

1967 Oakland 40 Houston 7	Green Bay Packers 21 Dallas 17
1968 New York Jets 27 Oakland 23	Baltimore 34 Cleveland 0
1969 Kansas City 17 Oakland 7	Minnesota 27 Cleveland 7

From 1970 the NFL has consisted of the AFC and the NFC, each with Eastern, Central and Western Divisions. End of season play-offs result in each Conference providing their own champions who meet in the Super Bowl.

AFC Championship	NFC Championship
1970 Baltimore 27 Oakland 17	Dallas 17 San Francisco 0
1971 Miami 21 Baltimore 0	Dallas 14 San Francisco 3
1972 Miami 21 Pittsburgh 17	Washington 26 Dallas 3
1973 Miami 27 Oakland 10	Minnesota 27 Dallas 10
1974 Pittsburgh 24 Oakland 13	Minnesota 30 Los Angeles 10
1975 Pittsburgh 16 Oakland 10	Dallas 37 Los Angeles 7
1976 Oakland 24 Pittsburgh 7	Minnesota 24 Los Angeles 13
1977 Denver 20 Oakland 17	Dallas 23 Minnesota 6
1978 Pittsburgh 34 Houston 5	Dallas 28 Los Angeles 0
1979 Pittsburgh 27 Houston 13	Los Angeles 9 Tampa Bay 0
1980 Oakland 34 San Diego 27	Philadelphia 20 Dallas 7
1981 Cincinnati 27 San Diego 7	San Francisco 28 Dallas 27
1982 Miami 14 New York Jets 0	Washington 31 Dallas 17
1983 Los Angeles Raiders 30 Seattle Seahawks 14	Washington 24 San Francisco 21
1984 Miami 45 Pittsburgh 28	San Francisco 23 Chicago 0
1985 New England 31 Miami 14	Chicago 24 Los Angeles Rams 0
1986 Denver 23 Cleveland 20	New York Giants 17 Washington 0
1987 Denver 38 Cleveland 33	Washington 17 Minnesota 10
1988 Cincinnati 21 Buffalo 10	San Francisco 28 Chicago 3

SUPERBOWL

1966 Green Bay Packers 35	Kansas City Chiefs 10
1967 Green Bay Packers 33	Oakland Raiders 14
1968 New York Jets 16	Baltimore Colts 7
1969 Kansas City Chiefs 23	Minnesota Vikings 7
1970 Baltimore Colts 16	Dallas Cowboys 13
1971 Dallas Cowboys 24	Miami Dolphins 3
1972 Miami Dolphins 14	Washington Redskins 7
1973 Miami Dolphins 24	Minnesota Vikings 7
1974 Pittsburgh Steelers 16	Minnesota Vikings 6
1975 Pittsburgh Steelers 21	Dallas Cowboys 17
1976 Oakland Raiders 32	Minnesota Vikings 14
1977 Dallas Cowboys 27	Denver Broncos 10
1978 Pittsburgh Steelers 35	Dallas Cowboys 31
1979 Pittsburgh Steelers 31	Los Angeles Rams 19
1980 Oakland Raiders 27	Philadelphia Eagles 10
1981 San Francisco 49ers 26	Cincinnati Bengals 21
1982 Washington Redskins 27	Miami Dolphins 17
1983 Los Angeles Raiders 38	Washington Redskins 9
1984 San Francisco 49ers 38	Miami Dolphins 16
1985 Chicago Bears 46	New England Patriots 10
1986 New York Giants 39	Denver Broncos 20
1987 Washington Redskins 42	Denver Broncos 10
1988 San Francisco 49ers 20	Cincinnati Bengals 16

Most Wins:
4 Pittsburgh Steelers

AFC and NFC Championship games and Superbowl are played in January. The years given are for the previous season's NFL competition.

AMERICAN FOOTBALL IN BRITAIN

The first known game of American Football in Britain took place in 1910 but it has only been since the television boom of the 1980s that it took off as an organised sport with the formation of the British American Football League, and subsequently the Budweiser league. The BAFL, however, folded in 1986.

SUMMERBOWL

The Summerbowl was the Championship Play-off Final of the British American Football League.

1985 London Ravens 45	Streatham Olympians 7
1986 Birmingham Bulls 23	Glasgow Lions 2
discontinued	

BUDWEISER BOWL

The Budweiser Bowl is the Championship Play-off Final of the Budweiser League.

1986 London Ravens 20	Streatham Olympians 12
1987 London Ravens 40	Manchester All Stars 23
1988 Birmingham Bulls 30	London Olympians 6

The Heisman Trophy is awarded to the outstanding College player of the Year. The 1985 winner, Bo Jackson of Auburn, also headed the Draft list, as drawn up by the professional teams. He was also head of the Baseball Draft and chose to play the latter sport. He became the first Heisman Trophy winner not to play pro football since Pete Dawkins, an Oxford Rugby Blue, in 1958. Jackson eventually joined the small band of dual US sportsmen by playing football for the Los Angeles Raiders.

Major NFL Career Records
Most games: 340 G. Blanda 1949-75
Most points: 2,002 G. Blanda 1949-75
Most touchdowns: 126 J. Brown 1957-65
Most field goals: 373 J. Stenerud 1967-85

RUSHING
Most yards gained: 16,726 W. Payton 1975-87

PASSING
Most passes completed: 3,686 F. Tarkenton 1961-78
Most yards gained: 47,003 F. Tarkenton 1961-78

Heisman Trophy
First awarded in 1935, the Heisman Trophy is awarded to the outstanding College footballer of the Year as determined by a poll of journalists.

Recent winners:
1970 J. Plunkett (Stanford)
1971 P. Sullivan (Auburn)
1972 J. Rodgers (Nebraska)
1973 J. Cappelletti (Penn State)
1974 A.. Griffin (Ohio State)
1975 A. Griffin (Ohio State)
1976 T. Dorset (Pittsburgh)
1977 E. Campbell (Texas)
1978 B. Sims (Oklahoma)
1979 C.. White (USC)
1980 G. Rogers (South Carolina)
1981 M. Allen (USC)
1982 H. Walker (Georgia)
1983 M. Rozier (Nebraska)
1984 D. Flutie (Boston College)
1985 B. Jackson (Auburn)
1986 V. Testaverde (Miami, Florida)
1987 T. Brown (Notre Dame)
1988 B. Sanders (Oklahoma State)

Most wins: 2 Archie Griffin

Angling must be the most international of all sports, as there can hardly be a country in the world where the sport is not practised. The oldest organised Angling club, the Ellem Club in Scotland, dates to 1829. The British National Championships were first held in 1906 and the International Confederation of Anglers was formed in Rome in 1952.

WORLD CHAMPIONSHIPS

The first World Championships were held in 1957, following the success of the European Championships inaugurated four years earlier.

Winners:

	Individual	Team
1957	Mandeli (ITA)	Italy
1958	Garroit (BEL)	Belgium
1959	R.Tesse (FRA)	France
1960	R.Tesse (FRA)	Belgium
1961	R.Legogue (FRA)	East Germany
1962	R.Tedasco (ITA)	Italy
1963	W.Lane (ENG)	France
1964	J.Fontanet (FRA)	France
1965	R.Tesse (FRA)	Romania
1966	H.Guiheneuf (FRA)	France
1967	J.Isenbaert (BEL)	Belgium
1968	G.Grebenstein (FRG)	France
1969	R.Harris (ENG)	Holland
1970	M.Van den Eynde (BEL)	Belgium
1971	D.Bassi (ITA)	Italy
1972	H.Levels (HOL)	France
1973	P.Michiels (BEL)	Belgium
1974	A.Richter (FRG)	France
1975	I.Heaps (ENG)	France
1976	D.Bassi (ITA)	Italy
1977	J.Mainil (BEL)	Luxembourg
1978	J -P.Fouquet (FRA)	France
1979	G.Heulard (FRA)	France
1980	R.Kremkus (FRG)	West Germany
1981	D.Thomas (ENG)	France
1982	K.Ashurst (ENG)	Holland
1983	R.Kremkus (FRG)	Belgium
1984	R.Smithers (IRE)	Luxembourg
1985	D.Roper (ENG)	England
1986	L.Wever (HOL)	Italy
1987	C. Branson (WAL)	England
1988	J -P.Fouquet (FRA)	England

Ancient man used Archery as a means of hunting some 10,000 years ago. It developed into a sport around the 3rd century AD, but did not become an organised sport, on similar lines to the competitions of today, until 1844 when the first British Championships were held at York. The world governing body, the Federation Internationale de Tir a l'Arc, was formed as recently as 1931.

WORLD CHAMPIONSHIPS
First held in 1931 the team competition was not instituted until 1957. The Championships have been a biennial event since 1959.

Men

	Individual	Team
1931	M.Sawicki(POL)	France
1932	L.Reith (BEL)	Poland
1933	D.Mackenzie (USA)	Belgium
1934	H.Kjellson (SWE)	Sweden
1935	A. van Kohlen (BEL)	Belgium
1936	E.Heilborn (SWE)	Czechoslovakia
1937	C. De Rons (BEL)	Poland
1938	F.Hadas (TCH)	Czechoslovakia
1939	R.Beday (FRA)	France
1946	E. Tang Holbek (DEN)	Denmark
1947	H.Deutgen (SWE)	Czechoslovakia
1948	H.Deutgen (SWE)	Sweden
1949	H.Deutgen (SWE)	Czechoslovakia
1950	H.Deutgen (SWE)	Sweden
1952	S.Andersson (SWE)	Sweden
1953	B.Lundgren (SWE)	Sweden
1955	N.Andersson (SWE)	Sweden
1957	O.K.Smathers (USA)	United States
1958	S.Thysell (SWE)	Finland
1959	J.Caspers (USA)	United States
1961	J.Thornton (USA)	United States
1963	C.Sandlin (USA)	United States
1965	M.Haikonen (FIN)	United States
1967	R.Rogers (USA)	United States
1969	H.Ward (USA)	United States
1971	J.Williams (USA)	United States
1973	V.Sidoruk (USSR)	United States
1975	D.Pace (USA)	United States
1977	R.McKinney (USA)	United States
1979	D.Pace (USA)	United States
1981	K.Laasonen (FIN)	United States
1983	R.McKinney (USA)	United States
1985	R.McKinney (USA)	South Korea
1987	V.Asheyez (USSR)	South Korea

Most Wins

Individual:	**Team:**
4 Hans Deutgen	14 United States

Women

	Individual	Team
1931	J.Spychajowa-Kurkowska (POL)	–
1932	J.Spychajowa-Kurkowska (POL)	–
1933	J.Spychajowa-Kurkowska (POL)	Poland
1934	J.Spychajowa-Kurkowska (POL)	Poland
1935	I.Catani (SWE)	Great Britain
1936	J.Spychajowa-Kurkowska (POL)	Poland
1937	E.Simon (GB)	Great Britain
1938	N.W.Martyr (GB)	Poland
1939	J.Spychajowa-Kurkowska (POL)	Poland
1946	P. de Wharton Burr (GB)	Czechoslovakia
1947	J.Spychajowa-Kurkowska (POL)	Great Britain
1948	P. de Wharton Burr (GB)	Finland
1949	B.Waterhouse (GB)	United States
1950	J.Lee (USA)	Finland
1952	J.Lee (USA)	United States
1953	J.Richards (USA)	Finland
1955	K.Wisniowski (POL)	Great Britain
1957	C.Meinhart (USA)	United States
1958	S.Johansson (SWE)	United States
1959	A.W.Corby (USA)	United States
1961	N.Vonderheide (USA)	United States
1963	V.Cook (USA)	United States
1965	M.Lindholm (FIN)	United States
1967	M.Mazynska (POL)	Poland
1969	D.Lidtstone (CAN)	USSR
1971	E.Gapchenko (USSR)	Poland
1973	L.Myers (USA)	USSR
1975	Z.Rustamova (USSR)	USSR
1977	L.Ryon (USA)	United States
1979	J -H.Kim (SKO)	South Korea
1981	N.Butusova (USSR)	USSR
1983	J -H.Kim (SKO)	South Korea
1985	I.Soldatova (USSR)	USSR
1987	Ma Xiagjuan (CHN)	USSR

Most Wins	Team:
7 Janina Spychajowa-Kurkowska	9 United States

OLYMPIC GAMES

Although Archery was included in the Olympics between 1900–08 and again in 1920; it has only been in its present form since 1972.

Winners since 1972:

	Men	Women
1972	J.Williams (USA)	D.Wilbur (USA)
1976	D.Pace (USA)	L.Ryon (USA)
1980	T.Poikolainen (FIN)	K.Losaberidze (USSR)
1984	D.Pace (USA)	H -S.Seo (SKO)
1988	J.Barrs (USA)	S -N.Kim (SKO)

The highest possible score under the present scoring system is 2880 points for a double round, and 1440 for a single round. The system for a single round consists of 36 arrows at targets at 30, 50, 70 and 90 metres (30, 50, 60 and 70 for women).
World records:

	Men			Women	
Single round:	1341	D. Pace (USA), 1979		1338	S -N.Kim (SKO), 1988
Double round:	2617	D. Pace (USA), 1983		2616	K. Jin-Ho (SKO), 1983
	2617	R. McKinney (USA), 1983			

The Chinese played a form of football, Tsu chu, over 2500 years ago but it was not until the reign of Edward II in 1314 that reference was made to the sport in England. He banned the playing of football because of the excessive noise people were making in the streets of London hustling over the footballs. Three subsequent British monarchs also banned the sport for one reason or another until it became an organised sport in the 19th century. The Football Association was formed in 1863 and the sport's popularity worldwide brought about the formation of F.I.F.A. in 1904.

WORLD CUP

First held in 1930 and subsequently held every four years, the coveted gold prize was the Jules Rimet Trophy which Brazil won outright after their third win in 1970. It was replaced by the F.I.F.A. World Cup in 1974.

Year	Winner	Runner up	Score	Venue
1930	Uruguay	Argentina	4-2	Uruguay
1934	Italy	Czechoslovakia	2-1	Italy
1938	Italy	Hungary	4-2	France
1950	Uruguay	Brazil	2-1	Brazil
1954	West Germany	Hungary	3-2	Switzerland
1958	Brazil	Sweden	5-2	Sweden
1962	Brazil	Czechoslovakia	3-1	Chile
1966	England	West Germany	4-2	England
1970	Brazil	Italy	4-1	Mexico
1974	West Germany	Holland	2-1	West Germany
1978	Argentina	Holland	3-1	Argentina
1982	Italy	West Germany	3-1	Spain
1986	Argentina	West Germany	3-2	Mexico

MOST WINS:
3 Brazil, Italy

EUROPEAN CHAMPIONSHIP

Like the World Cup, the European Championship is held every four years. Instituted in 1958, with the first final two years later, it was originally called the European Nations Cup. Teams play for the Henry Delauney Trophy, named after the former General Secretary of U.E.F.A. who devised the competition.

Year	Winner	Runner up	Score	Venue
1960	USSR	Yugoslavia	2-1	France
1964	Spain	USSR	2-1	Spain
1968	Italy	Yugoslavia	2-0	Italy (after 1-1 draw)
1972	West Germany	USSR	3-0	Belgium
1976	Czechoslovakia (Czechoslovakia won 5-3 on penalties)	West Germany	2-2	Yugoslavia
1980	West Germany	Belgium	2-1	Italy
1984	France	Spain	2-0	France
1988	Holland	USSR	2-0	West Germany

BRITISH INTERNATIONAL CHAMPIONSHIP
Formerly the Home International Championship, it was a fours nations competition involving the four home countries who played each other once, during the season. Because of its declining interest, the Championship ended in 1984.

Winners:

1883-84 Scotland
1884-85 Scotland
1885-86 England, Scotland
1886-87 Scotland
1887-88 England
1888-89 Scotland
1889-90 England, Scotland
1890-91 England
1891-92 England
1892-93 England
1893-94 Scotland
1894-95 England
1895-96 Scotland
1896-97 Scotland
1897-98 England
1898-99 England
1899-00 Scotland
1900-01 England
1901-02 Scotland
1902-03 England, Ireland, Scotland
1903-04 England
1904-05 England
1905-06 England, Scotland
1906-07 Wales
1907-08 England, Scotland
1908-09 England
1909-10 Scotland
1910-11 England
1911-12 England, Scotland
1912-13 England
1913-14 Ireland
1914-15 to 1918-19 Not Held
1919-20 Wales
1920-21 Scotland
1921-22 Scotland
1922-23 Scotland
1923-24 Wales
1924-25 Scotland
1925-26 Scotland
1926-27 England, Scotland
1927-28 Wales
1928-29 Scotland
1929-30 England
1930-31 England, Scotland
1931-32 England
1932-33 Wales

1933-34 Wales
1934-35 England, Scotland
1935-36 Scotland
1936-37 Wales
1937-38 England
1938-39 England, Scotland, Wales
1939-40 to 1945-46 Not Held
1946-47 England
1947-48 England
1948-49 Scotland
1949-50 England
1950-51 Scotland
1951-52 England, Wales
1952-53 England, Scotland
1953-54 England
1954-55 England
1955-56 England, N.Ireland, Scotland, Wales
1956-57 England
1957-58 England, N.Ireland
1958-59 England, N.Ireland
1959-60 England, Scotland, Wales
1960-61 England
1961-62 Scotland
1962-63 Scotland
1963-64 England, N.Ireland, Scotland
1964-65 England
1965-66 England
1966-67 Scotland
1967-68 England
1968-69 England
1969-70 England, Scotland, Wales
1970-71 England
1971-72 England, Scotland
1972-73 England
1973-74 England, Scotland
1974-75 England
1975-76 Scotland
1976-77 Scotland
1977-78 England
1978-79 England
1979-80 N.Ireland
1980-81 Not Completed
1981-82 England
1982-83 England
1983-84 N.Ireland

MOST OUTRIGHT WINS:
34 England

WORLD CLUB CHAMPIONSHIP

Instituted in 1960 it was originally a two-legged match between the winners of the European Champions Cup and the South American Championship. Since 1980, however, the match has been a one-legged affair played in Tokyo.

Results:

Year	Winners	Runners up	Score
1960	Real Madrid	Penarol	5-1 agg
1961	Penarol	Benfica	7-2 agg
1962	Santos	Benfica	8-4 agg
1963	Santos	AC Milan	7-6 agg
1964	Inter Milan	Independiente	3-1 agg
1965	Inter Milan	Independiente	3-0 agg
1966	Penarol	Real Madrid	4-0 agg
1967	Racing Club	Celtic	3-2 agg
1968	Estudiantes	Manchester U	2-1 agg
1969	AC Milan	Estudiantes	4-2 agg
1970	Feyenoord	Estudiantes	3-2 agg
1971	Nacional	Panathinaikos	3-2 agg
1972	Ajax	Independiente	4-1 agg
1973	Independiente (only one leg played)	Juventus	1-0
1974	Atletico Madrid	Independiente	2-1 agg
1975	Not Played		
1976	Bayern Munich	Cruzeiro	2-0 agg
1977	Boca Junios	Borussia Moenchengladbach	5-2 agg
1978	Not Played		
1979	Olimpia	Malmo	3-1 agg
1980	Nacional	Nottingham F	1-0
1981	Flamenco	Liverpool	3-0
1982	Penarol	Aston Villa	2-0
1983	Gremio	SV Hamburg	2-1
1984	Independiente	Liverpool	1-0
1985	Juventus (Juventus won 4-2 on penalties)	Argentinos Juniors	2-2
1986	River Plate	Steau Bucharest	1-0
1987	FC Porto	Penarol	2-1
1988	Nacional (Nacional won 7-6 on penalties)	PSV Eindhoven	2-2

MOST WINS: 3 Penarol; Nacional

(AFTER EXTRA TIME)

1989 A.C. MILAN 1

EUROPEAN CHAMPIONS CUP

Instituted in 1955 after a suggestion by Paris sports paper L'Equipe the European Cup has been held every year since and is contested by the League Champions of all the countries affiliated to U.E.F.A.

Year	Winners	Runners up	Score
1956	Real Madrid	Stade de Rheims	4-3
1957	Real Madrid	Fiorentina	2-0
1958	Real Madrid	AC Milan	3-2
1959	Real Madrid	Stade de Rheims	2-0
1960	Real Madrid	Eintracht Frankfurt	7-3
1961	Benfica	Barcelona	3-2
1962	Benfica	Real Madrid	5-3
1963	AC Milan	Benfica	2-1
1964	InterMilan	Real Madrid	3-1
1965	InterMilan	Benfica	1-0

1966	Real Madrid	Partizan Belgrade	2-1
1967	Celtic	Inter Milan	2-1
1968	Manchester U	Benfica	4-1
1969	AC Milan	Ajax	4-1
1970	Feyenoord	Celtic	2-1
1971	Ajax	Panathinaikos	2-0
1972	Ajax	Inter Milan	2-0
1973	Ajax	Juventus	1-0
1974	Bayern Munich (after 1-1 draw)	Atletico Madrid	4-0
1975	Bayern Munich	Leeds United	2-0
1976	Bayern Munich	St.Etienne	1-0
1977	Liverpool	Borussia Moenchengladbach	3-1
1978	Liverpool	FC Bruges	1-0
1979	Nottingham	Malmo	1-0
1980	Nottingham	SV Hamburg	1-0
1981	Liverpool	Real Madrid	1-0
1982	Aston Villa	Bayern Munich	1-0
1983	SV Hamburg	Juventus	1-0
1984	Liverpool (Liverpool won 4-2 on penalties)	AS Roma	1-1
1985	Juventus	Liverpool	1-0
1986	Steau Bucharest (Steau won 2-0 on penalties)	Barcelona	0-0
1987	Porto	Bayern Munich	2-1
1988	PSV Eindhoven (Eindhoven won 6-5 on penalties)	Benfica	0-0
1989	AC Milan	Steaua Bucharest	4-0

MOST WINS:
6 Real Madrid

EUROPEAN CUP WINNERS CUP
Instituted in 1960 the competition is open to national cup winners, or runners up if the winners are in the European Champions Cup.

Results:

Year	Winners	Runners up	Score
1961	Fiorentina	Rangers	4-1 agg
1962	Atletico Madrid	Fiorentina	4-1 agg
1963	Tottenham H	Atletico Madrid	5-1
1964	Sporting Lisbon (after 3-3 draw)	MTK Budapest	1-0
1965	West Ham U	Munich 1860	2-0
1966	Borussia Dortmund	Liverpool	2-1
1967	Bayern Munich	Rangers	1-0
1968	AC Milan	SV Hamburg	2-0
1969	Slovan Bratislava	Barcelona	3-2
1970	Manchester C	Gornik Zabrze	2-1
1971	Chelsea (after 1-1 draw)	Real Madrid	2-1
1972	Rangers	Moscow Dynamo	3-2
1973	AC Milan	Leeds United	1-0
1974	FC Magdeburg	AC Milan	2-0
1975	Dynamo Kiev	Ferencvaros	3-0
1976	Anderlecht	West Ham United	4-2

European Cup Winners Cup Cont.

1977	SV Hamburg	Anderlecht	2-0
1978	Anderlecht	Austria/WAC	4-0
1979	Barcelona	Fortuna Dusseldorf	4-3
1980	Valencia	Arsenal	0-0

(Valencia won 5-4 on penalties)

1981	Dynamo Tbilisi	Carl Zeis Jena	2-1
1982	Barcelona	Standard Liege	2-1
1983	Aberdeen	Real Madrid	2-1
1984	Juventus	Porto	2-1
1985	Everton	Rapid Vienna	3-1
1986	Dynamo Kiev	Atletico Madrid	3-0
1987	Ajax	Lokomotiv Leipzig	1-0
1988	Mechelen	Ajax	1-0
1989	Barcelona	Sampdoria	2-0

MOST WINS:

2 AC Milan, Anderlecht, Barcelona, Dynamo Kiev

UEFA CUP

The UEFA Cup started life as the Inter-Cities Fairs Cup in 1955 and was played over a three year period. Since 1960 however, it has been an annual tournament. It changed its name to the European Fairs Cup in 1966-67, and to its present name in 1971-72. The final is played over two legs.

Results:

Year	Winners	Runners up	Score
1958	Barcelona	London	8-2 agg
1960	Barcelona	Birmingham City	4-1 agg
1961	AS Roma	Birmingham City	4-2 agg
1962	Valencia	Barcelona	7-3 agg
1963	Valencia	Dynamo Zagreb	4-1 agg
1964	Real Zaragoza	Valencia	2-1

(only one game played)

1965	Ferencvaros	Juventus	1-0

(only one game played)

1966	Barcelona	Real Zaragoza	4-3 agg
1967	Dynamo Zagreb	Leeds United	2-0 agg
1968	Leeds United	Ferencvaros	1-0 agg
1969	Newcastle United	Ujpest Dózsa	6-2 agg
1970	Arsenal	Anderlecht	4-3 agg
1971	Leeds United	Juventus	3-3 agg

(Leeds won on the away goals rule)

1972	Tottenham H	Wolverhampton W	3-2 agg
1973	Liverpool	Borussia Moenchengladbach	3-2 agg
1974	Feyenoord	Tottenham H	4-2 agg
1975	Borussia Moenchengladbach	Twente Enschede	5-1 agg
1976	Liverpool	FC Bruges	4-3 agg
1977	Juventus	Atletico Bilbao	2-2 agg

(Juventus won on the away goals rule)

1978	PSV Eindhoven	Bastia	3-0 agg
1979	Borussia Moenchengladbach	Red Star Belgrade	2-1 agg
1980	Eintrach	Borussia Moenchengladbach	3-3 agg

(Eintracht won on the away goals rule)

1981	Ipswich Town	AZ 67 Alkmaar	5-4 agg
1982	IFK Gothenburg	SV Hamburg	4-0 agg
1983	Anderlecht	Benfica	2-1 agg

1984	Tottenham H	Anderlecht	2-2 agg
	(Tottenham won 4-3 on penalties)		
1985	Real Madrid	Videoton	3-1 agg
1986	Real Madrid	Cologne	5-3 agg
1987	IFK Gothenburg	Dundee U	2-1 agg
1988	Bayer Leverkusen	Espanol	3-3 agg
	(Leverkusen won 3-2 on penalties)		
1989	Napoli	VFB Stuttgart	5-4 agg

MOST WINS: 3 Barcelona

EUROPEAN SUPER CUP

An annual two legged match between the winners of the European Champions Cup and the European Cup Winners Cup.

Results:

Year	Winners	Runners up	Score
1972	Ajax	Rangers	6-3 agg
1973	Ajax	AC Milan	6-1 agg
1974	Bayern Munich	FC Magdeburg	5-3 agg
1975	Dynamo Kiev	Bayern Munich	3-0 agg
1976	Anderlecht	Bayern Munich	5-3 agg
1977	Liverpool	SV Hamburg	7-1 agg
1978	Anderlecht	Liverpool	4-3 agg
1979	Nottingham F	Barcelona	2-1 agg
1980	Valencia	Nottingham F	2-2 agg
	(Valencia won on the away goals rule)		
1981	Not Played		
1982	Aston Villa	Barcelona	3-1 agg
1983	Aberdeen	SV Hamburg	2-0 agg
1984	Juventus	Liverpool	2-0
	(One game only)		
1985	Not Played		
1986	Steau Bucharest	Dynamo Kiev	1-0
1987	FC Porto	Ajax	2-0 agg
1988	FC Mechelen	PSV Eindhoven	3-1 agg

MOST WINS:
2 Anderlecht, Ajax

F.A. CHALLENGE CUP

The most famous knockout cup tournament in the world, the FA Cup was instituted in 1871. There have been three different trophies over the years. The first trophy was stolen from a Birmingham shop window in 1895 while Aston Villa were the holders. The second trophy was presented to Lord Kinnaird on completion of 21 years as FA President in 1910 and the present trophy was first won by Bradford City in 1911.

Results:

Year	Winners	Runners up	Score
1872	Wanderers	Royal Engineers	1-0
1873	Wanderers	Oxford University	2-0
1874	Oxford University	Royal Engineers	2-0
1875	Royal Engineers	Old Etonians	2-0
	(after 1-1 draw)		
1876	Wanderers	Old Etonians	3-0
	(after 0-0 draw)		
1877	Wanderers	Oxford University	2-0
1878	Wanderers	Royal Engineers	3-1
1879	Old Etonians	Clapham Rovers	1-0

F.A. Challenge Cup Cont.

1880	Clapham Rovers	Oxford University	1-0
1881	Old Carthusians	Old Etonians	3-0
1882	Old Etonians	Blackburn R	1-0
1883	Blackburn O	Old Etonians	2-1
1884	Blackburn R	Queen's Park	2-1
1885	Blackburn R	Queen's Park	2-0
1886	Blackburn R (after 0-0 draw)	West Bromwich A	2-0
1887	Aston V	West Bromwich A	2-0
1888	West Bromwich A	Preston NE	2-1
1889	Preston NE	Wolverhampton W	3-0
1890	Blackburn R	Sheffield W	6-1
1891	Blackburn R	Notts C	3-1
1892	West Bromwich A	Aston V	3-0
1893	Wolverhampton W	Everton	1-0
1894	Notts C	Bolton W	4-1
1895	Aston V	West Bromwich A	1-0
1896	Sheffield W	Wolverhampton W	2-1
1897	Aston V	Everton	3-2
1898	Nottingham F	Derby C	3-1
1899	Sheffield U	Derby C	4-1
1900	Bury	Southampton	4-0
1901	Tottenham H (after 2-2 draw)	Sheffield U	3-1
1902	Sheffield U (after 1-1 draw)	Southampton	2-1
1903	Bury	Derby C	6-0
1904	Manchester C	Bolton W	1-0
1905	Aston V	Newcastle U	2-0
1906	Everton	Newcastle U	1-0
1907	Sheffield W	Everton	2-1
1908	Wolverhampton W	Newcastle U	3-1
1909	Manchester U	Bristol C	1-0
1910	Newcastle U (after 1-1 draw)	Barnsley	2-0
1911	Bradford C (after 0-0 draw)	Newcastle U	1-0
1912	Barnsley	West Bromwich A	2-0
1913	Aston V	Sunderland	1-0
1914	Burnley	Liverpool	1-0
1915	Sheffield U	Chelsea	3-0
1916-19	Not Held		
1920	Aston V	Huddersfield T	1-0
1921	Tottenham H	Wolverhampton W	1-0
1922	Huddersfield T	Preston NE	1-0
1923	Bolton W	West Ham U	2-0
1924	Newcastle U	Aston V	2-0
1925	Sheffield U	Cardiff C	1-0
1926	Bolton W	Manchester C	1-0
1927	Cardiff C	Arsenal	1-0
1928	Blackburn R	Huddersfield T	3-1
1929	Bolton W	Portsmouth	2-0
1930	Arsenal	Huddersfield T	2-0
1931	West Bromwich A	Birmingham C	2-1
1932	Newcastle U	Arsenal	2-1
1933	Everton	Manchester C	3-0
1934	Manchester C	Portsmouth	2-1

1935	Sheffield W	West Bromwich A	4-2
1936	Arsenal	Sheffield U	1-0
1937	Sunderland	Preston NE	3-1
1938	Preston NE	Huddersfield T	1-0
1939	Portsmouth	Wolverhampton W	4-1
1940-45	Not Held		
1946	Derby C	Charlton A	4-1
1947	Charlton A	Burnley	1-0
1948	Manchester U	Blackpool	4-2
1949	Wolverhampton W	Leicester C	3-1
1950	Arsenal	Liverpool	2-0
1951	Newcastle U	Blackpool	2-0
1952	Newcastle U	Arsenal	1-0
1953	Blackpool	Bolton W	4-3
1954	West Bromwich A	Preston NE	3-2
1955	Newcastle U	Manchester C	3-1
1956	Manchester C	Birmingham C	3-1
1957	Aston V	Manchester U	2-1
1958	Bolton W	Manchester U	2-0
1959	Nottingham F	Luton T	2-1
1960	Wolverhampton W	Blackburn R	3-0
1961	Tottenham H	Leicester C	2-0
1962	Tottenham H	Burnley	3-1
1963	Manchester U	Leicester C	3-1
1964	West Ham U	Preston NE	3-2
1965	Liverpool	Leeds U	2-1
1966	Everton	Sheffield W	3-2
1967	Tottenham H	Chelsea	2-1
1968	West Bromwich A	Everton	1-0
1969	Manchester C	Leicester C	1-0
1970	Chelsea (after 2-2 draw)	Leeds U	2-1
1971	Arsenal	Liverpool	2-1
1972	Leeds U	Arsenal	1-0
1973	Sunderland	Leeds U	1-0
1974	Liverpool	Newcastle U	3-0
1975	West Ham U	Fulham	2-0
1976	Southampton	Manchester U	1-0
1977	Manchester U	Liverpool	2-1
1978	Ipswich T	Arsenal	1-0
1979	Arsenal	Manchester U	3-2
1980	West Ham U	Arsenal	1-0
1981	Tottenham H (after 1-1 draw)	Manchester C	3-2
1982	Tottenham H (after 1-1 draw)	Queen's Park R	1-0
1983	Manchester U (after 2-2 draw)	Brighton & HA	4-0
1984	Everton	Watford	2-0
1985	Manchester U	Everton	1-0
1986	Liverpool	Everton	3-1
1987	Coventry C	Tottenham H	3-2
1988	Wimbledon	Liverpool	1-0
1989	Liverpool	Everton	3-2

MOST WINS: 7 Aston Villa, Tottenham Hotspur

LITTLEWOODS CUP

First contested in the 1960-61 season it was known as the Football League Cup until 1982 when it became the Milk Cup. It became the Littlewoods Cup in 1986. The final is now played at Wembley Stadium each year but, prior to 1967, the final was played over two legs on a home and away basis.

Results:

Year	Winners	Runners up	Score
1961	Aston V	Rotherham U	3-2 agg
1962	Norwich C	Rochdale	4-0 agg
1963	Birmingham C	Aston V	3-1 agg
1964	Leicester C	Stoke C	4-3 agg
1965	Chelsea	Leicester C	3-2 agg
1966	West Bromwich A	West Ham U	5-3 agg
1967	Queen's Park R	West Bromwich A	3-2
1968	Leeds U	Arsenal	1-0
1969	Swindon T	Arsenal	3-1
1970	Manchester C	West Bromwich A	2-1
1971	Tottenham H	Aston V	2-0
1972	Stoke C	Chelsea	2-1
1973	Tottenham H	Norwich C	1-0
1974	Wolverhampton W	Manchester C	2-1
1975	Aston V	Norwich C	1-0
1976	Manchester C	Newcastle U	2-1
1977	Aston V (after 0-0 and 1-1)	Everton	3-2
1978	Nottingham F (after 0-0 draw)	Liverpool	1-0
1979	Nottingham F	Southampton	3-2
1980	Wolverhampton W	Nottingham F	1-0
1981	Liverpool (after 1-1 draw)	West Ham U	2-1
1982	Liverpool	Tottenham H	3-1
1983	Liverpool	Manchester U	2-1
1984	Liverpool (after 0-0 draw)	Everton	1-0
1985	Norwich C	Sunderland	1-0
1986	Oxford U	Queen's Park R	3-0
1987	Arsenal	Liverpool	2-1
1988	Luton T	Arsenal	3-2
1989	Nottingham F	Luton T	3-1
1990	NOTTM FOREST	OLDHAM ATH	1-0

MOST WINS: 4 Liverpool, NOTTM FOREST.

FOOTBALL LEAGUE

Twelve clubs formed the original Football League in 1888-89. A second division was introduced in 1892-93 and a third division in 1920-21. When the League membership was increased the following season a third division (north) and third division (south) was introduced. These two divisions were replaced by the exisiting third and fourth divisions in 1958-59.

Champions:
Football League

1888-89	Preston NE	1890-91	Everton
1889-90	Preston NE	1891-92	Sunderland

	Division 1	Division 2
1892-93	Sunderland	Small Heath
1893-94	Aston V	Liverpool
1894-95	Sunderland	Bury
1895-96	Aston V	Liverpool
1896-97	Aston V	Notts C

1897-98	Sheffield U	Burnley
1898-99	Aston V	Manchester C
1899-00	Aston V	The Wednesday
1900-01	Liverpool	Grimsby T
1901-02	Sunderland	West Bromwich A
1902-03	The Wednesday	Manchester C
1903-04	The Wednesday	Preston NE
1904-05	Newcastle U	Liverpool
1905-06	Liverpool	Bristol C
1906-07	Newcastle U	Nottingham F
1907-08	Manchester U	Bradford C
1908-09	Newcastle U	Bolton W
1909-10	Aston V	Manchester C
1910-11	Manchester U	West Bromwich A
1911-12	Blackburn R	Derby C
1912-13	Sunderland	Preston NE
1913-14	Blackburn R	Notts C
1914-15	Everton	Derby C
1915-18	Not Held	
1919-20	West Bromwich A	Tottenham H

	Division 1	Division 2	Division 3
1920-21	Burnley	Birmingham	Crystal P

	Division 1	Division 2	Division 3(S)	Division 3(N)
1921-22	Liverpool	Nottingham F	Southampton	Stockport C
1922-23	Liverpool	Notts C	Bristol C	Nelson
1923-24	Huddersfield T	Leeds U	Portsmouth	Wolverhampton W
1924-25	Huddersfield T	Leicester C	Swansea T	Darlington H
1925-26	Huddersfield T	Sheffield W	Reading	Grimsby T
1926-27	Newcastle U	Middlesbrough	Bristol C	Stoke C
1927-28	Everton	Manchester C	Millwall	Bradford PA
1928-29	Sheffield W	Middlesbrough	Charlton A	Bradford C
1929-30	Sheffield W	Blackpool	Plymouth A	Port Vale
1930-31	Arsenal	Everton	Notts C	Chesterfield
1931-32	Everton	Wolverhampton W	Fulham	Lincoln C
1932-33	Arsenal	Stoke C	Brentford	Hull C
1933-34	Arsenal	Grimsby T	Norwich C	Barnsley
1934-35	Arsenal	Brentford	Charlton A	Doncaster R
1935-36	Sunderland	Manchester U	Coventry C	Chesterfield
1936-37	Manchester C	Leicester C	Luton T	Stockport C
1937-38	Arsenal	Aston V	Millwall	Tranmere R
1938-39	Everton	Blackburn R	Newport C	Barnsley
1939-40 to 1945-46 Not Held				
1946-47	Liverpool	Manchester C	Cardiff C	Doncaster R
1947-48	Arsenal	Birmingham C	Queen's Park R	Lincoln C
1948-49	Portsmouth	Fulham	Swansea T	Hull C
1949-50	Portsmouth	Tottenham H	Notts C	Doncaster R
1950-51	Tottenham H	Preston NE	Nottingham F	Rotherham U
1951-52	Manchester U	Sheffield W	Plymouth A	Lincoln C
1952-53	Arsenal	Sheffield U	Bristol R	Oldham A
1953-54	Wolverhampton W	Leicester C	Ipswich T	Port Vale
1954-55	Chelsea	Birmingham C	Bristol C	Barnsley
1955-56	Manchester U	Sheffield W	Leyton O	Grimsby T
1956-57	Manchester U	Leicester C	Ipswich T	Derby C
1957-58	Wolverhampton W	West Ham U	Brighton & HA	Scunthorpe U

Football League Champions Cont.

	Division 1	Division 2	Division 3	Division 4
1958-59	Wolverhampton W	Sheffield W	Plymouth A	Port Vale
1959-60	Burnley	Aston V	Southampton	Walsall
1960-61	Tottenham H	Ipswich T	Bury	Peterborough U
1961-62	Ipswich T	Liverpool	Portsmouth	Millwall
1962-63	Everton	Stoke C	Northampton T	Brentford
1963-64	Liverpool	Leeds U	Coventry C	Gillingham
1964-65	Manchester U	Newcastle U	Carlisle U	Brighton & HA
1965-66	Liverpool	Manchester C	Hull C	Doncaster R
1966-67	Manchester U	Coventry C	Queen's Park R	Stockport C
1967-68	Manchester C	Ipswich T	Oxford U	Luton T
1968-69	Leeds U	Derby C	Watford	Doncaster R
1969-70	Everton	Huddersfield T	Orient	Chesterfield
1970-71	Arsenal	Leicester C	Preston NE	Notts C
1971-72	Derby C	Norwich C	Aston V	Grimsby T
1972-73	Liverpool	Burnley	Bolton W	Southport
1973-74	Leeds U	Middlesbrough	Oldham A	Peterborough U
1974-75	Derby C	Manchester U	Blackburn R	Mansfield T
1975-76	Liverpool	Sunderland	Hereford U	Lincoln C
1976-77	Liverpool	Wolverhampton W	Mansfield T	Cambridge U
1977-78	Nottingham F	Bolton W	Wrexham	Watford
1978-79	Liverpool	Crystal P	Shrewsbury T	Reading
1979-80	Liverpool	Leicester C	Grimsby T	Huddersfield T
1980-81	Aston V	West Ham U	Rotherham U	Southend U
1981-82	Liverpool	Luton T	Burnley	Sheffield U
1982-83	Liverpool	Queen's Park R	Portsmouth	Wimbledon
1983-84	Liverpool	Chelsea	Oxford U	York C
1984-85	Everton	Oxford U	Bradford C	Chesterfield
1985-86	Liverpool	Norwich C	Reading	Swindon T
1986-87	Everton	Derby C	Bournemouth	Northampton T
1987-88	Liverpool	Millwall	Sunderland	Wolverhampton W
1988-89	Arsenal	Chelsea	Wolverhampton W	Rotherham U
1989-90	LIVERPOOL			EXETER CITY

MOST WINS

Div 1 18 Liverpool **Div 2** 6 Leicester C Manchester C **Div 3(S)** 3 Bristol C **Div 3(N)** 3 Barnsley
Div 3 2 Doncaster R Oxford U Lincoln Portsmouth
Div 4 2 Chesterfield Doncaster R Peterborough U

SCOTTISH LEAGUE

The Scottish League was formed in 1890-91 and, until its re-structuring in 1975, was run with two divisions from 1893. Since 1975, when the first division was renamed the Premier Division, three divisions have been in existence.

Champions:
Scottish League
1890-91 Dumbarton/Rangers
1891-92 Dumbarton
1892-93 Celtic

	Division 1	Division 2
1893-94	Celtic	Hibernian
1894-95	Hearts	Hibernian
1895-96	Celtic	Abercorn
1896-97	Hearts	Partick T
1897-98	Celtic	Kilmarnock
1898-99	Rangers	Kilmarnock
1899-00	Rangers	Partick T
1900-01	Rangers	St. Bernard's

1901-02	Rangers	Port Glasgow
1902-03	Hibernian	Airdrieonians
1903-04	Third Lanark	Hamilton A
1904-05	Celtic	Clyde
1905-06	Celtic	Leith A
1906-07	Celtic	St.Bernard's
1907-08	Celtic	Raith R
1908-09	Celtic	Abercorn
1909-10	Celtic	Leith A
1910-11	Rangers	Dumbarton
1911-12	Rangers	Ayr U
1912-13	Rangers	Ayr U
1913-14	Celtic	Cowdenbeath
1914-15	Celtic	Cowdenbeath
1915-16	Celtic	—
1916-17	Celtic	—
1917-18	Rangers	—
1918-19	Celtic	—
1919-20	Rangers	—
1920-21	Rangers	—
1921-22	Celtic	Alloa A
1922-23	Rangers	Queen's Park
1923-24	Rangers	St.Johnstone
1924-25	Rangers	Dundee U
1925-26	Celtic	Dunfermline A
1926-27	Rangers	Bo'ness
1927-28	Rangers	Ayr U
1928-29	Rangers	Dundee U
1929-30	Rangers	Leith A
1930-31	Rangers	Third Lanark
1931-32	Motherwell	East Stirling
1932-33	Rangers	Hibernian
1933-34	Rangers	Albion R
1934-35	Rangers	Third Lanark
1935-36	Celtic	Falkirk
1936-37	Rangers	Ayr U
1937-38	Celtic	Raith R
1938-39	Rangers	Cowdenbeath
1939-40 to 1945-46 Not Held		

	Division A	**Division B**
1946-47	Rangers	Dundee
1947-48	Hibernian	East Fife
1948-49	Rangers	Raith R
1949-50	Rangers	Morton
1950-51	Hibernian	Queen of the S
1951-52	Hibernian	Clyde
1952-53	Rangers	Stirling A
1953-54	Celtic	Mortherwell
1954-55	Aberdeen	Airdrieonians
1955-56	Rangers	Queen's Park

	Division 1	Division 2
1956-57	Rangers	Clyde
1957-58	Hearts	Stirling A
1958-59	Rangers	Ayr U
1959-60	Hearts	St.Johnstone
1960-61	Rangers	Stirling A
1961-62	Dundee	Clyde
1962-63	Rangers	St.Johnstone
1963-64	Rangers	Morton
1964-65	Kilmarnock	Stirling A
1965-66	Celtic	Ayr U
1966-67	Celtic	Morton
1967-68	Celtic	St.Mirren
1968-69	Celtic	Motherwell
1969-70	Celtic	Falkirk
1970-71	Celtic	Partick T
1971-72	Celtic	Dumbarton
1972-73	Celtic	Clyde
1973-74	Celtic	Airdrieonians
1974-75	Rangers	Falkirk

	Premier Division	Division 1	Division 2
1975-76	Rangers	Partick T	Clydebank
1976-77	Celtic	St.Mirren	Stirling A
1977-78	Rangers	Morton	Clyde
1978-79	Celtic	Dundee	Berwick R
1979-80	Aberdeen	Hearts	Falkirk
1980-81	Celtic	Hibernian	Queen's Park
1981-82	Celtic	Motherwell	Clyde
1982-83	Dundee U	St.Johnstone	Brechin C
1983-84	Aberdeen	Morton	Forfar A
1984-85	Aberdeen	Motherwell	Montrose
1985-86	Celtic	Hamilton A	Dunfermline A
1986-87	Rangers	Morton	Meadowbank
1987-88	Celtic	Hamilton A	Ayr U
1988-89	Rangers	Dunfermline	Albion R
1989-90	RANGERS	ST. JOHNSTONE	

MOST WINS:
Premier Div/Div 1 38 Rangers **Div1/2** 6 Ayr U **Div 2** 2 Clyde

SCOTTISH FA CUP

Instituted in 1873, the Scottish FA Cup has been dominated by the two Glasgow giants, Celtic and Rangers, in post-war years.

Year	Winners	Runners up	Score
1874	Queen's Park	Clydesdale	2-0
1875	Queen's Park	Renton	3-0
1876	Queen's Park (after 1-1 draw)	Third Lanark	2-0
1877	Vale of Leven (after 0-0 and 1-1)	Rangers	3-2
1878	Vale of Leven	Third Lanark	1-0
1879	Vale of Leven	Rangers	1-1

(Vale of Leven awarded cup after Rangers did not appear for replay)

1880	Queen's Park	Thornlibank	3-0
1881	Queen's Park	Dumbarton	3-1

(Dumbarton protested after first game won 2-1 by Queen's Park)

1882	Queen's Park (after 2-2 draw)	Dumbarton	4-1

1883	Dumbarton	Vale of Leven	2-1

(after 2-2 draw)

1884	Queen's Park	Vale of Leven	

(Queen's Park awarded the game after Vale of Leven failed to appear)

1885	Renton	Vale of Leven	3-1

(after 0-0 draw)

1886	Queen's Park	Renton	3-1
1887	Hibernian	Dumbarton	2-1
1888	Renton	Cambuslang	6-1
1889	Third Lanark	Celtic	2-1

(Replayed game on order of Scottish FA. Third Lanark won first game 3-0)

1890	Queen's Park	Vale of Leven	2-1

(after 1-1 draw)

1891	Hearts	Dumbarton	1-0
1892	Celtic	Queen's Park	5-1

(after protested game won by Celtic 1-0)

1893	Queen's Park	Celtic	2-1
1894	Rangers	Celtic	3-1
1895	St.Bernard's	Renton	2-1
1896	Hearts	Hibernian	3-1
1897	Rangers	Dumbarton	5-1
1898	Rangers	Kilmarnock	2-0
1899	Celtic	Rangers	2-0
1900	Celtic	Queen's Park	4-3
1901	Hearts	Celtic	4-3
1902	Hibernian	Celtic	1-0
1903	Rangers	Hearts	2-0

(after 1-1 and 0-0)

1904	Celtic	Rangers	3-2
1905	Third Lanark	Rangers	3-1

(after 0-0 draw)

1906	Hearts	Third Lanark	1-0
1907	Celtic	Hearts	3-0
1908	Celtic	St.Mirren	5-1

1909 Owing to riot in Celtic v Rangers final,
       after two drawn games 2-2 and 1-1, the cup was witheld

1910	Dundee	Clyde	2-1

(after 2-2 and 0-0)

1911	Celtic	Hamilton A	2-0

(after 0-0 draw)

1912	Celtic	Clyde	2-0
1913	Falkirk	Raith R	2-0
1914	Celtic	Hibernian	4-1

(after 0-0 draw)

1915-19 Not Held

1920	Kilmarnock	Albion R	3-2
1921	Partick T	Rangers	1-0
1922	Morton	Rangers	1-0
1923	Celtic	Hibernian	1-0
1924	Airdrieonians	Hibernian	2-0
1925	Celtic	Dundee	2-1
1926	St.Mirren	Celtic	2-0
1927	Celtic	East Fife	3-1
1928	Rangers	Celtic	4-0
1929	Kilmarnock	Rangers	2-0
1930	Rangers	Partick T	2-1

(after 0-0 draw)

Scottish F.A. Cup Cont.

Year	Winners	Runner up	Score
1931	Celtic (after 2-2 draw)	Motherwell	4-2
1932	Rangers (after 1-1 draw)	Kilmarnock	3-0
1933	Celtic	Motherwell	1-0
1934	Rangers	St.Mirren	5-0
1935	Rangers	Hamilton A	2-1
1936	Rangers	Third Lanark	1-0
1937	Celtic	Aberdeen	2-1
1938	East Fife (after 1-1 draw)	Kilmarnock	4-2
1939	Clyde	Motherwell	4-0
1940-46 Not Held			
1947	Aberdeen	Hibernian	2-1
1948	Rangers (after 1-1 draw)	Morton	1-0
1949	Rangers	Clyde	4-1
1950	Rangers	East Fife	3-0
1951	Celtic	Motherwell	1-0
1952	Motherwell	Dundee	4-0
1953	Rangers (after 1-1 draw)	Aberdeen	1-0
1954	Celtic	Aberdeen	2-1
1955	Clyde (after 1-1 draw)	Celtic	1-0
1956	Hearts	Celtic	3-1
1957	Falkirk (after 1-1 draw)	Kilmarnock	2-1
1958	Clyde	Hibernian	1-0
1959	St.Mirren	Aberdeen	3-1
1960	Rangers	Kilmarnock	2-0
1961	Dunfermline A (after 0-0 draw)	Celtic	2-0
1962	Rangers	St.Mirren	2-0
1963	Rangers (after 1-1 draw)	Celtic	3-0
1964	Rangers	Dundee	3-1
1965	Celtic	Dunfermline A	3-2
1966	Rangers (after 0-0 draw)	Celtic	1-0
1967	Celtic	Aberdeen	2-0
1968	Dunfermline A	Hearts	3-1
1969	Celtic	Rangers	4-0
1970	Aberdeen	Celtic	3-1
1971	Celtic (after 1-1 draw)	Rangers	2-1
1972	Celtic	Hibernian	6-1
1973	Rangers	Celtic	3-2
1974	Celtic	Dundee U	3-0
1975	Celtic	Airdrieonians	3-1
1976	Rangers	Hearts	3-1
1977	Celtic	Rangers	1-0
1978	Rangers	Aberdeen	2-1
1979	Rangers (after 0-0 and 0-0)	Hibernian	3-2

1980	Celtic	Rangers	1-0
1981	Rangers	Dundee U	4-1
	(after 0-0)		
1982	Aberdeen	Rangers	4-1
1983	Aberdeen	Rangers	1-0
1984	Aberdeen	Celtic	2-1
1985	Celtic	Dundee U	2-1
1986	Aberdeen	Hearts	3-0
1987	St Mirren	Dundee U	1-0
1988	Celtic	Dundee U	2-1
1989	Celtic	Rangers	1-0

MOST WINS:

29 Celtic

SCOTTISH LEAGUE CUP

Played annually since 1946-47 the Scottish League Cup has been known as the Skol Cup since 1984.

Year	Winners	Runner up	Score
1946-47	Rangers	Aberdeen	4-0
1947-48	East Fife	Falkirk	4-1
	(after 0-0 draw)		
1948-49	Rangers	Raith R	2-0
1949-50	East Fife	Dunfermline A	3-0
1950-51	Motherwell	Hibernian	3-0
1951-52	Dundee	Rangers	3-2
1952-53	Dundee	Kilmarnock	2-0
1953-54	East Fife	Partick T	3-2
1954-55	Hearts	Motherwell	4-2
1955-56	Aberdeen	St.Mirren	2-1
1956-57	Celtic	Partick T	3-0
	(after 0-0 draw)		
1957-58	Celtic	Rangers	7-1
1958-59	Hearts	Partick T	5-1
1959-60	Hearts	Third Lanark	2-1
1960-61	Rangers	Kilmarnock	2-0
1961-62	Rangers	Hearts	3-1
	(after 1-1 draw)		
1962-63	Hearts	Kilmarnock	1-0
1963-64	Rangers	Morton	5-0
1964-65	Rangers	Celtic	2-1
1965-66	Celtic	Rangers	2-1
1966-67	Celtic	Rangers	1-0
1967-68	Celtic	Dundee	5-3
1968-69	Celtic	Hibernian	6-2
1969-70	Celtic	St.Johnstone	1-0
1970-71	Rangers	Celtic	1-0
1971-72	Partick T	Celtic	4-1
1972-73	Hibernian	Celtic	2-1
1973-74	Dundee	Celtic	1-0
1974-75	Celtic	Hibernian	6-3
1975-76	Rangers	Celtic	1-0
1976-77	Aberdeen	Celtic	2-1
1977-78	Rangers	Celtic	2-1
1978-79	Rangers	Aberdeen	2-1

1979-80	Dundee U (after 0-0 draw)	Aberdeen	3-0
1980-81	Dundee U	Dundee	3-0
1981-82	Rangers	Dundee U	2-1
1982-83	Celtic	Rangers	2-1
1983-84	Rangers	Celtic	3-2
1984-85	Rangers	Dundee U	1-0
1985-86	Aberdeen	Hibernian	3-0
1986-87	Rangers	Celtic	2-1
1987-88	Rangers (Rangers won 5-3 on penalties)	Aberdeen	3-3
1988-89	Rangers	Aberdeen	3-2

MOST WINS:

16 Rangers

FA CHALLENGE TROPHY

Non-League football's most cherished competition, the prize for the two finalists each year is a trip to Wembley Stadium. First held in 1969-70.

Year	Winners	Runners up	Score
1970	Macclesfield T	Telford U	2-0
1971	Telford U	Hillingdon B	3-2
1972	Stafford R	Barnet	3-0
1973	Scarborough	Wigan A	2-1
1974	Morecambe	Dartford	2-1
1975	Matlock	Scarborough	4-0
1976	Scarborough	Stafford R	3-2
1977	Scarborough	Dagenham	2-1
1978	Altrincham	Leatherhead	3-1
1979	Stafford R	Kettering T	2-0
1980	Dagenham	Mossley	2-1
1981	Bishop's Stortford	Sutton U	1-0
1982	Enfield	Altrincham	1-0
1983	Telford U	Northwich V	2-1
1984	Northwich V (after 1-1 draw)	Bangor C	2-1
1985	Wealdstone	Boston U	2-1
1986	Altrincham	Runcorn	1-0
1987	Kidderminster H (after 0-0 draw)	Burton	2-1
1988	Enfield (after 0-0 draw)	Telford U	3-2
1989	Telford U	Macclesfield	1-0

MOST WINS:

3 Scarborough

OLYMPIC GAMES

Association Football was not played in the first Modern Olympics at Athens in 1896 but since 1900 it has been included in every celebration except the 1932 Los Angeles Games.

Champions:

1900 Great Britain	1952 Hungary
1904 Canada	1956 USSR
1908 Great Britain	1960 Yugoslavia

1912 Great Britain	1964 Hungary
1920 Belgium	1968 Hungary
1924 Uruguay	1972 Poland
1928 Uruguay	1976 East Germany
1932 Not Held	1980 Czechoslovakia
1936 Italy	1984 France
1948 Sweden	1988 USSR

MOST WINS:
3 Great Britain, Hungary

LEADING GOALSCORERS
Career: 1329 A. Friedenreich (BRA), 1909-35
World Cup (career): 14 G. Muller (FRG), 1970-74
        (one competition): 13 J. Fontaine (FRA), 1958
Football League (season):

Div 1	: 60	W. R. Dean (Everton), 1927-28
Div 2	: 59	G. Camsell (Middlesbrough), 1926-27
Div 3	: 39	D. Reeves (Southampton), 1959-60
Div 4	: 52	T. Bly (Peterborough V), 1960-61
Div 3 (S)	: 55	J. Payne (Luton T), 1936-37
Div 3 (N)	: 55	E. Harston (Mansfield T), 1936-37
Scottish League (season)	: 66	J. Smith (Ayr U), Div. 2, 1927-28

Athletics events date to the Ancient Olympic Games. There is evidence of athletics meetings in the middle ages but it started to become an organised sport in the middle of the 19th century. The governing body of international athletics, the International Amateur Athletic Federation, was founded in 1913.

OLYMPIC GAMES

Track and field athletics have been the principal sport at all Modern Olympic celebrations since the first at Athens in 1896.

Winners:

100 metres

Men	Women
1896 T.Burke (USA)	–
1900 F.Jarvis (USA)	–
1904 A.Hahn (USA)	–
1908 R.Walker (SAF)	–
1912 R.Craig (USA)	–
1920 C.Paddock (USA)	–
1924 H.Abrahams (GB)	–
1928 P.Williams (CAN)	E.Robinson (USA)
1932 E.Tolan (USA)	S.Walasiewicz (POL)
1936 J.Owens (USA)	H.Stephens (USA)
1948 H.Dillard (USA)	F.Blankers Koen (HOL)
1952 L.Remigino (USA)	M.Jackson (AUS)
1956 B-J.Morrow (USA)	B.Cuthbert (AUS)
1960 A.Hary (GER)	W.Rudolph (USA)
1964 R.Hayes (USA)	W.Tyus (USA)
1968 J.Hines (USA)	W.Tyus (USA)
1972 V.Borzov (USSR)	R.Stecher (GDR)
1976 H.Crawford (TRI)	A.Richter (FRG)
1980 A.Wells (GB)	L.Kondratyeva (USSR)
1984 C.Lewis (USA)	E.Ashford (USA)
1988 C.Lewis (USA)	F.Griffith-Joyner (USA)

200 metres

Men	Women
1900 W.Tewksbury (USA)	–
1904 A.Hahn (USA)	–
1908 R.Kerr (CAN)	–
1912 R.Craig (USA)	–
1920 A.Woodring (USA)	–
1924 J.Scholz (USA)	–
1928 P.Williams (CAN)	–
1932 E.Tolan (USA)	–
1936 J.Owens (USA)	
1948 M.Patton (USA)	F.Blankers-Koen (HOL)
1952 A.Stanfield (USA)	M.Jackson (AUS)
1956 B-J.Morrow (USA)	B.Cuthbert (AUS)
1960 L.Berutti (ITA)	W.Rudolph (USA)
1964 H.Carr (USA)	E.Maguire (USA)
1968 T.Smith (USA)	I.Szewinska (POL)
1972 V.Borzov (USSR)	R.Stecher (GDR)
1976 D.Quarrie (JAM)	B.Eckert (GDR)
1980 P.Mennea (ITA)	B.Wockel (nee Eckert) (GDR)
1984 C.Lewis (USA)	V.Brisco-Hooks (USA)
1988 J.DeLoach (USA)	F.Griffith-Joyner (USA)

400 metres

Men	Women
1896 T.Burke (USA)	–
1900 M.Long (USA)	–
1904 H.Hillman (USA)	–
1908 W.Halswelle (GB)	–
1912 C.Reidpath (USA)	–
1920 B.Rudd (SAF)	–
1924 E.Liddell (GB)	–
1928 R.Barbuti (USA)	–
1932 W.Carr (USA)	–
1936 A.Williams (USA)	–
1948 A.Wint (JAM)	–
1952 G.Rhoden (JAM)	–
1956 C.Jenkins (USA)	–
1960 O.Davis (USA)	
1964 M.Larrabee (USA)	B.Cuthbert (AUS)
1968 L.Evans (USA)	C.Besson (FRA)
1972 V.Matthews (USA)	M.Zehrt (GDR)
1976 A.Juantorena (CUB)	I.Szewinska (POL)
1980 V.Markin (USSR)	M.Koch (GDR)
1984 A.Babers (USA)	V.Brisco-Hooks (USA)
1988 S.Lewis (USA)	O.Bryzgina (USSR)

800 metres

Men	Women
1896 E.Flack (AUS)	–
1900 A.Tysoe (GB)	–
1904 J.Lightbody (USA)	–
1908 M.Sheppard (USA)	–
1912 J.Meredith (USA)	–
1920 A.Hill (GB)	–
1924 D.Lowe (GB)	–
1928 D.Lowe (GB)	L.Radke (GER)
1932 T.Hampson (GB)	–
1936 J.Woodruff (USA)	–
1948 M.Whitfield (USA)	–
1952 M.Whitfield (USA)	–
1956 T.Courtney (USA)	–
1960 P.Snell (NZ)	L.Shevtsova (USSR)
1964 P.Snell (NZ)	A.Packer (GB)
1968 R.Doubell (AUS)	M.Manning (USA)
1972 D.Wottle (USA)	H.Falck (FRG)
1976 A.Juantorena (CUB)	T.Kazankina (USSR)
1980 S.Ovett (GB)	N.Olizarenko (USSR)
1984 J.Cruz (BRA)	D.Melinte (ROM)
1988 P.Ereng (KEN)	S.Wodars (GDR)

1500 metres

Men	Women
1896 E.Flack (AUS)	–
1900 C.Bennett (GB)	–
1904 J.Lightbody (USA)	–
1908 M.Sheppard (USA)	–
1912 A.Jackson (GB)	–
1920 A.Hill (GB)	–
1924 P.Nurmi (FIN)	–
1928 H.Larva (FIN)	–
1932 L.Beccali (ITA)	–
1936 J.Lovelock (NZ)	–
1948 H.Eriksson (SWE)	–
1952 J.Barthel (LUX)	–
1956 R.Delany (IRL)	–
1960 H.Elliott (AUS)	–
1964 P.Snell (NZ)	–
1968 K.Keino (KEN)	–
1972 P.Vasala (FIN)	L.Bragina (USSR)
1976 J.Walker (NZ)	T.Kazankina (USSR)
1980 S.Coe (GB)	T.Kazankina (USSR)
1984 S.Coe (GB)	G.Dorio (ITA)
1988 P.Rono (KEN)	P.Ivan (ROM)

3000 metres
(Women only)

1984 M.Puica (ROM)
1988 T.Samolenko (USSR)

5000 metres
(Men only)

1912 H.Kolehmainen (FIN)
1920 J.Guillemot (FRA)
1924 P.Nurmi (FIN)
1928 V.Ritola (FIN)
1932 L.Lehtinen (FIN)
1936 G.Hockert (FIN)
1948 G.Rieff (BEL)
1952 E.Zatopek (TCH)
1956 V.Kuts (USSR)
1960 M.Halberg (NZ)
1964 B.Schul (USA)
1968 M.Gammoudi (TUN)
1972 L.Viren (FIN)
1976 L.Viren (FIN)
1980 M.Yifter (ETH)
1984 S.Aouita (MOR)
1988 J.Ngugi (KEN)

10,000 metres

Men	Women
1912 H.Kolehmainen (FIN)	
1920 P.Nurmi (FIN)	
1924 V.Ritola (FIN)	
1928 P.Nurmi (FIN)	
1932 J.Kusocinski (POL)	
1936 I.Salminen (FIN)	
1948 E.Zatopek (TCH)	
1952 E.Zatopek (TCH)	
1956 V.Kuts (USSR)	
1960 P.Bolotnikov (USSR)	
1964 W.Mills (USA)	
1968 N.Temu (KEN)	
1972 L.Viren (FIN)	
1976 L.Viren (FIN)	
1980 M.Yifter (ETH)	
1984 A.Cova (ITA)	
1988 M.B.Boutaib (MOR)	O.Bondarenko (USSR)

Marathon

Men	Women
1896 S.Louis (GRE)	–
1900 M.Theato (FRA)	–
1904 T.Hicks (USA)	–
1908 J.Hayes (USA)	–
1912 K.McArthur (SAF)	–
1920 H.Kolehmainen (FIN)	–
1924 A.Stenroos (FIN)	–
1928 M.El Ouafi (FRA)	–
1932 J.C.Zabala (ARG)	–
1936 K.Son (JAP)	–
1948 D.Cabrera (ARG)	–
1952 E.Zatopek (TCH)	–
1956 A.Mimoun (FRA)	–
1960 A.Bikila (ETH)	–
1964 A.Bikila (ETH)	–
1968 M.Wolde (ETH)	–
1972 F.Shorter (USA)	–
1976 W.Cierpinski (GDR)	–
1980 W.Cierpinski (GDR)	–
1984 C.Lopes (POR)	J.Benoit (USA)
1988 G.Bordin (ITA)	R.Mota (POR)

100 metres Hurdles
(Women only; 80 metres until 1968)

1932 M.Didrikson (USA)
1936 T.Valla (ITA)
1948 F.Blankers-Koen (HOL)
1952 S.Strickland (AUS)
1956 S.Strickland (AUS)
1960 I.Press (USSR)
1964 K.Balzer (GER)
1968 M.Caird (AUS)
1972 A.Ehrhardt (GDR)
1976 J.Schaller (GDR)
1980 V.Komisova (USSR)
1984 B.Fitzgerald-Brown (USA)
1988 J. Donkova (BUL)

110 metres Hurdles
(Men only)
1896 T.Curtis (USA)
1900 A.Kraenzlein (USA)
1904 F.Schule (USA)
1908 F.Smithson (USA)
1912 F.Kelly (USA)
1920 E.Thomson (CAN)
1924 D.Kinsey (USA)
1928 S.Atkinson (SAF)
1932 G.Saling (USA)
1936 F.Towns (USA)
1948 W.Porter (USA)
1952 H.Dillard (USA)
1956 L.Calhoun (USA)
1960 L.Calhoun (USA)
1964 H.Jones (USA)
1968 W.Davenport (USA)
1972 R.Milburn (USA)
1976 G.Drut (FRA)
1980 T.Munkelt (GDR)
1984 R.Kingdom (USA)
1988 R.Kingdom (USA)

400 metres Hurdles

Men	**Women**
1900 W.Tewksbury (USA)	–
1904 H.Hillman (USA)	–
1908 C.Bacon (USA)	–
1912 F.Kelly (USA)	–
1920 F.Loomis (USA)	–
1924 M.Taylor (USA)	–
1928 Lord Burghley (GB)	–
1932 B.Tisdall (IRE)	–
1936 G.Hardin (USA)	–
1948 R.Cochran (USA)	–
1952 C.Moore (USA)	–
1956 G.Davis (USA)	–
1960 G.Davis (USA)	–
1964 R.Cawley (USA)	–
1968 D.Hemery (GB)	–
1972 J.Akii-Bua (UGA)	–
1976 E.Moses (USA)	–
1980 V.Beck (GDR)	–
1984 E.Moses (USA)	N.El Moutawakel (MOR)
1988 A.Phillips (USA)	D.Flintoff-King (AUS)

3000 metres Steeplechase
(Men only; distance standardised at 3000 metres in 1920)
1900 G.Orton (CAN) J.Rimmer (GB)*
1904 J.Lightbody (USA)
1908 A.Russell (GB)
1920 P.Hodge (GB)
1924 V.Ritola (FIN)
1928 T.Loukola (FIN)
1932 V.Iso-Hollo (FIN)
1936 V.Iso-Hollo (FIN)
1948 T.Sjostrand (SWE)
1952 H.Ashenfelter (USA)
1956 C.Brasher (GB)
1960 Z.Krzyszkowiak (POL)
1964 G.Roelants (BEL)
1968 A.Biwott (KEN)
1972 K.Keino (KEN)
1976 A.Garderud (SWE)
1980 B.Malinowski (POL)
1984 J.Korir (KEN)
1988 J.Kariuki (KEN)
*two races, one over 2500m and the other over 4000m

4x100 metres Relay

Men	Women
1912 Great Britain	–
1920 United States	–
1924 United States	–
1928 United States	Canada
1932 United States	United States
1936 United States	United States
1948 United States	Netherlands
1952 United States	United States
1956 United States	Australia
1960 Germany	United States
1964 United States	Poland
1968 United States	United States
1972 United States	West Germany
1976 United States	East Germany
1980 USSR	East Germany
1984 United States	United States
1988 USSR	United States

4x400 metres Relay

Men	Women
1908 United States	–
1912 United States	–
1920 Great Britain	–
1924 United States	–
1928 United States	–
1932 United States	–
1936 Great Britain	–
1948 United States	–
1952 Jamaica	–
1956 United States	–
1960 United States	–
1964 United States	–

1968 United States	–
1972 Kenya	East Germany
1976 United States	East Germany
1980 USSR	USSR
1984 United States	United States
1988 United States	USSR

20,000 metres Walk
(Men only)
1956 L.Spirin (USSR)
1960 V.Golubnichiy (USSR)
1964 K.Matthews (GB)
1968 V.Golubnichiy (USSR)
1972 P.Frenkel (GDR)
1976 D.Bautista (MEX)
1980 M.Damilano (ITA)
1984 E.Canto (MEX)
1988 J.Pribilinec (TCH)

50,000 metres Walk
(Men only)
1932 T.Green (GB)
1936 H.Whitlock (GB)
1948 J.Ljunggren (SWE)
1952 G.Dordoni (ITA)
1956 N.Read (NZ)
1960 D.Thompson (GB)
1964 A.Pamich (ITA)
1968 C.Hohne (GDR)
1972 B.Kannenberg (FRG)
1980 H.Gauder (GDR)
1984 R.Gonzalez (Mex)
1988 V.Ivanenko (USSR)

High Jump

Men	Women
1896 E.Clark (USA)	–
1900 I.Baxter (USA)	–
1904 S.Jones (USA)	–
1908 H.Porter (USA)	–
1912 A.Richards (USA)	–
1920 R.Landon (USA)	–
1924 H.Osborn (USA)	–
1928 R.King (USA)	E.Catherwood (CAN)
1932 D.McNaughton (CAN)	J.Shiley (USA)
1936 C.Johnson (USA)	I.Csak (HUN)
1948 J.Winter (AUS)	A.Coachman (USA)
1952 W.Davis (USA)	E.Brand (SAF)
1956 C.Dumas (USA)	M.McDaniel (USA)
1960 R.Shavlakadze (USSR)	I.Balas (ROM)
1964 V.Brumel (USSR)	I.Balas (ROM)
1968 R.Fosbury (USA)	M.Rezkova (TCH)
1972 Y.Tarmak (USSR)	U.Meyfarth (FRG)
1976 J.Wszola (POL)	R.Ackermann (GDR)
1980 G.Wessig (GDR)	S.Simeoni (ITA)
1984 D.Moegenburg (FRG)	U.Meyfarth (FRG)
1988 G.Avdeyenko (USSR)	L.Ritter (USA)

Pole Vault
(Men only)
1896 W.Hoyt (USA)
1900 I.Baxter (USA)
1904 C.Dvorak (USA)
1908 E.Cooke (USA)
1912 H.Babcock (USA)
1916 Not held
1920 F.Foss (USA)
1924 L.Barnes (USA)
1928 S.Carr (USA)
1932 W.Miller (USA)
1936 E.Meadows (USA)
1948 G.Smith (USA)
1952 R.Richards (USA)
1956 R.Richards (USA)
1960 D.Bragg (USA)
1964 F.Hansen (USA)
1968 R.Seagren (USA)
1972 W.Nordwig (GDR)
1976 T.Slusarski (POL)
1980 W.Kozakiewicz (POL)
1984 P.Quinon (FRA)
1988 S.Bubka (USSR)

Long Jump

	Men	Women
1896	E.Clark (USA)	–
1900	A.Kraenzlein (USA)	–
1904	M.Prinstein (USA)	–
1908	F.Irons (USA)	–
1912	A.Gutterson (USA)	–
1920	W.Pettersson (SWE)	–
1924	W.De Hart Hubbard (USA)	–
1928	E.Hamm (USA)	–
1932	E.Gordon (USA)	–
1936	J.Owens (USA)	–
1948	W.Steele (USA)	O.Gyarmati (HUN)
1952	J.Biffle (USA)	Y.Williams (NZ)
1956	G.Bell (USA)	E.Krzesinska (POL)
1960	R.Boston (USA)	V.Krepkina (USSR)
1964	L.Davies (GB)	M.Rand (GB)
1968	B.Beamon (USA)	V.Viscopoleanu (ROM)
1972	R.Williams (USA)	H.Rosendahl (FRG)
1976	A.Robinson (USA)	A.Voigt (GDR)
1980	L.Dombrowski (GDR)	T.Kolpakova (USSR)
1984	C.Lewis (USA)	A.Stanciu (ROM)
1988	C.Lewis (USA)	J.Joyner-Kersee (USA)

Triple Jump
(Men only)
1896 J.Connolly (USA)
1900 M.Prinstein (USA)
1904 M.Prinstein (USA)
1908 T.Ahearne (GB)
1912 G.Lindblom (SWE)
1920 V.Tuulos (FIN)
1924 A.Winter (AUS)
1928 M.Oda (JAP)
1932 C.Nambu (JAP)
1936 N.Tajima (JAP)
1948 A.Ahman (SWE)
1952 A.Ferreira da Silva (BRA)
1956 A.Ferreira da Silva (BRA)
1960 J.Schmidt (POL)
1964 J.Schmidt (POL)
1968 V.Saneyev (USSR)
1972 V.Saneyev (USSR)
1976 V.Saneyev (USSR)
1980 J.Uudmae (USSR)
1984 A.Joyner (USA)
1988 H.Markov (BUL)

Shot Put

Men	Women
1896 R.Garrett (USA)	–
1900 R.Sheldon (USA)	–
1904 R.Rose (USA)	–
1908 R.Rose (USA)	–
1912 P.McDonald (USA)	–
1920 V.Porhola (FIN)	–
1924 C.Houser (USA)	–
1928 J.Kuck (USA)	–
1932 L.Sexton (USA)	–
1936 H.Woellke (GER)	–
1948 W.Thompson (USA)	M.Ostermeyer (FRA)
1952 P.O'Brien (USA)	G.Zybina (USSR)
1956 P.O'Brien (USA)	T.Tyshkevich (USSR)
1960 B.Nieder (USA)	T.Press (USSR)
1964 D.Long (USA)	T.Press (USSR)
1968 R.Matson (USA)	M.Gummel (GDR)
1972 W.Komar (POL)	N.Chizhova (USSR)
1976 U.Beyer (GDR)	I.Khristova (BUL)
1980 V.Kiselyev (USSR)	I.Slupianek (GDR)
1984 A.Andrei (ITA)	C.Losch (FRG)
1988 U.Timmerman (GDR)	N.Lisovskaya (USSR)

Discus

Men	Women
1896 R.Garrett (USA)	–
1900 R.Bauer (HUN)	–
1904 M.Sheridan (USA)	–
1908 M.Sheridan (USA)	–
1912 A.Taipale (FIN)	–
1920 E.Niklander (FIN)	–
1924 C.Houser (USA)	–
1928 C.Houser (USA)	H.Konopacka (POL)
1932 J.Anderson (USA)	L.Copeland (USA)
1936 K.Carpenter (USA)	G.Mauermayer (GER)
1948 A.Consolini (ITA)	M.Ostermeyer (FRA)
1952 S.Iness (USA)	M.Romashkova (USSR)
1956 A.Oerter (USA)	O.Fikotova (TCH)
1960 A.Oerter (USA)	N.Ponomaryeva (USSR)
1964 A.Oerter (USA)	T.Press (USSR)
1968 A.Oerter (USA)	L.Manoliu (ROM)
1972 L.Danek (TCH)	F.Melnik (USSR)
1976 M.Wilkins (USA)	E.Jahl (nee Schlaak) (GDR)
1980 V.Rashchupkin (USSR)	E.Jahl (GDR)
1984 R.Danneberg (FRG)	R.Stalman (HOL)
1988 J.Schult (GDR)	M.Hellman (GDR)

Hammer
(Men only)

1900 J.Flanagan (USA)
1904 J.Flanagan (USA)
1908 J.Flanagan (USA)
1912 M.McGrath (USA)
1920 P.Ryan (USA)
1924 F.Tootell (USA)
1928 P.O'Callaghan (IRE)
1932 P.O'Callaghan (IRE)
1936 K.Hein (GER)
1948 I.Nemeth (HUN)
1952 J.Csermak (HUN)
1956 H.Connolly (USA)
1960 V.Rudenkov (USSR)
1964 R.Klim (USSR)
1968 G.Zsivotzky (HUN)
1972 A.Bondarchuk (USSR)
1976 Y.Sedykh (USSR)
1980 Y.Sedykh (USSR)
1984 J.Tiainen (FIN)
1988 S.Litvinov (USSR)

Javelin

Men	Women
1908 E.Lemming (SWE)	–
1912 E.Lemming (SWE)	–
1920 J.Myyra (FIN)	–
1924 J.Myyra (FIN)	–
1928 E.Lundkvist (SWE)	–
1932 M.Jarvinen (FIN)	M.Didrikson (USA)
1936 G.Stock (GER)	T.Fleischer (GER)
1948 T.Rautavaara (FIN)	H.Bauma (AUT)
1952 C.Young (USA)	D.Zatopkova (TCH)
1956 E.Danielsen (NOR)	I.Jaunzeme (USSR)
1960 V.Tsibulenko (USSR)	E.Ozolina (USSR)
1964 P.Nevala (FIN)	M.Penes (ROM)
1968 J.Lusis (USSR)	A.Nemeth (HUN)
1972 K.Wolfermann (FRG)	R.Fuchs (GDR)
1976 M.Nemeth (HUN)	R.Fuchs (GDR)
1980 D.Kula (USSR)	M.Colon (CUB)
1984 A.Haerkoenen (FIN)	T.Sanderson (GB)
1988 T.Korjus (FIN)	P.Felke (GDR)

Decathlon
(Men only)

1904 T.Kiely (IRE)
1912 J.Thorpe (USA)
1920 H.Lovland (NOR)
1924 H.Osborn (USA)
1928 P.Yrjola (FIN)
1932 J.Bausch (USA)
1936 G.Morris (USA)
1948 R.Mathias (USA)
1952 R.Mathias (USA)
1956 M.Campbell (USA)
1960 R.Johnson (USA)
1964 W.Holdorf (GER)
1968 B.Toomey (USA)
1972 N.Avilov (USSR)
1976 B.Jenner (USA)
1980 D.Thompson (GB)
1984 D.Thompson (GB)
1988 |C.Shenk (GDR)

Heptathlon
(Women only; Pentathlon 1964-80)

1964 I.Press (USSR)
1968 I.Becker (FRG)
1972 M.Peters (GB)
1976 S.Siegl (GDR)
1980 N.Tkachenko (USSR)
1984 G.Nunn (AUS)
1988 J.Joyner-Kersee (USA)

Most Gold Medals
(Men):
10 Ray Ewry (Ewry won all his medals in the
now discontinued standing jumping events)

(Women):
4 Fanny Blankers-Koen, Betty Cuthbert, Barbel Wockel

LONDON MARATHON

With marathon running increasing in popularity in the 1980s, London followed other major cities by staging a race around the city in 1981. It has since become one of the leading races on the marathon calendar. Nearly 20,000 runners take part in the race each year.

Winners:

Men	Women
1981 I.Simonsen (NOR) & R.Beardsley (USA)	J.Smith (GB)
1982 H.Jones (GB)	J.Smith (GB)
1983 M.Gratton (GB)	G.Waitz (NOR)
1984 C.Spedding (GB)	I.Kristiansen (NOR)
1985 S.Jones (GB)	I.Kristiansen (NOR)
1986 T.Seko (JAP)	G.Waitz (NOR)
1987 H.Tanaguchi (JAP)	I.Kristiansen (NOR)
1988 H.Jorgensen (DEN)	I.Kristiansen (NOR)
1989 D.Wakiihuri (KEN)	V.Marot (GB)
1990 ALLISTER HUTTON (SCO)	WANDA PANFIL (POLAND)

WORLD CROSS COUNTRY CHAMPIONSHIP

Formerly the International Championship, it started in 1903 and consisted of runners from the four home countries. France competed from 1907 and it gradually became more of an international affair. It became known as the World Cross Country Championship in 1973 after the I.A.A.F. took the event under its control.

Winners (since 1973):

Men	Individual	Team
1973	P.Paivarinta (FIN)	Belgium
1974	E. De Beck (BEL)	Belgium
1975	I.Stewart (SCO)	New Zealand
1976	C.Lopes (POR)	England
1977	L.Schots (BEL)	Belgium
1978	J.Treacy (IRE)	France
1979	J.Treacy (IRE)	England
1980	C.Virgin (USA)	England
1981	C.Virgin (USA)	Ethiopia
1982	M.Kedir (ETH)	Ethiopia
1983	B.Debele (ETH)	Ethiopia
1984	C.Lopes (POR)	Ethiopia
1985	C.Lopes (POR)	Ethiopia
1986	J.Ngugi (KEN)	Kenya
1987	J.Ngugi (KEN)	Kenya
1988	J.Ngugi (KEN)	Kenya
1989	K.Metafeira (ETH)	Ethiopia

Women	Individual	Team
1973	P.Cacchi (ITA)	England
1974	P.Cacchi (ITA)	England
1975	J.Brown (USA)	United States
1976	C.Valero (SPA)	USSR
1977	C.Valero (SPA)	USSR
1978	G.Waitz (NOR)	Romania
1979	G.Waitz (NOR)	United States
1980	G.Waitz (NOR)	USSR
1981	G.Waitz (NOR)	USSR
1982	M.Puica (ROM)	USSR
1983	G.Waitz (NOR)	United States
1984	M.Puica (ROM)	United States
1985	Z.Budd (ENG)	United States

1986	Z.Budd (ENG)	England
1987	A.Sergent (FRA)	United States
1988	I.Kristiansen (NOR)	USSR
1989	S.Marchiano (USA)	USSR

WORLD CHAMPIONSHIPS

The first IAAF World Championships were held at Helsinki, Finland in 1983. Held every four years, the second championships were at Rome in 1987.

Men:	1983 Winners	1987 Winners
100 metres	C. Lewis (USA)	B. Johnson (CAN)
200 metres	C. Smith (USA)	C. Smith (USA)
400 metres	R. Cameron (JAM)	T. Schoenlebe (GDR)
800 metres	W. Wuelbeck (FRG)	B. Konchellah (KEN)
1500 metres	S. Cram (GB)	A. Bile (SOM)
5000 metres	E. Coghlan (IRE)	S. Aouita (MOR)
10000 metres	R. Cova (ITA)	P. Kipkoech (KEN)
Marathon	R. de Castella (AUS)	D. Waikihuru (KEN)
110m hurdles	G. Foster (USA)	G. Foster (USA)
400m hurdles	E. Moses (USA)	E. Moses (USA)
3000 steeplechase	P. Ilg (FRG)	F. Panetta (ITA)
4 x 100m relay	United States	United States
4 x 400m relay	USSR	United States
20 km walk	E. Canto (MEX)	M. Damilano (ITA)
50 km walk	R. Weigel (GDR)	H. Gauder (GDR)
High jump	G. Avdeenko (USSR)	P. Sjoeberg (SWE)
Long jump	C. Lewis (USA)	C. Lewis (USA)
Triple jump	Z. Hoffman (POL)	K. Markov (BUL)
Pole vault	S. Bubka (USSR)	S. Bubka (USSR)
Discus	I. Bugar (TCH)	J. Schult (GDR)
Hammer	S. Litvinov (USSR)	S. Litvinov (USSR)
Javelin	D. Michel (GDR)	S. Raty (FIN)
Decathlon	D. Thompson (GB)	T. Voss (GDR)
Shot Putt		W. Gunethoer (SWI)

Women:		
100 metres	M. Goehr (GDR)	S. Gladisch (GDR)
200 metres	M. Koch (GDR)	S. Gladisch (GDR)
400 metres	J. Kratochvilova (TCH)	O. Bryzgina (USSR)
800 metres	J. Kratochvilova (TCH)	S. Wodars (GDR)
1500 metres	M. Decker (USA)	T. Samolenko (USSR)
3000 metres	M. Decker (USA)	T. Samolenko (USSR)
Marathon	G. Waitz (NOR)	R. Mota (POR)
100 m hurdles	B. Jahn (GDR)	G. Zagorcheva (BUL)
400 m hurdles	E. Fesenko (USSR)	S. Busche (GDR)
4 x 100 m relay	GDR	United States
4 x 400 m relay	GDR	East Germany
High jump	T. Bykova (USSR)	S. Kostadinova (BUL)
Long jump	H. Daute (GDR)	J. Joyner-Kersee (USA)
Shot Putt	H. Fibingerova (TCH)	N. Lisovskaya (USSR)
Discus	M. Opitz (GDR)	M. Hellman (GDR)
Javelin	T. Lillak (FIN)	F. Whitbread (GB)
Heptathlon	R. Neubert (GDR)	J. Joyner-Kersee (USA)
10km Walk		I. Strakhova (USSR)

WORLD CUP

A team event for men's and women's teams from the five continents. It was first held at Dusseldorf in 1977 and has been held every two years since, with the exception of 1983 and 1987 when the World Championships were held.

Winners:

	Men	Women
1977	East Germany	Europe
1979	United States	East Germany
1981	Europe	East Germany
1983	Not held	
1985	United States	East Germany

EUROPEAN CUP

Like the World Cup, the European Cup is a team event for both men's and women's teams. The first championship was held in 1965 with the men's competition at Stuttgart and the women's at Kassel. The event is held every two years.

Winners:

	Men	Women
1965	USSR	USSR
1967	USSR	USSR
1970	East Germany	East Germany
1973	USSR	East Germany
1975	East Germany	East Germany
1977	East Germany	East Germany
1979	East Germany	East Germany
1981	East Germany	East Germany
1983	East Germany	East Germany
1985	USSR	USSR
1987	USSR	East Germany

BRITISH ATHLETICS LEAGUE

Originally called the National Athletics League, it was formed in 1969. The British Women's League was formed in 1975. Both men and women have League and Cup competitions each season. The knockout cup competition for men, the Gold Cup, was launched in 1973 and the women's knockout cup followed a year later.

Division One champions:

	Men	Women
1969	Birchfield Harriers	—
1970	Thames Valley Harriers	—
1971	Thames Valley Harriers	—
1972	Cardiff	—
1973	Cardiff	—
1974	Cardiff	—
1975	Wolverhampton & Bilston	Edinburgh Southern
1976	Wolverhampton & Bilston	Sale
1977	Wolverhampton & Bilston	Sale
1978	Wolverhampton & Bilston	Sale
1979	Wolverhampton & Bilston	Stretford
1980	Wolverhampton & Bilston	Bristol
1981	Wolverhampton & Bilston	Stretford
1982	Wolverhampton & Bilston	Notts AC
1983	Birchfield Harriers	Sale
1984	Haringey	Stretford
1985	Birchfield Harriers	Stretford
1986	Haringey	Sale
1987	Birchfield Harriers	Essex Ladies
1988	Haringey	Essex Ladies

Most wins (Men): 8 Wolverhampton & Bilston **(Women):** 5 Sale

Cup winners:

	Men	Women
1973	Wolverhampton & Bilston	—
1974	Cardiff	Mitcham
1975	Edinburgh Southern	Edinburgh Southern
1976	Wolverhampton & Bilston	Stretford
1977	Wolverhampton & Bilston	Stretford
1978	Shaftesbury	Stretford
1979	Wolverhampton & Bilston	Stretford
1980	Wolverhampton & Bilston	Stretford
1981	Haringey	Stretford
1982	Haringey	Borough of Hounslow
1983	Haringey	Borough of Hounslow
1984	Birchfields Harriers	Essex Ladies
1985	Shaftesbury	Essex Ladies
1986	Haringey	Essex Ladies
1987	Haringey	Essex Ladies
1988	Haringey	Stretford

Most wins (Men): 6 Haringey **(Women):** 7 Stretford

An 18-a-side game, it is tough and fast moving, and is played on an oval field approximately twice the size of a soccer pitch. The first organized game of Australian Rules Football was played between Scotch College and Melbourne Grammar School in Melbourne, in 1858.

VICTORIA FOOTBALL LEAGUE GRAND FINAL
The highlight of the Australian Rules Football season is the VFL Grand Final played at the Melbourne Cricket Ground, crowds in excess of 110,000 have attended the final.

1897 Essendon	1928 Collingwood	1959 Melbourne
1898 Fitzroy	1929 Collingwood	1960 Melbourne
1899 Fitzroy	1930 Collingwood	1961 Hawthorn
1900 Melbourne	1931 Geelong	1962 Essendon
1901 Essendon	1932 Richmond	1963 Geelong
1902 Collingwood	1933 South Melbourne	1964 Melbourne
1903 Collingwood	1934 Richmond	1965 Essendon
1904 Fitzroy	1935 Collingwood	1966 St. Kilda
1905 Fitzroy	1936 Collingwood	1967 Richmond
1906 Carlton	1937 Geelong	1968 Carlton
1907 Carlton	1938 Carlton	1969 Richmond
1908 Carlton	1939 Melbourne	1970 Carlton
1909 South Melbourne	1940 Melbourne	1971 Hawthorn
1910 Collingwood	1941 Melbourne	1972 Carlton
1911 Essendon	1942 Essendon	1973 Richmond
1912 Essendon	1943 Richmond	1974 Richmond
1913 Fitzroy	1944 Fitzroy	1975 North Melbourne
1914 Carlton	1945 Carlton	1976 Hawthorne
1915 Carlton	1946 Essendon	1977 North Melbourne
1916 Fitzroy	1947 Carlton	1978 Hawthorn
1917 Collingwood	1948 Melbourne	1979 Carlton
1918 South Melbourne	1949 Essendon	1980 Richmond
1919 Collingwood	1950 Essendon	1981 Carlton
1920 Richmond	1951 Geelong	1982 Carlton
1921 Richmond	1952 Geelong	1983 Hawthorn
1922 Fitzroy	1953 Collingwood	1984 Essendon
1923 Essendon	1954 Footscray	1985 Essendon
1924 Essendon	1955 Melbourne	1986 Hawthorn
1925 Geelong	1966 Melbourne	1987 Carlton
1926 Melbourne	1957 Melbourne	
1927 Collingwood	1958 Collingwood	

MOST WINS:
15 Carlton

The Chinese are reputed to have played a form of Badminton over 2000 years ago, but the roots of the modern game can be traced to Badminton Hall, Avon, the seat of the Duke of Beaufort, when house guests of the Duke used to amuse themselves playing the game in the 1870s. The game was taken to India, and it was there that the first set of rules were drawn up in 1877. The Badminton Association was formed in 1893.

THOMAS CUP

An international team competition for men's teams of six players; it was contested every three years until 1984 when it became a biennial event. The cup was donated by Sir George Thomas, winner of 21 All-England titles.

Winners:

1949 Malaya	1973 Indonesia
1952 Malaya	1976 Indonesia
1955 Malaya	1979 Indonesia
1958 Indonesia	1982 China
1961 Indonesia	1984 Indonesia
1964 Indonesia	1986 China
1967 Malaysia	1988 China
1970 Indonesia	

Most Wins: 8 Indonesia

UBER CUP

The women's equivalent of the Thomas Cup, it was also contested triennially until 1984 when it became a biennial event. The cup was presented by Betty Uber who represented England a then record 37 times between 1926–51.

Winners:

1957 United States	1975 Indonesia
1960 United States	1978 Japan
1963 United States	1981 Japan
1966 Japan	1984 China
1969 Japan	1986 China
1972 Japan	1988 China

Most Wins: 5 Japan

WORLD CHAMPIONSHIPS

Instituted in 1977 and initially held every three years, they are now held biennially.

Winners:

1977
Men's Singles	: F. Delfs (DEN)
Women's Singles	: L. Koppen (DEN)
Men's Doubles	: J. Wahjudi & T. Tjun (INA)
Women's Doubles	: E. Tuganoo & E. Vero (JAP)
Mixed Doubles	: S. Stovgaard & L. Koppen (DEN)

1980
Men's Singles	: R. Hartono (INA)
Women's Singles	: W. Verawaty (INA)
Men's Doubles	: A. Chandra & H. Christian (INA)
Women's Doubles	: N. Perry & J. Webster (GB)
Mixed Doubles	: H. Christian & I. Wigoeno (INA)

1983
Men's Singles   : I. Sugiarto (INA)
Women's Singles : L. Lingwei (CHN)
Men's Doubles   : S. Fladberg & J. Helledie (DEN)
Women's Doubles : L. Ying & W. Dixi (CHN)
Mixed Doubles   : T. Kihlstrom (SWE) & N. Perry (GB)
1985
Men's Singles   : H. Jian (CHN)
Women's Singles : H. Aiping (CHN)
Men's Doubles   : P. J. Bong & K. M. Soo (SKO)
Women's Doubles : H. Aiping & L. Lingwei (CHN)
Mixed Doubles   : P. J. Bong & S. Hee (SKO)
1987
Men's Singles   : Y. Yang (CHN)
Women's Singles : H. Aiping (CHN)
Men's Doubles   : L. Yongbo & T. Bingyi (CHN)
Women's Doubles : L. Ying & G. Weizhen (CHN)
Mixed Doubles   : W. Pengrin & S. Fanglin (CHN)
1989
Men's Singles   : Y. Yang (CHN)
Women's Singles : L. Lingwei (CHN)
Men's Doubles   : L. Yongbo & R. Bingyi (CHN)
Women's Doubles : L. Ying & G. Weizhen (CHN)
Mixed Doubles   : P.J. Bong & M.H. Chung (SKO)

Most Titles:
3 Han Aiping

ALL-ENGLAND CHAMPIONSHIP

Until the institution of the World Championships, the All-England Championship was Badminton's major event. In addition to the singles events, men's, women's and mixed doubles are also contested annually.

Men's Singles	Women's Singles
1900 S. Smith (ENG)	E. Thomson (ENG)
1901 H. Davies (ENG)	E. Thomson (ENG)
1902 R. Watling (ENG)	M. Lucas (ENG)
1903 R. Watling (ENG)	E. Thomson (ENG)
1904 H. Marrett (ENG)	E. Thomson (ENG)
1905 H. Marrett (ENG)	M. Lucas (ENG)
1906 N. Wood (ENG)	E. Thomson (ENG)
1907 N. Wood (ENG)	M. Lucas (ENG)
1908 H. Marrett (ENG)	M. Lucas (ENG)
1909 F. Chesterton (ENG)	M. Lucas (ENG)
1910 F. Chesterton (ENG)	M. Lucas (ENG)
1911 G. Sautter (ENG)	M. Larminie (ENG)
1912 F. Chesterton (ENG)	M. Larminie-Tragett (ENG)
1913 G. Sautter (ENG)	L. Radeglia (ENG)
1914 G. Sautter (ENG)	L. Radeglia (ENG)
1915–19 Not held	
1920 G. Thomas (ENG)	K. McKane (ENG)
1921 G. Thomas (ENG)	K. McKane (ENG)
1922 G. Thomas (ENG)	K. McKane (ENG)
1923 G. Thomas (ENG)	L. Radeglia (ENG)
1924 G. Mack (IRE)	K. McKane (ENG)
1925 F. Devlin (IRE)	M. Stocks (ENG)

All England Championship Cont.

Men's Singles	Women's Singles
1926 F. Devlin (IRE)	M. Barrett (ENG)
1927 F. Devlin (IRE)	M. Barrett (ENG)
1928 F. Devlin (IRE)	M. Larminie-Tragett (ENG)
1929 F. Devlin (IRE)	M. Barrett (ENG)
1930 D. Hulme (ENG)	M. Barrett (ENG)
1931 F. Devlin (IRE)	M. Barrett (ENG)
1932 R. Nichols (ENG)	L. Kingsbury (ENG)
1933 R. White (ENG)	A. Woodroffe (ENG)
1934 R. Nichols (ENG)	L. Kingsbury (ENG)
1935 R. White (ENG)	B. Uber (ENG)
1936 R. Nichols (ENG)	T. Kingsbury (ENG)
1937 R. Nichols (ENG)	T. Kingsbury (ENG)
1938 R. Nichols (ENG)	D. Young (ENG)
1939 T. Madsen (DEN)	D. Walton (CAN)
1940–46 Not held	
1947 C. Jepsen (SWE)	M. Ussing (DEN)
1948 J. Skaarup (DEN)	K. Thorndahl (DEN)
1949 D. Freeman (USA)	A. Jacobsen (DEN)
1950 W. P. Soon (MAL)	T. Olsen-Ahm (DEN)
1951 W. P. Soon (MAL)	A. Jacobsen (DEN)
1952 W. P. Soon (MAL)	T. Olsen-Ahm (DEN)
1953 E. Choong (MAL)	M. Ussing (DEN)
1954 E. Choong (MAL)	J. Devlin (USA)
1955 W. P. Soon (MAL)	M. Varner (USA)
1956 E. Choong (MAL)	M. Varner (USA)
1957 E. Choong (MAL)	J. Devlin (USA)
1958 E. Kops (DEN)	J. Devlin (USA)
1959 T. J. Hok (INA)	H. Ward (ENG)
1960 E. Kops (DEN)	J. Devlin (USA)
1961 E. Kops (DEN)	J. Devlin-Hashman (USA)
1962 E. Kops (DEN)	J. Devlin-Hashman (USA)
1963 E. Kops (DEN)	J. Devlin-Hashman (USA)
1964 K. Nielsen (DEN)	J. Devlin-Hashman (USA)
1965 E. Kops (DEN)	U. Smith (ENG)
1966 T. A. Huang (MAL)	J. Devlin-Hashman (USA)
1967 E. Kops (DEN)	J. Devlin-Hashman (USA)
1968 R. Hartono (INA)	E. Twedberg (SWE)
1969 R. Hartono (INA)	H. Yuki (JAP)
1970 R. Hartono (INA)	E. Takenaka (JAP)
1971 R. Hartono (INA)	E. Twedberg (SWE)
1972 R. Hartono (INA)	N. Nakayama (JAP)
1973 R. Hartono (INA)	M. Beck (ENG)
1974 R. Hartono (INA)	H. Yuki (JAP)
1975 S. Pri (DEN)	H. Yuki (JAP)
1976 R. Hartono (INA)	G. Gilks (ENG)
1977 F. Delfs (DEN)	H. Yuki (JAP)
1978 L. S. King (INA)	G. Gilks (ENG)
1979 L. S. King (INA)	L. Koppen (DEN)
1980 P. Padukone (INA)	L. Loppen (DEN)
1981 L. S. King (INA)	S -A. Hwang (SKO)
1982 M. Frost (DEN)	Z. Ailing (CHN)
1983 L. Jin (CHN)	Z. Ailing (CHN)
1984 M. Frost (DEN)	L. Lingwei (CHN)
1985 Z. Jinhua (CHN)	H. Aiping (CHN)

1986 M. Frost (DEN)	K. Yun–Ja (SKO)
1987 M. Frost (DEN)	K. Larsen (DEN)
1988 I. Frederiksen (DEN)	G. Jiaming (CHN)
1989 Y. Yang (CHN)	L. Lingwei (CHN)

Most Wins:
Men   8 Rudy Hartono
Women   10 Judy Devlin-Hashman

Shortest game: 9 mins — Miss N. Takagi (JPN) beat Miss P. Tumengkol (INA), 1969 Uber Cup
Most All-England titles   — men: 21 G. A. Thomas 1903-28
                              — women: 17 M. Lucas (GBR) 1899-1910
                                       17 J. Hashman (nee Devlin) (USA) 1954-67

Baseball derived itself from the English game of rounders and was first played in the 18th century. The first rules were drawn up in 1845 and the first match under the rules was a year later between the New York Base Ball Club and the sport's first organised club, the New York Knickerbockers.

WORLD SERIES

There are two Baseball leagues in America, the National League (NL) which was formed in 1876 and the American League (AL) which was formed in 1900. A total of 26 teams make up the two leagues and after a regular season of matches against other teams in their own league a series of play-offs decide which team shall represent each league in the best-of-seven-game World Series.

The letters in brackets indicate which league each side came from.

Year	Winners	Runners-up	Score
1903	Boston Red Sox (AL)	Pittsburgh Pirates (NL)	5–3
1904	Not held		
1905	New York Giants (NL)	Philadelphia Athletics (AL)	4–1
1906	Chicago White Sox (AL)	Chicago Cubs (NL)	4–2
1907	Chicago Cubs (NL)	Detriot Tigers (AL)	4–0(*)
1908	Chicago Cubs (NL)	Detriot Tigers (AL)	4–1
1909	Pittsburgh Pirates (NL)	Detriot Tigers (AL)	4–3
1910	Philadelphia Athletics (AL)	Chicago Cubs (NL)	4–1
1911	Philadelphia Athletics (AL)	New York Giants (NL)	4–2
1912	Boston Red Sox (AL)	New York Giants (NL)	4–3(*)
1913	Philadelphia Athletics (AL)	New York Giants (NL)	4–1
1914	Boston Braves (NL)	Philadelphia Athletics (AL)	4–0
1915	Boston Red Sox (AL)	Philadelphia Phillies (NL)	4–1
1916	Boston Red Sox (AL)	Brooklyn Dodgers (NL)	4–1
1917	Chicago White Sox (AL)	New York Giants (NL)	4–2
1918	Boston Red Sox (AL)	Chicago Cubs (NL)	4–2
1919	Cincinnati Reds (NL)	Chicago White Sox (AL)	5–3
1920	Cleveland Indians (AL)	Brooklyn Dodgers (NL)	5–2
1921	New York Giants (NL)	New York Yankees (AL)	4–3
1922	New York Giants (NL)	New York Yankees (AL)	4–0(*)
1923	New York Yankees (AL)	New York Giants (NL)	4–2
1924	Washington Senators (AL)	New York Giants (NL)	4–3
1925	Pittsburgh Pirates (NL)	Washington Senators (AL)	4–3
1926	St.Louis Cardinals (NL)	New York Yankees (AL)	4–3
1927	New York Yankees (AL)	Pittsburgh Pirates (NL)	4–0
1928	New York Yankees (AL)	St.Louis Cardinals (NL)	4–0
1929	Philadelphia Athletics (AL)	Chicago Cubs (NL)	4–1
1930	Philadelphia Athletics (AL)	St.Louis Cardinals (NL)	4–2
1931	St.Louis Cardinals (NL)	Philadelphia Athletics (AL)	4–3
1932	New York Yankees (AL)	Chicago Cubs (NL)	4–0
1933	New York Giants (NL)	Washington Senators (AL)	4–1
1934	St.Louis Cardinals (NL)	Detroit Tigers (AL)	4–3
1935	Detroit Tigers (AL)	Chicago Cubs (NL)	4–2
1936	New York Yankees (AL)	New York Giants (NL)	4–2
1937	New York Yankees (AL)	New York Giants (NL)	4–1
1938	New York Yankees (AL)	Chicago Cubs (NL)	4–0
1939	New York Yankees (AL)	Cincinnati Reds (NL)	4–0
1940	Cincinnati Reds (NL)	Detroit Tigers (AL)	4–3
1941	New York Yankees (AL)	Brooklyn Dodgers (NL)	4–1
1942	St.Louis Cardinals (NL)	New York Yankees (AL)	4–1

1943	New York Yankees (AL)	St.Louis Cardinals (NL)	4–1
1944	St.Louis Cardinals (NL)	St.Louis Browns (AL)	4–2
1945	Detroit Tigers (AL)	Chicago Cubs (NL)	4–3
1946	St. Louis Cardinals (NL)	Boston Red Sox (AL)	4–3
1947	New York Yankees (AL)	Brooklyn Dodgers (NL)	4–3
1948	Cleveland Indians (AL)	Boston Braves (NL)	4–2
1949	New York Yankees (AL)	Brooklyn Dodgers (NL)	4–1
1950	New York Yankees (AL)	Philadelphia Phillies (NL)	4–0
1951	New York Yankees (AL)	New York Giants (NL)	4–2
1952	New York Yankees (AL)	Brooklyn Dodgers (NL)	4–3
1953	New York Yankees (AL)	Brooklyn Dodgers (NL)	4–2
1954	New York Giants (NL)	Cleveland Indians (AL)	4–0
1955	Brooklyn Dodgers (NL)	New York Yankees (AL)	4–3
1956	New York Yankees (AL)	Brooklyn Dodgers (NL)	4–3
1957	Milwaukee Braves (NL)	New York Yankees (AL)	4–3
1958	New York Yankees (AL)	Milwaukee Braves (NL)	4–3
1959	Los Angeles Dodgers (NL)	Chicago White Sox (AL)	4–2
1960	Pittsburgh Pirates (NL)	New York Yankees (AL)	4–3
1961	New York Yankees (AL)	Cincinnati Reds (NL)	4–1
1962	New York Yankees (AL)	San Francisco Giants (NL)	4–3
1963	Los Angeles Dodgers (NL)	New York Yankees (AL)	4–0
1964	St.Louis Cardinals (NL)	New York Yankees (AL)	4–3
1965	Los Angeles Dodgers (NL)	Minnesota Twins (AL)	4–3
1966	Baltimore Orioles (AL)	Los Angeles Dodgers (NL)	4–0
1967	St.Louis Cardinals (NL)	Boston Red Sox (AL)	4–3
1968	Detroit Tigers (AL)	St.Louis Cardinals (NL)	4–3
1969	New York Mets (NL)	Baltimore Orioles (AL)	4–1
1970	Baltimore Orioles (AL)	Cincinnati Reds (NL)	4–1
1971	Pittsburgh Pirates (NL)	Baltimore Orioles (AL)	4–3
1972	Oakland 'A's (AL)	Cincinnati Reds (NL)	4–3
1973	Oakland 'A's (AL)	New York Mets (NL)	4–3
1974	Oakland 'A's (AL)	Los Angeles Dodgers (NL)	4–1
1975	Cincinnati Reds (NL)	Boston Red Sox (AL)	4–3
1976	Cincinnati Reds (NL)	New York Yankees (AL)	4–0
1977	New York Yankees (AL)	Los Angeles Dodgers (NL)	4–3
1978	New York Yankees (AL)	Los Angeles Dodgers (NL)	4–2
1979	Pittsburgh Pirates (NL)	Baltimore Orioles (AL)	4–3
1980	Philadelphia Phillies (NL)	Kansas City Royals (AL)	4–2
1981	Los Angeles Dodgers (NL)	New York Yankees (AL)	4–2
1982	St.Louis Cardinals (NL)	Milwaukee Brewers (AL)	4–3
1983	Baltimore Orioles (AL)	Philadelphia Phillies (NL)	4–1
1984	Detriot Tigers (AL)	San Diego Padres (NL)	4–1
1985	Kansas City Royals (AL)	St.Louis Cardinals (NL)	4–3
1986	New York Mets (NL)	Boston Red Sox (AL)	4–3
1987	Minnesota Twins (AL)	St. Louis Cardinals (NL)	4-3
1988	Los Angeles Dodgers (NL)	Boston Red Sox (AL)	4-1

(*) Includes one drawn game
Most Wins: 22 New York Yankees

THE RECORD BREAKERS:
Major League records:

Most runs in a career:	2245	T. Cobb, 1905-28
Best career batting average:	367	T. Cobb, 1905-28
Best season batting average:	438	H. Duffy, 1894
Total bases made in a career:	6856	H. Aaron, 1954-76
Total bases made in a season:	457	G. H. Ruth, 1921

Games won pitching in career:	511	D. T. Young, 1890-1911
Games won pitching in a season:	60	C. G. Radbourne, 1884
Most strikeouts in a career:	4373	L. N. Ryan 1968-87
Most strikeouts in a season:	383	L. N. Ryan 1973
Most World Series appearances:	14	L. P. Berra, 1947-63
Most home runs in a World Series game:	3	G. H. Ruth, 1926
	3	R. M. Jackson, 1977

Unlike many sports, Basketball can pin-point its birth to December 1891 when Dr.James Naismith invented the game at Springfield, Massachusetts.

OLYMPIC GAMES
Basketball has been played at each Olympic celebration since 1936, but women did not compete until 1976.

Men

1936 United States	1968 United States
1948 United States	1972 USSR
1952 United States	1976 United States
1956 United States	1980 Yugosolavia
1960 United States	1984 United States
1964 United States	1988 USSR

Most Wins:
9 United States

Women

1976 USSR	1988 United States
1980 USSR	
1984 United States	

Most Wins:
2 USSR; United States

WORLD CHAMPIONS
The first World Championships for men were held in 1950, and the first for women three years later. Both championships are now held every four years, and in between Olympic celebrations.

Men

1950 Argentina	1970 Yugoslavia
1954 United States	1974 USSR
1959 Brazil	1978 Yugoslavia
1963 Brazil	1982 USSR
1967 USSR	1986 United States

Most Wins:
3 USSR

Women

1953 United States	1971 USSR
1957 United States	1975 USSR
1959 USSR	1979 United States
1964 USSR	1983 USSR
1967 USSR	1987 United States

Most Wins:
6 USSR

Originally an outdoor game played on grass, the earliest reference to Billiards dates to the early 15th century. Louis XI of France is believed to have first taken the game indoors and onto a table. The game became popular in Britain at the turn of the 19th century and the governing body, The Billiards Association (now the Billiards & Snooker Control Council), was formed in 1885.

WORLD PROFESSIONAL CHAMPIONSHIP

Between 1870 and 1909 the champion put his title at stake by accepting challenges, in which case, only when the title changed hands is the new champion's name included in the list below. Between 1910–34 the championship was run on a tournament basis, it then became dormant but was revived on a challenge basis in 1951. In 1980 it was restored to a tournament event and, since 1982, has been held every year.

Winners:

1870 W. Cook (ENG)	1922 T. Newman (ENG)
1870 J. Roberts, Jnr (ENG)	1923 W. Smith (ENG)
1870 J. Bennett (ENG)	1924 T. Newman (ENG)
1871 J. Roberts, Jnr (ENG)	1925 T. Newman (ENG)
1871 W. Cook (ENG)	1926 T. Newman (ENG)
1875 J. Roberts, Jnr (ENG)	1927 T. Newman (ENG)
1880 J. Bennett (ENG)	1928 J. Davis (ENG)
1885 J. Roberts Jnr (ENG)	1929 J. Davis (ENG)
1889 C. Dawson (ENG)	1930 J. Davis (ENG)
1901 H. W. Stevenson (ENG)	1931 Not held
1901 C. Dawson (ENG),	1932 J. Davis (ENG)
1901 H. W. Stevenson (ENG)	1933 W. Lindrum (AUS)
1903 C. Dawson (ENG)	1934 W. Lindrum (AUS)
1908 M. Inman (ENG)	1951 C. McConachy (NZ)
1909 H. W. Stevenson (ENG)	1968 R. Williams (ENG)
1910 H. W. Stevenson (ENG)	1971 L. Driffield (ENG)
1911 H. W. Stevenson (ENG)	1971 R. Williams (ENG)
1912 M. Inman (ENG)	1980 F. Davis (ENG)
1913 M. Inman (ENG)	1981 Not held
1914 M. Inman (ENG)	1982 R. Williams (ENG)
1915–18 Not held	1983 R. Williams (ENG)
1919 M. Inman (ENG)	1984 M. Wildman (ENG)
1920 W. Smith (ENG)	1985 R. Edmonds (ENG)
1921 T. Newman (ENG)	1986 R. Foldvari (AUS)
	1987 N.Dagley (ENG)
	1988 N. Dagley (ENG)
	1989 MIKE RUSSELL (ENG)

Most Wins (Tournament event):
6 Tom Newman

One theory how Billiards got its name comes from a London pawnbroker named William Kew. Naturally he was know as Bill, and on rainy days he used to take down his pawnbroker's sign, three balls, in order to protect them. When bored, through lack of custom, he would push the balls around his shop with his yard-stick...hence the name Bill-Yard...a tall story maybe, but it could just be true!

WORLD AMATEUR CHAMPIONSHIP
First held in 1926, the event is held every two years.

1926 J. Earlham (ENG)	1962 R. Marshall (AUS)
1927 A. Prior (SAF)	1964 W. Jones (IND)
1929 L. Hayes (AUS)	1967 L. Driffield (ENG)
1931 L. Steeples (ENG)	1969 J. Karnehm (ENG)
1933 S. Lee (ENG)	1971 N. Dagley (ENG)
1935 H. Coles (WAL)	1973 M. Lafir (SRI)
1936 R. Marshall (AUS)	1975 N. Dagley (ENG)
1938 R. Marshall (AUS)	1977 M. Ferreira (IND)
1951 R. Marshall (AUS)	1979 P. Mifsud (MTA)
1952 L. Driffield (ENG)	1981 M. Ferreira (IND)
1954 T. Cleary (AUS)	1983 M. Ferreira (IND)
1958 W. Jones (IND)	1985 G. Sethi (IND)
1960 H. Beetham (ENG)	1987 G. Sethi (IND)

Most Wins:
4 Bob Marshall

BREAK RECORDS
Because the rules of Billiards have varied over the years, so have the break records. The following are some officially (and unofficially) recognised record breaks:

Official World record (since introduction of the 25-hazard rule in 1926)
    4,137   W. Lindrum, 1932
All-time record (using the outlawed 'cradle cannon')
    499,135   T. Reece, 1907
Record certified break (under 'anchor cannon' rule)
    42,746   W. Cook, 1907
Record under 'baulk-line' rule:
    1,784   J. Davis, 1936
Record official break by an amateur:
    1,149   M. Ferreira, 1978
Record under current 'two pot' rule:
    962 (Unfinished)   M. Ferreira, 1986
Highest break by a woman:
    197   R. Harrison, 1937

UNITED KINGDOM PROFESSIONAL CHAMPIONSHIP
Inaugurated in 1934 it has since led a chequered career but returned to the professional calendar in 1987.

Winners: (all British)

1934 J. Davis	1950 J. Barrie
1935 J. Davis	1951 F. Davis
1936 J. Davis	1952-78 Not held
1937 J. Davis	1979 R. Williams
1938 J. Davis	1980 J. Karnehm
1939 J. Davis	1981 R. Williams
1940-45 Not held	1982 Not held
1946 J. Barrie	1983 M. Wildman
1947 J. Davis	1984-86 Not held
1948 S. Smith	1987 N. Dagley
1949 Not held	1988 I. Williamson
	1989 P. Gilcrest

Most wins:
7 Joe Davis

Bobsleighing originated in Switzerland in 1888 when Englishman Wilson Smith join-ed two sleighs together with a wooden board in order to make his journey from St. Moritz to Celerina that much easier. The world's first purpose-built bob run was con-structed at St. Moritz in 1904 and the International Federation of Bobsleighing and Tobogganing was formed in 1923.

OLYMPIC GAMES
Bobsleighing was first held at the Winter Olympics in 1924 when the four-man event was held. The two-man competition followed eight years later. Bobsleighing has been held at every cele-bration since, with the exception of 1960.

Winners
Two-Man Bob

1932 United States	1964 Great Britain
1936 United States	1968 Italy
1948 Switzerland	1972 West Germany
1952 Germany	1976 East Germany
1956 Italy	1980 Switzerland
1960 Not held	1984 East Germany
	1988 USSR

Most Wins:
2 Italy, Switzerland, United States, East Germany, West Germany (inc one as Germany)

Four-Man Bob

1924 Switzerland	1960 Not held
1928 United States	1964 Canada
1932 United States	1968 Italy
1936 Switzerland	1972 Switzerland
1948 United States	1976 East Germany
1952 Germany	1980 East Germany
1956 Switzerland	1984 East Germany
	1988 Switzerland

Most Wins:
5 Switzerland

WORLD CHAMPIONSHIPS
The two-man bob world championship was first held in 1931, seven years after the four-man championships were introduced. Held every year, the Olympic Games winners are automatic world champions in Olympic years.

Winners
Two-Man Bob

1931 Germany	1937 Great Britain
1932 United States	1938 Germany
1933 Romania	1939 Belgium
1934 Romania	1940–46 Not held
1935 Switzerland	1947 Switzerland
1936 United States	1948 Switzerland

1949 Switzerland
1950 Switzerland
1951 Germany
1952 Germany
1953 Switzerland
1954 Italy
1955 Switzerland
1956 Italy
1957 Italy
1958 Italy
1959 Italy
1960 Italy
1961 Italy
1962 Italy
1963 Italy
1964 Great Britain
1965 Great Britain
1966 Italy
1967 Austria

Most Wins:
14 Italy, Switzerland

1968 Italy
1969 Italy
1970 West Germany
1971 Italy
1972 West Germany
1973 West Germany
1974 West Germany
1975 Italy
1976 East Germany
1977 Switzerland
1978 Switzerland
1979 Switzerland
1980 Switzerland
1981 East Germany
1982 Switzerland
1983 Switzerland
1984 East Germany
1985 East Germany
1986 East Germany
1987 Switzerland
1988 USSR
1989 East Germany

Four-Man Bob
1924 Switzerland
1925–26 Not held
1927 Great Britain
1928 United States
1929 Not held
1930 Italy
1931 Germany
1932 United States
1933 Not held
1934 Germany
1935 Germany
1936 Switzerland
1937 Great Britain
1938 Great Britain
1939 Switzerland
1940–46 Not held
1947 Switzerland
1948 United States
1949 United States
1950 United States
1951 Germany
1952 Germany
1953 United States
1954 Switzerland
1955 Switzerland
1956 Switzerland
1957 Switzerland
1958 West Germany

Most Wins:
17 Switzerland

1959 United States
1960 Italy
1961 Italy
1962 West Germany
1963 Italy
1964 Canada
1965 Canada
1966 Not held
1967 Romania
1968 Italy
1969 West Germany
1970 Italy
1971 Switzerland
1972 Switzerland
1973 Switzerland
1974 West Germany
1975 Switzerland
1976 East Germany
1977 East Germany
1978 East Germany
1979 West Germany
1980 East Germany
1981 East Germany
1982 Switzerland
1983 Switzerland
1984 East Germany
1985 East Germany
1986 Switzerland
1987 Switzerland
1988 Switzerland
1989 Switzerland

Because courses vary in length and design, it is difficult, and unfair, to maintain comparable speed records. The fastest recorded speed, however, is 85.4 mph (138 kph) by A. Strand (NOR), at Salen, Sweden in 1982.

The ancient Egyptians are believed to have played bowls around 5200BC but the earliest recorded green is at Southampton in 1299. Sir Francis Drake refused to commence battle with the Spanish Armada until he finished his game of bowls at Plymouth Hoe in 1588. The first set of bowls rules were drawn up in Scotland in 1848–49 by Glasgow solicitor W. W. Mitchell.

WORLD OUTDOOR CHAMPIONSHIPS
Instituted in 1966, the championships are now held every four years. The first women's championships were held in 1969.

Men

Singles
1966 D. Bryant (ENG)
1972 M. Evans (WAL)
1976 D. Watson (SAF)
1980 D. Bryant (ENG)
1984 P. Belliss (NZ)
1988 D. Bryant (ENG)

Pairs
1966 Australia
1972 Hong Kong
1976 South Africa
1980 Australia
1984 United States
1988 New Zealand

Triples
1966 Australia
1972 United States
1976 South Africa
1980 England
1984 Ireland
1988 New Zealand

Fours
1966 New Zealand
1972 England
1976 South Africa
1980 Hong Kong
1984 England
1988 Ireland

Leonard Trophy
(Presented to the winning team)

1966 Australia
1972 Scotland
1976 South Africa
1980 England
1984 Scotland
1988 England

Women

Singles
1969 G. Doyle (PNG)
1973 E. Wilke (NZ)
1977 E. Wilke (NZ)
1981 N. Shaw (ENG)
1985 M. Richardson (AUS)
1988 J. Ackland (WAL)

Pairs
1969 South Africa
1973 Australia
1977 Hong Kong
1981 Ireland
1985 Australia
1988 Ireland

Triples
1969 South Africa
1973 New Zealand
1977 Wales
1981 Hong Kong
1985 Australia
1988 Australia

Fours
1969 South Africa
1973 New Zealand
1977 Australia
1981 England
1985 Scotland
1988 Australia

Team Title
1969 South Africa
1973 New Zealand
1977 Australia
1981 England
1985 Australia
1988 England

WORLD INDOOR CHAMPIONSHIP

1979 D. Bryant (ENG)	1984 J. Baker (IRE)
1980 D. Bryant (ENG)	1985 T. Sullivan (WAL)
1981 D. Bryant (ENG)	1986 T. Allcock (ENG)
1982 J. Watson (SCO)	1987 T. Allcock (ENG)
1983 B. Sutherland (SCO)	1988 H. Duff (SCO)

Most Wins:
3 David Bryant

COMMONWEALTH GAMES
Because Bowls is not included in the Olympic Games programme, the Commonwealth Games is the sport's biggest international event after the World Championships.

Men
Singles

1930 R. Colquhoun (ENG)	1962 D. Bryant (ENG)
1934 R. Sprot (SCO)	1970 D. Bryant (ENG)
1938 H. Harvey (SAF)	1974 D. Bryant (ENG)
1950 J. Pirret (NZ)	1978 D. Bryant (ENG)
1954 R. Hodges (SRH)	1982 W. Wood (SCO)
1958 P. Danilowitz (SAF)	1986 I. Dickison (NZ)

Most Wins:
4 David Bryant

Pairs

1930 England	1962 New Zealand
1934 England	1970 England
1938 New Zealand	1974 Scotland
1950 New Zealand	1978 Hong Kong
1954 N. Ireland	1982 Scotland
1958 New Zealand	1986 Scotland

Fours

1930 England	1962 England
1934 England	1970 Hong Kong
1938 New Zealand	1974 New Zealand
1950 South Africa	1978 Hong Kong
1954 South Africa	1982 Australia
1958 England	1986 Wales

Women
Singles
1986 W. Line (ENG)

Pairs
1986 Northern Ireland

Women
Triples
1982 Zimbabwe

Fours
1986 Wales

THE WATERLOO HANDICAP

Played annually at Blackpool's Waterloo Hotel 'The Waterloo', as it is affectionately called, is one of Crown Green Bowling's classic tournaments. It was first held in 1907 and has been held continuously since 1910, with the exception of 1939 when the tournament was abandoned.

Winners:

1907 J. Rothwell	1947 W. Dalton
1908 G. Beatty	1948 A. E. Ringrose
1909 T. Meadows	1949 J. Egan
1910 Not Held	1950 H. Finch
1911 J. Peace	1951 J. Waterhouse
1912 T. Lowe	1952 L. Thompson
1913 G. Hart	1953 B. Kelly
1914 J. Rothwell	1954 B. Kelly
1915 W. Fairhurst	1955 J. Heyes
1916 J. Parkinson	1956 J. Sumner
1917 G. Barnes	1957 W. Lacy
1918 W. Simms	1958 F. Salisbury
1919 L. Moss	1959 W. Dawber
1920 E. Whiteside	1960 H. Bury
1921 J. Bagot	1961 J. Featherstone
1922 W. A. Smith	1962 J. Collier
1923 J. Martin	1963 T. Mayor
1924 R. Hill	1964 W. B. Heinkey
1925 J. Cox	1965 J. Pepper
1926 T. Roscoe	1966 R. Collier
1927 H. Waddecar	1967 E. Ashton
1928 T. Whittle	1968 B. Bennett
1929 C. Halpin	1969 G. T. Underwood
1930 J. Chadwick	1970 J. Everitt
1931 A. Gleave	1971 J. Bradbury
1932 T. E. Booth	1972 N. Burrows
1933 A. Ogden	1973 A. Murray
1934 W. Derbyshire	1974 W. Houghton
1935 C. Roberts	1975 J. Collen
1936 H. Yates	1976 K. Illingworth
1937 A. King	1977 L. Barrett
1938 J. W. Whitter	1978 A. Murray
1939 Abandoned	1979 B. Duncan
1940 A. Holden	1980 V. Lee
1941 W. J. Wilcock	1981 R. Nicholson
1942 T. Bimson	1982 D. Mercer
1943 S. Ivell	1983 S. Frith
1944 T. Tinkler	1984 S. Ellis
1945 W. Grace	1985 T. Johnstone
1946 C. Parkinson	1986 B. Duncan
	1987 B. Duncan
	1988 I. Gregory

MOST WINS:
3 Brian Duncan

The first President of the English Bowls Association in 1903 was none other than W.G. Grace, the most famous cricketer of all time.

From the beginning of time man has fought his fellow man but the first record of a boxing match was in Britain in 1681. In 1719 James Figg of Oxfordshire set up his school of arms in London and he is regarded as the first boxing champion. The first boxing rules were drawn up by John Broughton in 1743 and the famous Queensberry Rules, to which the sport adheres today, were drawn up in 1865.

WORLD CHAMPIONS

The first World Championship fight with gloves and under the Queensberry Rules was on 30 July 1884 when Irish-born Jack Dempsey beat George Fulljames of the United States for the middleweight title. The following is a list of all generally recognised world champions. Most weight divisions currently have three different champions as recognised by the WBA (World Boxing Association), WBC (World Boxing Council) and IBF (International Boxing Federation). The dates indicate when the title changed hands.

Champions:
Heavyweight

1882 John L.Sullivan (USA)
1892 James J.Corbett (USA)
1897 Bob Fitzsimmons (GB)
1899 James J.Jeffries (USA)
1905 Marvin Hart (USA)
1906 Tommy Burns (CAN)
1908 Jack Johnson (USA)
1915 Jess Willard (USA)
1919 Jack Dempsey (USA)
1926 Gene Tunney (USA)
1930 Max Schmeling (GER)
1932 Jack Sharkey (USA)
1933 Primo Carnera (ITA)
1934 Max Baer (USA)
1935 James J.Braddock (USA)
1937 Joe Louis (USA)
1949 Ezzard Charles (USA)
1951 Jersey Joe Walcott (USA)
1952 Rocky Marciano (USA)
1956 Floyd Patterson (USA)
1959 Ingemar Johansson (SWE)
1960 Floyd Patterson (USA)
1962 Sonny Liston (USA)
1964 Cassius Clay (USA)
1965 Ernie Terrell (USA) WBA

1968 Jimmy Ellis (USA) WBA
1970 Joe Frazier (USA)
1973 George Foreman (USA)
1974 Muhammad Ali (USA)
1978 Leon Spinks (USA)
1978 Ken Norton (USA) WBC
1978 Muhammad Ali (USA) WBA
1978 Larry Holmes (USA) WBC
1979 John Tate (USA) WBA
1980 Mike Weaver (USA) WBA
1982 Mike Dokes (USA) WBA
1983 Gerrie Coetzee (SAF) WBA
1984 Larry Holmes (USA) IBF
1984 Tim Witherspoon (USA) WBC
1984 Pinklon Thomas (USA) WBC
1984 Greg Page (USA) WBA
1985 Michael Spinks (USA) IBF
1985 Tony Tubbs (USA) WBA
1986 Tim Witherspoon (USA) WBA
1986 Trevor Berbick (JAM) WBC
1986 Mike Tyson (USA) WBC
1986 James Smith (USA) WBA
1987 Mike Tyson (USA) WBA/WBC
1987 Tony Tucker (USA) IBF
1987 Mike Tyson (USA)
1989 FRANCESCO DAMIANI (ITA) WBO

Cruiserweight

1979 Marvin Camel (USA) WBC
1980 Carlos de Leon (PR) WBC
1982 Ossie Ocasio (PR) WBA
1982 S.T.Gordon (USA) WBC
1983 Carlos de Leon (PR) WBC
1983 Marvin Camel (USA) IBF
1984 Lee Roy Murphy (USA) IBF
1984 Piet Crous (SAF) WBA
1985 Alfonso Ratliff (USA) WBC

1985 Dwight Muhammad Qawi (USA) WBA
1985 Bernard Benton (USA) WBC
1986 Carlos de Leon (PR) WBC
1986 Evander Holyfield (USA) WBA
1986 Rickey Parkey (USA) IBF
1987 Francesco Damiani (ITA) WBA
1987 Evander Holyfield (USA) IBF
1988 Evander Holyfield (USA)
1989 Taoufik Belbouli (FRA) IBF
1989 CARLOS DE LEON (PR) WBC
1989 GLENN McCRORY (GB) IBF

1990 JEFF LAMPKIN (USA) IBF

Light Heavyweight

1903 Jack Root (AUT)	1977 Miguel Cuello (ARG) WBC
1903 George Gardner (IRE)	1978 Mate Parlov (YUG) WBC
1903 Bob Fitzsimmons (GB)	1978 Mike Rossman (USA) WBA
1905 Jack O'Brien (USA)	1978 Marvin Johnson (USA) WBC
1912 Jack Dillon (USA)	1979 Victor Galindez (ARG) WBA
1916 Battling Levinsky (USA)	1979 Matthew Saad
1920 Georges Carpentier (FRA)	Muhammad (USA) WBC
1922 Battling Siki (SEN)	1979 Marvin Johnson (USA) WBA
1923 Mike McTigue (IRE)	1980 Eddie Mustaffa
1925 Paul Berlenbach (USA)	Muhammad (USA) WBA
1926 Jack Delaney (CAN)	1981 Michael Spinks (USA) WBA
1927 Jim Slattery (USA)	1981 Dwight Muhammad
1927 Tommy Loughran (USA)	Qawi (USA) WBC
1930 Jim Slattery (USA)	1983 Michael Spinks (USA)
1930 Maxie Rosenbloom (USA)	1985 J. B. Williamson (USA) WBC
1934 Bob Olin (USA)	1985 Slobodan Kacar (YUG) IBF
1935 John Henry Lewis (USA)	1986 Marvin Johnson (USA) WBA
1939 Melio Bettina (USA)	1986 Dennis Andries (GB) WBC
1939 Billy Conn (USA)	1986 Bobby Czyz (USA) IBF
1941 Anton Christoforidis (GRE)	1987 Thomas Hearns (USA) WBC
1941 Gus Lesnevich (USA)	1987 Leslie Stewart (JAM) WBA
1948 Freddie Mills (GB)	1987 Virgil Hill (USA) WBA
1950 Joey Maxim (USA)	1987 Prince Charles Williams (USA) IBF
1952 Archie Moore (USA)	1988 Donny Lalonde (CAN) WBC
1962 Harold Johnson (USA)	1988 Sugar Ray Leonard (USA) WBC
1963 Willie Pastrano (USA)	1989 Dennis Andries (GB) WBC
1965 Jose Torres (PR)	
1966 Dick Tiger (NIG)	
1968 Bob Foster (USA)	
1971 Vicente Rondon (VEN) WBA	
1974 John Conteh (GB) WBC	
1974 Victor Galindez (ARG) WBA	

Super-Middleweight

1984 Murray Sutherland (CAN) IBF	1988 Fulgencio Obelmejias (VEN) WBA
1984 Chong-Pal Park (SKO) WBA	1988 Sugar Ray Leonard (USA) WBC
1988 Graciano Rocchigiani (FRG) IBF	

Middleweight

1891 Nonpareil Jack Dempsey (IRE)	1926 Mickey Walker (USA)
1891 Bob Fitzsimmons (GB)	1931 Gorilla Jones (USA)
1897 Kid McCoy (USA)	1932 Marcel Thil (FRA)
1898 Tommy Ryan (USA)	1937 Fred Apostoli (USA)
1908 Stanley Ketchel (USA)	1939 Ceferino Garcia (PHI)
1908 Billy Papke (USA)	1940 Ken Overlin (USA)
1908 Stanley Ketchel (USA)	1941 Billy Soose (USA)
1910 Billy Papke (USA)	1941 Tony Zale (USA)
1911 Cyclone Thompson (USA)	1947 Rocky Graziano (USA)
1911 Billy Papke (USA)	1948 Tony Zale (USA)
1912 Frank Mantell (USA)	1948 Marcel Cerdan (ALG)
1912 Billy Papke (USA)	1949 Jake la Motta (USA)
1913 Frank Klaus (USA)	1951 Sugar Ray Robinson (USA)
1913 George Chip (USA)	1951 Randolph Turpin (GB)
1914 Al McCoy (USA)	1951 Sugar Ray Robinson (USA)
1917 Mike O'Dowd (USA)	1953 Carl Bobo Olson (HAW)
1920 Johnny Wilson (USA)	1955 Sugar Ray Robinson (USA)
1923 Harry Greb (USA)	1957 Gene Fullmer (USA)
1926 Tiger Flowers (USA)	1957 Sugar Ray Robinson (USA)

1957 Carmen Basilio (USA)
1958 Sugar Ray Robinson (USA)
1960 Paul Pender (USA)
1961 Terry Downes (GB)
1962 Paul Pender (USA)
1962 Dick Tiger (NIG)
1963 Joey Giardello (USA)
1965 Dick Tiger (NIG)
1966 Emile Griffith (VI)
1968 Nino Benvenuti (ITA)
1970 Carlos Monzon (ARG)
1974 Rodrigo Valdez (COL) WBC
1976 Carlos Monzon (ARG)

1977 Rodrigo Valdez (COL)
1978 Hugo Corro (ARG)
1979 Vito Antuofermo (ITA)
1980 Alan Minter (GB)
1980 Marvin Hagler (USA)
1987 Sugar Ray Leonard (USA) WBC
1987 Frank Tate (USA) IBF
1987 Sambu Kalambay (ZAI) WBA
1987 Thomas Hearns (USA) WBC
1988 Iran Barkley (USA) WBC
1988 Michael Nunn (USA) IBF
1989 Roberto Duran (PAN) WBC

Light-Middleweight

1962 Denny Moyer (USA)
1963 Ralph Dupas (USA)
1963 Sandro Mazzinghi (ITA)
1965 Nino Benvenuti (ITA)
1966 Ki-Soo Kim (KOR)
1968 Sandro Mazzinghi (ITA)
1969 Freddie Little (USA)
1970 Carmelo Bossi (ITA)
1971 Koichi Wajima (JAP)
1974 Oscar Albarado (USA)
1975 Koichi Wajima (JAP)
1975 Miguel de Oliviera (BRA) WBC
1975 Jae-Do Yuh (SKO) WBA
1975 Elisha Obed (BAH) WBC
1976 Koichi Wajima (JAP) WBA
1976 Jose Duran (SPA) WBA
1976 Eckhard Dagge (FRG) WBC
1976 Angel Castellini (ARG) WBA
1977 Eddie Gazo (NIC) WBA
1977 Rocky Mattioli (ITA) WBC
1978 Masashi Kudo (JAP) WBA

1979 Maurice Hope (GB) WBC
1979 Ayube Kalule (UGA) WBA
1981 Wilfred Benitez (USA) WBC
1981 Sugar Ray Leonard (USA) WBA
1981 Tadashi Mihara (JAP) WBA
1982 Davey Moore (USA) WBA
1982 Thomas Hearns (USA) WBC
1983 Roberto Duran (PAN) WBA
1984 Mark Medal (USA) IBF
1984 Mike McCallum (JAM) WBA
1984 Carlos Santos (PR) IBF
1986 Buster Drayton (USA) IBF
1986 Duane Thomas (USA) WBC
1987 Matthew Hilton (CAN) IBF
1987 Lupe Aquino (MEX) WBC
1988 Gianfranco Rossi (ITA) WBC
1988 Don Curry (USA) WBC
1988 Julian Jackson (VI) WBA
1988 Robert Hines (USA) IBF
1989 Darrin van Horn (USA) IBF

Welterweight

1892 Billy Smith (USA)
1894 Tommy Ryan (USA)
1898 Billy Smith (USA)
1900 Rube Ferns (USA)
1900 Matty Matthews (USA)
1901 Rube Ferns (USA)
1901 Joe Walcott (BAR)
1904 Dixie Kid (USA)
1905 Joe Walcott (BAR)
1906 Honey Mellody (USA)
1907 Mike Sullivan (USA)
1908 Harry Lewis (USA)
1914 Waldemar Holberg (DEN)
1914 Tom McCormick (IRE)
1914 Matt Wells (GB)
1915 Mike Glover (USA)
1915 Jack Britton (USA)
1915 Ted Kid Lewis (GB)

1916 Jack Britton (USA)
1917 Ted Kid Lewis (GB)
1919 Jack Britton (USA)
1922 Mickey Walker (USA)
1926 Pete Latzo (USA)
1927 Joe Dundee (ITA)
1928 Jack Thompson (USA)
1929 Jackie Fields (USA)
1930 Jack Thompson (USA)
1930 Tommy Freeman (USA)
1931 Jack Thompson (USA)
1931 Lou Brouillard (CAN)
1932 Jackie Fields (USA)
1933 Young Corbett III (ITA)
1933 Jimmy McLarnin (IRE)
1934 Barney Ross (USA)
1934 Jimmy McLarnin (IRE)
1935 Barney Ross (USA)

Welterweight cont'd

1938 Henry Armstrong (USA)
1940 Fritzie Zivic (USA)
1941 Red Cochrane (USA)
1946 Marty Servo (USA)
1946 Sugar Ray Robinson (USA)
1951 Johnny Bratton (USA)
1951 Kid Gavilan (CUB)
1954 Johnny Saxton (USA)
1955 Tony de Marco (USA)
1955 Carmen Basilio (USA)
1956 Johnny Saxton (USA)
1956 Carmen Basilio (USA)
1958 Virgil Atkins (USA)
1958 Don Jordon (DOM)
1960 Benny Kid Paret (CUB)
1961 Emile Griffith (VIR)
1961 Benny Kid Paret (CUB)
1962 Emile Griffith (VIR)
1963 Luis Rodriguez (CUB)
1963 Emile Griffith (VIR)
1966 Curtis Cokes (USA)
1969 Jose Napoles (CUB)
1970 Billy Backus (USA)
1971 Jose Napoles (CUB)

1975 Angel Espada (PR) WBA
1975 John H.Stracey (GB) WBC
1976 Carlos Palomino (MEX) WBC
1976 Pipino Cuevas (MEX) WBA
1979 Wilfred Benitez (USA) WBC
1979 Sugar Ray Leonard (USA) WBC
1980 Roberto Duran (PAN) WBC
1980 Thomas Hearns (USA) WBA
1980 Sugar Ray Leonard (USA) WBC
1981 Sugar Ray Leonard (USA)
1983 Don Curry (USA) WBA
1983 Milton McCrory (USA) WBC
1984 Don Curry (USA) IBF
1985 Don Curry (USA)
1986 Lloyd Honeyghan (GB)
1987 Mark Breland (USA) WBA
1987 Lloyd Honeyghan (GB) WBC/IBF
1987 Marlon Starling (USA) WBA
1987 Jorge Vaca (MEX) WBC
1988 Simon Brown (JAM) IBF
1988 Tomas Molinares (COL) WBA
1988 Lloyd Honeyghan (GB) WBC
1989 Mark Breland (USA) WBA
1989 Marlon Starling (USA) WBC

Junior-Welterweight

1922 Pinky Mitchell (USA)
1926 Mushy Callahan (USA)
1930 Jackie Kid Berg (GB)
1931 Tony Canzoneri (USA)
1932 Johnny Jaddick (USA)
1933 Battling Shaw (MEX)
1933 Tony Canzoneri (USA)
1933 Barney Ross (USA)
1946 Tippy Larkin (USA)
1959 Carlos Ortiz (PR)
1960 Duilio Loi (ITA)
1962 Eddie Perkins (USA)
1962 Duilio Loi (ITA)
1963 Roberto Cruz (PHI)
1963 Eddie Perkins (USA)
1965 Carlos Hernandez (VEN)
1966 Sandro Lopopolo (ITA)
1967 Paul Fuji (HAW)
1968 Nicolino Loche (ARG) WBA
1968 Pedro Adigue (PHI) WBC
1970 Bruno Arcari (ITA) WBC
1972 Alfonso Frazer (PAN) WBA
1972 Antonio Cervantes (COL) WBA
1974 Perico Fernandez (SPA) WBC
1975 Saensak Muangsurin (THA) WBC
1976 Wilfred Benitez (USA) WBA
1976 Miguel Velasquez (SPA) WBC
1976 Saensak Muangsurin (THA) WBC
1977 Antonio Cervantes (COL) WBA

1978 Sang-Hyun Kim (KOR) WBC
1980 Saoul Mamby (USA) WBC
1980 Aaron Pryor (USA) WBA
1982 Leroy Haley (USA) WBC
1983 Aaron Pryor (USA) IBF
1983 Bruce Curry (USA) WBC
1984 Johnny Bumphus (USA) WBA
1984 Billy Costello (USA) WBC
1984 Gene Hatcher (USA) WBA
1985 Ubaldo Sacco (ARG) WBA
1985 Lonnie Smith (USA) WBC
1986 Patrizio Oliva (ITA) WBA
1986 Gary Hinton (USA) IBF
1986 Rene Arredondo (MEX) WBC
1986 Tsuyoshi Hamada (JAP) WBC
1986 Joe Louis Manley (USA) IBF
1987 Terry Marsh (GB) IBF
1987 Juan Martin Coggi (ARG) WBA
1987 Rene Arredondo (MEX) WBC
1988 James Buddy McGirt (USA) IBF
1988 Roger Mayweather (USA) WBC
1988 Meldrick Taylor (USA) IBF
1989 HECTOR CAMACHO (   ) WBO

Lightweight

1896 George Lavigne (USA)
1899 Frank Erne (SWI)
1902 Joe Gans (USA)
1908 Battling Nelson (DEN)
1910 Ad Wolgast (USA)
1912 Willie Ritchie (USA)
1914 Freddie Welsh (GB)
1917 Benny Leonard (USA)
1925 Jimmy Goodrich (USA)
1925 Rocky Kansas (USA)
1926 Sammy Mandell (USA)
1930 Al Singer (USA)
1930 Tony Canzeroni (USA)
1933 Barney Ross (USA)
1935 Tony Canzeroni (USA)
1936 Lou Ambers (USA)
1938 Henry Armstrong (USA)
1939 Lou Ambers (USA)
1940 Lew Jenkins (USA)
1941 Sammy Angott (USA)
1942 Beau Jack (USA)
1943 Bob Montgomery (USA)
1943 Sammy Angott (USA)
1944 Juan Zurita (MEX)
1945 Ike Williams (USA)
1951 Jimmy Carter (USA)
1952 Lauro Salas (MEX)
1952 Jimmy Carter (USA)
1954 Paddy de Marco (USA)
1954 Jimmy Carter (USA)
1955 Wallace Bud Smith (USA)
1956 Joe Brown (USA)
1962 Carlos Ortiz (PR)
1965 Ismael Laguna (PAN)
1965 Carlos Ortiz (PR)

1968 Carlos Teo Cruz (DOM)
1969 Mando Ramos (USA)
1970 Ismael Laguna (PAN)
1970 Ken Buchanan (GB) WBA
1971 Pedro Carrasco (SPA) WBC
1972 Mando Ramos (USA) WBC
1972 Roberto Duran (PAN) WBA
1972 Chango Carmona (MEX) WBC
1972 Rodolfo Gonzalez (MEX) WBC
1974 Guts Ishimatsu (JAP) WBC
1976 Esteban de Jesus (PR) WBC
1978 Roberto Duran (PAN)
1979 Jim Watt (GB) WBC
1979 Ernesto Espana (VEN) WBA
1980 Hilmer Kenty (USA) WBA
1981 Sean O'Grady (USA) WBA
1981 Alexis Arguello (NIC) WBC
1981 Claude Noel (TRI) WBA
1981 Arturo Frias (USA) WBA
1982 Ray Mancini (USA) WBA
1983 Edwin Rosario (PR) WBC
1984 Charlie Brown (USA) IBF
1984 Livingstone Bramble (USA) WBA
1984 Harry Arroyo (USA) IBF
1984 Jose Luis Ramirez (MEX) WBC
1985 Jimmy Paul (USA) IBF
1985 Hector Camacho (PR) WBC
1986 Edwin Rosario (PR) WBA
1986 Greg Haugen (USA) IBF
1987 Vinny Pazienza (USA) IBF
1987 Jose Luis Ramirez (MEX) WBC
1987 Julio Cesar Chavez (MEX) WBA
1988 Greg Haugen (USA) IBF
1988 Julio Cesar Chavez (MEX) WBC/WBA
1989 Pernell Whitaker (USA) IBF

Junior-Lightweight

1921 Johnny Dundee (ITA)
1923 Jack Bernstein (USA)
1923 Johnny Dundee (ITA)
1924 Kid Sullivan (USA)
1925 Mike Balerino (USA)
1925 Tod Morgan (USA)
1929 Benny Bass (USSR)
1931 Kid Chocolate (CUB)
1933 Frankie Klick (USA)
1959 Harold Gomes (USA)
1960 Flash Elorde (PHI)
1967 Yoshiaki Numata (JAP)
1967 Hiroshi Kobayashi (JAP)
1969 Rene Barrientos (PHI) WBC
1970 Yoshiaki Numata (JAP) WBC
1971 Alfredo Marcano (VEN) WBA
1971 Ricardo Arredondo (MEX) WBC
1972 Ben Villaflor (PHI) WBA
1973 Kuniaki Shibata (JAP) WBA
1973 Ben Villaflor (PHI) WBA

1974 Kuniaki Shibata (JAP) WBC
1975 Alfredo Escalera (PR) WBC
1976 Sam Serrano (PR) WBA
1978 Alexis Arguello (NIC) WBC
1980 Yasutsune Uehara (JAP) WBA
1980 Rafael Limon (MEX) WBC
1981 Cornelius Boza Edwards (UGA) WBC
1981 Sam Serrano (PR) WBA
1981 Rolando Navarette (PHI) WBC
1982 Rafael Limon (MEX) WBC
1982 Bobby Chacon (USA) WBC
1983 Roger Mayweather (USA) WBA
1983 Hector Camacho (PR) WBC
1984 Rocky Lockridge (USA) WBA
1984 Hwan-Kil Yuh (SKO) IBF
1984 Julio Cesar Chavez (MEX) WBC
1985 Lester Ellis (AUS) IBF
1985 Wilfredo Gomez (PR) WBA
1985 Barry Michael (AUS) IBF
1986 Alfredo Layne (PAN) WBA

Junior-Lightweight cont'd

1986 Brian Mitchell (SAF) WBA
1987 Julio Cesar Chavez (MEX) WBC
1987 Rocky Lockridge (USA) IBF

1988 Azumah Nelson (GHA) WBC
1988 Tony Lopez (USA) IBF

Featherweight

1891 Young Griffo (AUS)
1892 George Dixon (CAN)
1897 Solly Smith (USA)
1898 Dave Sullivan (IRE)
1898 George Dixon (CAN)
1900 Terry McGovern (USA)
1901 Young Corbett II (USA)
1904 Jimmy Britt (USA)
1904 Brooklyn Tommy Sullivan (USA)
1906 Abe Attell (USA)
1912 Johnny Kilbane (USA)
1923 Eugene Criqui (FRA)
1923 Johnny Dundee (ITA)
1925 Kid Kaplan (USSR)
1927 Benny Bass (USSR)
1928 Tony Canzoneri (USA)
1928 Andre Routis (FRA)
1929 Battling Battalino (USA)
1932 Kid Chocolate (CUB)
1933 Freddie Miller (USA)
1936 Petey Sarron (USA)
1937 Henry Armstrong (USA)
1938 Joey Archibald (USA)
1940 Harry Jeffra (USA)
1941 Joey Archibald (USA)
1941 Chalky Wright (MEX)
1942 Willie Pep (USA)
1948 Sandy Saddler (USA)
1949 Willie Pep (USA)
1950 Sandy Saddler (USA)
1957 Hogan Kid Bassey (NIG)
1959 Davey Moore (USA)
1963 Sugar Ramos (CUB)
1964 Vicente Saldivar (MEX)
1968 Howard Winstone (GB) WBC
1968 Raul Rojas (USA) WBA
1968 Jose Legra (CUB) WBC

1968 Shozo Saijyo (JAP) WBA
1969 Johnny Famechon (FRA) WBC
1970 Vicente Saldivar (MEX) WBC
1970 Kuniaki Shibata (JAP) WBC
1971 Antonio Gomez (VEN) WBA
1972 Clemente Sanchez (MEX) WBC
1972 Ernesto Marcel (PAN) WBA
1972 Jose Legra (CUB) WBC
1973 Eder Jofre (BRA) WBC
1974 Ruben Olivares (MEX) WBA
1974 Bobby Chacon (USA) WBC
1974 Alexis Arguello (NIC) WBA
1975 Ruben Olivares (MEX) WBC
1975 David Kotey (GHA) WBC
1976 Danny Lopez (USA) WBC
1977 Rafael Ortega (PAN) WBA
1977 Cecilio Lastra (SPA) WBA
1978 Eusebio Pedroza (PAN) WBA
1980 Salvador Sanchez (MEX) WBC
1982 Juan Laporte (PR) WBC
1984 Min-Keum Oh (SKO) IBF
1984 Wilfredo Gomez (PR) WBC
1984 Azumah Nelson (GHA) WBC
1985 Barry McGuigan (IRE) WBA
1985 Ki-Young Chung (SKO) IBF
1986 Steve Cruz (USA) WBA
1986 Antonio Rivera (PR) IBF
1987 Antonio Esparragoza (VEN) WBA
1988 Calvin Gore (USA) IBF
1988 Jeff Fenech (AUS) WBC
1988 Jorge Paez (MEX) IBF

Junior-Featherweight

1922 Jack Kid Wolfe (USA)
1923 Carl Duane (USA)
1976 Rigoberto Riasco (PAN) WBC
1976 Royal Kobayashi (JAP) WBC
1976 Dong-Kyun Yum (SK) WBC
1977 Wilfredo Gomez (PR) WBC
1977 Soo-Hwan Hong (SK) WBA
1978 Ricardo Cardona (COL) WBA
1980 Leo Randolph (USA) WBA
1980 Sergio Palma (ARG) WBA
1982 Leo Cruz (DOM) WBA
1983 Jaime Garza (USA) WBC
1983 Bobby Berna (PHI) IBF
1984 Loris Stecca (ITA) WBA
1984 Seung-Il Suh (SKO) IBF

1984 Victor Callejas (PR) WBA
1984 Juan Meza (MEX) WBC
1985 Ji-Won Kim (SKO) IBF
1985 Lupe Pintor (MEX) WBC
1986 Samart Payakarun (THA) WBC
1987 Louis Espinoza (USA) WBA
1987 Seung-Hoon Lee (SKO) IBF
1987 Jeff Fenech (AUS) WBC
1987 Julio Gervacio (DOM) WBA
1988 Bernardo Pinango (VEN) WBA
1988 Daniel Zaragoza (MEX) WBC
1988 Jose Sanabria (VEN) IBF
1988 Juan Jose Estrada (MEX) WBA
1989 Fabrice Benichou (FRA) IBF

Bantamweight

1891 George Dixon (CAN)
1892 Billy Plimmer (GB)
1895 Pedlar Palmer (GB)
1899 Terry McGovern (USA)
1901 Harry Forbes (USA)
1903 Frankie Neil (USA)
1904 Joe Bowker (GB)
1905 Jimmy Walsh (USA)
1907 Owen Moran (GB)
1908 Johnny Coulon (CAN)
1914 Kid Williams (DEN)
1917 Pete Herman (USA)
1920 Joe Lynch (USA)
1921 Pete Herman (USA)
1921 Johnny Buff (USA)
1922 Joe Lynch (USA)
1924 Abe Goldstein (USA)
1924 Eddie Martin (USA)
1925 Charlie Rosenberg (USA)
1927 Bud Taylor (USA)
1928 Bushy Graham (ITA)
1929 Al Brown (PAN)
1935 Baltazar Sangchilli (SPA)
1936 Tony Marino (USA)
1936 Sixto Escobar (SPA)
1937 Harry Jeffra (USA)
1938 Sixto Escobar (SPA)
1940 Lou Salica (USA)
1942 Manuel Ortiz (USA)
1947 Harold Dade (USA)
1947 Manuel Ortiz (USA)
1950 Vic Toweel (SAF)
1952 Jimmy Carruthers (AUS)
1954 Robert Cohen (ALG)
1956 Mario D'Agata (ITA)
1957 Alphonse Halimi (ALG)

1959 Joe Becerra (MEX)
1960 Eder Jofre (BRA)
1965 Fighting Harada (JAP)
1968 Lionel Rose (AUS)
1969 Ruben Olivares (MEX)
1970 Chucho Castillo (MEX)
1971 Ruben Olivares (MEX)
1972 Rafael Herrera (MEX)
1972 Enrique Pinder (PAN)
1973 Romeo Anaya (MEX) WBA
1973 Rafael Herrera (MEX) WBC
1973 Arnold Taylor (SAF) WBA
1974 Soo-Hwan Hong (SKO) WBA
1974 Rodolfo Martinez (MEX) WBC
1975 Alfonso Zamora (MEX) WBA
1976 Carlos Zarate (MEX) WBC
1977 Jorge Lujan (PAN) WBA
1979 Lupe Pintor (MEX) WBC
1980 Julian Solis (PR) WBA
1980 Jeff Chandler (USA) WBA
1983 Alberto Davila (USA) WBC
1984 Richard Sandoval (USA) WBA
1984 Satoshi Shingaki (JAP) IBF
1985 Jeff Fenech (AUS) IBF
1985 Daniel Zaragoza (MEX) WBC
1985 Miguel Lora (COL) WBC
1986 Gaby Canizales (USA) WBA
1986 Bernardo Pinango (VEN) WBA
1987 Takuya Muguruma (JAP) WBA
1987 Kelvin Seabrooks (USA) IBF
1987 Chang-Young Park (SKO) WBA
1987 Wilfredo Vasquez (PR) WBA
1988 Kaokor Galaxy (THA) WBA
1988 Orlando Canizales (USA) IBF
1988 Sung-Kil Moon (SKO) WBA
1988 Raul Perez (MEX) WBC

Super-Flyweight

1980 Rafael Orono (VEN) WBC
1981 Chul-Ho Kim (SK) WBC
1981 Gustavo Ballas (ARG) WBA
1981 Rafael Pedroza (PAN) WBA
1982 Jiro Watanabe (JAP) WBA
1982 Rafael Orono (VEN) WBC
1983 Payao Poontarat (THA) WBC
1983 Joo-Do Chun (SKO) IBF
1984 Jiro Watanabe (JAP) WBC
1984 Kaosai Galaxy (THA) WBA

1985 Ellyas Pical (INA) IBF
1986 Cesar Polanco (DOM) IBF
1986 Gilberto Roman (MEX) WBC
1986 Tae-Il Chang (SKO) IBF
1986 Ellyas Pical (INA) IBF
1987 Santos Laciar (ARG) WBC
1987 Jesus Rojas (COL) WBC
1988 Gilberto Roman (MEX) WBC

Flyweight

1913 Sid Smith (GB)
1913 Bill Ladbury (GB)
1914 Percy Jones (GB)
1915 Joe Symonds (GB)
1916 Jimmy Wilde (GB)
1923 Pancho Villa (PHI)
1925 Fidel la Barba (USA)
1928 Frankie Genaro (USA)
1929 Emile Pladner (FRA)
1929 Frankie Genaro (USA)
1931 Young Perez (TUN)
1932 Jackie Brown (ENG)
1935 Benny Lynch (GB)
1938 Peter Kane (GB)
1943 Jackie Paterson (GB)
1948 Rinty Monaghan (GB)
1950 Terry Allen (GB)
1950 Dado Marino (HAW)
1952 Yoshio Shirai (JAP)
1954 Pascual Perez (ARG)
1960 Pone Kingpetch (THA)
1962 Fighting Harada (JAP)
1963 Pone Kingpetch (THA)
1963 Hiroyuki Ebihara (JAP)
1964 Pone Kingpetch (THA)
1965 Salvatore Burruni (ITA)
1966 Horacio Accavallo (ARG) WBA
1966 Walter McGowan (GB) WBC
1966 Chartchai Chionoi (THA) WBC
1969 Efren Torres (MEX) WBC
1969 Hiroyuki Ebihara (JAP) WBA
1969 Bernabe Villacampo (PHI) WBA
1970 Chartchai Chionoi (THA) WBC
1970 Berkrerk Chartvanchai (THA) WBA
1970 Masao Ohba (JAP) WBA
1970 Erbito Salavarria (PHI) WBC
1972 Venice Borkorsor (THA) WBC
1973 Chartchai Chionoi (THA) WBA

1973 Betulio Gonzalez (VEN) WBC
1974 Shoji Oguma (JAP) WBC
1974 Susumu Hanagata (JAP) WBA
1975 Miguel Canto (MEX) WBC
1975 Erbito Salavarria (PHI) WBA
1976 Alfonso Lopez (PAN) WBA
1976 Guty Espadas (MEX) WBA
1978 Betulio Gonzalez (VEN) WBA
1979 Chan-Hee Park (SKO) WBC
1979 Luis Ibarra (PAN) WBA
1980 Tae-Shik Kim (SKO) WBA
1980 Shoji Oguma (JAP) WBC
1980 Peter Mathebula (SAF) WBA
1981 Santos Laciar (ARG) WBA
1981 Antonio Avelar (MEX) WBC
1981 Luis Ibarra (PAN) WBA
1981 Juan Herrera (MEX) WBA
1982 Prudencio Cardona (COL) WBC
1982 Santos Laciar (ARG) WBA
1982 Freddie Castillo (MEX) WBC
1982 Eleoncio Mercedes (DOM) WBC
1983 Charlie Magri (GB) WBC
1983 Frank Cedeno (PHI) WBC
1983 Soon-Chun Kwon (SKO) IBF
1984 Koji Kobayashi (JAP) WBC
1984 Gabriel Bernal (MEX) WBC
1984 Sot Chitalada (THA) WBC
1985 Hilario Zapata (PAN) WBA
1985 Chong-Kwan Chung (SKO) IBF
1986 Bi-Won Chung (SKO) IBF
1986 Hi-Sup Shin (SKO) IBF
1987 Fidel Bassa (COL) WBA
1987 Dodie Penalosa (PHI) IBF
1987 Chang-Ho Choi (SKO) IBF
1988 Rolando Bohol (PHI) IBF
1988 Yung-Kang Kim (SKO) WBC
1988 Duke McKenzie (GB) IBF

Light-Flyweight
1975 Franco Udella (ITA) WBC
1975 Jaime Rios (PAN) WBA
1975 Luis Estaba (VEN) WBC
1976 Juan Jose Guzman (DOM) WBA
1976 Yoko Gushiken (JAP) WBA
1978 Freddie Castillo (MEX) WBC
1978 Netrnoi Vorasingh (THA) WBC
1978 Sung-Jun Kim (SKO) WBC
1980 Shigeo Nakajima (JAP) WBC
1980 Hilario Zapata (PAN) WBC
1981 Pedro Flores (MEX) WBA
1981 Hwan-Jim Kim (SKO) WBA
1981 Katsuo Takashiki (JAP) WBA
1982 Amado Ursua (MEX) WBC
1982 Tadashi Tomori (JAP) WBC
1982 Hilario Zapata (PAN) WBC
1983 Jung-Koo Chang (KOR) WBC
1983 Lupe Madera (MEX) WBA
1983 Dodie Penalosa (PHI) IBF
1984 Francisco Quiroz (DOM) WBA
1985 Joey Olivo (USA) WBA
1985 Myung-Woo Yuh (SKO) WBA
1986 Chong-Hwan Choi (SKO) IBF
1988 Tacy Macalos (PHI) IBF
1988 German Torres (MEX) WBC
1989 Yol-Woo Lee (SKO) WBC

Straw-weight
1987 Kyung-Yung Lee (SKO) WBC
1988 Leo Gamez (DOM) WBA
1988 Hiroki Ioka (JAP) WBC
1988 Samuth Sithnaruepol (THA) IBF
1988 Napa Kiatwanchai (THA) WBC

OLYMPIC GAMES

Boxing has been included in every Olympic celebration since 1904, with the exception of 1912. There were 12 weight categories at the 1988 Seoul Olympics. The following is a list of all Olympic champions.

Super-heavyweight (over 200½lb)
1984 T. Biggs (USA)
1988 L. Lewis (CAN)

Heavyweight
1904 Samuel Berger (USA)
1908 A.L.Oldham (GB)
1912 Not held
1920 Ronald Rawson (GB)
1924 Otto von Porat (NOR)
1928 Arturo Rodriguez Jurado (ARG)
1932 Santiago Lovell (ARG)
1936 Herbert Runge (GER)
1948 Rafael Iglesias (ARG)
1952 Hayes Sanders (USA)
1956 Peter Rademacher (USA)
1960 Franco de Piccoli (ITA)
1964 Joe Frazier (USA)
1968 George Foreman (USA)
1972 Teofilo Stevenson (CUB)
1976 Teofilo Stevenson (CUB)
1980 Teofilo Stevenson (CUB)
1984 Henry Tillman (USA)
1988 R. Mercer (USA)

Light-heavyweight (179lb)

1920	E. Eagan (USA)	1960	C. Clay (USA)
1924	H. Mitchell (GB)	1964	C. Pinto (ITA)
1928	V. Avendano (ARG)	1968	D. Poznyak (USSR)
1932	D. Carstens (SAF)	1972	M. Parlov (YUG)
1936	R. Michelot (FRA)	1976	L. Spinks (USA)
1948	G. Hunter (SAF)	1980	S. Kacar (YUG)
1952	N. Lee (USA)	1984	A. Jospovic (YUG)
1956	J. Boyd (USA)	1988	A. Maynard (USA)

Middleweight (165½lb)

1904	C. Meyer (USA)	1956	G. Schatkov (USSR)
1908	J. Douglas (GB)	1960	E. Crook (USA)
1920	H. Mallin (GB)	1964	V. Popentschenko (USSR)
1924	H. Mallin (GB)	1968	C. Finnegan (GB)
1928	P. Toscani (ITA)	1972	V. Lemechev (USSR)
1932	C. Barth (USA)	1976	M. Spinks (USA)
1936	J. Despeaux (FRA)	1980	J. Gomez (CUB)
1948	L. Papp (HUN)	1984	Sin-Joon Sup (SKO)
1952	F. Patterson (USA)	1988	H. Maske (GDR)

Light-middleweight (156lb)

1952	L. Papp (HUN)	1972	D. Kottysch (FRG)
1956	L. Papp (HUN)	1976	J. Rybicki (POL)
1960	W. McClure (USA)	1980	A. Martinez (CUB)
1964	B. Lagutin (USSR)	1984	F. Tate (USA)
1968	B. Lagutin (USSR)	1988	S -H. Park (SKO)

Welterweight (148lb)

1904	A. Young (USA)	1956	N. Lince (ROM)
1920	A. Schneider (CAN)	1960	G. Benvenuti (ITA)
1924	J. Delarge (BEL)	1964	M. Kasprzyk (POL)
1928	E. Morgan (NZ)	1968	M. Wolke (GDR)
1932	E. Flynn (USA)	1972	E. Correa (CUB)
1936	S. Stuvio (FIN)	1976	J. Bachfield (GDR)
1948	J. Torma (TCH)	1980	A. Aldama (CUB)
1952	Z. Chychla (POL)	1984	M. Breland (USA)
		1988	R. Wangila (KEN)

Light-welterweight (140lb)

1952	C. Adkins (USA)	1972	R. Seales (USA)
1956	V. Yengibaryan (USSR)	1976	R. Leonard (USA)
1960	B. Nemecek (TCH)	1980	P. Oliva (ITA)
1964	J. Kulej (POL)	1984	J. Page (USA)
1968	J. Kulej (POL)	1988	V. Yanovski (USSR)

Lightweight (132lb)

1904	H. Spanger (USA)	1956	D. McTaggart (GB)
1908	F. Grace (GB)	1960	K. Pazdzior (POL)
1920	S. Mosberg (USA)	1964	J. Grudzien (POL)
1924	H. Nielsen (DEN)	1968	R. Harris (USA)
1928	C. Orlandi (ITA)	1972	J. Sczepanski (POL)
1932	L. Stevens (SAF)	1976	H. Davis (USA)
1936	I. Harangi (HUN)	1980	A. Herrera (CUB)
1948	G. Dreyer (SAF)	1984	P. Whitaker (USA)
1952	A. Bolognesi (ITA)	1988	A. Zvelow (GDR)

Featherweight (126lb)

1904	O. Kirk (USA)	1956	V. Safronov (USSR)
1908	R. Gunn (GB)	1960	F. Musso (ITA)
1920	P. Fritsch (FRA)	1964	S. Stepashkin (USSR)
1924	J. Fields (USA)	1968	A. Roldan (MEX)
1928	L. van Klaveren (HOL)	1972	B. Kuznetsov (USSR)
1932	C. Robledo (ARG)	1976	A. Herrera (CUB)
1936	O. Casanovas (ARG)	1980	R. Fink (GDR)
1948	E. Formenti (ITA)	1984	M. Taylor (USA)
1952	J. Zachara (TCH)	1988	G. Parisi (ITA)

Bantamweight (119½lb)

1904	O. Kirk (USA)	1956	W. Behrendti (FRG)
1908	H. Thomas (GB)	1960	O. Grigoyev (USSR)
1920	C. Walker (SAF)	1964	T. Sajurai (JAP)
1924	W. Smith (SAF)	1968	V. Sokolov (USSR)
1928	V. Tamagnini (ITA)	1972	O. Martinez (CUB)
1932	H. Gwynne (CAN)	1976	Yong-Jo Gu (NKO)
1936	U. Sergo (ITA)	1980	J. Hernandez (CUB)
1948	T. Csik (HUN)	1984	M. Stecca (ITA)
1952	P. Hamalainen (FIN)	1988	K. McKinney (USA)

Flyweight (112½lb)

1904	D. Finnegan (USA)	1956	T. Spinks (GB)
1920	F. De Genaro (USA)	1960	G. Torok (HUN)
1924	F. LaBarba (USA)	1964	F. Atzori (ITA)
1928	A. Kocsis (HUN)	1968	R. Delgado (MEX)
1932	I. Enekes (HUN)	1972	G. Kostadinov (BUL)
1936	W. Kaiser (FRG)	1976	L. Randolph (USA)
1948	P. Perez (ARG)	1980	P. Lessov (BUL)
1952	N. Brooks (USA)	1984	S. McCrory (USA)
		1988	K -S. Kim (SKO)

Light-flyweight (106lb)

1968	F. Rodriguez (VEN)	1980	A. Sabirov (USSR)
1972	G. Gedo (HUN)	1984	P. Gonzales (USA)
1976	J. Hernandez (CUB)	1988	I. Hristov (BUL)

Canoeing became popular as a sport in the mid-19th century, and the Royal Canoe Club in Britain was founded in 1866. There are two types of Canoe used in international competition, the Kayak and the Canadian.

OLYMPIC GAMES

A demonstration sport at the 1924 Olympics, Canoeing became a full Olympic sport in 1936.

Winners:
500 metres Kayak Singles

Men	Women
1948 –	K.Hoff (DEN)
1952 –	S.Saimo (FIN)
1956 –	E.Dementyeva (USSR)
1960 –	A.Seredina (USSR)
1964 –	L.Khvedosyuk (USSR)
1968 –	L.Pinayeva (USSR)
1972 –	Y.Ryabchinskaya (USSR)
1976 V.Diba (ROM)	C.Zirzow (GDR)
1980 V.Parfenovich (USSR)	B.Fischer (GDR)
1984 I.Ferguson (NZ)	A.Anderson (SWE)
1988 Z. Gyulay (HUN)	V. Guecheva (BUL)

1000 metres Kayak Singles
Men

1936 G.Hradetzky (AUT)	1968 M.Hesz (HUN)
1948 G.Fredriksson (SWE)	1972 A.Shaparenko (USSR)
1952 G.Fredriksson (SWE)	1976 R.Helm (GDR)
1956 G.Fredriksson (SWE)	1980 R.Helm (GDR)
1960 E.Hansen (DEN)	1984 A.Thompson (NZ)
1964 R.Peterson (SWE)	1988 G. Barton (USA)

500 metres Kayak Pairs

Men	Women
1960 –	USSR
1964 –	West Germany
1968 –	West Germany
1972 –	USSR
1976 East Germany	USSR
1980 USSR	East Germany
1984 New Zealand	Sweden
1988 New Zealand	East Germany

1000 metres Kayak Pairs
Men

1936 Austria	1968 USSR
1948 Sweden	1972 USSR
1952 Finland	1976 USSR
1956 West Germany	1980 USSR
1960 Sweden	1984 Canada
1964 Sweden	1988 United States

1000 metres Kayak Fours
Men

1964 USSR	1976 USSR
1968 Norway	1980 East Germany
1972 USSR	1984 New Zealand
	1988 Hungary

500 metres Kayak Fours
Women

1984 Romania   East Germany

1000 metres Canadian Singles
Men

1936 F.Amyot (CAN)	1968 T.Tatai (HUN)
1948 J.Holecek (TCH)	1972 I.Patzaichin (ROM)
1952 J.Holecek (TCH)	1976 M.Ljubek (YUG)
1956 L.Rotman (ROM)	1980 L.Lubenov (BUL)
1960 J.Parti (HUN)	1984 U.Eicke (FRG)
1964 J.Eschert (FRG)	1988 I. Clementiev (USSR)

500 metres Canadian Singles
Men

1976 A.Rogov (USSR)
1980 S.Postrekhin (USSR)
1984 L.Cain (CAN)
1988 O. Heukrodt (GDR)

1000 metres Canadian Pairs
Men

1936 Czechoslovakia	1968 Romania
1948 Czechoslovakia	1972 USSR
1952 Denmark	1976 USSR
1956 Romania	1980 Romania
1960 USSR	1984 Romania
1964 USSR	1988 USSR

500 metres Canadian Pairs
Men

1976 USSR
1980 Hungary
1984 Yugoslavia
1988 USSR

Most Gold Medals:
6 Gerd Fredriksson

Gerd Fredriksson (SWE), Rudiger Helm (GDR) and Ivan Patzaichin (ROM) have all won 13 world titles (including Olympics), but they fall a long way short of the 20 won by Birgit Schmidt (nee Fischer) between 1978-87.

A military game, Chess was mentioned in Indian and Persian literature in the 6th century. The game eventually spread across Europe and came to Britain with the Norman conquest.

WORLD CHAMPIONS

Although world champions are recorded from 1851, the championships did not become officially recognised until 1866. It is only since the death of champion Alexandre Alekhine in 1946 that the championship has been run on an organised basis.

Winners:
Men

1851 A. Anderssen (GER)	1957 V. Smyslov (USSR)
1858 P. Morphy (USA)	1958 M. Botvinnik (USSR)
1862 A. Anderssen (GER)	1960 M. Tal (USSR)
1866 W. Steinitz (AUT)	1961 M. Botvinnik (USSR)
1894 E. Lasker (GER)	1963 T. Petrosian (USSR)
1921 J. Capablanca (CUB)	1969 B. Spassky (USSR)
1927 A. Alekhine (FRA)	1972 R. Fischer (USA)
1935 M. Euwe (HOL)	1975 A. Karpov (USSR)
1937 A. Alekhine (FRA)	1985 G. Kasparov (USSR))
1948 M. Botvinnik (USSR)	

Longest Reigning Champion:
27 years Emanuel Lasker

Women

1927 V. Menchik-Stevenson (GB)	1958 E. Bykova (USSR)
1950 L. Rudenko (USSR)	1962 N. Gaprindashvili (USSR)
1953 E. Bykova (USSR)	1978 M. Chiburdanidze (USSR)
1956 O. Rubtsova (USSR)	

Longest Reigning Champion:
17 years Vera Menchik-Stevenson

The first record of a Chess Club was in 1747 when members met at Slaughter's Coffee House, London.

The two finalists in the 1978 Wormwood Scrubs chess championship were Ian Brady and John Stonehouse...

Chess coverage is popular in many of today's better class newspapers. But the first paper to carry a regular chess column was the *Liverpool Mercury*, who started a weekly column in 1813. *Bell's Life in London,* 22 years later, was the first national newspaper to have a chess column. The following year, the first chess magazine appeared in Paris. It was called *La Palamede.*

The idea of the Commonwealth Games was first suggested by a Yorkshireman, the Reverend Astley Cooper in 1891, but it was not until 39 years later that his original idea came to fruition. The first Games, then known as the British Empire Games, were held at Hamilton, Canada, between 16-23 August 1930.

The following is a list of all the cities that have staged the Commonwealth Games.

Year Venue

1930 Hamilton, Canada	1962 Perth, Australia
1934 London, England	1966 Kingston, Jamaica
1938 Sydney, Australia	1970 Edinburgh, Scotland
1942–1946 Not held	1974 Christchurch, New Zealand
1950 Auckland, New Zealand	1978 Edmonton, Canada
1954 Vancouver, Canada	1982 Brisbane, Australia
1958 Cardiff, Wales	1986 Edinburgh, Scotland
	1990 Auckland, New Zealand

GOLD MEDALLISTS

The following is a table of all gold medal winning nations:

373 England	6 Uganda
345 Australia	4 Hong Kong
252 Canada	4 Singapore
77 New Zealand	3 Bahamas
60 South Africa	3 Tanzania
51 Scotland	3 Zimbabwe (incl. N & S Rhodesia)
29 Kenya	2 Fiji
24 India	2 Guyana (incl. British Guiana)
22 Wales	2 Isle of Man
20 Pakistan	2 Sri Lanka (formerly Ceylon)
18 Jamaica	2 Zambia
14 Nigeria	1 Barbados
14 Northern Ireland	1 St. Vincent
12 Ghana	
8 Malaysia	
7 Trinidad	

SPORTS

The following ten sports were contested at the 1986 Games in Edinburgh:
Athletics, Badminton, Bowls, Boxing, Cycling, Rowing, Shooting, Swimming & Diving, Weightlifting and Wrestling.
In addition, the following sports have been included in the Games over the years but are now discontinued:
Archery, Fencing, Gymnastics

Although a bat and ball game resembling cricket was probably played in the 13th century, it was not until the 17th century that the game took a format not dissimilar to that played today. The Marylebone Cricket Club (the M.C.C.) was formed in 1787.

COUNTY CHAMPIONSHIP

The early County Championships were decided by the least number of games lost. It was not until 1890 that the Championship was officially organised with a points system.

Champions:
1864 Surrey
1865 Nottinghamshire
1866 Middlesex
1867 Yorkshire
1868 Nottinghamshire
1869 Nottinghamshire & Yorkshire (shared)
1870 Yorkshire
1871 Nottinghamshire
1872 Nottinghamshire
1873 Gloucestershire & Nottinghamshire (shared)
1874 Gloucestershire
1875 Nottinghamshire
1876 Gloucestershire
1877 Gloucestershire
1878 Undecided
1879 Lancashire & Nottinghamshire (shared)
1880 Nottinghamshire
1881 Lancashire
1882 Lancashire & Nottinghamshire (shared)
1883 Nottinghamshire
1884 Nottinghamshire
1885 Nottinghamshire
1886 Nottinghamshire
1887 Surrey
1888 Surrey
1889 Lancashire, Nottinghamshire & Surrey (shared)
1890 Surrey
1891 Surrey
1892 Surrey
1893 Yorkshire
1894 Surrey
1895 Surrey
1896 Yorkshire
1897 Lancashire
1898 Yorkshire
1899 Surrey
1900 Yorkshire
1901 Yorkshire
1902 Yorkshire
1903 Middlesex
1904 Lancashire
1905 Yorkshire

1906 Kent
1907 Nottinghamshire
1908 Yorkshire
1909 Kent
1910 Kent
1911 Warwickshire
1912 Yorkshire
1913 Kent
1914 Surrey
1915–18 Not held
1919 Yorkshire
1920 Middlesex
1921 Middlesex
1922 Yorkshire
1923 Yorkshire
1924 Yorkshire
1925 Yorkshire
1926 Lancashire
1927 Lancashire
1928 Lancashire
1929 Nottinghamshire
1930 Lancashire
1931 Yorkshire
1932 Yorkshire
1933 Yorkshire
1934 Lancashire
1935 Yorkshire
1936 Derbyshire
1937 Yorkshire
1938 Yorkshire
1939 Yorkshire
1940–45 Not held
1946 Yorkshire
1947 Middlesex
1948 Glamorgan
1949 Middlesex & Yorkshire (shared)
1950 Lancashire & Surrey (shared)
1951 Warwickshire

1952 Surrey
1953 Surrey
1954 Surrey
1955 Surrey
1956 Surrey
1957 Surrey
1958 Surrey
1959 Yorkshire
1960 Yorkshire
1961 Hampshire
1962 Yorkshire
1963 Yorkshire
1964 Worcestershire
1965 Worcestershire
1966 Yorkshire
1967 Yorkshire
1968 Yorkshire
1969 Glamorgan
1970 Kent
1971 Surrey
1972 Warwickshire
1973 Hampshire
1974 Worcestershire
1975 Leicestershire
1976 Middlesex
1977 Kent & Middlesex (shared)
1978 Kent
1979 Essex
1980 Middlesex
1981 Nottinghamshire
1982 Middlesex
1983 Essex
1984 Essex
1985 Middlesex
1986 Essex
1987 Nottinghamshire
1988 Worcestershire

Most Outright Wins:
31 Yorkshire

NATWEST BANK TROPHY

A 60-over one day knockout competition, it was introduced in 1963 and was known as the Gillette Cup until acquiring new sponsors in 1981. The Final of the competition is played at Lord's.

Gillette Cup

Year	Winners	Runners up	Winning Margin
1963	Sussex	Worcestershire	14 runs
1964	Sussex	Warwickshire	8 wickets
1965	Yorkshire	Surrey	175 runs
1966	Warwickshire	Worcestershire	5 wickets
1967	Kent	Somerset	32 runs
1968	Warwickshire	Sussex	4 wickets
1969	Yorkshire	Derbyshire	69 runs
1970	Lancashire	Sussex	6 wickets
1971	Lancashire	Kent	24 runs
1972	Lancashire	Warwickshire	4 wickets
1973	Gloucestershire	Sussex	40 runs
1974	Kent	Lancashire	4 wickets
1975	Lancashire	Middlesex	7 wickets
1976	Northamptonshire	Lancashire	4 wickets
1977	Middlesex	Glamorgan	5 wickets
1978	Sussex	Somerset	5 wickets
1979	Somerset	Northamptonshire	45 runs
1980	Middlesex	Surrey	7 wickets

NatWest Bank Trophy

Year	Winners	Runners up	Winning Margin
1981	Derbyshire	Northamptonshire	fewer wickets lost −scores level
1982	Surrey	Warwickshire	9 wickets
1983	Somerset	Kent	24 runs
1984	Middlesex	Kent	4 wickets
1985	Essex	Nottinghamshire	1 run
1986	Sussex	Lancashire	7 wickets
1987	Nottinghamshire	Northamptonshire	3 wickets
1988	Middlesex	Worcestershire	3 wickets

Most Wins:

4 Lancashire, Sussex, Middlesex

REFUGE ASSURANCE LEAGUE

Introduced in 1969 as the John Player League, matches consist of 40 overs per team and all matches are played on a Sunday.

Champions:

1969 Lancashire
1970 Lancashire
1971 Worcestershire
1972 Kent
1973 Kent
1974 Leicestershire
1975 Hampshire
1976 Kent
1977 Leicestershire
1978 Hampshire
1979 Somerset
1980 Warwickshire
1981 Essex
1982 Sussex
1983 Yorkshire
1984 Essex
1985 Essex
1986 Hampshire
1987 Worcestershire
1988 Worcestershire

Most Wins:

3 Essex, Kent, Hampshire, Worcestershire

REFUGE ASSURANCE CUP FINAL
A knockout tournament involving the top four teams in the Refuge Assurance League, it was inaugurated in 1988.

Finals:

1988 Lancashire beat Worcestershire by 52 runs

BENSON & HEDGES CUP
A limited 55-over competition. Teams are divided into four groups and play other teams in their group. The top two in each group qualify for the quarter finals when it becomes a knockout competition. The final is played at Lord's.

Year	Winners	Runners up	Winning Margin
1972	Leicestershire	Yorkshire	5 wickets
1973	Kent	Worcestershire	39 runs
1974	Surrey	Leicestershire	27 runs
1975	Leicestershire	Middlesex	5 wickets
1976	Kent	Worcestershire	43 runs
1977	Gloucestershire	Kent	64 runs
1978	Kent	Derbyshire	6 wickets
1979	Essex	Surrey	35 runs
1980	Northamptonshire	Essex	6 runs
1981	Somerset	Surrey	7 wickets
1982	Somerset	Nottinghamshire	9 wickets
1983	Middlesex	Essex	4 runs
1984	Lancashire	Warwickshire	6 wickets
1985	Leicestershire	Essex	5 wickets
1986	Middlesex	Kent	2 runs
1987	Yorkshire	Northamptonshire	Fewer wickets lost
1988	Hampshire	Derbyshire	7 wickets

Most Wins:

3 Leicestershire, Kent

WORLD CUP
The first ICC World Cup was held in England in 1975. Held every four years, all subsequent competitions have also been played in England, but the 1987 event was staged in Pakistan and India.

Finals:

Year	Winners	Runners up	Winning margin
1975	West Indies	Australia	17 runs
1979	West Indies	England	92 runs
1983	India	West Indies	43 runs
1987	Australia	England	7 runs

Most Wins:

2 West Indies

TEST CRICKET SUMMARY:
Since 1876–77 more than 1000 Test Matches have been played. The following is each country's record against all other countries. (Correct as at 1 March 1989)

	Played	Won		Drawn	Tied
England v Australia	263	E88	A97	78	-
England v South Africa	102	E46	SA18	38	-
England v West Indies	95	E21	WI39	35	-
England v India	75	E30	I11	34	-
England v New Zealand	66	E30	NZ4	32	-
England v Pakistan	47	E13	P5	29	-
England v Sri Lanka	3	E2	SL0	1	-

Australia v South Africa	53	A29	SA11	13	-
Australia v West Indies	65	A28	WI22	15	1
Australia v India	45	A20	I8	16	1
Australia v New Zealand	24	A10	NZ5	9	-
Australia v Pakistan	31	A11	P9	11	-
Australia v Sri Lanka	2	A2	SL0	0	-
South Africa v New Zealand	17	SA9	NL2	6	-
West Indies v India	58	WI23	I6	29	-
West Indies v New Zealand	24	WI8	NZ4	12	-
West Indies v Pakistan	25	WI9	P6	10	-
India v New Zealand	28	I12	NZ5	11	-
India v Pakistan	40	I4	P7	29	-
India v Sri Lanka	7	I2	SL1	4	-
New Zealand v Pakistan	30	NZ3	P10	17	-
New Zealand v Sri Lanka	6	NZ4	SL0	2	-
Pakistan v Sri Lanka	9	P5	SL1	3	-

MAJOR CRICKET RECORDS First Class Cricket

Team records
Highest total: 1,107 Victoria v New South Wales 1926–27
Lowest total: 12 Oxford University v MCC & Ground 1877
12 Northamptonshire v Gloucestershire 1907

Individual Records
Batting:
Highest individual score:
499 Hanif Mohammad 1958–59
Most centuries in a career:
197 J. B. Hobbs
Most centuries in a season:
18 D. C. S. Compton 1947
Most runs in a career:
61,237 J. B. Hobbs
Most runs in a season:
3,816 D. C. S. Compton 1947
Most runs in an over:
36 G. S. Sobers 1968
36 R. J. Shastri 1984–85
Most runs in a day:
345 C. G. McCartney 1921
Fastest half century:
8 mins C. C. Inman 1965
Fastest century:
35 mins P. G. H. Fender 1920   S.J. O'Shaughnessy 1983
Fastest double century:
113 mins R. J. Shastri 1984–85
Fastest triple century:
181 mins D. C. S. Compton 1948–49
Record partnership:
577 V. S. Hazare & Gul Mahomed 1946–47
Bowling:
Most wickets in a career:
4,187 W. Rhodes
Most wickets in a season:
304 A. P. Freeman 1928
Most wickets in a match:
19 J. C. Laker 1956
Most wickets in a day:
17 C. Blythe 1907; 17 H. Verity 1933; 17 T. W. Goddard 1939

Most hat tricks:
7 D. V. P. Wright
Best analysis:
10–10 H. Verity 1932

Wicketkeeping

Most dismissals in a career:
1,648 R. W. Taylor
Most dismissals in a season:
127 L. E. G. Ames 1929
Most dismissals in a match:
12 E. Pooley 1868
12 D. Tallon 1938–39
12 H. B. Taber 1968–69
Most dismissals in an innings:
8 A. T. W. Grout 1959–60
8 D. E. East 1985

Fielding (Excluding wicketkeepers)

Most catches in a career:
1,018 F. E. Woolley

Most catches in a season:
78 W. R. Hammond 1928
Most catches in a match:
10 W. R. Hammond 1928
Most catches in an innings:
7 M. J. Stewart 1957
7 A. S. Brown 1966

Test Cricket
Team records
Highest total:
903–7 dec. England v Australia 1938
Lowest total:
26 New Zealand v England 1954–55

Batting:
Highest individual score:
365* G. S. Sobers (West Indies) 1957–58
Most centuries in a career:
34 S. M. Gavaskar (India)
Most runs in a career:
10,122 S. M. Gavaskar (India)
Most runs in a series:
974 D. G. Bradman (Australia) 1930
Most runs in a calendar year:
1,710 I. V. A. Richards (West Indies) 1976
Most runs in a day:
309 D. G. Bradman (Australia) 1930
Fastest half century:
28 mins J. T. Brown (England) 1894–95
Fastest century:
70 mins J. M. Gregory (Australia) 1921–22
Fastest double century:
214 mins D. G. Bradman (Australia) 1930
Fastest triple century:
287 mins W. R. Hammond (England) 1932–33

Record partnership:
451 W. H. Ponsford & D. G. Bradman (Australia) 1934
451 Mudassar Nazar & Javed Miandad (Pakistan) 1982-83

Bowling:
Most wickets in a career:
396 R. J. Hadlee (New Zealand)
Most wickets in a series:
49 S. F. Barnes (England) 1913–14
Most wickets in a match:
19 J. C. Laker (England) 1956
Most wickets in an innings:
10 J. C. Laker (England) 1956
Best analysis:
19–90 J. C. Laker (England) 1956
Wicketkeeping
Most dismissals in a career:
355 R. W. Marsh (Australia)
Most dismissals in a series:
28 R. W. Marsh (Australia) 1982–83
Most dismissals in a match:
10 R. W. Taylor (England) 1979–80
Most dismissals in an innings:
7 Wasim Bari (Pakistan) 1978–79
7 R. W. Taylor (England) 1979–80

Fielding (Excluding wicketkeepers)
Most catches in a career:
122 G. S. Chappell (Australia)
Most catches in a series:
15 J. M. Gregory (Australia) 1920–21
Most catches in a match:
7 G. S. Chappell (Australia) 1974–75
7 Yajurvindra Singh (India) 1976–77
Most catches in an innings:
5 V. Y. Richardson (Australia) 1935–36
5 Yajurvindra Singh (India) 1976–77

* – Not out
(Records correct up to 1 March 1989)

BATTING/BOWLING AVERAGES:

Since 1894, the leaders in the batting & bowling averages in England have been:
(Qualifications; Batting, min. 20 innings; Bowling, min, 50 wickets)

	Batting		Bowling	
1894	38.23	W. Brockwell (Surrey)	9.35	A. D. Pougher (Leics)
1895	51.20	A. C. MacLaren (Lancs)	13.94	C. L. Townsent Gloucs)
1896	57.91	K. S. Ranjitsinhji (Sussex)	14.26	T. R. McKibbin (Australia)
1897	51.55	N. S. Druce (Surrey)	13.84	A. E. Trott (MCC)
1898	60.95	W. G. Quaife (Warwicks)	14.05	J. T. Hearne (Middlesex)
1899	91.23	R. M. Poore (Hants)	17.09	A. E. Trott (Middlesex)
1900	87.57	K. S. Ranjitsinhji (Sussex)	13.81	W. Rhodes (Yorks)
1901	78.67	C. B. Fry (Sussex)	15.12	W. Rhodes (Yorks)
1902	50.00	A. Shrewsbury (Notts)	12.55	S. Haigh (Yorks)
1903	81.30	C. B. Fry (Sussex)	13.67	W. Mead (Essex)
1904	74.17	K. S. Ranjitsinhji (Sussex)	17.90	W. C. Smith (Surrey)
1905	70.02	C. B. Fry (Sussex)	15.37	S. Haigh (Yorks)
1906	67.05	C. J. Burnup (Kent)	12.26	W Huddlestone (Lancs)
1907	46.74	C. B. Fry (Sussex)	11.79	R. O. Schwarz (S. Africa)
1908	54.05	B. J. T. Bosanquet (Middlesex)	11.01	J. B. King (Philadelphia)
1909	46.04	W. Bardsley (Australia)	12.43	W. C. Smith (Surrey)
1910	46.33	J. T. Tyldesley (Lancs)	12.79	J. T. Hearne (Middlesex)
1911	72.00	C. B. Fry (Hants)	16.71	G. J. Thompson (Northants)
1912	56.85	C. B. Fry (Hants)	11.33	S. F. Barnes (Staffs)
1913	50.51	C. P. Mead (Hants)	15.90	B. G. Melle (Oxford U)
1914	60.45	J. W. Hearne (Middlesex)	15.19	C. Blythe (Kent)
1915-18	No championship			
1919	63.08	G. Gunn (Notts)	14.42	W. Rhodes (Yorks)
1920	61.46	E. Hendren (Middlesex)	13.18	W. Rhodes (Yorks)
1921	69.10	C. P. Mead (Hants)	11.19	E. R. Wilson (Yorks)
1922	66.83	E. Hendren (Middlesex)	12.19	W. Rhodes (Yorks)
1923	77.17	E. Hendren (Middlesex)	11.54	W. Rhodes (Yorks)
1924	59.48	A. Sandham (Surrey)	13.23	G. G. Macaulay (Yorks)
1925	70.32	J. B. Hobbs (Surrey)	14.91	C. W. L. Parker (Gloucs)
1926	77.60	J. B. Hobbs (Surrey)	14.86	W. Rhodes (Yorks)
1927	75.58	C. Hallows (Lancs)	16.95	H. Larwood (Notts)
1928	82.00	J. B. Hobbs (Surrey)	14.51	H. Larwood (Notts)
1929	66.55	J. B. Hobbs (Surrey)	15.57	R. Tyldesley (Lancs)
1930	98.66	D. G. Bradman (Australia)	12.42	H. Verity (Yorks)
1931	96.96	H. Sutcliffe (Yorks)	12.03	H. Larwood (Notts)
1932	74.13	H. Sutcliffe (Yorks)	12.86	H. Larwood (Notts)
1933	67.81	W. R. Hammond (Gloucs)	13.43	H. Verity (Yorks)
1934	84.16	D. G. Bradman (Australia)	17.04	W. J. O'Reilly (Australia)
1935	49.35	W. R. Hammond (Gloucs)	14.36	H. Verity (Yorks)
1936	56.94	W. R. Hammond (Gouocs)	12.97	H. Larwood (Notts)
1937	65.04	W. R. Hammond (Gloucs)	15.68	H. Verity (Yorks)
1938	115.66	D. G. Bradman (Australia)	15.23	W. E. Bowes (Yorks)
1939	72.70	G. Headley (W. Indies)	13.13	H. Verity (Yorks)
1940-45	No championship			
1946	84.90	W. R. Hammond (Gloucs)	11.61	A. Booth (Yorks)
1947	90.85	D. C. S. Compton (Middlesex)	16.44	J. C. Clay (Glamorgan)
1948	89.92	D. G. Bradman (Australia)	15.68	R. Lindwall (Australia)
1949	72.61	J. Hardstaff, Jnr. (Notts)	19.18	T. W. Goddard (Gloucs)
1950	79.65	E. D. Weekes (W. Indies)	13.59	R. Tattersall (Lancs)
1951	68.79	P. B. H. May (Surrey)	14.14	R. Appleyard (Yorks)

	Batting			Bowling
1952	64.62	D. S. Sheppard (Sussex)	13.78	F. S. Trueman (Yorks)
1953	65.80	R. N. Harvey (Australia)	15.28	L. Jackson (Derbys)
1954	58.62	D. C. S. Compton (Middlesex)	14.13	J. B. Statham (Lancs)
1955	58.46	D. J. McGlew (S. Africa)	13.01	R. Appleyard (Yorks)
1956	52.52	K. Mackay (Australia)	12.46	G. A. R. Lock (Surrey)
1957	61.76	P. B. H. May (Surrey)	12.02	G. A. R. Lock (Surrey)
1958	63.74	P. B. H. May (Surrey)	10.99	L. Jackson (Derbys)
1959	57.94	M. J. K. Smith (Warwicks)	15.01	J. B. Statham (Lancs)
1960	55.66	R. Subba Row (Northants)	12.31	J. B. Statham (Lancs)
1961	61.18	W. M. Lawry (Australia)	17.79	J. A. Flavell (Worcs)
1962	54.02	T. W. Graveney (Gloucs)	17.13	C. Cook (Gloucs)
1963	47.60	G. S. Sobers (W. Indies)	12.83	C. Griffith (W. Indies)
1964	62.40	K. F. Barrington (Surrey)	13.00	J. A. Standen (Worcs)
1965	63.42	M. C. Cowdrey (Kent)	11.04	H. J. Rhodes (Derbys)
1966	61.31	G. S. Sobers (W. Indies)	13.80	D. L. Underwood (Kent)
1967	68.63	K. F. Barrington (Kent)	12.39	D. L. Underwood (Kent)
1968	64.65	G. Boycott (Yorks)	12.95	O. S. Wheatley (Glamorgan)
1969	69.93	J. H. Edrich (Surrey)	14.82	A. Ward (Derbys)
1970	75.73	G. S. Sobers (Notts)	19.16	D. J. Shepherd (Glamorgan)
1971	100.12	G. Boycott (Yorks)	17.12	G. G. Arnold (Surrey)
1972	72.35	G. Boycott (Yorks)	16.55	M. J. Proctor (Gloucs)
1973	67.11	G. M. Turner (N. Zealand)	15.84	T. W. Cartwright (Warwicks)
1974	63.39	C. H. Lloyd (Lancs)	13.62	A. M. E. Roberts (Hants)
1975	82.53	R. B. Kanhai (Warwicks)	15.80	A. M. E. Roberts (Hants)
1976	75.11	Zaheer Abbas (Gloucs)	14.38	M. A. Holding (W. Indies)
1977	68.04	G. Boycott (Yorks)	15.94	M. Hendrick (Derbys)
1978	66.82	C. E. B. Rice (Notts)	14.49	D. L. Underwood (Kent)
1979	102.53	G. Boycott (Yorks)	13.83	J. Garner (Somerset)
1980	66.55	A. J. Lamb (Northants)	14.72	V. A. P. van der Bijl (Middlesex)
1981	86.69	Zaheer Abbas (Gloucs)	14.89	R. J. Hadlee (Notts)
1982	70.23	Zaheer Abbas (Gloucs)	14.57	R. J. Hadlee (Notts)
1983	75.25	I. V. A. Richards (Somerset)	16.28	J. K. Lever (Essex)
1984	68.39	M. W. Gatting (Middlesex)	14.05	R. J. Hadlee (Notts)
1985	76.50	I. V. A. Richards (Somerset)	17.20	R. M. Ellison (Kent)
1986	67.83	C. G. Greenidge (Hants)	15.08	M. D. Marshall (Hants)
1987	67.79	M. D. Crowe (Somerset)	12.64	R. J. Hadlee (Notts)
1988	77.75	R. Harper (West Indies)	12.16	M. D. Marshall (West Indies)

SHEFFIELD SHIELD

An Australian Inter-State championship the competition is named after Lord Sheffield who presented the trophy. First held in 1892-93. Since 1982-83 the leading two teams in the championship have met in the Sheffield Shield Final.

Winners:

1892-93	Victoria	1902-03	New South Wales
1893-94	South Australia	1903-04	New South Wales
1894-95	Victoria	1904-05	New South Wales
1895-96	New South Wales	1905-06	New South Wales
1896-97	New South Wales	1906-07	New South Wales
1897-98	Victoria	1907-08	Victoria
1898-99	Victoria	1908-09	New South Wales
1899-00	New South Wales	1909-10	South Australia
1900-01	Victoria	1910-11	New South Wales
1901-02	New South Wales	1911-12	New South Wales

1912-13 South Australia	1955-56 New South Wales
1913-14 New South Wales	1956-57 New South Wales
1914-15 Victoria	1957-58 New South Wales
1915-19 Not held	1958-59 New South Wales
1919-20 New South Wales	1959-60 New South Wales
1920-21 New South Wales	1960-61 New South Wales
1921-22 Victoria	1961-62 New South Wales
1922-23 New South Wales	1962-63 Victoria
1923-24 Victoria	1963-64 South Australia
1924-25 Victoria	1964-65 New South Wales
1925-26 New South Wales	1965-66 New South Wales
1926-27 South Australia	1966-67 Victoria
1927-28 Victoria	1967-68 Western Australia
1928-29 New South Wales	1968-69 South Australia
1929-30 Victoria	1969-70 Victoria
1930-31 Victoria	1970-71 South Australia
1931-32 New South Wales	1971-72 Western Australia
1932-33 New South Wales	1972-73 Western Australia
1933-34 Victoria	1973-74 Victoria
1934-35 Victoria	1974-75 Western Australia
1935-36 South Australia	1975-76 South Australia
1936-37 Victoria	1976-77 Western Australia
1937-38 New South Wales	1977-78 Western Australia
1938-39 South Australia	1978-79 Victoria
1939-40 New South Wales	1979-80 Victoria
1940-46 Not held	1980-81 Western Australia
1946-47 Victoria	1981-82 South Australia
1947-48 Western Australia	1982-83 New South Wales
1948-49 New South Wales	1983-84 Western Australia
1949-50 New South Wales	1984-85 New South Wales
1950-51 Victoria	1985-86 New South Wales
1951-52 New South Wales	1986-87 Western Australia
1952-53 South Australia	1987-88 Queensland
1953-54 New South Wales	1988-89 Western Australia
1954-55 New South Wales	

Most wins: 39 New South Wales

RED STRIPE CUP

The leading domestic competition in the West Indies, it is an Inter-Territorial competition sponsored by Red Stripe. It was formerly the Shell Shield. First held in 1965-66.

Winners:

1965-66 Barbados	1976-77 Barbados
1966-67 Barbados	1977-78 Barbados
1967-68 Not held	1978-79 Barbados
1968-69 Jamaica	1979-80 Barbados
1969-70 Trinidad	1980-81 Combined Islands
1970-71 Trinidad	1981-82 Barbados
1971-72 Barbados	1982-83 Guyana
1972-73 Guyana	1983-84 Barbados
1973-74 Barbados	1985-85 Trinidad & Tobago
1974-75 Guyana	1985-86 Barbados
1975-76 Trinidad/Barbados	1986-87 Guyana
	1987-88 Jamaica
Most wins: 11 Barbados	1988-89 Jamaica

SHELL TROPHY

Originally called the Plunket Shield, named after the former Governor General of New Zealand, Lord Plunket, who presented the trophy in 1906. It was originally organised on a challenge basis between the provinces of New Zealand, but in 1922 a league system was introduced. The competition became known as the Shell Trophy in 1976.

Winners:

Challenge system
1907 Canterbury
1907-11 Auckland
1911-12 Canterbury
1912-13 Auckland
1913-18 Canterbury
1918-19 Wellington
1919-20 Canterbury
1920-21 Auckland
1921   Wellington

League System
1921-22 Auckland
1922-23 Canterbury
1923-34 Wellington
1924-25 Otago
1925-26 Wellington
1926-27 Auckland
1927-28 Wellington
1928-29 Auckland
1929-30 Wellington
1930-31 Canterbury
1931-32 Wellington
1932-33 Otago
1933-34 Auckland
1934-35 Canterbury
1935-36 Wellington
1936-37 Auckland
1937-38 Auckland
1938-39 Auckland
1939-40 Auckland
1945-46 Canterbury
1946-47 Auckland
1947-48 Otago
1948-49 Canterbury
1949-50 Wellington

1950-51 Otago
1951-52 Canterbury
1952-53 Otago
1953-54 Central Districts
1954-55 Wellington
1955-56 Canterbury
1956-57 Wellington
1957-58 Otago
1958-59 Auckland
1959-60 Canterbury
1960-61 Wellington
1961-62 Wellington
1962-63 Northern Districts
1963-64 Auckland
1964-65 Canterbury
1965-66 Wellington
1966-67 Central Districts
1967-68 Central Districts
1968-69 Auckland
1969-70 Otago
1970-71 Central Districts
1971-72 Otago
1972-73 Wellington
1973-74 Wellington
1974-75 Otago
1975-76 Canterbury
1976-77 Otago
1977-78 Auckland
1978-79 Otago
1979-80 Northern Districts
1980-81 Auckland
1981-82 Wellington
1982-83 Wellington
1983-84 Canterbury
1984-85 Wellington
1985-86 Otago
1986-87 Central Districts
1987-88 Otago
1988-89 Auckland

Most wins (since 1922): 17 Wellington

CURRIE CUP

South Africa's Inter-Provincial Championship since 1889-90, the trophy was donated by shipowner Sir Donald Currie. The Cup has been contested annually since 1965-66, prior to that there was no competition if there was a touring side to South Africa.

Winners

1889-90 Transvaal	1954-55 Natal
1890-91 Griqualand West	1955-56 Western Province
1892-93 Wester Province	1958-59 Transvaal
1893-94 Western Province	1959-60 Natal
1894-95 Transvaal	1960-61 Natal
1896-97 Western Province	1962-63 Natal
1897-98 Western Province	1963-64 Natal
1902-03 Transvaal	1965-66 Natal/Transvaal
1903-04 Transvaal	1966-67 Natal
1904-05 Transvaal	1967-68 Natal
1906-07 Transvaal	1968-69 Transvaal
1908-09 Western Province	1969-70 Transvaal/Western Province
1910-11 Natal	1970-71 Transvaal
1912-13 Natal	1971-72 Transvaal
1920-21 Western Province	1972-73 Transvaal
1921-22 Transvaal/Natal/Western Province	1973-74 Natal
1923-24 Transvaal	1974-75 Western Province
1925-26 Transvaal	1975-76 Natal
1926-27 Transvaal	1976-77 Natal
1929-30 Transvaal	1977-78 Western Province
1931-32 Western Province	1978-79 Transvaal
1933-34 Natal	1979-80 Transvaal
1934-35 Transvaal	1980-81 Natal
1936-37 Natal	1981-82 Western Province
1937-38 Natal/Transvaal	1982-83 Transvaal
1946-47 Natal	1983-84 Transvaal
1947-48 Natal	1984-85 Transvaal
1950-51 Transvaal	1985-86 Western Province
1951-52 Natal	1986-87 Transvaal
1952-53 Western Province	1987-88 Transvaal
	1988-89 Eastern Province

Most wins: 24 Transvaal

RANJI TROPHY

The Ranji Trophy was established in 1934 and is named after the former England test cricketer, Kumar Shri Ranjitsinhji. It is India's premier competition and all competing States and Provinces play on a zonal basis before taking part in a knockout tournament.

Winners:

1934-35 Bombay	1944-45 Bombay
1935-36 Bombay	1945-46 Holkar
1936-37 Nawanagar	1946-47 Baroda
1937-38 Hyberabad	1948-49 Bombay
1938-39 Bengal	1949-50 Baroda
1939-40 Maharashtra	1950-51 Holkar
1940-41 Maharashtra	1951-52 Bombay
1941-42 Bombay	1952-53 Holkar
1942-43 Baroda	1953-54 Bombay
1943-44 Western India States	1954-55 Madras

1955-56 Bombay	1970-71 Bombay
1960-61 Bombay	1971-72 Bombay
1961-62 Bombay	1972-73 Bombay
1962-63 Bombay	1973-74 Karnataka
1963-64 Bombay	1974-75 Bombay
1964-65 Bombay	1975-76 Bombay
1965-66 Bombay	1976-77 Bombay
1966-67 Bombay	1977-78 Karnataka
1967-68 Bombay	1978-79 Delhi
1968-69 Bombay	1979-80 Delhi
1969-70 Bombay	1980-81 Bombay
1956-57 Bombay	1981-82 Delhi
1957-58 Baroda	1982-83 Karnataka
1958-59 Bombay	1983-84 Bombay
1959-60 Bombay	1984-85 Bombay
	1985-86 Delhi
Most wins: 30 Bombay	1986-87 Hyderabad
	1987-88 Tamil Nadu

QUAID-E-AZAM TROPHY

Pakistan's principal championship, it came into being in 1953 and the trophy is named after the country's first Governor General Quaid-e-Azam, Mohammad Ali Jinnah.

Winners:

1953-54 Bahawalpur	1972-73 Railways
1954-55 Karachi	1973-74 Railways
1956-57 Punjab	1974-75 Punjab 'A'
1957-58 Bahawalpur	1975-76 National Bank
1958-59 Karachi	1976-77 United Bank
1959-60 Karachi	1977-78 Habib Bank
1960-61 Karachi 'B'	1978-79 National Bank
1961-62 Karachi 'A'	1979-80 Pakistan International Airlines
1963-64 Karachi Blues	1980-81 United Bank
1964-65 Karachi Blues	1981-82 National Bank
1966-67 Karachi	1982-83 United Bank
1968-69 Lahore	1983-84 National Bank
1969-70 Pakistan International Airlines	1984-85 United Bank
1970-71 Karachi Blues	1985-86 Karachi
	1986-87 National Bank
	1987-88 Pia

Most wins: 5 National Bank

WOMEN'S CRICKET

Women's cricket has been played since 1745. The first test match was at Brisbane in 1934 when the Australians played England. The International Women's Cricket Council (IWCC) was formed in 1958.

WORLD CUP

A World Cup for women's teams was contested three times between 1973 and 1982.
Winners:
1973 England
1978 Australia
1982 Australia

WOMEN'S COUNTY CHAMPIONSHIP

The first official women's County Championship was played in 1988 with the leading two teams contesting the final.
Result:
1988 Yorkshire beat Surrey by 3 wickets

WOMEN'S RECORDS:

Highest Innings:
224 not out M. Bryant, Visitors v Residents, at Eastbourne, Sussex (1901)
Highest Test Innings:
193 D. Annetts, Australia v England, at Cottingham, W. Yorkshire (1987)
Highest Test Partnership:
309 (3rd wicket) D. Annetts & L. Reefer, Australia, as above.
Most Runs in Test Career:
1,814 R. Flint (nee Heyhoe), England (1960-79)
Most Wickets in Test Career:
77 M. Duggan, England (1949-63)
Best Bowling:
10-0 R. Humphries, Dalton Ladies v Woodfield SC, at Huddersfield, W. Yorks (1931);
10-0 R. White, Wallington LCC v Beaconsfield LCC, at Wallington (1962)
Best Bowling (Test Match):
7-6 M. Duggan, England v Australia, at St. Kilda, Melbourne (1958)
Highest Team Score:
567 Tarana v Rockley, at Rockley, New South Wales, Australia (1896)
Highest Team Score (Test Match):
503-5 dec England v New Zealand, at Christchurch (1935)
Lowest Test Innings:
35 England v Australia, at St. Kilda, Melbourne (1958)

The Dutch are believed to have first played Curling in the 16th century and they took the game to Scotland were it became very popular. Canada was next to take to the sport and the first series of international matches between the two countries started in 1903. The sport's governing body, the Royal Caledonian Curling Club was founded in 1838.

WORLD CHAMPIONSHIP

First contested in 1959 for the Scotch Cup, the Championship was for the Air Canada Silver Broom trophy from 1968-1986, and the President's Cup in 1987. The women's championship was instituted in 1979.

Men

1959 Canada	1973 Sweden
1960 Canada	1974 United States
1961 Canada	1975 Switzerland
1962 Canada	1976 USA
1963 Canada	1977 Sweden
1964 Canada	1978 United States
1965 United States	1979 Norway
1966 Canada	1980 Canada
1967 Scotland	1981 Switzerland
1968 Canada	1982 Canada
1969 Canada	1983 Canada
1970 Canada	1984 Norway
1971 Canada	1985 Canada
1972 Canada	1986 Canada
	1987 Canada
Most Wins:	1988 Norway
19 Canada	1989 Canada

Women

1979 Switzerland	1983 Switzerland
1980 Canada	1984 Canada
1981 Sweden	1985 Canada
1982 Denmark	1986 Canada
	1987 Canada
	1988 West Germany
Most Wins:	1989 Canada
6 Canada	

Curling is appropriately known as the 'Roaring Game' because of the sound made by the stone as it travels across the ice.

Some of the terminology used in curling is unique to that sport and expressions like: Burnt; Crampit; Foot-score; Hack; Hog; House and Soop will often be heard during a game.

The forerunner of the bicycle, the *celereifere*, was demonstrated in 1791 in the garden of the Palais Royale in Paris. It consisted of a wooden horse mounted on two wheels. Throughout the 19th century the bicycle developed and in 1867 the first cycling club, the Liverpool Velocipede Club, was formed. The first-ever cycle race was a 1200 metre race at the Parc St. Cloud, Paris, and won by Englishman James Moore.

TOUR DE FRANCE

Without doubt, the Tour de France is the greatest cycle race in the world. It was first held in 1903 and the winning rider has to cover over 3,000 miles in three weeks.

Winners:

1903 M. Garin (FRA)
1904 H. Cornet (FRA)
1905 L. Trousselier (FRA)
1906 R. Pottier (FRA)
1907 L. Petit-Breton (FRA)
1908 L. Petit-Breton (FRA)
1909 F. Faber (LUX)
1910 O. Lapize (FRA)
1911 G. Garrigou (FRA)
1912 O. Defraye (BEL)
1913 P. Thys (BEL)
1914 P. Thys (BEL)
1915–18 Not held
1919 F. Lambot (BEL)
1920 P. Thys (BEL)
1921 L. Scieur (BEL)
1922 F. Lambot (BEL)
1923 H. Pelissier (FRA)
1924 O. Bottecchia (ITA)
1925 O. Bottecchia (ITA)
1926 L. Buysse (BEL)
1927 N. Frantz (LUX)
1928 N. Frantz (LUX)
1929 M. De Waele (BEL)
1930 A. Leducq (FRA)
1931 A. Magne (FRA)
1932 A. Leducq (FRA)
1933 G. Speicher (FRA)
1934 A. Magne (FRA)
1935 R. Maes (BEL)
1936 S. Maes (BEL)
1937 R. Lapebie (FRA)
1938 G. Bartali (ITA)
1939 S. Maes (BEL)
1940–46 Not held
1947 J. Robic (FRA)
1948 G. Bartali (ITA)
1949 F. Coppi (ITA)

1950 F. Kubler (SWI)
1951 H. Koblet (SWI)
1952 F. Coppi (ITA)
1953 L. Bobet (FRA)
1954 L. Bobet (FRA)
1955 L. Bobet (FRA)
1956 R. Walkowiak (FRA)
1957 J. Anquetil (FRA)
1958 C. Gaul (LUX)
1959 F. Bahamontes (SPA)
1960 G. Nencini (ITA)
1961 J. Anquetil (FRA)
1962 J. Anquetil (FRA)
1963 J. Anquetil (FRA)
1964 J. Anquetil (FRA)
1965 F. Gimondi (ITA)
1966 L. Aimar (FRA)
1967 R. Pingeon (FRA)
1968 J. Janssen (HOL)
1969 E. Merckx (BEL)
1970 E. Merckx (BEL)
1971 E. Merckx (BEL)
1972 E. Merckx (BEL)
1973 L. Ocana (SPA)
1974 E. Merckx (BEL)
1975 B. Thevenet (FRA)
1976 L. van Impe (BEL)
1977 B. Thevenet (FRA)
1978 B. Hinault (FRA)
1979 B. Hinault (FRA)
1980 J. Zoetemelk (HOL)
1981 B. Hinault (FRA)
1982 B. Hinault (FRA)
1983 L. Fignon (FRA)
1984 L. Fignon (FRA)
1985 B. Hinault (FRA)
1986 G. LeMond (USA)
1987 S. Roche (IRE)
1988 P. Delgado (SPA)

Most Wins:
5 Jacques Anquetil, Eddy Merckx, Bernard Hinault

Women
1984 M. Martin (USA)
1985 M. Canins (ITA)
1986 M. Canins (ITA)
1987 J. Longo (FRA)
1988 J. Longo (FRA)

Most wins: 2 Maria Canins, Jeannie Longo

TOUR DE FRANCE RECORDS
Fastest average speed: 23.51 mph (37.84 kph) B. Hinault (FRA), 1981
Longest race: 3569 miles (5745 km), 1926

TOUR OF BRITAIN (Milk Race)
Until 1983 the Milk Race was an amateur event but it has since gone open. First held in 1951, it was originally sponsored by the *Daily Express* but has been sponsored by the Milk Marketing Board since 1958 when the race resumed after a two year lay-off.

Winners:

1951 I. Steel (GB)	1970 J. Mainus (TCH)
1952 K. Russell (GB)	1971 F. Den Hertog (HOL)
1953 G. Thomas (GB)	1972 H. Kuiper (HOL)
1954 E. Tamburlini (FRA)	1973 P. Van Katwijk (HOL)
1955 A. Hewson (GB)	1974 R. Schuiten (HOL)
1956–57 Not held	1975 B. Johansson (SWE)
1958 R. Durlacher (AUT)	1976 B. Nickson (GB)
1959 W. Bradley (GB)	1977 S. Gusseinov (USSR)
1960 W. Bradley (GB)	1978 J. Brzezny (POL)
1961 W. Holmes (GB)	1979 Y. Kashirin (USSR)
1962 E. Pokorny (POL)	1980 I. Mitchtenko (USSR)
1963 P. Chisman (GB)	1981 S. Krivocheyev (USSR)
1964 A. Metcalfe (GB)	1982 Y. Kashirin (USSR)
1965 L. West (GB)	1983 M. Eaton (USA)
1966 J. Gawliczek (POL)	1984 O. Czougeda (USSR)
1967 L. West (GB)	1985 E. van Lancker (BEL)
1968 G. Petterson (SWE)	1986 J. McLoughlin (GB)
1969 F. Den Hertog (HOL)	1987 M. Elliott (GB)
	1988 V. Zhdanov (USSR)

Most wins: 2 Bill Bradley, Les West, Fedor Den Hertog, Yuri Kasharin

WORLD PROFESSIONAL CHAMPIONSHIPS

The first official world track championships were held in Chicago in 1893 and the first road race championship at Germany's famous Nurburgring in 1927. The first professional cyclo-cross world championships were at Zurich in 1967. Between 1950–66 it was an open event.

Professional Road Race Champions

1927 A. Binda (ITA)	1960 R. van Looy (BEL)
1928 G. Ronsse (BEL)	1961 R. van Looy (BEL)
1929 G. Ronsse (BEL)	1962 J. Stablinski (FRA)
1930 A. Binda (ITA)	1963 R. Beheyt (BEL)
1931 L. Guerra (ITA)	1964 J. Janssen (HOL)
1932 A. Binda (ITA)	1965 T. Simpson (GB)
1933 G. Speicher (FRA)	1966 R. Altig (FRG)
1934 K. Kaers (BEL)	1967 E. Merckx (BEL)
1935 J. Aerts (BEL)	1968 V. Adorni (ITA)
1936 A. Magne (FRA)	1969 H. Ottenbros (HOL)
1937 E. Meulenberg (BEL)	1970 J.-P. Monsere (BEL)
1938 M. Kint (BEL)	1971 E. Merckx (BEL)
1939–45 Not held	1972 M. Basso (ITA)
1946 H. Knecht (SWI)	1973 F. Gimondi (ITA)
1947 T. Middlekamp (HOL)	1974 E. Merckx (BEL)
1948 A. Schotte (BEL)	1975 H. Kuiper (HOL)
1949 R. van Steenbergen (BEL)	1976 F. Maertens (BEL)
1950 A. Schotte (BEL)	1977 F. Moser (ITA)
1951 F. Kubler (SWI)	1978 G. Knetemann (HOL)
1952 H. Muller (GER)	1979 J. Rass (HOL)
1953 F. Coppi (ITA)	1980 B. Hinault (FRA)
1954 L. Bobet (FRA)	1981 F. Maertens (BEL)
1955 S. Ockers (BEL)	1982 G. Saronni (ITA)
1956 R. van Steenbergen (BEL)	1983 G. LeMond (USA)
1957 R. van Steenbergen (BEL)	1984 C. Criquielon (BEL)
1958 E. Baldini (ITA)	1985 J. Zoetemelk (HOL)
1959 A. Darrigade (FRA)	1986 M. Argentin (ITA)
	1987 S. Roche (IRE)
	1988 M. Fondrest (ITA)

Most Wins:

3 Alfredo Binda, Eddie Merckx, Rik van Steenbergen

PROFESSIONAL WORLD SPEED RECORDS

5km	5:44.70	G. Braun (FRG), 1986
10km	11:39.72	F. Moser (ITA), 1984
20km	23:21.59	F. Moser (ITA), 1984
100km (unpaced):	2h 11:21.43	B. Meister (SWI), 1986
100km (motor paced):	1h 10:50.94	A. Romanov (USSR), 1987

TOUR OF ITALY
After the Tour de France the Tour of Italy (Giro d'Italia) is the most prestigious of the major continental tours.

Winners:

1909 L. Canna (ITA)	1953 F. Coppi (ITA)
1910 C. Galetti (ITA)	1954 C. Clerici (SWI)
1911 C. Galetti (ITA)	1955 F. Magni (ITA)
1912 Team Atala (only a team prize awarded)	1956 C. Gaul (LUX)
1913 C. Oriani (ITA)	1957 G. Nencini (ITA)
1914 A. Calzolari (ITA)	1958 E. Baldani (ITA)
1915-18 Not held	1959 C. Gaul (LUX)
1919 C. Girardengo (ITA)	1960 J. Anquetil (FRA)
1920 G. Belloni (ITA)	1961 A. Pambianco (ITA)
1921 G. Brunero (ITA)	1962 F. Balmamion (ITA)
1922 G. Brunero (ITA)	1963 F. Balmamion (ITA)
1923 C. Girardengo (ITA)	1964 J. Anquetil (FRA)
1924 G. Enrici (ITA)	1965 V. Adorni (ITA)
1925 A. Binda (ITA)	1966 G. Motta (ITA)
1926 G. Brunero (ITA)	1967 F. Gimondi (ITA)
1927 A. Binda (ITA)	1968 E. Merckx (BEL)
1928 A. Binda (ITA)	1969 F. Gimondi (ITA)
1929 A. Binda (ITA)	1970 E. Merckx (BEL)
1930 L. Marchisio (ITA)	1971 G. Petterson (SWE)
1931 F. Camusso (ITA)	1972 E. Merckx (BEL)
1932 A. Pesenti (ITA)	1973 E. Merckx (BEL)
1933 A. Binda (ITA)	1974 E. Merckx (BEL)
1934 L. Guerra (ITA)	1975 F. Bertoglio (ITA)
1935 V. Bergamaschi (ITA)	1976 F. Gimondi (ITA)
1936 G. Bartali (ITA)	1977 M. Pollentier (BEL)
1937 G. Bartali (ITA)	1978 J. de Muynck (BEL)
1938 G. Bartali (ITA)	1979 G. Saronni (ITA)
1939 G. Bartali (ITA)	1980 B. Hinault (FRA)
1940 F. Coppi (ITA)	1981 G. Battaglin (ITA)
1941-45 Not held	1982 B. Hinault (FRA)
1946 G. Bartali (ITA)	1983 G. Saronni (ITA)
1947 F. Coppi (ITA)	1984 F. Moser (ITA)
1948 F. Magni (ITA)	1985 B. Hinault (FRA)
1949 F. Coppi (ITA)	1986 R. Visentini (ITA)
1950 H. Koblet (SWI)	1987 S. Roche (IRE)
1951 F. Magni (ITA)	1988 A. Hampsten (USA)
1952 F. Coppi (ITA)	

MOST WINS:
5 Alfredo Binda, Fausto Coppi, Eddy Merckx

TOUR OF SPAIN
The third major continental Tour, the Tour of Spain (Vuelta de Espana) is the first major tour of the season.

Winners:

1935 G. Deloor (BEL)	1943-44 Not held
1936 G. Deloor (BEL)	1945 D. Rodriguez (SPA)
1937-40 Not held	1946 D. Langarica (SPA)
1941 J. Berrendero (SPA)	1947 E. Van Dyck (BEL)
1942 J. Berrendero (SPA)	1948 B. Ruiz (SPA)

1949 Not held
1950 E. Rodriguez (SPA)
1951-54 Not held
1955 J. Dotto (SPA)
1956 A. Contero (ITA)
1957 J. Lorono (SPA)
1958 J. Stablinski (FRA)
1959 A. Suarez (SPA)
1960 F. de Mulder (BEL)
1961 A. Soler (SPA)
1962 R. Altig (FRG)
1963 J. Anquetil (FRA)
1964 R. Poulidor (FRA)
1965 R. Wolfshohl (FRG)
1966 F. Gabicagogeascoa (SPA)
1967 J. Janssen (HOL)
1968 F. Gimondi (ITA)
1969 R. Pingeon (FRA)
1970 L. Ocana (SPA)

1971 F. Bracke (BEL)
1972 J-M. Fuente (SPA)
1973 E. Merckx (BEL)
1974 J-M. Fuente (SPA)
1975 G. Tamames (SPA)
1976 J. Pesarrodona (SPA)
1977 F. Maertens (BEL)
1978 B. Hinault (FRA)
1979 J. Zoetemelk (HOL)
1980 F. Ruperez (SPA)
1981 G. Battaglin (ITA)
1982 M. Lejaretta (SPA)
1983 B. Hinault (FRA)
1984 E. Caritoux (FRA)
1985 P. Delgado (SPA)
1986 A. Pino (SPA)
1987 L. Herrera (COL)
1988 S. Kelly (IRE)
1989 P. Delgado (SPA)

MOST WINS:
2 Gustav Deloor, Julio Berrendero,
Jose-Manuel Fuente, Bernard Hinault

WORLD CYCLO-CROSS CHAMPIONSHIPS
First held in Paris in 1950. Between then and 1967 it was an Open event, but since then amateurs and professionals have made their own races.

Open
1950 J. Robic (FRA)
1951 J. Ronedeaux (FRA)
1952 J. Ronedeaux (FRA)
1953 J. Ronedeaux (FRA)
1954 A. Dufraisse (FRA)
1955 A. Dufraisse (FRA)
1956 A. Dufraisse (FRA)
1957 A. Dufraisse (FRA)
1958 A. Dufraisse (FRA)

1959 R. Longo (ITA)
1960 R. Wolfshohl (FRG)
1961 R. Wolfshohl (FRG)
1962 R. Longo (ITA)
1963 R. Wolfshohl (FRG)
1964 R. Longo (ITA)
1965 R. Longo (ITA)
1966 E. de Vlaeminck (BEL)

Professional
1967 R. Longo (ITA)
1968 E. de Vlaeminck (BEL)
1969 E. de Vlaeminck (BEL)
1970 E. de Vlaeminck (BEL)
1971 E. de Vlaeminck (BEL)
1972 E. de Vlaeminck (BEL)
1973 E. de Vlaeminck (BEL)
1974 A. van Damme (BEL)
1975 R. de Vlaeminck (BEL)
1976 A. Zweifel (SWI)
1977 A. Zweifel (SWI)
1978 A. Zweifel (SWI)

1979 A.. Zweifel (SWI)
1980 R. Liboton (BEL)
1981 H. Stamsnijder (HOL)
1982 R. Liboton (BEL)
1983 R. Liboton (BEL)
1984 R. Liboton (BEL)
1985 K-P. Thaler (FRG)
1986 A. Zweifel (SWI)
1987 K-P. Thaler (FRG)
1988 P. Richard (SWI)
1989 D. De Bie (BEL)

MOST WINS:
7 Eric de Vlaeminck

The Pilgrim Fathers are reputed to have played darts on the Mayflower on their way to the New World. But it has been known in its present form since 1896 when Brian Gamlin of Lancashire devised the present numbering system on the dart board. The National Darts Association was formed in 1924.

WORLD PROFESSIONAL CHAMPIONSHIP

The premier event for Professional players, the first championship was held in Nottingham in 1978.

Winners:

1978 L.Rees (WAL)	1983 K.Deller (ENG)
1979 J.Lowe (ENG)	1984 E.Bristow (ENG)
1980 E.Bristow (ENG)	1985 E.Bristow (ENG)
1981 E.Bristow (ENG)	1986 E.Bristow (ENG)
1982 J.Wilson (SCO)	1987 J. Lowe (ENG)
	1988 B. Anderson (ENG)
	1989 J. Wilson (SCO)

Most Wins:
5 Eric Bristow

WORLD MASTERS
First held in 1974.

Winners:

1974 C.Inglis (ENG)	1981 E.Bristow (ENG)
1975 A.Evans (WAL)	1982 D.Whitcombe (ENG)
1976 J.Lowe (ENG)	1983 E.Bristow (ENG)
1977 E.Bristow (ENG)	1984 E.Bristow (ENG)
1978 R.Davies (WAL)	1985 D.Whitcombe (ENG)
1979 E.Bristow (ENG)	1986 B. Anderson (ENG)
1980 J.Lowe (ENG)	1987 B. Anderson (ENG)
	1988 B. Anderson (ENG)

Most Wins:
5 Eric Bristow

WORLD CUP
Played every two years, the first World Cup was at Wembley in 1977. The winning nation is the one with the most points after a singles, pairs, and fours competition.

Individual	**Team**
1977 L.Rees (WAL)	1977 Wales
1979 N.Virachkul (USA)	1979 England
1981 J.Lowe (ENG)	1981 England
1983 E.Bristow (ENG)	1983 England
1985 E.Bristow (ENG)	1985 England
1987 E. Bristow (ENG)	1987 England
Most Wins:	**Most Wins:**
3 Eric Bristow	5 England

NATIONS CUP

A tournament for three-man teams, the first Nations Cup was organised in 1977.

Winners:

1977 Scotland	1982 England
1978 Sweden	1983 England
1979 England	1984 England
1980 England	1985 Finland
1981 Scotland	1986 England
	1987 England
Most Wins:	1988 England
8 England	

NEWS OF THE WORLD CHAMPIONSHIP

Because of the intensity of the competition, with thousands of darts players from all over Britain competing, the *News Of The World* tournament is one of the hardest events to win, and one that the leading professionals still like to win if they can. The first tournament was in 1927 but in the London area only. The first National championship was in 1948 and won by Harry Leadbetter from St.Helens.

Winners:

1948 H.Leadbetter	1968 B.Duddy
1949 J.Royce	1969 B.Twomlow
1950 D.Newberry	1970 H.Barney
1951 H.Perryman	1971 D.Filkins
1952 T.Gibbons	1972 B.Netherton
1953 J.Carr	1973 I.Hodgkinson
1954 O.James	1974 P.Chapman
1955 T.Reddington	1975 D.White
1956 T.Peachey	1976 B.Lennard
1957 A.Mullins	1977 M.Norris
1958 T.Gibbons	1978 S.Lord (SWE)
1959 A.Welch	1979 B.George
1960 T.Reddington	1980 S.Lord (SWE)
1961 A.Adamson	1981 J.Lowe
1962 E.Brown	1982 R.Morgan
1963 R.Rumney	1983 E.Bristow
1964 T.Barrett	1984 E.Bristow
1965 T.Barrett	1985 D.Lee
1966 W.Ellis	1986 B.George
1967 W.Seaton	1987 M. Gregory
	1988 M. Gregory

Most Wins:

2 Tommy Gibbons, Tom Reddington, Tom Barrett, Stefan Lord, Eric Bristow, Bobby George, Mike Gregory

NINE-DART FINSIH

The lowest possible finish for a game of 501 is nine darts.
John Lowe won £102,000 for a nine-dart finish in the 1984 World Match—Play Championship. His nine darts were: 60-60-60-60-60-60-51-54-36. The least number of darts required to complete a game of 301 is six.

MARATHON

Highest score in 24-hours: 496,949 I. Brown (Lanark, Scotland), 1988

WOMEN'S DARTS

WORLD CUP
Inaugurated in 1983 and played alongside the men's tournament.
Winners:

Individual	Team
1983 S. Reitan (USA)	1983 England
1985 L. Batten (GB)	1985 England
1987 V. Maycum (HOL)	1987 United States

WORLD MASTERS
An annual event.
Winners:

1984 K. Wones (ENG)
1985 L. Barnett (NZ)
1986 K. Wones (ENG)
1987 A. Thomas (WAL)
1988 M. Solomons (ENG)

BRITISH OPEN
Inaugurated in 1979, and held every year.
Winners:

1979 J. Campbell (SCO)
1980 L. Batten (ENG)
1981 A. M. Davies (WAL)
1982 M. Flowers (ENG)
1983 S. Earnshaw (ENG)
1984 A. M. Davies (ENG)
1985 L. Batten (ENG)
1986 G. Sutton (ENG)
1987 S. Colclough (ENG)
1988 J. Stubbs (ENG)
1989 C. McCullough (SCO)

The earliest known show jumping competition was at the Agricultural Hall, London, in 1869 although some sources say that jumping obstacles on horseback took place at a Paris show three years earlier. The British Show Jumping Association was formed in 1923.

WORLD CHAMPIONSHIPS
World Championships exist for the three Equestrian disciplines: Three-Day Eventing, Show Jumping and Dressage. The Show Jumping championship in 1953 was the first to be introduced.

SHOW JUMPING
Men

1953 F.Goyoago (SPA)	1970 D.Broome (GB)
1954 H.-G.Winkler (FRG)	1974 H.Steenken (FRG)
1955 H.-G.Winkler (FRG)	1978 G.Wiltfang (FRG)
1956 R.d'Inzeo (ITA)	1982 N.Koof (FRG)
1960 R.d'Inzeo (ITA)	1986 G.Greenhough (CAN)
1966 P.d'Oriola (FRA)	

Most Wins:
2 Hans-Gunter Winkler, Raimond d'Inzeo

Women
1965 M.Coakes (GB)
1970 J.Lefebvre (FRA)
1974 J.Lefebvre-Tissot (FRA)
(Since 1978 women have competed in the same championship as men)

Most Wins:
2 Janou Lefebvre-Tissot

Team
1978 Great Britain
1982 France
1986 United States

THREE-DAY EVENT
Individual

1966 C.Moratorio (ARG)	1978 B.Davidson (USA)
1970 M.Gordon-Watson (GB)	1982 L.Green (GB)
1974 B.Davidson (USA)	1986 V.Leng (GB)

Most Wins:
2 Bruce Davidson

Team

1966 Ireland	1978 Canada
1970 Great Britain	1982 Great Britain
1974 United States	1986 Great Britain

Most Wins:
3 Great Britain

DRESSAGE
Individual
1966 J.Neckarmann (FRG)
1970 E.Petouchkova (USSR)
1974 R.Klimke (FRG)

1978 C.Stuckelberger (SWI)
1982 R.Klimke (FRG)
1986 A.Jensen (FRG)

Most Wins:
2 Reiner Klimke

Team
1966 West Germany
1970 USSR
1974 West Germany

1978 West Germany
1982 West Germany
1986 West Germany

Most Wins:
5 West Germany

EUROPEAN SHOW JUMPING CHAMPIONSHIPS
First held in 1957; men and women had separate competitions until 1975.

Winners:
Men
1957 H.-G.Winkler (FRG)
1958 F.Thiedemann (FRG)
1959 P.d'Inzeo (ITA)
1961 D.Broome (GB)
1962 C.D.Barker (GB)
1963 G.Mancinelli (ITA)
1965 H.Schridde (FRG)
1966 N.Pessoa (BRA)
1967 D.Broome (GB)

1969 D.Broome (GB)
1971 H.Steenken (FRG)
1973 P.McMahon (GB)
1975 A.Schockemohle (FRG)
1977 J.Heins (HOL)
1979 G.Wiltfang (FRG)
1981 P.Schockemohle (FRG)
1983 P.Schockemohle (FRG)
1985 P.Schockemohle (FRG)
1987 P.Durand (FRA)

Most Wins:
3 David Broome, Paul Schockemohle

Women
1957 P.Smythe (GB)
1958 G.Serventi (ITA)
1959 A.Townsend (GB)
1960 S.Cohen (GB)
1961 P.Smythe (GB)
1962 P.Smythe (GB)
1963 P.Smythe (GB)

1966 J.Lefebvre (FRA)
1967 K.Kusner (USA)
1968 A.Drummond-Hay (GB)
1969 I.Kellett (IRE)
1971 A.Moore (GB)
1973 A.Moore (GB)

Most Wins:
4 Pat Smythe

OLYMPIC GAMES
Showjumping was included in the 1900 Olympic Games while both the Dressage and Three Day Event made their debut in 1912.

SHOW JUMPING
Individual

1900 A.Haegeman (BEL)	1956 H.-G.Winkler (GER)
1912 J.Cariou (FRA)	1960 R.d'Inzeo (ITA)
1920 T.Lequio (ITA)	1964 P.d'Oriola (FRA)
1924 A.Gemuseus (SWI)	1968 W.Steinkraus (USA)
1928 F.Ventura (TCH)	1972 G.Mancinelli (ITA)
1932 T.Nishi (JAP)	1976 A.Schockemohle (FRG)
1936 K.Hasse (GER)	1980 J.Kowalczyk (POL)
1948 H.Mariles-Cortes (MEX)	1984 J.Fargis (USA)
1952 P.d'Oriola (FRA)	1988 P.Durand (FRA)

Most Wins:
2 Pierre d'Oriola

Team

1912 Sweden	1956 West Germany
1920 Sweden	1960 West Germany
1924 Sweden	1964 West Germany
1928 Spain	1968 Canada
1932 not completed	1972 West Germany
1936 Germany	1976 France
1948 Mexico	1980 USSR
1952 Great Britian	1984 United States
	1988 West Germany

Most Wins:
6 West Germany (incl. one as Germany)

THREE-DAY EVENT
Individual

1912 A.Nordlander (SWE)	1956 P.Kastenman (SWE)
1920 H.Morner (SWE)	1960 L.Morgan (USA)
1924 A.van der Voort van Zijp (HOL)	1964 M.Checcoli (ITA)
1928 C.Pahud de Mortanges (HOL)	1968 J.-J.Guyon (FRA)
1932 C.Pahud de Mortanges (HOL)	1972 R.Meade (GB)
1936 L.Stubbendorff (GER)	1976 E.Coffin (USA)
1948 B.Chevallier (FRA)	1980 F.Roman (ITA)
1952 H.von Blixen-Finecke (SWE)	1984 M.Todd (NZ)
	1988 M.Todd (NZ)

Most Wins:
2 Charles Pahud de Mortanges, Mark Todd

Team

1912 Sweden	1956 Great Britain
1920 Sweden	1960 Australia
1924 Holland	1964 Italy
1928 Holland	1968 Great Britain
1932 United States	1972 Great Britain
1936 Germany	1976 United States
1948 United States	1980 USSR
1952 Sweden	1984 United States
	1988 West Germany

Most Wins:
4 United States

DRESSAGE
Individual

1912 C.Bonde (SWE)	1956 H.St.Cyr (SWE)
1920 J.Lundblad (SWE)	1960 S.Filatov (USSR)
1924 E.Linder (SWE)	1964 H.Chammartin (SWI)
1928 C.von Langen (GER)	1968 I.Kizimov (USSR)
1932 X.Legsae (FRA)	1972 L.Linsenhoff (FRG)
1936 H.Pollay (GER)	1976 C.Stuckelberger (SWI)
1948 H.Moser (SWI)	1980 E.Theurer (AUT)
1952 H.St.Cyr (SWE)	1984 R.Klimke (FRG)
	1988 N.Uphoff (FRG)

Most Wins:
2 Henri St.Cyr

Team

1928 Germany	1964 West Germany
1932 France	1968 West Germany
1936 Germany	1972 USSR
1948 France	1976 West Germany
1952 Sweden	1980 USSR
1956 Sweden	1984 West Germany
1960 Not held	1988 West Germany

Most Wins:
7 West Germany (incl. two as Germany)

BADMINTON HORSE TRIALS
One of the classic Three-Day events, the Badminton Horse Trials take place in the grounds of Badminton House in Gloucestershire, home of the Beaufort family. The first Badminton was in 1949.

Winners:

1949 J.Shedden (GB)	1969 R.Walker (GB)
1950 Capt.J.A.Collings (GB)	1970 R.Meade (GB)
1951 Capt.H.Schwarzenbach (SWI)	1971 Lt.M.Phillips (GB)
1952 Capt.M.A.Darley (IRE)	1972 Lt.M.Phillips (GB)
1953 Maj.L.Rook (GB)	1973 L.Prior-Palmer (GB)
1954 M.Hough (GB)	1974 Capt.M.Phillips (GB)
1955 Maj.F.W.C.Weldon (GB)*	1975 Cancelled after dressage
1956 Maj.F.W.C.Weldon (GB)	1976 L.Prior-Palmer (GB)
1957 S.Willcox (GB)	1977 L.Prior-Palmer (GB)
1958 S.Willcox (GB)	1978 J.Holderness-Roddam (GB)
1959 S.Waddington-Willcox (GB)	1979 L.Prior-Palmer (GB)
1960 W.Roycroft (AUS)	1980 M.Todd (NZ)
1961 L.Morgan (AUS)	1981 Capt.M.Phillips (GB)
1962 A.Drummond-Hay (GB)	1982 R.Meade (GB)
1963 S.Fleet (GB)‡	1983 L.Green (GB)
1964 Capt.J.R.Templer (GB)	1984 L.Green (GB)
1965 Maj.E.A.Boylan (IRE)	1985 V.Holgate (GB)
1966 Not held	1986 I.Stark (GB)
1967 C.Ross-Taylor (GB)	1987 Not held
1968 J.Bullen (GB)	1988 I.Stark (GB)
	1989 V.Leng (GB)

Most Wins:
6 Lucinda Green (née Prior-Palmer)
* Held at Windsor.
‡ Reduced to One Day Event because of the weather.

BURGHLEY HORSE TRIALS

Held each September on the estate surrounding Burghley House in Lincolnshire, the Burghley Horse Trials is the major event of the autumn trials season. Burghley House was the home of the former Olympic athlete, the Marquis of Exeter. The European Championships have three times been held at the Burghley meeting.

Winners:

1961 A.Drummond-Hay (GB)	1974 World Championship
1962 J.Templar (GB)–	1975 A.Pattinson (GB)
European Championship	1976 J.Holderness-Roddam (GB)
1963 Capt.H.Freeman-Jackson (IRE)	1977 L.Prior-Palmer (GB)
1964 R.Meade (GB)	1978 L.Clarke-Sutherland (GB)
1965 Capt.J.J.Beale (GB)	1979 A.Hoy (AUS)
1966 World Championship	1980 R.Walker (GB)
1967 L.Sutherland (GB)	1981 L.Prior-Palmer (GB)
1968 S.Willcox (GB)	1982 R.Walker (GB)
1969 G.Watson (GB)	1983 V.Holgate (GB)
1970 J.Bradwell (GB)	1984 V.Holgate (GB)
1971 HRH Princess Anne–	1985 V.Holgate (GB)–
European Championship	European Championship
1972 J.Hodgson (GB)	1986 V.Leng (GB)
1973 Capt.M.Phillips (GB)	1987 M.Todd (NZ)
	1988 J.Thelwall (GB)

Most Wins:
3 Virginia Leng (née Holgate) (plus one European Championship win)

BRITISH SHOW JUMPING DERBY

Held annually at the All-England Jumping Centre, Hickstead in Sussex; the first Derby was in 1961.

Winners:

1961 S.Hayes (IRE)	1974 H.Smith (GB)
1962 P.Smythe (GB)	1975 P.Darragh (IRE)
1963 N.Pessoa (BRA)	1976 E.Macken (IRE)
1964 S.Hayes (IRE)	1977 E.Macken (IRE)
1965 N.Pessoa (BRA)	1978 E.Macken (IRE)
1966 D.Broome (GB)	1979 E.Macken (IRE)
1967 M.Coakes (GB)	1980 M.Whitaker (GB)
1968 A.Westwood (GB)	1981 H.Smith (GB)
1969 A.Drummond-Hay (GB)	1982 P.Schockemohle (FRG)
1970 H.Smith (GB)	1983 J.Whitaker (GB)
1971 H.Smith (GB)	1984 J.Ledingham (IRE)
1972 H.Snoek (FRG)	1985 P.Schockemohle (FRG)
1973 M.Dawes (GB)	1986 P.Schockemohle (FRG)
	1987 N.Skelton (GB)
	1988 N.Skelton (GB)

Most Wins:
4 Harvey Smith, Eddie Macken

KING GEORGE V CUP

The leading event for male showjumpers at the Royal International Horse Show each year. First held in 1911.

Post war winners:

1947 P. J. d'Oriola (FRA)			
1948 H. Llewellyn (GB)		1968 H.-G. Winkler (FRG)	
1949 B. Butler (GB)		1969 T. Edgar (GB)	
1950 H. Llewellyn (GB)		1970 H. Smith (GB)	
1951 K. Barry (IRE)		1971 G. Wiltfang (FRG)	
1952 D. C. Figuero (SPA)		1972 D. Broome (GB)	
1953 H. Llewellyn (GB)		1973 P. McMahon (GB)	
1954 F. Thiedemann (FRG)		1974 F. Chapot (USA)	
1955 L. Cartesegua (ITA)		1975 A.. Schockemohle (FRG)	
1956 W. Steinkraus (USA)		1976 M. Saywell (GB)	
1957 P. d'Inzeo (ITA)		1977 D. Broome (GB)	
1958 H. Wiley (USA)		1978 J. McVean (AUS)	
1959 H. Wiley (USA)		1979 R. Smith (GB)	
1960 D. Broome (GB)		1980 D. Bowen (GB)	
1961 P. d'Inzeo (ITA)		1981 D. Broome (GB)	
1962 P. d'Inzeo (ITA)		1982 M. Whitaker (GB)	
1963 T. Wade (IRE)		1983 P. Schockemohle (FRG)	
1964 W. Steinkraus (USA)		1984 N. Skelton (GB)	
1965 H.-G. Winkler (FRG)		1985 M. Pyrah (GB)	
1966 D. Broome (GB)		1986 J. Whitaker (GB)	
1967 P. Robeson (GB)		1987 M.Pyrah (GB)	
		1988 R.Smith (GB)	

Most wins: 5 David Broome

QUEEN ELIZABETH II CUP

The principal event for female riders at the Royal International Horse Show. The event was inaugurated in 1949.

1949 I. Kellett (IRE)			
1950 G. Palethorpe (GB)		1969 A. Westwood (GB)	
1951 I. Kellett (IRE)		1970 A. Drummond-Hay (GB)	
1952 G. Rich (GB)		1971 M. Mould (GB)	
1953 M. Delfosse (GB)		1972 A. Moore (GB)	
1954 J. Bonnaud (FRA)		1973 A. Moore (GB) & A. Dawes (GB)	
1955 D. Palethorpe (GB)		1974 J. Davenport (GB)	
1956 D. Palethorpe (GB)		1975 J. Davenport (GB)	
1957 E. Anderson (GB)		1976 M. Mould (GB)	
1958 P. Smythe (GB)		1977 L. Edgar (GB)	
1959 A. Clement (FRG)		1978 C. Bradley (GB)	
1960 S. Cohen (GB)		1979 L. Edgar (GB)	
1961 S. F. Howard (GB)		1980 C. Bradley (GB)	
1962 J. Crago (GB)		1981 L. Edgar (GB)	
1963 J. Nash (GB)		1982 L. Edgar (GB)	
1964 G. Makin (GB)		1983 J. Germany (GB)	
1965 M. Coakes (GB)		1984 V. Whitaker (GB)	
1966 A. Roger Smith (GB)		1985 S. Pountain (GB)	
1967 B. Jennaway (GB)		1986 L. Edgar (GB)	
1968 M. Chapot (USA)		1987 S.Greenwood (GB)	
Most wins: 5 Liz Edgar		1988 J.Hunter (GB)	

The sword has been used as a weapon since ancient times and even as a sport it dates back 3000 years. The three present day swords, the Épée, Foil and Sabre are more recent innovations and the Foil, the oldest of the three, was introduced in the 17th century.

OLYMPIC GAMES

Men's fencing has been part of every Olympic programme since 1896. Women did not compete until 1924 and, unlike the men, they contest only one discipline, the Foil.

Foil Individual

Men	Women
1896 E.Gravelotte (FRA)	–
1900 E.Coste (FRA)	–
1904 R.Fonst (CUB)	–
1912 N.Nadi (ITA)	–
1920 N.Nadi (ITA)	–
1924 R.Ducret (FRA)	E.Osiier (DEN)
1928 L.Gaudin (FRA)	H.Mayer (GER)
1932 G.Marzi (ITA)	E.Preis (AUT)
1936 G.Gaudini (ITA)	I.Elek (HUN)
1948 J.Buhan (FRA)	I.Elek (HUN)
1952 C.d'Oriola (FRA)	I.Camber (ITA)
1956 C.d'Oriola (FRA)	G.Sheen (GB)
1960 V.Zhdanovich (USSR)	H.Schmid (GER)
1964 E.Franke (POL)	I.UjlakiRejto (HUN)
1968 I.Drimba (ROM)	E.Novikova (USSR)
1972 W.Woyda (POL)	A.RagnoLonzi (ITA)
1976 F.Dal Zotto (ITA)	I.Schwarczenberger (HUN)
1980 V.Smirnov (USSR)	P.Trinquet (FRA)
1984 M.Numa (ITA)	J.Luan (CHN)
1988 S.Cerioni (ITA)	A.Fichtel (FRG)

Foil Team

Men	Women
1904 Cuba	–
1920 Italy	–
1924 France	–
1928 Italy	–
1932 France	–
1936 Italy	–
1948 France	–
1952 France	–
1956 Italy	–
1960 USSR	USSR
1964 USSR	Hungary
1968 France	USSR
1972 Poland	USSR
1976 East Germany	USSR
1980 France	France
1984 Italy	West Germany
1988 USSR	West Germany

Épée Individual

1900 R.Fonst (CUB)	1952 E.Mangiarotti (ITA)
1904 R.Fonst (CUB)	1956 C.Pavesi (ITA)
1908 G.Alibert (FRA)	1960 G.Delfino (ITA)
1912 P.Anspach (BEL)	1964 G.Kriss (USSR)
1920 A.Massard (FRA)	1968 G.Kulscar (HUN)
1924 C.Delporte (BEL)	1972 C.Fenyvesi (HUN)
1928 L.Gaudin (FRA)	1976 A.Pusch (FRG)
1932 G.Cornaggia-Medici (ITA)	1980 J.Harmenberg (SWE)
1936 F.Riccardi (ITA)	1984 P.Boisse (FRA)
1948 L.Cantone (ITA)	1988 A.Schmitt (FRG)

Épée Team

1908 France	1956 Italy
1912 Belgium	1960 Italy
1920 Italy	1964 Hungary
1924 France	1968 Hungary
1928 Italy	1972 Hungary
1932 France	1976 Sweden
1936 Italy	1980 France
1948 France	1984 West Germany
1952 Italy	1988 France

Sabre Individual

1896 J.Georgiadis (GRE)	1948 A.Gerevich (HUN)
1900 G.de la Falaise (FRA)	1952 P.Kovacs (HUN)
1904 M.Diaz (CUB)	1956 R.Karpati (HUN)
1908 J.Fuchs (HUN)	1960 R.Karpati (HUN)
1912 J.Fuchs (HUN)	1964 T.Pezsa (HUN)
1920 N.Badi (ITA)	1968 J.Pawlowski (POL)
1924 S.Posta (HUN)	1972 V.Sidiak (USSR)
1928 O.Tersztyanszky (HUN)	1976 V.Krovopouskov (USSR)
1932 G.Piller (HUN)	1980 V.Krovopouskov (USSR)
1936 E.Kabos (HUN)	1984 J -F. Lamour (FRA)
	1988 J -F.Lamour (FRA)

Sabre Team

1908 Hungary	1956 Hungary
1912 Hungary	1960 Hungary
1920 Italy	1964 USSR
1924 Italy	1968 USSR
1928 Hungary	1972 Italy
1932 Hungary	1976 USSR
1936 Hungary	1980 USSR
1948 Hungary	1984 Italy
1952 Hungary	1988 Hungary

Most Individual Gold Medals:
3 Ramon Fonst, Nedo Nadi

Football was first mentioned in Ireland in 1527 but it, together with other ball games, was banned because it interfered with archery practice. The first reference to a game resembling Gaelic Football was in 1712 when reference was made to a match between native villages Swords and Lusk. The Gaelic Athletic Association was formed in 1884 and a standardised set of rules was drawn up.

ALL IRELAND CHAMPIONSHIP
Played at Dublin's Croke Park on the fourth Sunday in September, the first All Ireland Championship was in 1887. The winning team receives the Sam Maguire Trophy

Winners:

1887 Limerick	1920 Tipperary	1953 Kerry
1888 Unfinished	1921 Dublin	1954 Meath
1889 Tipperary	1922 Dublin	1955 Kerry
1890 Cork	1923 Dublin	1956 Galway
1891 Dublin	1924 Kerry	1957 Louth
1892 Dublin	1925 Galway	1958 Dublin
1893 Wexford	1926 Kerry	1959 Kerry
1894 Dublin	1927 Kildare	1960 Down
1895 Tipperary	1928 Kildare	1961 Down
1896 Limerick	1929 Kerry	1962 Kerry
1897 Dublin	1930 Kerry	1963 Dublin
1898 Dublin	1931 Kerry	1964 Galway
1899 Dublin	1932 Kerry	1965 Galway
1900 Tipperary	1933 Cavan	1966 Galway
1901 Dublin	1934 Galway	1967 Meath
1902 Dublin	1935 Cavan	1968 Down
1903 Kerry	1936 Mayo	1969 Kerry
1904 Kerry	1937 Kerry	1970 Kerry
1905 Kildare	1938 Galway	1971 Offaly
1906 Dublin	1939 Kerry	1972 Offaly
1907 Dublin	1940 Kerry	1973 Cork
1908 Dublin	1941 Kerry	1974 Dublin
1909 Kerry	1942 Dublin	1975 Kerry
1910 Louth	1943 Roscommon	1976 Dublin
1911 Cork	1944 Roscommon	1977 Dublin
1912 Louth	1945 Cork	1978 Kerry
1913 Kerry	1946 Kerry	1979 Kerry
1914 Kerry	1947 Cavan	1980 Kerry
1915 Wexford	1948 Cavan	1981 Kerry
1916 Wexford	1949 Meath	1982 Offaly
1917 Wexford	1950 Mayo	1983 Dublin
1918 Wexford	1951 Mayo	1984 Kerry
1919 Kildare	1952 Cavan	1985 Kerry
		1986 Kerry
		1987 Meath
		1988 Meath

Most Wins:
30 Kerry

All Ireland finals:
Record score: 27-15 Dublin v Armagh, 1977

The exact roots of golf are uncertain. The Chinese played a form of golf 1800 years ago, and the French, Dutch and Belgians played something resembling the sport in the Middle Ages. Scotland also claims to have been the inventor of the game and their claims are strong because of reference to the sport in the times of James III and IV and by Mary Queen of Scots who played the game. Scotland is regarded as the home of golf and the world's first golf club, the Honourable Company of Edinburgh golfers, was founded in 1744. The ruling body of the sport, in the eyes of most countries, is the Royal & Ancient situated at St.Andrews.

BRITISH OPEN

Regarded as the world's leading tournament the event has been played almost continuously since 1860. One tradition of the Open is that the championship takes place on a seaside links course.

Winners:

1860 W.Park, Snr (GB)	1898 H.Vardon (GB)
1861 T.Morris, Snr (GB)	1899 H.Vardon (GB)
1862 T.Morris, Snr (GB)	1900 J.H.Taylor (GB)
1863 W.Park, Snr (GB)	1901 J.H.Braid (GB)
1864 T.Morris, Snr (GB)	1902 A.Herd (GB)
1865 A.Strath (GB)	1903 H.Vardon (GB)
1866 W.Park, Snr (GB)	1904 J.White (GB)
1867 T.Morris, Snr (GB)	1905 J.Braid (GB)
1868 T.Morris, Jnr (GB)	1906 J.Braid (GB)
1869 T.Morris, Jnr (GB)	1907 A.Massy (FRA)
1870 T.Morris, Jnr (GB)	1908 J.Braid (GB)
1871 Not held	1909 J.H.Taylor (GB)
1872 T.Morris, Jnr (GB)	1910 J.Braid (GB)
1873 T.Kidd (GB)	1911 H.Vardon (GB)
1874 M.Park (GB)	1912 E.Ray (GB)
1875 W.Park, Snr (GB)	1913 J.H.Taylor (GB)
1876 R.Martin (GB)	1914 H.Vardon (GB)
1877 J.Anderson (GB)	1915–19 Not held
1878 J.Anderson (GB)	1920 G.Duncan (GB)
1879 J.Anderson (GB)	1921 J.Hutchinson (USA)
1880 R.Ferguson (GB)	1922 W.Hagen (USA)
1881 R.Ferguson (GB)	1923 A.Havers (GB)
1882 R.Ferguson (GB)	1924 W.Hagen (USA)
1883 W.Fernie (GB)	1925 J.Barnes (USA)
1884 J.Simpson (GB)	1926 R.T.Jones (USA)
1885 R.Martin (GB)	1927 R.T.Jones (USA)
1886 D.Brown (GB)	1928 W.Hagen (USA)
1887 W.Park, Jnr (GB)	1929 W.Hagen (USA)
1888 J.Burns (GB)	1930 R.T.Jones (USA)
1889 W.Park, Jnr (GB)	1931 T.Armour (USA)
1890 J.Ball (GB)	1932 G.Sarazen (USA)
1891 H.Kirkaldy (GB)	1933 D.Shute (USA)
1892 H.H.Hilton (GB)	1934 T.H.Cotton (GB)
1893 W.Auchterlonie (GB)	1935 A.Perry (GB)
1894 J.H.Taylor (GB)	1936 A.Padgham (GB)
1895 J.H.Taylor (GB)	1937 T.H.Cotton (GB)
1896 H.Vardon (GB)	1938 R.Whitcombe (GB)
1897 H.H.Hilton (GB)	1939 R.Burton (GB)

1940–45 Not held	1966 J.W.Nicklaus (USA)
1946 S.Snead (USA)	1967 R.de Vicenzo (ARG)
1947 F.Daly (GB)	1968 G.Player (SAF)
1948 T.H.Cotton (GB)	1969 A.Jacklin (GB)
1949 A.D.Locke (SAF)	1970 J.W.Nicklaus (USA)
1950 A.D.Locke (SAF)	1971 L.Trevino (USA)
1951 M.Faulkner (GB)	1972 L.Trevino (USA)
1952 A.D.Locke (SAF)	1973 T.Weiskopf (USA)
1953 B.Hogan (USA)	1974 G.Player (SAF)
1954 P.Thomson (AUS)	1975 T.Watson (USA)
1955 P.Thomson (AUS)	1976 J.Miller (USA)
1956 P.Thomson (AUS)	1977 T.Watson (USA)
1957 A.D.Locke (SAF)	1978 J.W.Nicklaus (USA)
1958 P.Thomson (AUS)	1979 S.Ballesteros (SPA)
1959 G.Player (SAF)	1980 T.Watson (USA)
1960 K.Nagle (AUS)	1981 B.Rogers (USA)
1961 A.D.Palmer (USA)	1982 T.Watson (USA)
1962 A.D.Palmer (USA)	1983 T.Watson (USA)
1963 R.Charles (NZ)	1984 S.Ballesteros (SPA)
1964 A.Lema (USA)	1985 A.W.Lyle (GB)
1965 P.Thomson (AUS)	1986 G.Norman (AUS)
	1987 N.Faldo (GB)

Most Wins:
6 Harry Vardon

1988 S.Ballesteros (SPA)

WORLD MATCHPLAY CHAMPIONSHIP

The number of entrants is restricted to 12 in this end-of-season matchplay event played at Wentworth.

Year	Winner	Runner-up	Score
1964	A.D.Palmer (USA)	N.C.Coles (GB)	2 & 1
1965	G.Player (SAF)	P.Thomson (AUS)	3 & 2
1966	G.Player (SAF)	J.W.Nicklaus (USA)	6 & 4
1967	A.D.Palmer (USA)	P.Thomson (AUS)	1 hole
1968	G.Player (SAF)	R.Charles (NZ)	1 hole
1969	R.Charles (NZ)	G.Littler (USA)	at 37th
1970	J.W.Nicklaus (USA)	L.Trevino (USA)	2 & 1
1971	G.Player (SAF)	J.W.Nicklaus (USA)	5 & 4
1972	T.Weiskopf (USA)	L.Trevino (USA)	4 & 3
1973	G.Player (SAF)	G.Marsh (AUS)	at 40th
1974	H.Irwin (USA)	G.Player (SAF)	3 & 1
1975	H.Irwin (USA)	A.Geiberger (USA)	4 & 2
1976	D.Graham (AUS)	H.Irwin (USA)	at 38th
1977	G.Marsh (AUS)	R.Floyd (USA)	5 & 3
1978	I.Aoki (JAP)	S.Owen (NZ)	3 & 2
1979	B.Rogers (USA)	I.Aoki (JAP)	1 hole
1980	G.Norman (AUS)	A.W.Lyle (GB)	1 hole
1981	S.Ballesteros (SPA)	B.Crenshaw (USA)	1 hole
1982	S.Ballesteros (SPA)	A.W.Lyle (GB)	at 37th
1983	G.Norman (AUS)	N.Faldo (GB)	3 & 2
1984	S.Ballesteros (SPA)	B.Langer (FRG)	2 & 1
1985	S.Ballesteros (SPA)	B.Langer (FRG)	6 & 5
1986	G.Norman (AUS)	A.W.Lyle (GB)	2 & 1
1987	I.Woosnam (GB)	A.W.Lyle (GB)	1 hole
1988	A.W.Lyle (GB)	N.Faldo (GB)	2 & 1

Most Wins:
5 Gary Player

WORLD CUP

The World Cup was the idea of American industrialist Jay Hopkins who saw the need for another competition to rival the Ryder Cup, but allowing entry to professionals from any country. Teams consist of just two players.

Year	Winning Team	Leading Indvidual
1953	Argentina	A.Cerda (ARG)
1954	Australia	S.Leonard (CAN)
1955	United States	E.Furgol (USA)
1956	United States	B.Hogan (USA)
1957	Japan	T.Nakamura (JAP)
1958	Ireland	A.Miguel (SPA)
1959	Australia	S.Leonard (CAN)
1960	United States	F.van Donck (BEL)
1961	United States	S.Snead (USA)
1962	United States	R. de Vicenzo (ARG)
1963	United States	J.W.Nicklaus (USA)
1964	United States	J.W.Nicklaus (USA)
1965	South Africa	G.Player (SAF)
1966	United States	G.Knudson (CAN)
1967	United States	A.D.Palmer (USA)
1968	Canada	A.Balding (CAN)
1969	United States	L.Trevino (USA)
1970	Australia	R. de Vicenzo (ARG)
1971	United States	J.W.Nicklaus (USA)
1972	Taiwan	Min Nan Hsieh (TAI)
1973	United States	J.Miller (USA)
1974	South Africa	B.Cole (SAF)
1975	United States	J.Miller (USA)
1976	Spain	E.Acosta (MEX)
1977	Spain	G.Player (SAF)
1978	United States	J.Mahaffey (USA)
1979	United States	H.Irwin (USA)
1980	Canada	A.W.Lyle (SCO)
1981	Not held	
1982	Spain	M.Pinero (SPA)
1983	United States	D.Barr (CAN)
1984	Spain	J.-M.Canizares (SPA)
1985	Canada	H.Clark (ENG)
1986	Not Held	
1987	Wales	I.Woosnam (WAL)
1988	United States	B.Crenshaw (USA)

Most Wins:
(Team) 16 United States
(Ind) 3 Jack Nicklaus

US MASTERS

The brainchild of the legendary amateur Bobby Jones, the first Masters was held in 1934. To play in the Masters is by invitation only, and the cream of the world's players compete for the coveted green jacket which forms part of the winner's prize. All winners from United States unless otherwise stated.

1934	H.Smith	1940	J.Demaret
1935	G.Sarazen	1941	C.Wood
1936	H.Smith	1942	B.Nelson
1937	B.Nelson	1943–45	Not held
1938	H.Picard	1946	H.Keiser
1939	R.Guldahl	1947	J.Demaret

1948	C.Harmon	1969	G.Archer
1949	S.Snead	1970	W.Casper
1950	J.Demaret	1971	C.Coody
1951	B.Hogan	1972	J.W.Nicklaus
1952	S.Snead	1973	T.Aaron
1953	B.Hogan	1974	G.Player (SAF)
1954	S.Snead	1975	J.W.Nicklaus
1955	C.Middlecoff	1976	R.Floyd
1956	J.Burke	1977	T.Watson
1957	D.Ford	1978	G.Player (SAF)
1958	A.D.Palmer	1979	F.Zoeller
1959	A.Wall, Jnr	1980	S.Ballesteros (SPA)
1960	A.D.Palmer	1981	T.Watson
1961	G.Player (SAF)	1982	C.Stadler
1962	A.D.Palmer	1983	S.Ballesteros (SPA)
1963	J.W.Nicklaus	1984	B.Crenshaw
1964	A.D.Palmer	1985	B.Langer (FRG)
1965	J.W.Nicklaus	1986	J.W.Nicklaus
1966	J.W.Nicklaus	1987	L.Mize
1967	G.Brewer	1988	A.W.Lyle (GB)
1968	B.Goalby	1989	N.Faldo (GB)

Most Wins:
6 Jack Nicklaus

RYDER CUP

Following the success of two matches played between the United States and British professionals in 1921 and 1926, wealthy Englishman Samuel Ryder put up a trophy to be contested every two years by the two nations. Since 1979 European golfers have been allowed to compete and the Great Britain team became known as Europe.

Year	Venue	Winners	Score
1927	Worcester, Massachusetts	United States	9½–2½
1929	Moortown, Yorkshire	Great Britain	7–5
1931	Scioto, Ohio	United States	9–3
1933	Southport & Ainsdale, Lancs	Great Britain	6½–5½
1935	Ridgewood, New Jersey	United States	9–3
1937	Southport & Ainsdale, Lancs	United States	8–4
1947	Portland, Oregon	United States	11–1
1949	Ganton, Yorkshire	United States	7–5
1951	Pinehurst, North Carolina	United States	9½–2½
1953	Wentworth, Surrey	United States	6½–5½
1955	Thunderbird G&CC, California	United States	8–4
1957	Lindrick, Yorkshire	Great Britain	7½–4½
1959	Eldorado CC, California	United States	8½–3½
1961	Royal Lytham, Lancs	United States	14½–9½
1963	Atlanta, Georgia	United States	23–9
1965	Royal Birkdale, Lancs	United States	19½–12½
1967	Houston, Texas	United States	23½–8½
1969	Royal Birkdale, Lancs		Draw 16–16
1971	St.Louis, Missouri	United States	18½–13½
1973	Muirfield, Scotland	United States	19–13
1975	Laurel Valley, Pennsylvania	United States	21–11
1977	Royal Lytham, Lancs	United States	12½–7½

1979	Greenbrier, West Virginia	United States	17–11
1981	Walton Heath, Surrey	United States	18½–9½
1983	PGA National, Florida	United States	14½–13½
1985	The Belfry, Sutton Coldfield	Europe	16½–11½
1987	Muirfield Village, Ohio	Europe	15-13

Most Wins:
21 United States

UNITED STATES OPEN

The toughest of all of the four major championships to win, the US Open was first held at Newport, Rhode Island in 1895.

All winners from United States unless otherwise stated.

1895	H.Rawlins	1936	T.Manero
1896	J.Foulis	1937	R.Guldahl
1897	J.Lloyd	1938	R.Guldahl
1898	F.Herd	1939	B.Nelson
1899	W.Smith	1940	L.Little
1900	H.Vardon (GB)	1941	C.Wood
1901	W.Anderson	1942–45	Not held
1902	L.Auchterlonie	1946	L.Mangrum
1903	W.Anderson	1947	L.Worsham
1904	W.Anderson	1948	B.Hogan
1905	W.Anderson	1949	C.Middlecoff
1906	A.Smith	1950	B.Hogan
1907	A.Ross	1951	B.Hogan
1908	F.McLeod	1952	J.Boros
1909	G.Sargent	1953	B.Hogan
1910	A.Smith	1954	E.Furgol
1911	J.McDermott	1955	J.Fleck
1912	J.McDermott	1956	C.Middlecoff
1913	F.Ouimet	1957	D.Mayer
1914	W.Hagen	1958	T.Bolt
1915	J.Travers	1959	W.Casper
1916	C.Evans, Jnr	1960	A.D.Palmer
1917–18	Not held	1961	G.Littler
1919	W.Hagen	1962	J.W.Nicklaus
1920	E.Ray (GB)	1963	J.Boros
1921	J.M.Barnes	1964	K.Venturi
1922	G.Sarazen	1965	G.Player (SAF)
1923	R.T.Jones	1966	W.Casper
1924	C.Walker	1967	J.W.Nicklaus
1925	W.MacFarlane	1968	L.Trevino
1926	R.T.Jones	1969	O.Moody
1927	T.Armour	1970	A.W.Jacklin (GB)
1928	J.Farrell	1971	L.Trevino
1929	R.T.Jones	1972	J.W.Nicklaus
1930	R.T.Jones	1973	J.Miller
1931	B.Burke	1974	H.Irwin
1932	G.Sarazen	1975	L.Graham
1933	J.Goodman	1976	J.Pate
1934	O.Dutra	1977	H.Green
1935	S.Parks, Jnr	1978	A.North

1979 H.Irwin	1983 L.Nelson
1980 J.W.Nicklaus	1984 F.Zoeller
1981 D.Graham (AUS)	1985 A.North
1982 T.Watson	1986 R.Floyd
	1987 S. Simpson
	1988 C.Strange

Most Wins:
4 Willie Anderson, Bobby Jones, Ben Hogan, Jack Nicklaus

UNITED STATES PGA CHAMPIONSHIP
First held in 1916, the championship was a matchplay event until 1928 when it became a stroke play competition over four rounds.

All winners from United States unless otherwise stated.

1916 J.M.Barnes	1952 J.Turnesa
1917–18 Not held	1953 W.Burkemo
1919 J.M.Barnes	1954 C.Harbert
1920 J.Hutchinson	1955 D.Ford
1921 W.Hagen	1956 J.Burke
1922 G.Sarazen	1957 L.Hebert
1923 G.Sarazen	1958 D.Finsterwald
1924 W.Hagen	1959 B.Rosburg
1925 W.Hagen	1960 J.Hebert
1926 W.Hagen	1961 J.Barber
1927 W.Hagen	1962 G.Player (SAF)
1928 L.Diegel	1963 J.W.Nicklaus
1929 L.Diegel	1964 B.Nichols
1930 T.Armour	1965 D.Marr
1931 T.Creavy	1966 A.Geiberger
1932 O.Dutra	1967 D.January
1933 G.Sarazen	1968 J.Boros
1934 P.Runyan	1969 R.Floyd
1935 J.Revolta	1970 D.Stockton
1936 D.Shute	1971 J.W.Nicklaus
1937 D.Shute	1972 G.Player (SAF)
1938 P.Runyan	1973 J.W.Nicklaus
1939 H.Picard	1974 L.Trevino
1940 B.Nelson	1975 J.W.Nicklaus
1941 V.Ghezzi	1976 D.Stockton
1942 S.Snead	1977 L.Wadkins
1943 Not held	1978 J.Mahaffey
1944 B.Hamilton	1979 D.Graham (AUS)
1945 B.Nelson	1980 J.W.Nicklaus
1946 B.Hogan	1981 L.Nelson
1947 J.Ferrier	1982 R.Floyd
1948 B.Hogan	1983 H.Sutton
1949 S.Snead	1984 L.Trevino
1950 C.Harper	1985 H.Green
1951 S.Snead	1986 R.Tway
	1987 L.Nelson
	1988 J.Sluman

Most Wins:
5 Walter Hagen, Jack Nicklaus

LEADING MONEY WINNERS

The following is a list of leading money winners, season by season, in Europe and the United States.

Europe

1961 B.Hunt (GB) £4,492	1974 P.Oosterhuis (GB) £32,127
1962 P.Thomson (AUS) £5,764	1975 D.Hayes (SAF) £20,507
1963 B.Hunt (GB) £7,209	1976 S.Ballesteros (SPA) £39,504
1964 N.C.Coles (GB) £7,890	1977 S.Ballesteros (SPA) £46,436
1965 P.Thomson (AUS) £7,011	1978 S.Ballesteros (SPA) £54,348
1966 B.Devlin (AUS) £13,205	1979 A.W.Lyle (GB) £49,233
1967 G.Brewer (USA) £20,235	1980 G.Norman (AUS) £74,829
1968 G.Brewer (USA) £23,107	1981 B.Langer (FRG) £95,991
1969 W.Casper (USA) £23,483	1982 A.W.Lyle (GB) £86,141
1970 C.O'Connor (IRE) £31,532	1983 N.Faldo (GB) £140,761
1971 G.Player (SAF) £11,281	1984 B.Langer (FRG) £160,883
1972 R.Charles (NZ) £18,538	1985 A.W.Lyle (GB) £199,020
1973 A.W.Jacklin (GB) £24,839	1986 S.Ballesteros (SPA) £259,275
	1987 I.Woosnam (GB) £439,075
	1988 S.Ballesteros (SPA) £451,559

Most times leading winner:
4 Severiano Ballesteros

United States

All winners from United States unless otherwise stated

1934 P.Runyan $6,767	1961 G.Player (SAF) $64,450
1935 J.Revolta $9,543	1962 A.D.Palmer $81,448
1936 H.Smith $7,682	1963 A.D.Palmer $128,230
1937 H.Cooper $14,138	1964 J.W.Nicklaus $113,284
1938 S.Snead $19,534	1965 J.W.Nicklaus $140,752
1939 H.Picard $10,303	1966 W.Casper $121,944
1940 B.Hogan $10,655	1967 J.W.Nicklaus $188,998
1941 B.Hogan $18,358	1968 W.Casper $205,168
1942 B.Hogan $13,143	1969 F.Beard $164,707
1943 Statistics not compiled	1970 L.Trevino $157,037
1944 B.Nelson $37,967	1971 J.W.Nicklaus $244,490
1945 B.Nelson $63,335	1972 J.W.Nicklaus $320,542
1946 B.Hogan $42,556	1973 J.W.Nicklaus $308,362
1947 J.Demaret $27,936	1974 J.Miller $353,021
1948 B.Hogan $32,112	1975 J.W.Nicklaus $298,149
1949 S.Snead $31,593	1976 J.W.Nicklaus $266,438
1950 S.Snead $35,758	1977 T.Watson $310,653
1951 L.Mangrum $26,088	1978 T.Watson $362,428
1952 J.Boros $37,032	1979 T.Watson $462,636
1953 L.Worsham $34,002	1980 T.Watson $530,808
1954 B.Toski $65,819	1981 T.Kite $375,698
1955 J.Boros $63,121	1982 C.Stadler $446,462
1956 E.Kroll $72,835	1983 H.Sutton $426,668
1957 D.Mayer $65,835	1984 T.Watson $476,260
1958 A.D.Palmer $42,607	1985 C.Strange $542,321
1959 A.Wall $53,167	1986 G. Norman (Aus) $653,296
1960 A.D.Palmer $75,262	1987 C.Strange $925,941
	1988 C.Strange $1,147,644

Most times leading winner:
8 Jack Nicklaus

MAJOR CHAMPIONSHIP RECORDS

	18 Holes		72 Holes	
British Open	63	M. Hayes (USA), 1977	268	T. Watson (USA), 1977
	63	I. Aoki (JPN), 1980		
	63	G. Norman (AUS), 1986		
US Open	63	J. Miller (USA), 1973	272	J.W.Nicklaus (USA), 1980
	63	T. Weiskopf (USA), 1980		
	63	J.W.Nicklaus (USA), 1980		
US Masters	63	N. Price (SAF), 1986	271	J.W.Nicklaus (USA), 1965
			271	R. Floyd (USA), 1976
US PGA	63	B. Crampton (AUS), 1975	271	B. Nichols (USA), 1964
	63	G. Player (SAF), 1984		

DUNHILL CUP

An annual knockout three-man team event played at St. Andrews. Inaugurated in 1985.

Finals:

1985	Australia beat United States	3-0
1986	Australia beat Japan	3-0
1987	England beat Scotland	2-1
1988	Ireland beat Australia	2-1

WALKER CUP

The forerunner of the Ryder Cup, the Walker Cup was instituted in 1922, the year after an unofficial match between amateur teams from Great Britain and the United States. It was the idea of George Herbert Walker, a former president of the United States Golf Association. Held every two years, the venue alternates between Britain and the United States.

Results:

Year	Venue	Winners	Score
1922	Long Island, New York	USA	8-4
1923	St. Andrews, Scotland	USA	6½-5½
1924	Garden City, New York	USA	9-3
1926	St. Andrews, Scotland	USA	6½-5½
1928	Chicago GC, Illinois	USA	11-1
1930	Royal St. George's, Sandwich	USA	10-2
1932	Brookline, Massachusetts	USA	9½-2½
1934	St. Andrews, Scotland	USA	9½-2½
1936	Pine Valley, New Jersey	USA	10½-1½
1938	St. Andrews, Scotland	GB	7½-4½
1947	St. Andrews, Scotland	USA	8-4
1949	Winged Foot, New York	USA	10-2
1951	Royal Birkdale, Southport	USA	7½-4½
1953	Kittansett, Massachusetts	USA	9-3
1955	St. Andrews, Scotland	USA	10-2
1957	Minikhada, Minnesota	USA	8½-3½
1959	Muirfield, Scotland	USA	9-3
1961	Seattle, Washington	USA	11-1
1963	Turnberry, Scotland	USA	14-10
1965	Baltimore, Maryland	Drawn	12-12
1967	Royal St. George's, Sandwich	USA	15-9
1969	Milwaukee, Wisconsin	USA	13-11
1971	St. Andrews, Scotland	GB	13-11

1973	Brookline, Massachusetts	USA	14-10
1975	St. Andrews, Scotland	USA	15½-8½
1977	Shinnecock Hills, New York	USA	16-8
1979	Muirfield, Scotland	USA	15½-8½
1981	Cypress Point, California	USA	15-9
1983	Royal Liverpool, Hoylake	USA	13½-10½
1985	Pine Valley, Philadelphia	USA	13-11
1987	Sunningdale, Berkshire	USA	16½-7½

Wins: 28 United States; 2 Great Britain, 1 Drawn

US WOMEN'S OPEN

An annual event first held in 1946. It was a match-play competition in the first year, but has been a stroke-play event ever since.

All winners from United States unless otherwise stated.

1946 P.Berg	1968 S.Berning
1947 B.Jameson	1969 D.Caponi
1948 M. Zaharias	1970 D.Caponi
1949 L.Suggs	1971 J.Carner
1950 M.Zaharias	1972 S.Berning
1951 B.Rawls	1973 S.Berning
1952 L.Suggs	1974 S.Haynie
1953 B.Rawls	1975 S.Palmer
1954 M.Zaharias	1976 J.Carner
1955 F.Crocker	1977 H.Stacy
1956 K.Cornelius	1978 H.Stacy
1957 B.Rawls	1979 J.Britz
1958 M.Wright	1980 A.Alcott
1959 M.Wright	1981 P.Bradley
1960 B.Rawls	1982 J.Alex
1961 M.Wright	1983 J.Stephenson
1962 M.Lindstrom	1984 H.Stacy
1963 M.Mills	1985 K.Baker
1964 M.Wright	1986 J.Geddes
1965 C.Mann	1987 L.Davies (GB)
1966 S.Spuzich	1988 L.Nuemann
1967 C.Lacoste (FRA)	

Most Wins:
4 Mickey Wright; Betsy Rawls

BRITISH WOMEN'S OPEN

An annual stroke-play competition, it was inaugurated in 1976.

1976 J.Lee Smith (GB)
1977 V.Saunders (GB)
1978 J.Melville (GB)
1979 A.Sheard (SAF)
1980 D.Massey (USA)
1981 D.Massey (USA)
1982 M.Figueras-Dotti (SPA)
1983 Not held
1984 A.Okamoto (JAP)
1985 B.King (USA)
1986 L.Davies (GB)
1987 A.Nicholas (GB)
1988 C.Dibnah (GB)

Most Wins:
2 Debbie Massey

CAREER EARNINGS

(as at 1 January 1989)

US TOUR

(all United States)

$5,005,825	Jack Nicklaus
$4,974,825	Tom Watson
$4,263,133	Curtis Strange
$4,205,413	Tom Kite
$3,707,586	Lanny Wadkins
$3,673,980	Ben Crenshaw
$3,541,888	Ray Floyd
$3,341,789	Lee Trevino
$3,076,854	Hale Irwin
$2,807,345	Bruce Lietzke

EUROPEAN TOUR

£1,693,384	Severiano Ballesteros (SPA)
£1,187,082	Nick Faldo (ENG)
£1,170,705	Sandy Lyle (SCO)
£1,099,110	Ian Woosnam (WAL)
£937,854	Bernhard Langer (FRG)
£846,584	Howard Clark (ENG)
£834,037	Sam Torrance (SCO)
£696,562	Greg Norman (AUS)
£633,519	Gordon Brand Jr (SCO)
£602,033	Des Smyth (IRE)

Golf holes have a collection of beautiful and strange names. But the most famous of all named courses is Augusta, Georgia, home of the US Masters. Each hole is named after the flower, plant or shrub that grows alongside it, and such names as Tea Olive, Pink Dogwood and White Dogwood decorate the most beautiful course in the world.

The first attempts to race greyhounds at the end of the 19th century were unsuccessful because of the lack of facilities to propel the hare. However, after attempts by the Americans in 1906 to pull a hare by motorcycle, a mechanical hare on an oval track was designed. The first regular track was opened at Emeryville, California in 1919. The first track with a mechanical hare in Britain was at Belle Vue, Manchester, and opened in 1926.

GREYHOUND DERBY

The sport's leading race, the Derby normally takes place in June each year after a series of elimination races in the months leading up to the final. The Derby used to have its home at the White City until the London stadium's closure. It is now held at Wimbledon.

Winners:

1927 Entry Badge	1959 Mile Bush Pride
1928 Boher Ash	1960 Duleek Dandy
1929 Mick the Miller	1961 Palm's Printer
1930 Mick the Miller	1962 The Grand Canal
1931 Seldom Led	1963 Lucky Boy Boy
1932 Wild Woolley	1964 Hack Up Chieftain
1933 Future Cutlet	1965 Chittering Clapton
1934 Davesland	1966 Faithful Hope
1935 Greta Ranee	1967 Tric Trac
1936 Fine Jubilee	1968 Camera Flash
1937 Wattle Bark	1969 Sand Star
1938 Lone Keel	1970 John Silver
1939 Highland Rum	1971 Dolores Rocket
1940 G.R.Archduke	1972 Patricia's Hope
1941–44 Not held	1973 Patricia's Hope
1945 Ballyhennessy Seal	1974 Jimsun
1946 Mondays News	1975 Tartan Khan
1947 Trevs Perfection	1976 Mutts Silver
1948 Priceless Border	1977 Balliniska Band
1949 Narrogar Ann	1978 Lacca Champion
1950 Ballmac Ball	1979 Sarah's Bunny
1951 Ballylanigan Tanist	1980 Indian Joe
1952 Endless Gossip	1981 Parkdown Jet
1953 Daws Dancer	1982 Laurie's Panther
1954 Pauls Fun	1983 I'm Slippy
1955 Rushton Mack	1984 Whisper Wishes
1956 Dunmore King	1985 Pagan Swallow
1957 Ford Spartan	1986 Tico
1958 Pigalle Wonder	1987 Signal Spark
	1988 Hit the Lid

Most Wins:
2 Mick the Miller, Patricia's Hope

The ancient Greeks and Romans were exponents of gymnastics and excelled at the Ancient Olympic Games over 2000 years ago. Modern techniques, however, were developed in Germany towards the latter part of the 18th century. The sport spread to Britain 100 years later and the Amateur Gymnastics Association was formed in 1888.

OLYMPIC GAMES

Although Gymnastics was held at the inaugural Modern Olympics in 1896, overall team or individual competitions were not contested. The individual competition was first held in 1900 and the team competition followed at the next celebration. The women's events were first held in 1928 but it was not until 1952 that medals were awarded for individual competition.

Men

	Team	Overall Individual
1900	–	G.Sandras (FRA)
1904	United States	J.Lenhart (AUT)
1908	Sweden	A.Braglia (ITA)
1912	Italy	A.Braglia (ITA)
1920	Italy	G.Zampori (ITA)
1924	Italy	L.Stukelj (YUG)
1928	Switzerland	G.Miez (SWI)
1932	Italy	R.Neri (ITA)
1936	Germany	A.Schwarzmann (GER)
1948	Finland	V.Huhtanen (FIN)
1952	USSR	V.Chukarin (USSR)
1956	USSR	V.Chukarin (USSR)
1960	Japan	B.Shaklin (USSR)
1964	Japan	Y.Endo (JAP)
1968	Japan	S.Kato (JAP)
1972	Japan	S.Kato (JAP)
1976	Japan	N.Andrianov (USSR)
1980	USSR	A.Ditiatin (USSR)
1984	United States	K.Gushiken (JAP)
1988	USSR	V.Artimov (USSR)

Most Wins (Team): 5 Japan
Individual 2 Alberto Braglia, Viktor Chukarin, Sawao Kato

Women

	Team	Overall Individual
1928	Holland	–
1936	Germany	–
1948	Czechoslovakia	–
1952	USSR	M.Gorokhovskaya (USSR)
1956	USSR	L.Latynina (USSR)
1960	USSR	L.Latynina (USSR)
1964	USSR	V.Caslavska (TCH)
1968	USSR	V.Caslavska (TCH)
1972	USSR	L.Tourischeva (USSR)
1976	USSR	N.Comaneci (ROM)
1980	USSR	E.Davydova (USSR)
1984	Romania	M -L.Retton (USA)
1988	USSR	E.Shoushounova (USSR)

Most Wins (Team): 9 USSR
Individual 2 Larissa Latynina, Vera Caslavska

WORLD CHAMPIONSHIPS

First held for men in 1903, they were originally held biennially but, from 1922, they were held every four years in between the Olympics. Since 1979 they have reverted to being held every two years. The first women's championships were held in 1934.

Men

	Team	Overall Individual
1903	France	J.Martinez (FRA)
1905	France	M.Lalue (FRA)
1907	Czechoslovakia	J.Cada (TCH)
1909	France	M.Torres (FRA)
1911	Czechoslovakia	F.Steiner (TCH)
1913	Czechoslovakia	M.Torres (FRA)
1922	Czechoslovakia	P.Sumi (YUG) & F.Pechacek (TCH)
1926	Czechoslovakia	P.Sumi (YUG)
1930	Czechoslovakia	J.Primozic (YUG)
1934	None	E.Mack (SWI)
1938	Czechoslovakia	J.Gajdos (TCH)
1950	Switzerland	W.Lehmann (SWI)
1954	USSR	V.Chukarin (USSR) & V.Mouratov (USSR)
1958	USSR	B.Shakhlin (USSR)
1962	Japan	Y.Titov (USSR)
1966	Japan	M.Voronin (USSR)
1970	Japan	E.Kenmotsu (JAP)
1974	Japan	S.Kasamatsu (JAP)
1978	Japan	N.Andrianov (USSR)
1979	USSR	A.Ditiatin (USSR)
1981	USSR	Y.Korolev (USSR)
1983	China	D.Belozertchev (USSR)
1985	USSR	Y.Korolev (USSR)
1987	USSR	D.Belozertchev (USSR)

Most Wins (Team): 7 Czechoslovakia

Individual 2 Marcos Torres, Peter Sumi, Yuri Korolev

Women

	Team	Overall Individual
1934	Czechoslovakia	V.Dekanova (TCH)
1938	Czechoslovakia	V.Dekanova (TCH)
1950	Sweden	H.Rakoczy (POL)
1954	USSR	G.Roudiko (USSR)
1958	USSR	L.Latynina (USSR)
1962	USSR	L.Latynina (USSR)
1966	Czechoslovakia	V.Caslavska (TCH)
1970	USSR	L.Tourischeva (USSR)
1974	USSR	L.Tourischeva (USSR)
1978	USSR	E.Mukhina (USSR)
1979	Romania	N.Kim (USSR)
1981	USSR	O.Bitcherova (USSR)
1983	USSR	N.Yurchenko (USSR)
1985	USSR	E.Shoushounova (USSR)
1987	Romania	A.Dobre (ROM)

Most Wins (Team): 9 USSR

Individual 2 Vlasta Dekanova, Larissa Latynina, Vera Caslavska Lyudmila Tourischeva

WORLD CUP
First held in 1975
Overall Champions

Men	Women
1975 N. Andrianov (USSR)	L. Tourescheva
1977 N. Andrianov (USSR) &	M. Filatova (USSR)
V. Markelov (USSR)	
1978 A. Ditiatin (USSR)	M. Filatova (USSR)
1979 A. Ditiatin (USSR)	S. Zakharova (USSR)
1982 Li Ning (CHN)	O. Bicherova (USSR) &
	N. Yurchenko (USSR)
1986 Y. Korolev (USSR) &	E.Shoushounova (USSR)
Li Ning (CHN)	

EUROPEAN CHAMPIONSHIPS
First held in 1955
Overall Champions

Men	Women
1955 B. Shakhlin (USSR)	—
1957 J. Blume (SPA)	L. Latynina (USSR)
1959 Y. Titov (USSR)	N. Kot (POL)
1961 M. Cerar (YUG)	L. Latynina (USSR)
1963 M. Cerar (YUG)	M. Bilic (YUG)
1965 F. Menichelli (ITA)	V. Caslavska (TCH)
1967 M. Voronin (USSR)	V. Caslavska (TCH)
1969 M. Voronin (USSR)	K. Janz
1971 V. Klimenko (USSR)	L. Tourischeva (USSR) &
	T. Lazakovich
1973 V. Klimenko (USSR)	L. Tourischeva (USSR)
1975 N. Andrianov (USSR)	N. Comaneci (ROM)
1977 V. Markelov (USSR)	N. Comaneci (ROM)
1979 S. Deltchev (BUL)	N. Comaneci (ROM)
1981 A.. Tkachev (USSR)	M. Gnauck (GDR)
1983 D. Belozerchev (USSR)	O. Bicherova (USSR)
1985 D. Belozerchev (USSR)	E. Shoushounova (USSR)
1987 V. Lyukin (USSR)	D. Silivas (ROM)

Like many sports, Handball can be linked to the Ancient Greeks but it was not developed in its present form until 1890 when introduced by German Konrad Koch. It was not until after the First World War that interest in the game grew and in 1928 the International Amateur Handball Federation was founded with 11 member nations.

OLYMPIC GAMES

Handball as an 11-a-side outdoor game was introduced into the 1936 Berlin Olympics but when it was next included in the Olympic programme, in 1972, it was an indoor seven-a-side game. The first women's Olympic competition was in 1976.

Men
1936 Germany
1972 Yugoslavia
1976 USSR
1980 East Germany
1984 Yugoslavia
1988 USSR

Most wins:
2 Yugoslavia, USSR

Women
1976 USSR
1980 USSR
1984 Yugoslavia
1988 South Korea

Most Wins:
2 USSR

Only two people have won three Olympic handball medals: R. Voina and A. Cosma were both members of the Romanian team that won bronze medals in 1972 and 1980, and a silver medal in 1976.

East Germany's final point in their thrilling overtime win over the Soviet Union in the 1980 Olympic final was scored by Hans-Georg Beyer. At the exact same time his brother Udo was winning the shot put bronze medal in the athletics stadium. Two days later their sister Gisela came fourth in the discus.

It is believed the Egyptians played Hockey nearly 4000 years ago and the Greeks played a form of Hockey about 500 BC. Reference was made to the sport in England in the 12th century but it was not until the 19th century that the word 'Hockey' was first used to describe the sport. The first club was the Blackheath Football and Hockey Club, founded in 1861. The Hockey Association was formed in 1886 and the international body, the F.I.H. was formed in 1924.

OLYMPIC GAMES
Hockey became an Olympic sport in London in 1908 and has been a continuous sport since 1928. Women had their first competition in 1980.

Men

1908 England	1960 Pakistan
1920 Great Britain	1964 India
1928 India	1968 Pakistan
1932 India	1972 West Germany
1936 India	1976 New Zealand
1948 India	1980 India
1952 India	1984 Pakistan
1956 India	1988 Great Britain

Most Wins:
8 India

Women

1980 Zimbabwe	1988 Australia
1984 Holland	

WORLD CUP
The first FIH World Cup for men was organised in 1971. Originally a biennial event, it is now played every four years. The first women's World Cup was in 1974.

Men

1971 Pakistan	1978 Pakistan
1973 Holland	1982 Pakistan
1975 India	1986 Australia

Most Wins:
3 Pakistan

Women

1974 Holland	1981 West Germany
1976 West Germany	1983 Holland
1978 Holland	1986 Holland

Most Wins:
4 Holland

WORLD CHAMPIONSHIP

Separate to the World Cup, the International Federation of Women's Hockey Associations organised a World Championship in 1975 and 1979.

Winners:
1975 England
1979 Holland

The captain of the Australian hockey team at the 1984 Los Angeles Olympics was Rick Charlesworth, Member of Parliament, and former first class cricketer.

Great Britain only qualified for the 1984 Los Angeles Olympics as a result of Russia's withdrawal, but they were the sensation of the Games, winning the bronze medal.

The highest score in an international hockey match was set during the 1932 Olympic Games when India beat the host nation, the United States 24-1. The highest score in a women's international is 23-0 when England beat France in 1923.
The most individual goals scored in a senior match is 21 by Ms. E. M. Blakelock during Ross Ladies' 40-0 win over Wyeside in 1929.

HOCKEY ASSOCIATION CUP

Contested annually since 1972, it is the English Club Championship.

Winners:

1972 Hounslow	1982 Southgate
1973 Hounslow	1983 Neston
1974 Southgate	1984 East Grinstead
1975 Southgate	1985 Southgate
1976 Nottingham	1986 Southgate
1977 Slough	1987 Southgate
1978 Guildford	1988 Southgate
1979 Slough	1989 Hounslow
1980 Slough	
1981 Slough	

Most Wins:
7 Southgate

ENGLISH NATIONAL INTER-LEAGUE

A championship involving the winners of all major English Leagues. It was first held in 1975.

Winners:

1975 Bedfordshire Eagles	1984 Neston
1976 Slough	1985 East Grinstead
1977 Southgate	1986 East Grinstead
1978 Southgate	1987 Slough
1979 Isca	1988 Southgate
1980 Slough	1989 St Albans
1981 Slough	
1982 Slough	
1983 Slough	

Most Wins:
6 Slough

NATIONAL WOMEN'S CLUB CHAMPIONSHIP
The women's equivalent of the Hockey Association Cup. It was first contested in 1979.

Winners:

1979 Chelmsford	1985 Ipswich
1980 Norton	1986 Slough
1981 Sutton Coldfield	1987 Ealing
1982 Slough	1988 Ealing
1983 Slough	1989 Ealing
1984 Sheffield	

Most Wins:
3 Slough
3 Ealing

COUNTY CHAMPIONSHIP
Inaugurated in the 1957-58 season, the first final was played in 1958. The women's championship was inaugurated in 1968-69.

Men	Women
1958 Lincolnshire	—
1959 Middlesex	—
1960 Hertfordshire	—
1961 Middlesex	—
1962 Durham	—
1963 Surrey	—
1964 Kent	—
1965 Kent	—
1966 Cheshire	—
1967 Wiltshire	—
1968 Wiltshire	—
1969 Lancashire	Lancashire & Hertfordshire
1970 Wiltshire	Lancashire
1971 Staffordshire	Lancashire & Hertfordshire
1972 Wiltshire	Essex
1973 Surrey	Lancashire
1974 Hertfordshire	Lancashire
1975 Kent	Leicestershire & Surrey
1976 Hertfordshire	Lancashire
1977 Middlesex	Lancashire
1978 Lancashire	Hertfordshire
1979 Kent	Lancashire
1980 Buckinghamshire	Suffolk & Leicestershire
1981 Middlesex	Staffordshire
1982 Buckinghamshire	Suffolk
1983 Lancashire	Leicestershire
1984 Yorkshire	Middlesex
1985 Worcestershire	Lancashire
1986 Surrey	Middlesex
1987 Worcestershire	Staffordshire
1988 Middlesex	Kent
1989 Middlesex	Kent

Most Wins:	**Most Wins:**
6 Middlesex	9 Lancashire

There is evidence that Horse Racing took place in Ancient Egypt more than 3000 years ago, and racing on horseback formed part of the Ancient Olympic programme. The first regular race meetings were held around Smithfield, London, in the 12th century and the oldest racecourse in Britain is Chester's Roodee which staged its first meeting on 9 February 1540.

THE DERBY
The most famous race in the world it is run at Epsom (apart from two wartime spells on Newmarket's July course, 1915–18, 1940–45) and covers a distance of 1 1/2 miles and, like all five English Classics, is for three-year-olds only. It is open to colts and fillies. The race is named after the 12th Earl of Derby.

Winners:

Year	Winner	Jockey	Year	Winner	Jockey
1780	Diomed	S.Arnull	1819	Tiresias	W.Clift
1781	Young Eclipse	C.Hindley	1820	Sailor	S.Chifney,jnr
1782	Assassin	S.Arnull	1821	Gustavus	S.Day
1783	Saltram	C.Hindley	1822	Moses	T.Goodisson
1784	Serjeant	J.Arnull	1823	Emilius	F.Buckle
1785	Aimwell	C.Hindley	1824	Cedric	J.Robinson
1786	Noble	J.White	1825	Middleton	J.Robinson
1787	Sir Peter Teazle	S.Arnull	1826	Lap-dog	G.Dockeray
1788	Sir Thomas	W.South	1827	Mameluke	J.Robinson
1789	Skyscraper	S.Chifney,snr	1828	Cadland	J.Robinson
1790	Rhadamanthus	J.Arnull	1829	Frederick	J.Forth
1791	Eager	M.Stephenson	1830	Priam	S.Day
1792	John Bull	F.Buckle	1831	Spaniel	W.Wheatley
1793	Waxy	W.Clift	1832	St.Giles	W.Scott
1794	Daedalus	F.Buckle	1833	Dangerous	J.Chapple
1795	Spread Eagle	A.Wheatley	1834	Plenipotentiary	P.Conolly
1796	Didelot	J.Arnull	1835	Mundig	W.Scott
1797	Unnamed colt	J.Singleton	1836	Bay Middleton	J.Robinson
1798	Sir Harry	S.Arnull	1837	Phosphorus	G.Edwards
1799	Archduke	J.Arnull	1838	Amato	J.Chapple
1800	Champion	W.Clift	1839	Bloomsbury	S.Templeman
1801	Eleanor	J.Saunders	1840	Little Wonder	W.MacDonald
1802	Tyrant	F.Buckle	1841	Coronation	P.Conolly
1803	Ditto	W.Clift	1842	Atilla	W.Scott
1804	Hannibal	W.Arnull	1843	Cotherstone	W.Scott
1805	Cardinal Beaufort	D.Fitzpatrick	1844	Orlando	N.Flatman
1806	Paris	J.Shepherd	1845	The Merry Monarch	F.Bell
1807	Election	J.Arnull	1846	Pyrrhus the First	S.Day
1808	Pan	F.Collinson	1847	Cossack	S.Templeman
1809	Pope	T.Goodisson	1848	Surplice	S.Templeman
1810	Whalebone	W.Clift	1849	The Flying Dutchman	C.Marlow
1811	Phantom	F.Buckle	1850	Voltigeur	J.Marson
1812	Octavius	W.Arnull	1851	Teddington	J.Marson
1813	Smolensko	T.Goodisson	1852	Daniel O'Rourke	F.Butler
1814	Blucher	W.Arnull	1853	West Australian	F.Butler
1815	Whisker	T.Goodisson	1854	Andover	A.Day
1816	Prince Leopold	W.Wheatley	1855	Wild Dayrell	R.Sherwood
1817	Azor	J.Robinson	1856	Ellington	T.Aldcroft
1818	Sam	S.Chifney,jnr	1857	Blink Bonny	J.Charlton

The Derby Winners Cont.

Year	Winner	Jockey	Year	Winner	Jockey
1858	Beadsman	J.Wells	1914	Durbar II	M.MacGee
1859	Musjid	J.Wells	1915	Pommern	S.Donoghue
1860	Thormanby	H.Custance	1916	Fifinella	J.Childs
1861	Kettledrum	R.Bullock	1917	Gay Crusader	S.Donoghue
1862	Caractacus	J.Parsons	1918	Gainsborough	J.Childs
1863	Macaroni	T.Challoner	1919	Grand Parade	F.Templeman
1864	Blair Athol	J.Snowden	1920	Spion Kop	F.O'Neill
1865	Gladiateur	H.Grimshaw	1921	Humorist	S.Donoghue
1866	Lord Lyon	H.Custance	1922	Captain Cuttle	S.Donoghue
1867	Hermit	J.Daley	1923	Papyrus	S.Donoghue
1868	Blue Gown	J.Wells	1924	Sansovino	T.Weston
1869	Pretender	J.Osborne	1925	Manna	S.Donoghue
1870	Kingcraft	T.French	1926	Coronach	J.Childs
1871	Favonius	T.French	1927	Call Boy	E.C.Elliott
1872	Cremorne	C.Maidment	1928	Felstead	H.Wragg
1873	Doncaster	F.Webb	1929	Trigo	J.Marshall
1874	George Frederick	H.Custance	1930	Blenheim	H.Wragg
1875	Galopin	J.Morris	1931	Cameronian	F.Fox
1876	Kisber	C.Maidment	1932	April the Fifth	F.Lane
1877	Silvio	F.Archer	1933	Hyperion	T.Weston
1878	Sefton	H.Constable	1934	Windsor Lad	C.Smirke
1879	Sir Bevys	G.Fordham	1935	Bahram	F.Fox
1880	Bend Or	F.Archer	1936	Mahmoud	C.Smirke
1881	Iroquois	F.Archer	1937	Mid-day Sun	M.Beary
1882	Shotover	T.Cannon	1938	Bois Roussel	E.C.Elliott
1883	St.Blaise	C.Wood	1939	Blue Peter	E.Smith
1884	St.Gatien &	C.Wood	1940	Pont l'Eveque	S.Wragg
	Harvester (deadheated)	S.Loates	1941	Owen Tudor	W.Nevett
1885	Melton	F.Archer	1942	Watling Street	H.Wragg
1886	Ormonde	F.Archer	1943	Straight Deal	T.Carey
1887	Merry Hampton	J.Watts	1944	Ocean Swell	W.Nevett
1888	Ayrshire	F.Barrett	1945	Dante	W.Nevett
1889	Donovan	T.Loates	1946	Airborne	T.Lowrey
1890	Sainfoin	J.Watts	1947	Pearl Diver	G.Bridgland
1891	Common	G.Barrett	1948	My Love	W.Johnstone
1892	Sir Hugo	F.Allsopp	1949	Nimbus	C.Elliott
1893	Isinglass	T.Loates	1950	Galcador	W.Johnstone
1894	Ladas	J.Watts	1951	Arctic Prince	C.Spares
1895	Sir Visto	S.Loates	1952	Tulyar	C.Smirke
1896	Persimmon	J.Watts	1953	Pinza	G.Richards
1897	Galtee More	C.Wood	1954	Never Say Die	L.Piggott
1898	Jeddah	O.Madden	1955	Phil Drake	F.Palmer
1899	Flying Fox	M.Cannon	1956	Lavandin	W.Johnstone
1900	Diamond Jubilee	H.Jones	1957	Crepello	L.Piggott
1901	Volodyovski	L.Reiff	1958	Hard Ridden	C.Smirke
1902	Ard Patrick	J.H.Martin	1959	Parthia	H.Carr
1903	Rock Sand	D.Maher	1960	St.Paddy	L.Piggott
1904	St.Amant	K.Cannon	1961	Psidium	R.Poincelet
1905	Cicero	D.Maher	1962	Larkspur	N.Sellwood
1906	Spearmint	D.Maher	1963	Relko	Y.SaintMartin
1907	Orby	J.Reiff	1964	Santa Claus	A.Breasley
1908	Signorinetta	W.Bullock	1965	Sea Bird II	T.P.Glennon
1909	Minoru	H.Jones	1966	Charlottown	A.Breasley
1910	Lemberg	B.Dillon	1967	Royal Palace	G.Moore
1911	Sunstar	G.Stern	1968	Sir Ivor	L.Piggott
1912	Tagalie	J.Reiff	1969	Blakeney	E.Johnson
1913	Aboyeur	E.Piper	1970	Nijinsky	L.Piggott

Year	Winner	Jockey	Year	Winner	Jockey
1971	Mill Reef	G.Lewis	1981	Shergar	W.Swinburn
1972	Roberto	L.Piggott	1982	Golden Fleece	P.Eddery
1973	Morston	E.Hide	1983	Teenoso	L.Piggott
1974	Snow Knight	B.Taylor	1984	Secreto	C.Roche
1975	Grundy	P.Eddery	1985	Slip Anchor	S.Cauthen
1976	Empery	L.Piggott	1986	Shahrastani	W.Swinburn
1977	The Minstrel	L.Piggott	1987	Reference Point	S.Cauthen
1978	Shirley Heights	G.Starkey	1988	Kahyasi	R.Cochrane
1979	Troy	W.Carson	1989	Nashwan	W. Carson
1980	Henbit	W.Carson			

Most Wins (Jockey):
9 Lester Piggott

THE OAKS
A 1½ mile race over the Epsom course (moved to Newmarket during the wars), this English Classic is only open to three-year-old fillies. The race is named after the Epsom home of the 12th Earl of Derby.

Winners:

Year	Winner	Jockey	Year	Winner	Jockey
1779	Bridget	R.Goodisson	1812	Manuella	W.Peirse
1780	Tetotum	R.Goodisson	1813	Music	T.Goodisson
1781	Faith	R.Goodisson	1814	Medora	S.Barnard
1782	Ceres	S.Chifney,snr	1815	Minuet	T.Goodisson
1783	Maid of the Oaks	S.Chifney,snr	1816	Landscape	S.Chifney,jnr
1784	Stella	C.Hindley	1817	Neva	F.Buckle
1785	Trifle	J.Bird	1818	Corinne	F.Buckle
1786	Yellow Filly	J.Edwards	1819	Shoveler	S.Chifney,jnr
1787	Annette	D.Fitzpatrick	1820	Caroline	H.Edwards
1788	Nightshade	D.Fitzpatrick	1821	Augusta	J.Robinson
1789	Tag	S.Chifney,snr	1822	Pastille	H.Edwards
1790	Hippolyta	S.Chifney,snr	1823	Zinc	F.Buckle
1791	Portia	J.Singleton	1824	Cobweb	J.Robinson
1792	Volante	C.Hindley	1825	Wings	S.Chifney,jnr
1793	Caelia	J.Singleton	1826	Lilias	T.Lye
1794	Hermione	S.Arnull	1827	Gulnare	F.Boyce
1795	Platina	D.Fitzpatrick	1828	Turquoise	J.B.Day
1796	Parisot	J.Arnull	1829	Green Mantle	G.Dockeray
1797	Nike	F.Buckle	1830	Variation	G.Edwards
1798	Bellissima	F.Buckle	1831	Oxygen	J.B.Day
1799	Bellina	F.Buckle	1832	Galata	P.Conolly
1800	Ephemera	D.Fitzpatrick	1833	Vespa	J.Chapple
1801	Eleanor	J.Saunders	1834	Pussy	J.B.Day
1802	Scotia	F.Buckle	1835	Queen of Trumps	T.Lye
1803	Theophania	F.Buckle	1836	Cyprian	W.Scott
1804	Pelisse	W.Clift	1837	Miss Letty	J.Holmes
1805	Meteora	F.Buckle	1838	Industry	W.Scott
1806	Bronze	W.Edwards	1839	Deception	J.B.Day
1807	Briseis	S.Chifney,jnr	1840	Crucifix	J.B.Day
1808	Morel	W.Clift	1841	Ghuznee	W.Scott
1809	Maid of Orleans	B.Moss	1842	Our Nell	T.Lye
1810	Oriana	W.Peirse	1843	Poison	F.Butler
1811	Sorcery	S.Chifney,jnr	1844	The Princess	F.Butler

Year	Winner	Jockey	Year	Winner	Jockey
1845	Refraction	H.Bell	1900	La Roche	M.Cannon
1846	Mendicant	S.Day	1901	Cap and Bells II	M.Henry
1847	Miami	S.Templeman	1902	Sceptre	H.Randall
1848	Cymba	S.Templeman	1903	Our Lassie	M.Cannon
1849	Lady Evelyn	F.Butler	1904	Pretty Polly	W.Lane
1850	Rhedycina	F.Butler	1905	Cherry Lass	H.Jones
1851	Iris	F.Butler	1906	Keystone II	D.Maher
1852	Songstress	F.Butler	1907	Glass Doll	H.Randall
1853	Catherine Hayes	C.Marlow	1908	Signorinetta	W.Bullock
1854	Mincemeat	J.Charlton	1909	Perola	F.Wootton
1855	Marchioness	S.Templeman	1910	Rosedrop	C.Trigg
1856	Mincepie	A.Day	1911	Cherimoya	F.Winter
1857	Blink Bonny	J.Charlton	1912	Mirska	J.Childs
1858	Governess	T.Ashmall	1913	Jest	F.Rickaby,jnr
1859	Summerside	G.Fordham	1914	Princess Dorrie	W.Huxley
1860	Butterfly	J.Snowden	1915	Snow Marten	W.Griggs
1861	Brown Duchess	L.Snowden	1916	Fifinella	J.Childs
1862	Feu de Joie	T.Chaloner	1917	Sunny Jane	O.Madden
1863	Queen Bertha	T.Aldcroft	1918	My Dear	S.Donoghue
1864	Fille de L'Air	A.Edwards	1919	Bayuda	J.Childs
1865	Regalia	J.Norman	1920	Charlebelle	A.Whalley
1866	Tormentor	J.Mann	1921	Love in Idleness	J.Childs
1867	Hippia	J.Daley	1922	Pogrom	E.Gardner
1868	Formosa	G.Fordham	1923	Brownhylda	V.Smyth
1869	Brigantine	T.Cannon	1924	Straitlace	F.O'Neill
1870	Gamos	G.Fordham	1925	Saucy Sue	F.Bullock
1871	Hannah	C.Maidment	1926	Short Story	R.A.Jones
1872	Reine	G.Fordham	1927	Beam	T.Weston
1873	Marie Stuart	T.Cannon	1928	Toboggan	T.Weston
1874	Apology	J.Osborne	1929	Pennycomequick	H.Jellis
1875	Spinaway	F.Archer	1930	Rose of England	G.Richards
1876	Enguerrande &	Hudson	1931	Brulette	E.C.Elliott
	Camelia (deadheated)	T.Glover	1932	Udaipur	M.Beary
1877	Placida	H.Jeffery	1933	Chatelaine	S.Wragg
1878	Jannette	F.Archer	1934	Light Brocade	B.Carslake
1879	Wheel of Fortune	F.Archer	1935	Quashed	H.Jellis
1880	Jenny Howlet	J.Snowden	1936	Lovely Rosa	T.Weston
1881	Thebais	G.Fordham	1937	Exhibitionnist	S.Donoghue
1882	Geheimniss	T.Cannon	1938	Rockfel	H.Wragg
1883	Bonny Jean	J.Watts	1939	Galatea II	R.A.Jones
1884	Busybody	T.Cannon	1940	Godiva	D.Marks
1885	Lonely	F.Archer	1941	Commotion	H.Wragg
1886	Miss Jummy	J.Watts	1942	Sun Chariot	G.Richards
1887	Rêve d'Or	C.Wood	1943	Why Hurry	E.C.Elliott
1888	Seabreeze	J.Robinson	1944	Hycilla	G.Bridgland
1889	L'Abbesse de Jouarre	J.Woodburn	1945	Sun Stream	H.Wragg
1890	Memoir	J.Watts	1946	Steady Aim	H.Wragg
1891	Mimi	F.Rickaby	1947	Imprudence	W.Johnstone
1892	La Fleche	G.Barrett	1948	Masaka	W.Nevitt
1893	Mrs Butterwick	J.Watts	1949	Musidora	E.Britt
1894	Amiable	W.Bradford	1950	Asmena	W.Johnstone
1895	La Sagesse	S.Loates	1951	Neasham Belle	S.Clayton
1896	Canterbury Pilgrim	F.Rickaby	1952	Frieze	E.Britt
1897	Limasol	W.Bradford	1953	Ambiguity	J.Mercer
1898	Airs and Graces	W.Bradford	1954	Sun Cap	W.Johnstone
1899	Musa	O.Madden	1955	Meld	H.Carr

Year	Winner	Jockey	Year	Winner	Jockey
1956	Sicarelle	F.Palmer	1972	Ginevra	T.Murray
1957	Carrozza	L.Piggott	1973	Mysterious	G.Lewis
1958	Bella Paola	M.Garcia	1974	Polygamy	P.Eddery
1959	Petit Etoile	L.Piggott	1975	Juliette Marny	L.Piggott
1960	Never Too Late	R.Poincelet	1976	Pawneese	Y.Saint-Martin
1961	Sweet Solera	W.Rickaby	1977	Dunfermline	W.Carson
1962	Monade	Y.SaintMartin	1978	Fair Salinia	G.Starkey
1963	Noblesse	G.Bougoure	1979	Scintillate	P.Eddery
1964	Homeward Bound	G.Starkey	1980	Bireme	W.Carson
1965	Long Look	J.Purtell	1981	Blue Wind	L.Piggott
1966	Valoris	L.Piggott	1982	Time Charter	W.Newnes
1967	Pia	E.Hide	1983	Sun Princess	W.Carson
1968	La Lagune	G.Thiboeuf	1984	Circus Plume	L.Piggott
1969	Sleeping Partner	J.Gorton	1985	Oh So Sharp	S.Cauthen
1970	Lupe	A.Barclay	1986	Midway Lady	R.Cochrane
1971	Altesse Royale	G.Lewis	1987	Unite	W.Swinburn
			1988	Diminuendo	S.Cauthen

Most Wins (Jockey):
9 Frank Buckle

1000 GUINEAS
A race for three-year-old fillies over one mile, the One Thousand Guineas is the first Classic of the English season, and is run at Newmarket.
Winners:

Year	Winner	Jockey	Year	Winner	Jockey
1814	Charlotte	W.Clift	1842	Firebrand	S.Rogers
1815	Unnamed filly	W.Clift	1843	Extempore	S.Chifney,jnr
1816	Rhoda	S.Barnard	1844	Sorella	J.Robinson
1817	Neva	W.Arnull	1845	Picnic	W.Abdale
1818	Corinne	F.Buckle	1846	Mendicant	S.Day
1819	Catgut	Not known	1847	Clementina	E.Flatman
1820	Rowena	F.Buckle	1848	Canezou	F.Butler
1821	Zeal	F.Buckle	1849	The Flea	A.Day
1822	Whizgig	F.Buckle	1850	Lady Orford	F.Butler
1823	Zinc	F.Buckle	1851	Aphrodite	J.Marson
1824	Cobweb	J.Robinson	1852	Kate	A.Day
1825	Tontine	Not known	1853	Mentmore Lass	J.Charlton
1826	Problem	J.B.Day	1854	Virago	J.Wells
1827	Arab	F.Buckle	1855	Habena	S.Rogers
1828	Zoe	J.Robinson	1856	Manganese	J.Osborne
1829	Young Mouse	W.Arnull	1857	Imperieuse	N.Flatman
1830	Charlotte West	J.Robinson	1858	Governess	T.Ashmall
1831	Galantine	P.Conolly	1859	Mayonaise	G.Fordham
1832	Galata	W.Arnull	1860	Sagitta	T.Aldcroft
1833	Tarantella	E.Wright	1861	Nemesis	G.Fordham
1834	May-Day	J.B.Day	1862	Hurricane	T.Ashmall
1835	Preserve	E.Flatman	1863	Lady Augusta	A.Edwards
1836	Destiny	J.B.Day	1864	Tomato	J.Wells
1837	Chapeau d'Espagne	J.B.Day	1865	Siberia	G.Fordham
1838	Barcarolle	E.Edwards	1866	Repulse	T.Cannon
1839	Cara	G.Edwards	1867	Achievement	H.Custance
1840	Crucifix	J.B.Day	1868	Formosa	G.Fordham
1841	Potentia	J.Robinson	1869	Scottish Queen	G.Fordham

Year	Winner	Jockey	Year	Winner	Jockey
1870	Hester	J.Grimshaw	1927	Cresta Run	A.Balding
1871	Hannah	C.Maidment	1928	Scuttle	J.Childs
1872	Reine	H.Parry	1929	Taj Mah	W.Sibbritt
1873	Cecilia	J.Morris	1930	Fair Isle	T.Weston
1874	Apology	J.Osborne	1931	Four Course	E.C.Elliott
1875	Spinaway	F.Archer	1932	Kandy	E.C.Elliott
1876	Camelia	T.Glover	1933	Brown Betty	J.Childs
1877	Belphoebe	H.Jeffery	1934	Campanula	H.Wragg
1878	Pilgrimage	T.Cannon	1935	Mesa	W.Johnstone
1879	Wheel of Fortune	F.Archer	1936	Tide-way	R.Perryman
1880	Elizabeth	C.Wood	1937	Exhibitionnist	S.Donoghue
1881	Thebais	G.Fordham	1938	Rockfel	S.Wragg
1882	St.Marguerite	C.Wood	1939	Galatea II	R.A.Jones
1883	Hauteur	G.Fordham	1940	Godiva	D.Marks
1884	Busybody	T.Cannon	1941	Dancing Time	R.Perryman
1885	Farewell	G.Barrett	1942	Sun Chariot	G.Richards
1886	Miss Jummy	J.Watts	1943	Herringbone	H.Wragg
1887	Rêve d'Or	C.Wood	1944	Picture Play	E.C.Elliott
1888	Briarroot	W.Warne	1945	Sun Stream	H.Wragg
1889	Minthe	J.Woodburn	1946	Hypericum	D.Smith
1890	Semolina	J.Watts	1947	Imprudence	W.Johnstone
1891	Mimi	F.Rickaby	1948	Queenpot	G.Richards
1892	La Fleche	G.Barrett	1949	Musidora	E.Brit
1893	Siffleuse	T.Loates	1950	Camaree	W.Johnstone
1894	Amiable	W.Bradford	1951	Belle of All	G.Richards
1895	Galeottia	F.Pratt	1952	Zabara	K.Gethin
1896	Thais	J.Watts	1953	Happy Laughter	E.Mercer
1897	Chelandry	J.Watts	1954	Festoon	A.Breasley
1898	Nun Nicer	S.Loates	1955	Meld	H.Carr
1899	Sibola	J.Sloan	1956	Honeylight	E.Britt
1900	Winifreda	S.Loates	1957	Rose Royale II	C.Smirke
1901	Aida	D.Maher	1958	Bella Paola	S.Boullenger
1902	Sceptre	H.Randall	1959	Petite Etoile	D.Smith
1903	Quintessence	H.Randall	1960	Never Too Late	R.Poincelet
1904	Pretty Polly	W.Lane	1961	Sweet Solera	W.Rickaby
1905	Cherry Lass	G.McCall	1962	Abermaid	W.Williamson
1906	Flair	B.Dillon	1963	Hula Dancer	R.Poincelet
1907	Witch Elm	B.Lynham	1964	Pourparler	G.Bougoure
1908	Rhodora	L.Lyne	1965	Night Off	W.Williamson
1909	Electra	B.Dillon	1966	Glad Rags	P.Cook
1910	Winkipop	B.Lynham	1967	Fleet	G.Moore
1911	Atmah	F.Fox	1968	Caergwrle	A.Barclay
1912	Tagalie	L.Hewitt	1969	Full Dress II	R.Hutchinson
1913	Jest	F.Rickaby,jnr	1970	Humble Duty	L.Piggott
1914	Princess Dorrie	W.Huxley	1971	Altesse Royale	Y.Saint-Martin
1915	Vaucluse	F.Rickaby,jnr	1972	Waterloo	E.Hide
1916	Canyon	F.Rickaby,jnr	1973	Mysterious	G.Lewis
1917	Diadem	F.Rickaby,jnr	1974	Highclere	J.Mercer
1918	Ferry	B.Carslake	1975	Nocturnal Spree	J.Roe
1919	Roseway	A.Whalley	1976	Flying Water	Y.Saint-Martin
1920	Cinna	W.Griggs	1977	Mrs McArdy	E.Hide
1921	Bettina	G.Bellhouse	1978	Enstone Spark	E.Johnson
1922	Silver Urn	B.Carslake	1979	One in a Million	J.Mercer
1923	Tranquil	E.Gardner	1980	Quick As Lightning	B.Rouse
1924	Plack	E.C.Elliott	1981	Fairy Footsteps	L.Piggott
1925	Saucy Sue	F.Bullock	1982	On The House	J.Reid
1926	Pillion	R.Perryman	1983	Ma Biche	F.Head

Year	Winner	Jockey	Year	Winner	Jockey
1984	Pebbles	P.Robinson	1986	Midway Lady	R.Cochrane
1985	Oh So Sharp	S.Cauthen	1987	Miesque	F.Head
			1988	Ravinella	G.Moore
			1989	Musical Bliss	W.Swinburn

Most Wins (Jockey):
7 George Fordham

2000 GUINEAS
The Two Thousand Guineas is the other early season Classic and is run over one mile at Newmarket. It is for three-year-olds only.

Winners:

Year	Winner	Jockey	Year	Winner	Jockey
1809	Wizard	W.Clift	1854	The Hermit	A.Day
1810	Hephestion	F.Buckle	1855	Lord of the Isles	T.Aldcroft
1811	Trophonius	S.Barnard	1856	Fazzoletto	N.Flatman
1812	Cwrw	S.Chifney,jnr	1857	Vedette	J.Osborne
1813	Smolensko	H.Miller	1858	Fitzroland	J.Wells
1814	Olive	W.Arnull	1859	Promised Land	A.Day
1815	Tigris	W.Arnull	1860	The Wizard	T.Ashmall
1816	Nectar	W.Arnull	1861	Diophantus	A.Edwards
1817	Manfred	W.Wheatley	1862	The Marquis	T.Ashmall
1818	Interpreter	W.Clift	1863	Macaroni	T.Chaloner
1819	Antar	E.Edwards	1864	General Peel	T.Aldcroft
1820	Pindarrie	F.Buckle	1865	Gladiateur	H.Grimshaw
1821	Reginald	F.Buckle	1866	Lord Lyon	R.Thomas
1822	Pastilla	F.Buckle	1867	Vauban	G.Fordham
1823	Nicolo	W.Wheatley	1868	Moslem &	T.Chaloner
1824	Schahriar	W.Wheatley		Formosa (deadheated)	G.Fordham
1825	Enamel	J.Robinson	1869	Pretender	J.Osborne
1826	Dervise	J.B.Day	1870	Macgregor	J.Daley
1827	Turcoman	F.Buckle	1871	Bothwell	J.Osborne
1828	Cadland	J.Robinson	1872	Prince Charlie	J.Osborne
1829	Patron	F.Boyce	1873	Gang Forward	T.Chaloner
1830	Augustus	P.Conolly	1874	Atlantic	F.Archer
1831	Riddlesworth	J.Robinson	1875	Camballo	J.Osborne
1832	Archibald	A.Pavis	1876	Petrarch	H.Luke
1833	Clearwell	J.Robinson	1877	Chamant	J.Goater
1834	Glencoe	J.Robinson	1878	Pilgrimage	T.Cannon
1835	Ibrahim	J.Robinson	1879	Charibert	F.Archer
1836	Bay Middleton	J.Robinson	1880	Petronel	G.Fordham
1837	Achmet	E.Edwards	1881	Peregrine	F.Webb
1838	Grey Momus	J.B.Day	1882	Shotover	T.Cannon
1839	The Corsair	W.Wakefield	1883	Galliard	F.Archer
1840	Crucifix	J.B.Day	1884	Scot Free	W.Platt
1841	Ralph	J.B.Day	1885	Paradox	F.Archer
1842	Meteor	W.Scott	1886	Ormonde	G.Barrett
1843	Cotherstone	W.Scott	1887	Enterprise	T.Cannon
1844	The Ugly Buck	J.Day,jnr	1888	Ayrshire	J.Osborne
1845	Idas	N.Flatman	1889	Enthusiast	T.Cannon
1846	Sir Tatton Sykes	W.Scott	1890	Surefoot	J.Liddiard
1847	Conyngham	J.Robinson	1891	Common	G.Barrett
1848	Flatcatcher	J.Robinson	1892	Bona Vista	W.Robinson
1849	Nunnykirk	F.Butler	1893	Isinglass	T.Loates
1850	Pitsford	A.Day	1894	Ladas	J.Watts
1851	Hernandez	N.Flatman	1895	Kirkconnel	J.Watts
1852	Stockwell	J.Norman	1896	St.Frusquin	T.Loates
1853	West Australian	F.Butler	1897	Galtee More	C.Wood

Year	Winner	Jockey	Year	Winner	Jockey
1898	Disraeli	S.Loates	1943	Kingsway	S.Wragg
1899	Flying Fox	M.Cannon	1944	Garden Path	H.Wragg
1900	Diamond Jubilee	H.Jones	1945	Court Martial	G.Richards
1901	Handicapper	W.Halsey	1946	Happy Knight	T.Weston
1902	Sceptre	H.Randall	1947	Tudor Minstrel	G.Richards
1903	Rock Sand	J.Martin	1948	My Babu	C.Smirke
1904	St.Amant	K.Cannon	1949	Nimbus	C.Elliott
1905	Vedas	H.Jones	1950	Palestine	C.Smirke
1906	Gorgos	H.Jones	1951	Ki Ming	A.Breasley
1907	Slieve Gallion	W.Higgs	1952	Thunderhead II	R.Poincelet
1908	Norman III	O.Madden	1953	Nearula	E.Britt
1909	Minoru	H.Jones	1954	Darius	E.Mercer
1910	Neil Gow	D.Maher	1955	Our Babu	D.Smith
1911	Sunstar	G.Stern	1956	Gilles de Retz	F.Barlow
1912	Sweeper II	D.Maher	1957	Crepello	L.Piggott
1913	Louvois	J.Reiff	1958	Pall Mall	D.Smith
1914	Kennymore	G.Stern	1959	Taboun	G.Moore
1915	Pommern	S.Donoghue	1960	Martial	R.Hutchinson
1916	Clarissimus	J.Clark	1961	Rockavon	N.Stirk
1917	Gay Crusader	S.Donoghue	1962	Privy Councillor	W.Rickaby
1918	Gainsborough	J.Childs	1963	Only For Life	J.Lindley
1919	The Panther	R.Cooper	1964	Baldric II	W.Pyers
1920	Tetratema	B.Carslake	1965	Niksar	D.Keith
1921	Craig an Eran	J.Brennan	1966	Kashmir II	J.Lindley
1922	St.Louis	G.Archibald	1967	Royal Palace	G.Moore
1923	Ellangowan	E.C.Elliott	1968	Sir Ivor	L.Piggott
1924	Diophon	G.Hulme	1969	Right Tack	G.Lewis
1925	Manna	S.Donoghue	1970	Nijinsky	L.Piggott
1926	Colorado	T.Weston	1971	Brigadier Gerard	J.Mercer
1927	Adam's Apple	J.Leach	1972	High Top	W.Carson
1928	Flamingo	E.C.Elliott	1973	Mon Fils	F.Durr
1929	Mr.Jinks	H.Beasley	1974	Nonoalco	Y.Saint-Martin
1930	Diolite	F.Fox	1975	Bolkonski	G.Dettori
1931	Cameronian	J.Childs	1976	Wollow	G.Dettori
1932	Orwell	R.A.Jones	1977	Nebbiolo	G.Curran
1933	Rodosto	R.Brethes	1978	Roland Gardens	F.Durr
1934	Colombo	W.Johnstone	1979	Tap On Wood	S.Cauthen
1935	Bahram	F.Fox	1980	Known Fact	W.Carson
1936	Pay Up	R.Dick	1981	To-Agori-Mou	G.Starkey
1937	Le Ksar	C.Semblat	1982	Zino	F.Head
1938	Pasch	G.Richards	1983	Lomond	P.Eddery
1939	Blue Peter	E.Smith	1984	El Gran Senor	P.Eddery
1940	Djebel	E.C.Elliott	1985	Shadeed	L.Piggott
1941	Lambert Simnel	E.C.Elliott	1986	Dancing Brave	G.Starkey
1942	Big Game	G.Richards	1987	Don't Forget Me	W.Carson
			1988	Doyoun	W.Swinburn
			1989	Nashwan	W.Carson

Most Wins (Jockey):
9 Jem Robinson

ST. LEGER

The oldest of the five Classics, it is run over 1 mile 6 furlongs 127 yds at Doncaster each September (although it has moved in wartime to the Rowley Mile, Newmarket (1915–18), Thirsk (1940), Manchester (1941), July course, Newmarket (1942–44), and in 1945 to York). The race is open to three year old colts and fillies.

Winners:

Year	Winner	Jockey	Year	Winner	Jockey
1776	Allabaculia	J.Singleton	1826	Tarrare	G.Nelson
1777	Bourbon	J.Cade	1827	Matilda	J.Robinson
1778	Hollandaise	G.Herring	1828	The Colonel	W.Scott
1779	Tommy	G.Lowry,snr	1829	Rowton	W.Scott
1780	Ruler	J.Mangle	1830	Birmingham	P.Conolly
1781	Serina	R.Foster	1831	Chorister	J.B.Day
1782	Imperatrix	G.Searle	1832	Margrave	J.Robinson
1783	Phoenomenon	A.Hall	1833	Rockingham	S.Darling
1784	Omphale	J.Kirton	1834	Touchstone	G.Calloway
1785	Cowslip	G.Searle	1835	Queen of Trumps	T.Lye
1786	Paragon	J.Mangle	1836	Elis	J.B.Day
1787	Spadille	J.Mangle	1837	Mango	S.Day,jnr
1788	Young Flora	J.Mangle	1838	Don John	W.Scott
1789	Pewett	W.Wilson	1839	Charles the Twelfth	W.Scott
1790	Ambidexter	G.Searle	1840	Launcelot	W.Scott
1791	Young Traveller	J.Jackson	1841	Satirist	W.Scott
1792	Tartar	J.Mangle	1842	The Blue Bonnet	T.Lye
1793	Ninety-Three	W.Peirse	1843	Nutwith	J.Marson
1794	Beningbrough	J.Jackson	1844	Foig a Ballagh	H.Bell
1795	Hambletonian	R.D.Boyce	1845	The Baron	F.Butler
1796	Ambrosio	J.Jackson	1846	Sir Tatton Sykes	W.Scott
1797	Lounger	J.Shepherd	1847	Van Tromp	J.Marson
1798	Symmetry	J.Jackson	1848	Surplice	E.Flatman
1799	Cockfighter	T.Fields	1849	The Flying Dutchman	C.Marlow
1800	Champion	F.Buckle	1850	Voltigeur	J.Marson
1801	Quiz	J.Shepherd	1851	Newminster	S.Templeman
1802	Orville	J.Singleton,jnr	1852	Stockwell	J.Norman
1803	Remembrancer	B.Smith	1853	West Australian	F.Butler
1804	Sancho	F.Buckle	1854	Knight of St.George	R.Basham
1805	Staveley	J.Jackson	1855	Saucebox	J.Wells
1806	Fyldener	T.Carr	1856	Warlock	N.Flatman
1807	Paulina	W.Clift	1857	Imperieuse	N.Flatman
1808	Petronius	B.Smith	1858	Sunbeam	L.Snowden
1809	Ashton	B.Smith	1859	Gamester	T.Aldcroft
1810	Octavian	W.Clift	1860	St.Albans	L.Snowden
1811	Soothsayer	B.Smith	1861	Caller Ou	T.Chaloner
1812	Otterington	R.Johnson	1862	The Marquis	T.Chaloner
1813	Altisidora	J.Jackson	1863	Lord Clifden	J.Osborne
1814	William	J.Shepherd	1864	Blair Athol	J.Snowden
1815	Fihlo da Puta	J.Jackson	1865	Gladiateur	H.Grimshaw
1816	The Duchess	B.Smith	1866	Lord Lyon	H.Custance
1817	Ebor	R.Johnson	1867	Achievement	T.Chaloner
1818	Reveller	R.Johnson	1868	Formosa	T.Chaloner
1819	Antonio	J.Nicholson	1869	Pero Gomez	J.Wells
1820	St.Patrick	R.Johnson	1870	Hawthornden	J.Grimshaw
1821	Jack Spigot	W.Scott	1871	Hannah	C.Maidment
1822	Theodore	J.Jackson	1872	Wenlock	C.Maidment
1823	Barefoot	T.Goodisson	1873	Marie Stuart	T.Osborne
1824	Jerry	B.Smith	1874	Apology	J.Osborne
1825	Memnon	W.Scott	1875	Craig Millar	T.Chaloner

St. Leger Winners Cont.

Year	Winner	Jockey	Year	Winner	Jockey
1876	Petrarch	J.Goater	1930	Singapore	G.Richards
1877	Silvio	F.Archer	1931	Sandwich	H.Wragg
1878	Jannette	F.Archer	1932	Firdaussi	F.Fox
1879	Rayon d'Or	J.Goater	1933	Hyperion	T.Weston
1880	Robert the Devil	T.Cannon	1934	Windsor Lad	C.Smirke
1881	Iroquois	F.Archer	1935	Bahram	C.Smirke
1882	Dutch Oven	F.Archer	1936	Boswell	P.Beasley
1883	Ossian	J.Watts	1937	Chulmleigh	G.Richards
1884	The Lambkin	J.Watts	1938	Scottish Union	B.Carslake
1885	Melton	F.Archer	1939	Not held	
1886	Ormonde	F.Archer	1940	Turkhan	G.Richards
1887	Kilwarlin	W.T.Robinson	1941	Sun Castle	G.Bridgland
1888	Seabreeze	W.T.Robinson	1942	Sun Chariot	G.Richards
1889	Donovan	F.Barrett	1943	Herringbone	H.Wragg
1890	Memoir	J.Watts	1944	Tehran	G.Richards
1891	Common	G.Barrett	1945	Chamossaire	T.Lowrey
1892	La Fleche	J.Watts	1946	Airborne	T.Lowrey
1893	Isinglass	T.Loates	1947	Sayajirao	E.Britt
1894	Throstle	M.Cannon	1948	Black Tarquin	E.Britt
1895	Sir Visto	S.Loates	1949	Ridge Wood	M.Beary
1896	Persimmon	J.Watts	1950	Scratch II	W.Johnstone
1897	Galtee More	C.Wood	1951	Talma II	W.Johnstone
1898	Wildfowler	C.Wood	1952	Tulyar	C.Smirke
1899	Flying Fox	M.Cannon	1953	Premonition	E.Smith
1900	Diamond Jubilee	H.Jones	1954	Never Say Die	C.Smirke
1901	Doricles	K.Cannon	1955	Meld	H.Carr
1902	Sceptre	F.W.Hardy	1956	Cambremer	F.Palmer
1903	Rock Sand	D.Maher	1957	Ballymoss	T.Burns
1904	Pretty Polly	W.Lane	1958	Alcide	H.Carr
1905	Challacombe	O.Madden	1959	Cantelo	E.Hide
1906	Troutbeck	G.Stern	1960	St.Paddy	L.Piggott
1907	Wool Winder	W.Halsey	1961	Aurelius	L.Piggott
1908	Your Majesty	W.Griggs	1962	Hethersett	H.Carr
1909	Bayardo	D.Maher	1963	Ragusa	G.Bougoure
1910	Swynford	F.Wootton	1964	Indiana	J.Lindley
1911	Prince Palatine	F.O'Neill	1965	Provoke	J.Mercer
1912	Tracery	G.Bellhouse	1966	Sodium	F.Durr
1913	Night Hawk	E.Wheatley	1967	Ribocco	L.Piggott
1914	Black Jester	W.Griggs	1968	Ribero	L.Piggott
1915	Pommern	S.Donoghue	1969	Intermezzo	R.Hutchinson
1916	Hurry On	C.Childs	1970	Nijinsky	L.Piggott
1917	Gay Crusader	S.Donoghue	1971	Athens Wood	L.Piggott
1918	Gainsborough	J.Childs	1972	Boucher	L.Piggott
1919	Keysoe	B.Carslake	1973	Peleid	F.Durr
1920	Caligula	A.Smith	1974	Bustino	J.Mercer
1921	Polemarch	J.Childs	1975	Bruni	A.Murray
1922	Royal Lancer	R.A.Jones	1976	Crow	Y.Saint-Martin
1923	Tranquil	T.Weston	1977	Dunfermline	W.Carson
1924	Salmon-Trout	B.Carslake	1978	Julio Mariner	E.Hide
1925	Solario	J.Childs	1979	Son of Love	A.Lequeux
1926	Coronach	J.Childs	1980	Light Cavalry	J.Mercer
1927	Book Law	H.Jelliss	1981	Cut Above	J.Mercer
1928	Fairway	T.Weston	1982	Touching Wood	P.Cook
1929	Trigo	M.Beary	1983	Sun Princess	W.Carson

1984	Commanche Run	L.Piggott	1986	Moon Madness	P.Eddery
1985	Oh So Sharp	S.Cauthen	1987	Reference Point	S.Cauthen
			1988	Minster Son	W.Carson

Most Wins (Jockey):
9 Bill Scott

GRAND NATIONAL

Originally run at a course in Maghull, some four miles from the present site at Aintree, the first race was in 1836 and won by The Duke, who won again in 1837. The first race at Aintree was in 1839 and the race became known as the Grand National in 1847. Three substitute races, 1916–18, were run at Gatwick.

Winners:

Year	Winner	Jockey	Year	Winner	Jockey
1839	Lottery	J.Mason	1882	Seaman	Lord Manners
1840	Jerry	Mr.B.Bretherton	1883	Zoedone Count	K.Kinsky
1841	Charity	H.N.Powell	1884	Voluptuary	Mr.E.Wilson
1842	Gaylad	T.Oliver	1885	Roquefort	Mr.E.Wilson
1843	Vanguard	T.Oliver	1886	Old Joe	T.Skelton
1844	Discount	H.Crickmere	1887	Gamecock	W.Daniels
1845	Cure-all	W.Loft	1888	Playfair	G.Mawson
1846	Pioneer	W.Taylor	1889	Frigate	Mr.T.Beasley
1847	Mathew	D.Wynne	1890	Ilex	A.Nightingall
1848	Chandler	Capt.Little	1891	Come Away	Mr.H.Beasley
1849	Peter Simple	T.Cunningham	1892	Father O'Flynn	Capt.R.Owen
1850	Abd-el-Kader	C.Green	1893	Cloister	W.Dollery
1851	Abd-el-Kader	T.Abbott	1894	Why Not	A.Nightingall
1852	Miss Mowbray	Mr.A.Goodman	1895	Wild Man from Borneo	Mr.J.Widger
1853	Peter Simple	T.Oliver	1896	The Soarer	Mr.D.Campbell
1854	Bourton	Tasker	1897	Manifesto	T.Kavanagh
1855	Wanderer	J.Hanlon	1898	Drogheda	J.Gourley
1856	Freetrader	G.Stevens	1899	Manifesto	G.Williamson
1857	Emigrant	C.Boyce	1900	Ambush II	A.Anthony
1858	Little Charley	W.Archer	1901	Grudon	A.Nightingall
1859	Half Caste	C.Green	1902	Shannon Lass	D.Read
1860	Anatis	Mr.T.Pickernell	1903	Drumcree	P.Woodland
1861	Jealousy	J.Kendall	1904	Moifaa	A.Birch
1862	Huntsman	H.Lamplugh	1905	Kirkland	F.Mason
1863	Emblem	G.Stevens	1906	Ascetic's Silver	Hon.A.Hastings
1864	Emblematic	G.Stevens	1907	Eremon	A.Newey
1865	Alcibiade	Capt.Coventry	1908	Rubio	H.Bletsoe
1866	Salamander	Mr.A.Goodman	1909	Lutteur III	G.Parfrement
1867	Cortolvin	J.Page	1910	Jenkinstown	R.Chadwick
1868	The Lamb	Mr.G.Ede	1911	Glenside	J.Anthony
1869	The Colonel	G.Stevens	1912	Jerry M	E.Piggott
1870	The Colonel	G.Stevens	1913	Covertcoat	P.Woodland
1871	The Lamb	Mr.T.Pickernell	1914	Sunloch	W.Smith
1872	Casse Tête	J.Page	1915	Ally. Sloper	J.Anthony
1873	Disturbance	Mr.M.Richardson	1916	Vermouth	J.Reardon
1874	Reugny	Mr.M.Richardson	1917	Ballymacad	E.Driscoll
1875	Pathfinder	Mr.T.Pickernell	1918	Poethlyn	E.Piggott
1876	Regal	J.Cannon	1919	Poethlyn	E.Piggott
1877	Austerlitz	Mr.F.Hobson	1920	Troytown	J.Anthony
1878	Shifnal	J.Jones	1921	Shaun Spadah	F.Rees
1879	The Liberator	Mr.G.Moore	1922	Music Hall	L.Rees
1880	Empress	Mr.T.Beasley	1923	Sergeant Murphy	Capt.G.Bennett
1881	Woodbrook	Mr.T.Beasley	1924	Master Robert	R.Trudgill

Grand National Winners Cont.

Year	Winner	Jockey	Year	Winner	Jockey
1925	Double Chance	Maj.J.Wilson	1959	Oxo	M.Scudamore
1926	Jack Horner	W.Watkinson	1960	Merryman II	G.Scott
1927	Sprig	T.E.Leader	1961	Nicolaus Silver	B.Beasley
1928	Tipperary Tim	W.P.Dutton	1962	Kilmore	F.Winter
1929	Gregalach	R.Everett	1963	Ayala	P.Buckley
1930	Shaun Goilin	T.Cullinan	1964	Team Spirit	W.Robinson
1931	Grakle	R.Lyall	1965	Jay Trump	T.Smith
1932	Forbra	J.Hamey	1966	Anglo	T.Norman
1933	Kellsboro' Jack	D.Williams	1967	Foinavon	J.Buckingham
1934	Golden Miller	G.Wilson	1968	Red Alligator	B.Fletcher
1935	Reynoldstown	F.Furlong	1969	Highland Wedding	E.Harty
1936	Reynoldstown	F.Walwyn	1970	Gay Trip	P.Taaffe
1937	Royal Mail	E.Williams	1971	Specify	J.Cook
1938	Battleship	B.Hobbs	1972	Well To Do	G.Thorner
1939	Workman	T.Hyde	1973	Red Rum	B.Fletcher
1940	Bogskar	M.Jones	1974	Red Rum	B.Fletcher
1941–45	Not held		1975	L'Escargot	T.Carberry
1946	Lovely Cottage	Capt.R.Petre	1976	Rag Trade	J.Burke
1947	Caughoo	E.Dempsey	1977	Red Rum	T.Stack
1948	Sheila's Cottage	A.Thompson	1978	Lucius	B.Davies
1949	Russian Hero	L.McMorrow	1979	Rubstic	M.Barnes
1950	Freebooter	J.Power	1980	Ben Nevis	Mr.C.Fenwick
1951	Nickel Coin	J.Bullock	1981	Aldaniti	B.Champion
1952	Teal	A.Thompson	1982	Grittar	Mr.D.Saunders
1953	Early Mist	B.Marshall	1983	Corbiere	B.de Haan
1954	Royal Tan	B.Marshall	1984	Hallo Dandy	N.Doughty
1955	Quare Times	P.Taaffe	1985	Last Suspect	H.Davies
1956	E.S.B.	D.Dick	1986	West Tip	R.Dunwoody
1957	Sundew	F.Winter	1987	Maori Venture	S.Knight
1958	Mr.What	A.Freeman	1988	Rhyme 'N Reason	B.Powell
			1989	Little Polveir	J.Frost

Most Wins
(Horse):
3 Red Rum
(Jockey):
5 George Stevens

CHELTENHAM GOLD CUP

The Cheltenham Gold Cup is the highlight of the Festival Meeting at Cheltenham every March. The Gold Cup was first contested in 1924 and the race currently covers just over 3¼ miles.

Winners:

Year	Winner	Jockey	Year	Winner	Jockey
1924	Red Splash	F.Rees	1957	Linwell	M.Scudamore
1925	Ballinode	T.Leader	1958	Kerstin	S.Hayhurst
1926	Koko	J.Hamey	1959	Roddy Owen	B.Beasley
1927	Thrown In	Mr.H.Grosvenor	1960	Pas Seul	W.Rees
1928	Patron Saint	F.Rees	1961	Saffron Tartan	F.Winter
1929	Easter Hero	F.Rees	1962	Mandarin	F.Winter
1930	Easter Hero	T.Cullinan	1963	Mill House	W.Robinson
1931	Not held		1964	Arkle	P.Taaffe
1932	Golden Miller	T.Leader	1965	Arkle	P.Taaffe
1933	Golden Miller	W.Stott	1966	Arkle	P.Taaffe
1934	Golden Miller	G.Wilson	1967	Woodland Venture	T.Biddlecombe
1935	Golden Miller	G.Wilson	1968	Fort Leney	P.Taaffe
1936	Golden Miller	E.Williams	1969	What a Myth	P.Kelleway
1937	Not held		1970	L'Escargot	T.Carberry
1938	Morse Code	D.Morgan	1971	L'Escargot	T.Carberry
1939	Brendan's Cottage	G.Owen	1972	Glencaraig Lady	F.Berry
1940	Roman Hackle	E.Williams	1973	The Dikler	R.Barry
1941	Poet Prince	R.Burford	1974	Captain Christy	H.Beasley
1942	Medoc II	H.Nicholson	1975	Ten Up	T.Carberry
1943–44	Not held		1976	Royal Frolic	J.Burke
1945	Red Rower	D.Jones	1977	Davy Lad	D.Hughes
1946	Prince Regent	T.Hyde	1978	Midnight Court	J.Francome
1947	Fortina	Mr.R.Black	1979	Alverton	J.J.O'Neill
1948	Cottage Rake	A.Brabazon	1980	Master Smudge	R.Hoare
1949	Cottage Rake	A.Brabazon	1981	Little Owl	Mr.A.J.Wilson
1950	Cottage Rake	A.Brabazon	1982	Silver Buck	R.Earnshaw
1951	Silver Fame	M.Molony	1983	Bregawn	G.Bradley
1952	Mont Tremblant	D.Dick	1984	Burrough Hill Lad	P.Tuck
1953	Knock Hard	T.Molony	1985	Forgive'N'Forget	M.Dwyer
1954	Four Ten	T.Cusack	1986	Dawn Run	J.J.O'Neill
1955	Gay Donald	A.Grantham	1987	The Thinker	R. Lamb
1956	Limber Hill	J.Power	1988	Charter Party	R.Dunwoody
			1989	Desert Orchid	S.Sherwood

Most Wins
(Horse):
5 Golden Miller
(Jockey)
4 Pat Taaffe

CHAMPION HURDLE

First run in 1927, the Champion Hurdle is run at Cheltenham during the March Festival. It is run over two miles.

Winners:

Year	Winner	Jockey	Year	Winner	Jockey
1927	Blaris	G.Duller	1958	Bandalore	G.Slack
1928	Brown Jack	L.Rees	1959	Fare Time	F.Winter
1929	Royal Falcon	F.Rees	1960	Another Flash	H.Beasley
1930	Brown Tony	T.Cullinan	1961	Eborneezer	F.Winter
1931	Not held		1962	Anzio	W.Robinson
1932	Insurance	T.Leader	1963	Winning Fair	A.Lillingston
1933	Insurance	W.Stott	1964	Magic Court	P.McCarron
1934	Chenango	D.Morgan	1965	Kirriemuir	G.Robinson
1935	Lion Courage	G.Wilson	1966	Salmon Spray	J.Haine
1936	Victor Norman	H.Nicholson	1967	Saucy Kit	R.Edwards
1937	Free Fare	G.Pellerin	1968	Persian War	J.Uttley
1938	Our Hope	Capt.R.Harding	1969	Persian War	J.Uttley
1939	African Sister	K.Piggott	1970	Persian War	J.Uttley
1940	Solford	S.Magee	1971	Bula	P.Kelleway
1941	Seneca	R.Smyth	1972	Bula	P.Kelleway
1942	Forestation	R.Smyth	1973	Comedy of Errors	K.White
1943–44	Not held		1974	Lanzarote	R.Pitman
1945	Brains Trust	F.Rimell	1975	Comedy of Errors	W.Smith
1946	Distell	R.O'Ryan	1976	Night Nurse	P.Broderick
1947	National Spririt	D.Morgan	1977	Night Nurse	P.Broderick
1948	National Spirit	R.Smyth	1978	Monksfield	T.Kinane
1949	Hatton's Grace	A.Brabazon	1979	Monksfield	D.Hughes
1950	Hatton's Grace	A.Brabazon	1980	Sea Pigeon	J.J.O'Neill
1951	Hatton's Grace	T.Molony	1981	Sea Pigeon	J.Francome
1952	Sir Ken	T.Molony	1982	For Auction	C.Magnier
1953	Sir Ken	T.Molony	1983	Gaye Brief	R.Linley
1954	Sir Ken	T.Molony	1984	Dawn Run	J.J.O'Neill
1955	Clair Soleil	F.Winter	1985	See You Then	S.Smith Eccles
1956	Doorknocker	H.Sprague	1986	See You Then	S.Smith Eccles
1957	Merry Deal	G.Underwood	1987	See You Then	S.Smith Eccles
			1988	Celtic Shot	P.Scudamore
			1989	Beech Road	R.Guest

Most Wins

(Horse):
3 Hatton's Grace, Sir Ken, Persian War, See You Then

(Jockey):
4 Tim Molony

PRIX DE L'ARC DE TRIOMPHE

An end of season test for Europe's top horses, the Prix de l'Arc de Triomphe was established in 1920 and is run over 2400 metres at Longchamps.

Winners:

Year	Horse	Jockey
1920	Comrade	F.Bullock
1921	Ksar	G.Stern
1922	Ksar	F.Bullock
1923	Parth	F.O'Neill
1924	Massine	F.Sharpe
1925	Priori	M.Allemand
1926	Biribi	D.Torterolo
1927	Mon Talisman	C.H.Semblat
1928	Kantar	J. Kettering
1929	Ortello	P.Caprioli
1930	Motrico	M.Fruhinsholtz
1931	Pearl Cap	C.H.Semblat
1932	Motrico	C.H.Semblat
1933	Crapom	P.Caprioli
1934	Brantome	C. Bouillon
1935	Samos	W.Sibbritt
1936	Corrida	E.C.Elliott
1937	Corrida	E.C.Elliott
1938	Eclair au Chocolat	C.Bouillon
1939-40	Not held	
1941	La Pacha	P.Francolon
1942	Djebel	J.Doyasbere
1943	Verso II	G.Duforez
1944	Ardan	J.Doyasbere
1945	Nikellora	W.Johnstone
1946	Caracalla	E.C.Elliott
1947	Le Paillon	F.Rochetti
1948	Migoli	C.Smirke
1949	Coronation	R.Poincelet
1950	Tantieme	J.Doyasbere
1951	Tantieme	J.Doyasbere
1952	Nuccio	R. Poincelet
1953	La Sorellina	M.Larraun
1954	Sica Boy	W.Johnstone
1955	Ribot	E.Camici
1956	Ribot	E.Camici
1957	Oroso	S.Boullenger
1958	Ballymoss	A.Breasley
1959	Saint Crespin	G.Moore
1960	Puissant Chef	M.Garcia
1961	Molvedo	E.Camici
1962	Soltikoff	M.Depalmas
1963	Exbury	J.Deforge
1964	Prince Royal II	R.Poincelet
1965	Sea Bird II	T.P.Glennon
1966	Bon Mot	F.Head
1967	Topyo	W.Pyers
1968	Vaguely Noble	W.Williamson
1969	Levmoss	W.Williamson
1970	Sassafras	Y.Saint-Martin
1971	Mill Reef	G.Lewis
1972	San San	F.Head
1973	Rheingold	L.Piggott
1974	Allez France	Y.Saint-Martin

Prix de L'Arc de Triomphe cont.

Year	Winner	Jockey
1975	Star Appeal	G.Starkey
1976	Ivanjica	F.Head
1977	Alleged	L.Piggott
1978	Alleged	L.Piggott
1979	Three Troikas	F.Head
1980	Detriot	P.Eddery
1981	Gold River	G.W.Moore
1982	Akiyda	Y.Saint-Martin
1983	All Along	W.Swinburn
1984	Sagace	Y.Saint-Martin
1985	Rainbow Quest	P.Eddery
1986	Dancing Brave	P.Eddery
1987	Trempolino	P.Eddery
1988	Tony Bin	J.Reid

Most Wins
(Horse):
2 Ksar, Motrico, Corrida, Tantieme, Ribot, Alleged
(Jockey):
4 Jacko Doyasbere, Freddy Head, Yves Saint-Martin

Prior to 1972 only six fillies had won the Arc. Since then, however, there have been EIGHT winners from the female species. The full list of fillies who have won the race is: Pearl Cap (1931), Samos (1935), Corrida (1936-7), Nikellora (1945), Coronation (1949), La Sorellina (1953), San San (1972), Allez France (1974), Ivanjica (1976), Three Troikas (1979), Detroit (1980), Gold River (1981), Akiyda (1982), All Along (1983).

THE BREEDERS' CUP

After the Triple Crown, the Breeders' Cup is the most important series of races in the United States. Conducted throughout the season, the leading horses gather for one meeting at the end of the season (November) and race for total prize money of $10 million. The leading race is the Breeders' Cup Classic with $3 million prize money. The series was inaugurated in 1984.

Winners:

Year	Winner	Jockey	Year	Winner	Jockey

BREEDERS' CUP SPRINT (6f)   **BREEDERS' CUP DISTAFF (1¼m)**

Year	Winner	Jockey	Year	Winner	Jockey
1984	Ellio	C.Perret	1984	Princess Rooney	E.Delahoussaye
1985	Precisionist	C.McCarron	1985	Life's Magic	A.Cordero
1986	Smile	J.Vasquez	1986	Lady's Secret	P.Day
1987	Very Subtle	P.Valenzuela	1987	Sacahuista	R.Romero
1988	Gulch	A.Cordero	1988	Personal Ensign	R.Romero

BREEDERS' CUP MILE   **BREEDERS' CUP CLASSIC (1¼m)**

Year	Winner	Jockey	Year	Winner	Jockey
1984	Royal Heroine	F.Toro	1984	Wild Again	P.Day
1985	Cozzene	W.Guerra	1985	Proud Truth	J.Velasquez
1986	Last Tycon	Y.St.Martin	1986	Skywalker	L.Pincay
1987	Miesque	F.Head	1987	Ferdinand	W.Shoemaker
1988	Miesque	F.Head	1988	Alysheba	C.McCarron

BREEDERS' CUP JUVENILE (1m 1f)   **BREEDERS' CUP TURF (1½m)**

Year	Winner	Jockey	Year	Winner	Jockey
1984	Chiefs Crown	D.MacBeth	1984	Lashkari	Y.St.Martin
1985	Tasso	L.Pincay	1985	Pebbles	P.Eddery
1986	Capote	L.Pincay	1986	Manila	J.Santos
1987	Success Express	J.Santos	1987	Theatrical	P.Day
1988	Is It True?	L.Pincay	1988	Great Communicator	R.Sibille

BREEDERS' CUP JUVENILE FILLIES (1m 1f)

Year	Winner	Jockey
1984	Outstandingly	W.Guerra
1985	Twilight Ridge	J.Velasquez
1986	Brave Raj	P.Valenzuela
1987	Epitome	P.Day
1988	Open Mind	A.Cordero

Most Wins
(Horse):
2 Miesque
(Jockey):
4 Laffit Pincay jnr; Pat Day

CHAMPION JOCKEYS (NATIONAL HUNT)

The following is a list of champion National Hunt jockeys in Britain, together with their winning totals, since 1900. Prior to the 1925–26 season the figure was taken for the calendar year but it was then changed to encompass the riding season.

Year	Jockey	Winners	Year	Jockey	Winners
1900	Mr.H.S.Sidney	53	1945–46	T.F.Rimell	54
1901	F.Mason	58	1946–47	J.Dowdeswell	58
1902	F.Mason	67	1947–48	B.Marshall	66
1903	P.Woodland	54	1948–49	T.Molony	60
1904	F.Mason	59	1949–50	T.Molony	95
1905	F.Mason	73	1950–51	T.Molony	83
1906	F.Mason	58	1951–52	T.Molony	99
1907	F.Mason	59	1952–53	F.Winter	121
1908	P.Cowley	65	1953–54	R.Francis	76
1909	R.Gordon	45	1954–55	T.Molony	67
1910	E.Piggott	67	1955–56	F.Winter	74
1911	W.Payne	76	1956–57	F.Winter	80
1912	I.Anthony	78	1957–58	F.Winter	82
1913	E.Piggott	60	1958–59	T.Brookshaw	83
1914	Mr.J.R.Anthony	60	1959–60	S.Mellor	68
1915	E.Piggott	44	1960–61	S.Mellor	118
1916	C.Hawkins	17	1961–62	S.Mellor	80
1917	W.Smith	15	1962–63	J.Gifford	70
1918	G.Duller	17	1963–64	J.Gifford	94
1919	Mr.H.Brown	48	1964–65	T.Biddlecombe	114
1920	F.B.Rees	64	1965–66	T.Biddlecombe	102
1921	F.B.Rees	65	1966–67	J.Gifford	122
1922	J.Anthony	78	1967–68	J.Gifford	82
1923	F.B.Rees	64	1968–69	B.R.Davies	77
1924	F.B.Rees	108		T.Biddlecombe	77
1925	E.Foster	76	1969–70	B.R.Davies	91
1925–26	T.Leader	61	1970–71	G.Thorner	74
1926–27	F.B.Rees	59	1971–72	B.R.Davies	89
1927–28	W.Stott	88	1972–73	R.Barry	125
1928–29	W.Stott	76	1973–74	R.Barry	94
1929–30	W.Stott	77	1974–75	T.Stack	82
1930–31	W.Stott	81	1975–76	J.Francome	96
1931–32	W.Stott	77	1976–77	T.Stack	97
1932–33	G.Wilson	61	1977–78	J.J.O'Neill	149
1933–34	G.Wilson	56	1978–79	J.Francome	95
1934–35	G.Wilson	73	1979–80	J.J.O'Neill	115
1935–36	G.Wilson	57	1980–81	J.Francome	105
1936–37	G.Wilson	45	1981–82	J.Francome	120
1937–38	G.Wilson	59		P.Scudamore	120
1938–39	T.F.Rimell	61	1982–83	J.Francome	106
1939–40	T.F.Rimell	24	1983–84	J.Francome	131
1940–41	G.Wilson	22	1984–85	J.Francome	101
1941–42	R.Smyth	12	1985–86	P.Scudamore	91
1942–44	Not held		1986–87	P.Scudamore	123
1944–45	H.Nicholson	15	1987-88	P.Scudamore	132
	T.F.Rimell	15			

Most Times Champion:
7 John Francome, Gerry Wilson
Most Wins In Season:
149 J.J.O'Neill

CHAMPION JOCKEYS (FLAT)

The following is a list of Champion Jockeys on the flat in Britain since 1900, showing the number of winners each has ridden

Year	Champion	Winners	Year	Champion	Winners
1900	L.Reiff	143	1943	G.Richards	65
1901	O.Madden	130	1944	G.Richards	88
1902	W.Lane	170	1945	G.Richards	104
1903	O.Madden	154	1946	G.Richards	212
1904	O.Madden	161	1947	G.Richards	269
1905	E.Wheatley	124	1948	G.Richards	224
1906	W.Higgs	149	1949	G.Richards	261
1907	W.Higgs	146	1950	G.Richards	201
1908	D.Maher	139	1951	G.Richards	227
1909	F.Wootton	165	1952	G.Richards	231
1910	F.Wootton	137	1953	G.Richards	191
1911	F.Wootton	187	1954	D.Smith	129
1912	F.Wootton	118	1955	D.Smith	168
1913	D.Maher	115	1956	D.Smith	155
1914	S.Donoghue	129	1957	A.Breasley	173
1915	S.Donoghue	62	1958	D.Smith	165
1916	S.Donoghue	43	1959	D.Smith	157
1917	S.Donoghue	42	1960	L.Piggott	170
1918	S.Donoghue	66	1961	A.Breasley	171
1919	S.Donoghue	129	1962	A.Breasley	179
1920	S.Donoghue	143	1963	A.Breasley	176
1921	S.Donoghue	141	1964	L.Piggott	140
1922	S.Donoghue	102	1965	L.Piggott	166
1923	S.Donoghue	89	1966	L.Piggott	191
	C.Elliott	89	1967	L.Piggott	117
1924	C.Elliott	106	1968	L.Piggott	139
1925	G.Richards	118	1969	L.Piggott	163
1926	T.Weston	95	1970	L.Piggott	162
1927	G.Richards	164	1971	L.Piggott	162
1928	G.Richards	148	1972	W.Carson	132
1929	G.Richards	135	1973	W.Carson	163
1930	F.Fox	129	1974	P.Eddery	148
1931	G.Richards	145	1975	P.Eddery	164
1932	G.Richards	190	1976	P.Eddery	162
1933	G.Richards	259	1977	P.Eddery	176
1934	G.Richards	212	1978	W.Carson	182
1935	G.Richards	217	1979	J.Mercer	164
1936	G.Richards	174	1980	W.Carson	165
1937	G.Richards	216	1981	L.Piggott	179
1938	G.Richards	200	1982	L.Piggott	188
1939	G.Richards	155	1983	W.Carson	159
1940	G.Richards	68	1984	S.Cauthen	130
1941	H.Wragg	71	1985	S.Cauthen	195
1942	G.Richards	67	1986	P.Eddery	177
			1987	S.Cauthen	197
			1988	P.Eddery	183

Most Times Champion:
26 Gordon Richards
Most Wins In Season:
269 Gordon Richards

RACING IN AUSTRALIA
MELBOURNE CUP
Like the Epsom Derby, the highlight of the racing calendar in Australia, the Melbourne Cup, is a social occasion. Run on the first Tuesday each November it was first raced in 1861.

Year	Winner	Jockey
1861	Archer	J. Cutts
1862	Archer	J. Cutts
1863	Banker	H. Chifney
1864	Lantern	S. Davis
1865	Toryboy	E. Cavanagh
1866	The Barb	W. Davis
1867	Tim Whiffler	J. Driscoll
1868	Glencoe	C. Stanley
1869	Warrior	J. Morrison
1870	Nimblefoot	J. Day
1871	The Pearl	J. Cavanagh
1872	The Quack	W. Enderson
1873	Don Juan	W. Wilson
1874	Haricot	P. Pigott
1875	Wollomai	R. Batty
1876	Briseis	P. St. Albans
1877	Chester	P. Pigott
1878	Calamia	T. Brown
1879	Darriwell	S. Cracknell
1880	Grand Flaneur	T. Hales
1881	Zulu	James Gough
1882	The Assyrian	C. Hutchens
1883	Martini Henry	J. Williamson
1884	Malua	A. Robertson
1885	Sheet Anchor	M. O'Brien
1886	Arsenal	W. English
1887	Dunlop	T. Sanders
1888	Mentor	M. O'Brien
1889	Bravo	J. Anwin
1890	Carbine	R. Ramage
1891	Malvolio	G. Redfearn
1892	Glenloth	G. Robson
1893	Tarcoola	H. Cripps
1894	Patron	H. Dawes
1895	Auraria	J. Stevenson
1896	Newhaven	H. Gardiner
1897	Gaulus	S. Callinan
1898	The Grafter	John Gough
1899	Merriwee	V. Turner
1900	Clean Sweep	A. Richardson
1901	Revenue	F. Dunn
1902	The Victory	R. Lewis
1903	Lord Cardigan	N. Godby
1904	Acrasia	T. Clayton
1905	Blue Spec	F. Bullock
1906	Poseidon	T. Clayton
1907	Apologue	W. Evans
1908	Lord Nolan	J. Flynn
1909	Prince Foote	W. McLachlan
1910	Comedy King	W. McLachlan
1911	The Parisian	R. Cameron
1912	Piastre	A. Shanahan
1913	Posinatus	A. Shanahan
1914	Kingsburgh	G. Meddick

Year	Winner	Jockey
1915	Patrobas	R. Lewis
1916	Sasanof	F. Foley
1917	Westcourt	W. McLachlan
1918	Night Watch	W. Duncan
1919	Artilleryman	R. Lewis
1920	Poitrel	K. Bracken
1921	Sister Olive	E. O'Sullivan
1922	King Ingoda	A. Wilson
1923	Bitalli	A. Wilson
1924	Backwood	P. Brown
1925	Windbag	J. Munro
1926	Spearfelt	H. Cairns
1927	Trivalve	R. Lewis
1928	Statesman	J. Munro
1929	Nightmarch	R. Reed
1930	Phar Lap	J. Pike
1931	White Nose	N. Percival
1932	Peter Pan	W. Duncan
1933	Hall Mark	J. O'Sullivan
1934	Peter Pan	D. Munro
1935	Marabou	K. Voitre
1936	Wotan	O. Phillips
1937	The Trump	A. Reed
1938	Catalogue	F. Shean
1939	Rivette	E. Preston
1940	Old Rowley	A. Knox
1941	Skipton	W. Cook
1942	Colonus	H. McCloud
1943	Dark Felt	V. Hartney
1944	Sirius	D. Munro
1945	Rainbird	B. Cook
1946	Russia	D. Munro
1947	Hiraji	P. Purtell
1948	Rimfire	R. Neville
1949	Foxzami	W. Fellows
1950	Comic Court	T. P. Glennon
1951	Delta	N. Sellwood
1952	Dalray	W. Williamson
1953	Wodalla	J. Purtell
1954	Rising Fast	J. Purtell
1955	Toparoa	N. Sellwood
1956	Evening Peal	G. Podmore
1957	Straight Draw	N. McGrowdie
1958	Baystone	M. Schumacher
1959	Macdougal	T. P. Glennon
1960	Hi Jinx	W. Smith
1961	Lord Fury	R. Selkrig
1962	Even Stevens	L. Cole
1963	Gatum Gatum	J. Johnson
1964	Polo Prince	R. Taylor
1965	Light Fingers	R. Higgins
1966	Galilee	J. Miller
1967	Red Handed	R. Higgins
1968	Rain Lover	J. Johnson
1969	Rain Lover	J. Johnson
1970	Baghdad Note	E. Didham
1971	Silver Knight	B. Marshall
1972	Piping Lane	J. Letts
1973	Gala Supreme	F. Reys

Melbourne Cup Cont.

Year	Winner	Jockey
1974	Think Big	H. White
1975	Think Big	H. White
1976	Van der Hum	R. Skelton
1977	Gold and Black	J. Duggan
1978	Arwon	H. White
1979	Hyperno	H. White
1980	Beldale Ball	J. Letts
1981	Just a Dash	P. Cook
1982	Gurner's Lane	M. Dittman
1983	Kiwi	J. Cassidy
1984	Black Night	P. Cook
1985	What A Nuisance	P. Hyland
1986	At Talaq	M. Clarke
1987	Kensei	L. Olsen
1988	Empire Rose	T. Allan

MOST WINS: JOCKEY
4. Bobby Lewis, Harry White

MOST WINS: HORSE
2 Archer, Peter Pan, Rain Lover, Think Big

RECORD TIMES:
The record times for the major races are:

Derby:	2:33.80	Mahmoud (1936) [hand timed]
	2.33.84	Kahyasi (1988) [electronically timed]
Oaks:	2:34.21	Time Charter (1982)
St. Leger:	3:01.6	Coronach (1926) and Windsor Lad (1934)
1000 Guineas	1:36.85	Oh So Sharp (1985)
2000 Guineas	1:35.8	My Babu (1948)
Grand National:	9:01.9	Red Rum (1973)

The Derby is named after Lord Derby, but it could well have been called 'The Bunbury', because the name of the race was decided on the toss of a coin between Lord Derby and his great friend Sir Charles Bunbury. Derby won and thus we were saved the embarassment of having the 'English Bunbury', 'French Bunbury' or even the 'Kentucky Bunbury' ... Consolation came for Sir Charles as his horse Diomed won the first running of the new race in 1780.

Hurling has been played in Ireland for more than 600 years and indeed the sport was outlawed in 1367 by the statute of Kilkenny. Standardisation of the rules came about in 1884 following the formation of the Gaelic Athletic Association.

ALL-IRELAND HURLING CHAMPIONSHIPS

The highlight of the Hurling season in Ireland is the All-Ireland final at Croke Park, Dublin, on the first Sunday of September. The winning team receives the McCarthy Cup.

Winners:

1887 Tipperary	1920 Dublin	1953 Cork
1888 Unfinished	1921 Limerick	1954 Cork
1889 Dublin	1922 Kilkenny	1955 Wexford
1890 Cork	1923 Galway	1956 Wexford
1891 Kerry	1924 Dublin	1957 Kilkenny
1892 Cork	1925 Tipperary	1958 Tipperary
1893 Cork	1926 Cork	1959 Waterford
1894 Cork	1927 Dublin	1960 Wexford
1895 Tipperary	1928 Cork	1961 Tipperary
1896 Tipperary	1929 Cork	1962 Tipperary
1897 Limerick	1930 Tipperary	1963 Kilkenny
1898 Tipperary	1931 Cork	1964 Tipperary
1899 Tipperary	1932 Kilkenny	1965 Tipperary
1900 Tipperary	1933 Kilkenny	1966 Cork
1901 London Irish	1934 Limerick	1967 Kilkenny
1902 Cork	1935 Kilkenny	1968 Wexford
1903 Cork	1936 Limerick	1969 Kilkenny
1904 Kilkenny	1937 Tipperary	1970 Cork
1905 Kilkenny	1938 Dublin	1971 Tipperary
1906 Tipperary	1939 Kilkenny	1972 Kilkenny
1907 Kilkenny	1940 Limerick	1973 Limerick
1908 Tipperary	1941 Cork	1974 Kilkenny
1909 Kilkenny	1942 Cork	1975 Kilkenny
1910 Wexford	1943 Cork	1976 Cork
1911 Kilkenny	1944 Cork	1977 Cork
1912 Kilkenny	1945 Tipperary	1978 Cork
1913 Kilkenny	1946 Cork	1979 Kilkenny
1914 Clare	1947 Kilkenny	1980 Galway
1915 Laois	1948 Waterford	1981 Offaly
1916 Tipperary	1949 Tipperary	1982 Kilkenny
1917 Dublin	1950 Tipperary	1983 Kilkenny
1918 Limerick	1951 Tipperary	1984 Cork
1919 Cork	1952 Cork	1985 Offaly
		1986 Cork
		1987 Galway
		1988 Galway

Most Wins:
25 Cork

Most appearances in All-Ireland Final:
    10 Christy Ring (Cork and Munster)
    10 John Doyle (Tipperary)
Most appearances on winning team:
    8 Christy Ring (Cork) 1941-54
    8 John Doyle (Tipperary) 1949-65
Biggest win:
    Cork 39 Wexford 25 (1970)

One of the world's fastest games, Ice Hockey was first played in Canada in the mid-19th century, but several cities claim to have originated the game. By the latter part of the century many leagues had developed throughout Canada and the United States. The US Amateur Hockey League was formed in 1896 and at the turn of the century the sport came to Britain and spread across Europe. The International Ice Hockey Federation was formed in Belgium in 1908.

OLYMPIC GAMES
Ice Hockey was included in the Summer Olympics at Antwerp in 1920 but since 1924 it has been included in the Winter Olympics programme.

Winners:

1920 Canada	1960 United States
1924 Canada	1964 USSR
1928 Canada	1968 USSR
1932 Canada	1972 USSR
1936 Great Britain	1976 USSR
1948 Canada	1980 United States
1952 Canada	1984 USSR
1956 USSR	1988 USSR

Most Wins:
7 USSR

WORLD CHAMPIONSHIPS
In 1920, 1924 and 1928 the Olympic champions were also classed as World Champions. A separate World Championship has existed since 1930 and in Olympic years between 1932-68 the Olympic champions were also World Champions. Since 1980 there have been no championships in Olympic years.

Winners:

1920 Canada	1956 USSR
1924 Canada	1957 Sweden
1928 Canada	1958 Canada
1930 Canada	1959 Canada
1931 Canada	1960 United States
1932 Canada	1961 Canada
1933 United States	1962 Sweden
1934 Canada	1963 USSR
1935 Canada	1964 USSR
1936 Great Britain	1965 USSR
1937 Canada	1966 USSR
1938 Canada	1967 USSR
1939 Canada	1968 USSR
1947 Czechoslovakia	1969 USSR
1948 Canada	1970 USSR
1949 Czechoslovakia	1971 USSR
1950 Canada	1972 Czechoslovakia
1951 Canada	1973 USSR
1952 Canada	1974 USSR
1953 Sweden	1975 USSR
1954 USSR	1976 Czechoslovakia
1955 Canada	

1977 Czechoslovakia	1983 USSR
1978 USSR	1985 Czechoslovakia
1979 USSR	1986 USSR
1981 USSR	1987 Sweden
1982 USSR	

Most Wins:

20 USSR

STANLEY CUP

The Stanley Cup was presented by Canada's Governor-General Lord Stanley in 1893. It was originally a trophy for the Amateur Championship of Canada but since 1910 it has been presented to the winning team in the National Hockey Association League.

Winners:

1893–94 Montreal AAA	1932–33 New York Rangers
1894–95 Montreal Victorias	1933–34 Chicago Black Hawks
1895–96 Montreal Victorias	1934–35 Montreal Maroons
1896–97 Montreal Victorias	1935–36 Detroit Red Wings
1897–98 Montreal Victorias	1936–37 Detroit Red Wings
1898–99 Montreal Victorias	1937–38 Chicago Black Hawks
1899–00 Montreal Shamrocks	1938–39 Boston Bruins
1900–01 Winnipeg Victorias	1939–40 New York Rangers
1901–02 Montreal AAA	1940–41 Boston Bruins
1902–03 Ottawa Silver Seven	1941–42 Toronto Maple Leafs
1903–04 Ottawa Silver Seven	1942–43 Detroit Red Wings
1904–05 Ottawa Silver Seven	1943–44 Montreal Canadiens
1905–06 Montreal Wanderers	1944–45 Toronto Maple Leafs
1906–07 Kenora Thistles	1945–46 Montreal Canadiens
1906–07 Montreal Wanderers	1946–47 Toronto Maple Leafs
(Cup contested twice in 1906–07)	1947–48 Toronto Maple Leafs
1907–08 Montreal Wanderers	1948–49 Toronto Maple Leafs
1908–09 Ottawa Senators	1949–50 Detroit Red Wings
1909–10 Montreal Wanderers	1950–51 Toronto Maple Leafs
1910–11 Ottawa Senators	1951–52 Detroit Red Wings
1911–12 Quebec Bulldogs	1952–53 Montreal Canadiens
1912–13 Quebec Bulldogs	1953–54 Detroit Red Wings
1913–14 Toronto Ontarios	1954–55 Detroit Red Wings
1914–15 Vancouver Millionaires	1955–56 Montreal Canadiens
1915–16 Montreal Canadiens	1956–57 Montreal Canadiens
1916–17 Seattle Metropolitans	1957–58 Montreal Canadiens
1917–18 Toronto Arenas	1958–59 Montreal Canadiens
1918–19 Not held	1959–60 Montreal Canadiens
1919–20 Ottawa Senators	1960–61 Chicago Black Hawks
1920–21 Ottawa Senators	1961–62 Toronto Maple Leafs
1921–22 Toronto St.Patricks	1962–63 Toronto Maple Leafs
1922–23 Ottawa Senators	1963–64 Toronto Maple Leafs
1923–24 Montreal Canadiens	1964–65 Montreal Canadiens
1924–25 Victoria Cougars	1965–66 Montreal Canadiens
1925–26 Montreal Maroons	1966–67 Toronto Maple Leafs
1926–27 Ottawa Senators	1967–68 Montreal Canadiens
1927–28 New York Rangers	1968–69 Montreal Canadiens
1928–29 Boston Bruins	1969–70 Boston Bruins
1929–30 Montreal Canadiens	1970–71 Montreal Canadiens
1930–31 Montreal Canadiens	1971–72 Boston Bruins
1931–32 Toronto Maple Leafs	1972–73 Montreal Canadiens

1973–74 Philadelphia Flyers
1974–75 Philadelphia Flyers
1975–76 Montreal Canadiens
1976–77 Montreal Canadiens
1977–78 Montreal Canadiens
1978–79 Montreal Canadiens
1979–80 New York Islanders

1980–81 New York Islanders
1981–82 New York Islanders
1982–83 New York Islanders
1983–84 Edmonton Oilers
1984–85 Edmonton Oilers
1985–86 Montreal Canadiens
1986–87 Edmonton Oilers
1987-88 Edmonton Oilers

Most Wins:
23 Montreal Canadiens

BRITISH CLUB CHAMPIONSHIP

The British Club Championship was introduced in 1982 and is a play-off involving the leading teams in the British League.

Winners:
1982 Dundee Rockets
1983 Dundee Rockets
1984 Dundee Rockets

1985 Fife Flyers
1986 Murrayfield Racers
1987 Durham Wasps

Most Wins:
3 Dundee Rockets

Several tennis players have represented their country at Ice Hockey. Ilie Nastase played for Romania and Jaroslav Drobny won a silver medal with the Czechoslovakian team at the 1948 Winter Olympics. But Ion Tiriac can go one better...in addition to playing Ice Hockey for his country, he has driven in the Monte Carlo Rally!

Although reference has been made to Ice Skating going back more than 1500 years, the first skating club was the Edinburgh Skating Club which was formed around 1742. The sport's governing body, the International Skating Union, was formed in 1892, sixteen years after the building of the first mechanically refrigerated ice rink at the Glaciarium, King's Road, Chelsea.

OLYMPIC GAMES
Figure skating was first included in the 1908 London Olympic Games.

Winners:
Figure Skating

Men	Women
1908 U.Salchow (SWE)	M.Syers (GB)
1920 G.Grafstrom (SWE)	M.Julin-Mauroy (SWE)
1924 G.Grafstrom (SWE)	H.Planck-Szabo (AUT)
1928 G.Grafstrom (SWE)	S.Henie (NOR)
1932 K.Schafer (AUT)	S.Henie (NOR)
1936 K.Schafer (AUT)	S.Henie (NOR)
1948 R.Button (USA)	B.Scott (CAN)
1952 R.Button (USA)	J.Altwegg (GB)
1956 H.A.Jenkins (USA)	T.Albright (USA)
1960 D.Jenkins (USA)	C.Heiss (USA)
1964 M.Schnelldorfer (GER)	S.Dijkstra (HOL)
1968 W.Schwarz (AUT)	P.Fleming (USA)
1972 O.Nepela (TCH)	B.Schuba (AUT)
1976 J.Curry (GB)	D.Hamill (USA)
1980 R.Cousins (GB)	A.Potzsch (GDR)
1984 S.Hamilton (USA)	K.Witt (GDR)
1988 B.Boitano (USA)	K.Witt (GDR)

Most Wins

(Men):	(Women):
3 Gillis Grafstrom	3 Sonja Henie

Pairs

1908 A.Hubler/H.Burger (GER)	1956 E.Schwarz/K.Oppelt (AUT)
1920 L.Jakobsson/W.Jakobsson (FIN)	1960 B.Wagner/R.Paul (CAN)
1924 H.Engelmann/A.Berger (AUT)	1964 L.Belousova/O.Protopopov (USSR)
1928 A.Joly/P.Brunet (FRA)	1968 L.Belousova/O.Protopopov (USSR)
1932 A.Brunet/P.Brunet (FRA)	1972 I.Rodnina/A.Ulanov (USSR)
1936 M.Herber/E.Baier (GER)	1976 I.Rodnina/A.Zaitsev (USSR)
1948 M.Lannoy/P.Baugniet (BEL)	1980 I.Rodnina/A.Zaitsev (USSR)
1952 R.Falk/P.Falk (GER)	1984 E.Valova/O.Vasiliev (USSR)
	1988 E.Gordeyeva/S.Grinlov (USSR)

Most Wins
3 Irina Rodnina

Dance
1976 L.Pakhomova/A.Gorshkov (USSR)
1980 N.Linichuck/G.Karponosov (USSR)
1984 J.Torvill/C.Dean (GB)
1988 N.Bestemianova/A.Bukin (USSR)

WORLD CHAMPIONSHIPS
The first World Championships were held at St.Petersburg (now Leningrad) in 1896.

Figure Skating

Men	Women
1896 G.Fuchs (GER)	–
1897 G.Hugel (AUT)	–
1898 H.Grenander (SWE)	–
1899 G.Hugel (AUT)	–
1900 G.Hugel (AUT)	–
1901 U.Salchow (SWE)	–
1902 U.Salchow (SWE)	–
1903 U.Salchow (SWE)	–
1904 U.Salchow (SWE)	–
1905 U.Salchow (SWE)	–
1906 G.Fuchs (GER)	M.Syers (GB)
1907 U.Salchow (SWE)	M.Syers (GB)
1908 U.Salchow (SWE)	L.Kronberger (HUN)
1909 U.Salchow (SWE)	L.Kronberger (HUN)
1910 U.Salchow (SWE)	L.Kronberger (HUN)
1911 U.Salchow (SWE)	L.Kronberger (HUN)
1912 F.Kachler (AUT)	M.Horvath (HUN)
1913 F.Kachler (AUT)	M.Horvath (HUN)
1914 G.Sandhal (SWE)	M.Horvath (HUN)
1915–21 Not held	
1922 G.Grafstrom (SWE)	H.Plank (AUT)
1923 F.Kachler (AUT)	H.Plank (AUT)
1924 G.Grafstrom (SWE)	H.Plank (AUT)
1925 W.Bockl (AUT)	J.Szabo (AUT)
1926 W.Bockl (AUT)	J.Szabo (AUT)
1927 W.Bockl (AUT)	S.Henie (NOR)
1928 W.Bockl (AUT)	S.Henie (NOR)
1929 G.Grafstrom (SWE)	S.Henie (NOR)
1930 K.Schafer (AUT)	S.Henie (NOR)
1931 K.Schafer (AUT)	S.Henie (NOR)
1932 K.Schafer (AUT)	S.Henie (NOR)
1933 K.Schafer (AUT)	S.Henie (NOR)
1934 K.Schafer (AUT)	S.Henie (NOR)
1935 K.Schafer (AUT)	S.Henie (NOR)
1936 K.Schafer (AUT)	S.Henie (NOR)
1937 F.Kaspar (AUT)	C.Colledge (GB)
1938 F.Kaspar (AUT)	M.Taylor (GB)
1939 G.Sharp (GB)	M.Taylor (GB)
1940–46 Not held	
1947 H.Gerschwiler (SWI)	B.Scott (CAN)
1948 R.Button (USA)	B.Scott (CAN)
1949 R.Button (USA)	A.Vrzanova (TCH)
1950 R.Button (USA)	A.Vrzanova (TCH)
1951 R.Button (USA)	J.Altwegg (GB)
1952 R.Button (USA)	J. du Bief (FRA)
1953 H.Jenkins (USA)	T.Albright (USA)
1954 H.Jenkins (USA)	G.Busch (GER)
1955 H.Jenkins (USA)	T.Albright (USA)
1956 H.Jenkins (USA)	C.Heiss (USA)
1957 D.Jenkins (USA)	C.Heiss (USA)
1958 D.Jenkins (USA)	C.Heiss (USA)
1959 D.Jenkins (USA)	C.Heiss (USA)
1960 A.Giletti (FRA)	C.Heiss (USA)
1961 Not held	
1962 D.Jackson (CAN)	S.Dijkstra (HOL)

1963 D.McPherson (CAN)	S.Dijkstra (HOL)
1964 M.Schnelldorfer (GER)	S.Dijkstra (HOL)
1965 A.Calmat (FRA)	P.Burka (CAN)
1966 E.Danzer (AUT)	P.Fleming (USA)
1967 E.Danzer (AUT)	P.Fleming (USA)
1968 E.Danzer (AUT)	P.Fleming (USA)
1969 T.Wood (USA)	G.Seyfert (GDR)
1970 T.Wood (USA)	G.Seyfert (GDR)
1971 O.Nepela (TCH)	B.Schuba (AUT)
1972 O.Nepela (TCH)	B.Schuba (AUT)
1973 O.Nepela (TCH)	K.Magnussen (CAN)
1974 J.Hoffmann (GDR)	C.Errath (GDR)
1975 S.Volkov (USSR)	D.de Leeuw (HOL)
1976 J.Curry (GB)	D.Hamill (USA)
1977 V.Kovalyev (USSR)	L.Fratianne (USA)
1978 C.Tickner (USA)	A.Potzsch (GDR)
1979 V.Kovalyev (USSR)	L.Fratianne (USA)
1980 J.Hoffmann (GDR)	A.Potzsch (GDR)
1981 S.Hamilton (USA)	D.Biellmann (SWI)
1982 S.Hamilton (USA)	E.Zayak (USA)
1983 S.Hamilton (USA)	R.Sumners (USA)
1984 S.Hamilton (USA)	K.Witt (GDR)
1985 A.Fadeev (USSR)	K.Witt (GDR)
1986 B.Boitano (USA)	D.Thomas (USA)
1987 B.Orser (CAN)	K.Witt (GDR)
1988 B.Boitano (USA)	K.Witt (GDR)
1989 K.Browning (CAN)	M.Ito (JAP)

Most Wins

(Men): **(Women):**
10 Ulrich Salchow 10 Sonja Henie

Pairs

1908 F.Hubler/H.Burger (GER)	1947 M.Lannoy/P.Baugniet (BEL)
1909 P.Johnson/J.Johnson (GB)	1948 M.Lannoy/P.Baugniet (BEL)
1910 F.Hubler/H.Burger (GER)	1949 A.Kekessy/A.Kiraly (HUN)
1911 L.Eilers/W.Jakobsson (FIN)	1950 K.Kennedy/P.Kennedy (USA)
1912 J.Johnson/J.Johnson (GB)	1951 R.Baran/P.Falk (GER)
1913 H.Engelmann/K.Mejscrik (AUT)	1952 R.Falk/P.Falk (GER)
1914 L.Jakobsson/W.Jakobsson (FIN)	1953 J.Nicks/J.Nicks (GB)
1915-21 Not held	1954 F.Dafoe/N.Bowden (CAN)
1922 N.Engelmann/H.Berger (AUT)	1955 F.Dafoe/N.Bowden (CAN)
1923 L.Jakobsson/W.Jakobsson (FIN)	1956 S.Schwarz/K.Oppelt (AUT)
1924 H.Englemann/H.Berger (AUT)	1957 B.Wagner/R.Paul (CAN)
1925 J.Szabo/L.Wrede (AUT)	1958 B.Wagner/R.Paul (CAN)
1926 A.Joly/P.Brunet (FRA)	1959 B.Wagner/R.Paul (CAN)
1927 J.Szabo/L.Wrede (AUT)	1960 B.Wagner/R.Paul (CAN)
1928 A.Joly/P.Brunet (FRA)	1961 Not held
1929 L.Scholz/O.Kaiser (AUT)	1962 M.Jelinek/O.Jelinek (CAN)
1930 A.Brunet/P.Brunet (FRA)	1963 M.Kilius/H-G.Baumler (FRG)
1931 E.Rotter/L.Szollas (HUN)	1964 M.Kilius/H-G.Baumler (FRG)
1932 A.Brunet/P.Brunet (FRA)	1965 L.Protopopov/O.Protopopov (USSR)
1933 E.Rotter/L.Szollas (HUN)	1966 L.Protopopov/O.Protopopov (USSR)
1934 E.Rotter/L.Szollas (HUN)	1967 L.Protopopov/O.Protopopov (USSR)
1935 E.Rotter/L.Szollas (HUN)	1968 L.Protopopov/O.Protopopov (USSR)
1936 M.Herber/E.Baier (GER)	1969 I.Rodnina/A.Ulanov (USSR)
1937 M.Herber/E.Baier (GER)	1970 I.Rodnina/A.Ulanov (USSR)
1938 M.Herber/E.Baier (GER)	1971 I.Rodnina/A.Ulanov (USSR)
1939 M.Herber/E.Baier (GER)	1972 I.Rodnina/A.Ulanov (USSR)
1940–46 Not held	1973 I.Rodnina/A.Zaitsev (USSR)

World Championship Winners Cont.

1974 I.Rodnina/A.Zaitsev (USSR)
1975 I.Rodnina/A.Zaitsev (USSR)
1976 I.Rodnina/A.Zaitsev (USSR)
1977 I.Rodnina/A.Zaitsev (USSR)
1978 I.Rodnina/A.Zaitsev (USSR)
1979 T.Babilonia/R.Gardner (USA)
1980 M.Tcherkasova/S.Shakrai (USSR)

1981 I.Vorobyeva/I.Lisovsky (USSR)
1982 S.Baess/T.Thierbach (GDR)
1983 E.Valova/O.Vasiliev (USSR)
1984 E.Valova/O.Vasiliev (USSR)
1985 E.Valova/O.Vasiliev (USSR)
1986 E.Gordeeva/S.Grinkov (USSR)
1987 E.Gordeeva/S.Grinkov (USSR)
1988 E.Valova/O.Vasiliev (USSR)
1989 E.Gordeeva/S.Grinkov (USSR)

Most Wins:
10 Irina Rodnina

Dance

1950 L.Waring/M.McGean (USA)
1951 J.Westwood/L.Demmy (GB)
1952 J.Westwood/L.Demmy (GB)
1953 J.Westwood/L.Demmy (GB)
1954 J.Westwood/L.Demmy (GB)
1955 J.Westwood/L.Demmy (GB)
1956 P.Weight/P.Thomas (GB)
1957 J.Markham/C.Jones (GB)
1958 J.Markham/C.Jones (GB)
1959 D.Denny/C.Jones (GB)
1960 D.Denny/C.Jones (GB)
1961 Not held
1962 E.Romanova/P.Roman (TCH)
1963 E.Romanova/P.Roman (TCH)
1964 E.Romanova/P.Roman (TCH)
1965 E.Romanova/P.Roman (TCH)
1966 D.Towler/B.Ford (GB)
1967 D.Towler/B.Ford (GB)
1968 D.Towler/B.Ford (GB)

1969 D.Towler/B.Ford (GB)
1970 L.Pakhomova/A.Gorshkov (USSR)
1971 L.Pakhomova/A.Gorshkov (USSR)
1972 L.Pakhomova/A.Gorshkov (USSR)
1973 L.Pakhomova/A.Gorshkov (USSR)
1974 L.Pakhomova/A.Gorshkov (USSR)
1975 I.Moiseyeva/A.Minenkov (USSR)
1976 L.Pakhomova/A.Gorshkov (USSR)
1977 I.Moiseyeva/A.Minenkov (USSR)
1978 N.Linichuk/G.Karponosov (USSR)
1979 N.Linichuk/G.Karponosov (USSR)
1980 K.Regoczy/A.Sallay (HUN)
1981 J.Torvill/C.Dean (GB)
1982 J.Torvill/C.Dean (GB)
1983 J.Torvill/C.Dean (GB)
1984 J.Torvill/C.Dean (GB)
1985 N.Bestemianova/A.Bukin (USSR)
1986 N.Bestemianova/A.Bukin (USSR)
1987 N.Bestemianova/A.Bukin (USSR)
1988 N.Bestemianova/A.Bukin (USSR)

Most Wins:
6 Ludmila Pakhomova, Alexsandr Gorshkov

One of the many sports that have developed from the Japanese martial arts, Judo was devised by Jigoro Kano in 1882. The International Judo Federation was formed in 1951.

WORLD CHAMPIONSHIPS
The first three World Championships only consisted of an Open class. When the championship became a biennial event in 1965 six classes were introduced and in 1979 the weight divisions were altered to provide eight classes. There was no championship in 1977.

Winners:

Open
1956 S.Natsui (JAP)
1958 K.Sone (JAP)
1961 A.Geesink (HOL)
1965 I.Inokuma (JAP)
1967 M.Matsunaga (JAP)
1969 M.Shinomaki (JAP)
1971 M.Shinomaki (JAP)
1963 K.Ninomiya (JAP)
1975 H.Uemura (JAP)
1979 S.Endo (JAP)
1981 Y.Yamashita (JAP)
1983 A.Parisi (FRA)
1985 Y.Masaki (JAP)
1987 N.Ogawa (JAP)

Over 95kg
1965 A.Geesink (HOL)
1967 W.Ruska (HOL)
1969 S.Suma (JAP)
1971 W.Ruska (HOL)
1973 C.Tagaki (JAP)
1975 S.Endo (JAP)
1979 Y.Yamashita (JAP)
1981 Y.Yamashita (JAP)
1983 Y.Yamashita (JAP)
1985 Y.C.Cho (SKO)
1987 G.Vertichev (USSR)

Under 95kg
1967 N.Sato (JAP)
1969 F.Sasahara (JAP)
1971 F.Sasahara (JAP)
1973 N.Sato (JAP)
1975 J-L.Rouge (FRA)
1979 T.Khubuluri (USSR)
1981 T.Khubuluri (USSR)
1983 V.Divisenko (USSR)
1985 H.Sugai (JAP)
1987 H.Sugai (JAP)

Under 86kg
1965 I.Okano (JAP)
1967 E.Maruki (JAP)
1969 I.Sonoda (JAP)
1971 S.Fujii (JAP)
1973 S.Fujii (JAP)
1975 S.Fujii (JAP)
1979 D.Ultsch (GDR)
1981 B.Tchoullouyan (FRA)
1983 D.Ultsch (GDR)
1985 P.Seisenbacher (AUT)
1987 F.Canu (FRA)

Under 78kg
1967 H.Minatoya (JAP)
1969 H.Minatoya (JAP)
1971 H.Tsuzawa (JAP)
1973 K.Nomura (JAP)
1975 V.Nevzorov (USSR)
1979 S.Fujii (JAP)
1981 N.Adams (GB)
1983 N.Hikage (JAP)
1985 N.Hikage (JAP)
1987 H.Okada (JAP)

Under 71kg
1965 H.Matsuda (JAP)
1967 T.Shigeokoa (JAP)
1969 Y.Sonoda (JAP)
1971 T.Kawaguchi (JAP)
1973 Y.Minamo (JAP)
1975 Y.Minamo (JAP)
1979 K.Katsuki (JAP)
1981 Chong Hak Park (SKO)
1983 H.Nakanichi (JAP)
1985 A.Byeong-Keun (SKO)
1987 M.Swain (USA)

Under 65kg
1979 N.Soludukhin (USSR)
1981 K.Kashiwazaki (JAP)
1983 N.Soludukhin (USSR)
1985 Y.Sokolov (USSR)
1987 H.Yamamoto (JAP)

Under 60kg
1965 H.Minatoya (JAP)
1967 T.Shigeoka (JAP)
1969 Y.Sonoda (JAP)
1971 T.Kawaguchi (JAP)
1973 Y.Minamo (JAP)
1975 Y.Minamo (JAP)
1979 T.Ray (FRA)
1981 Y.Moriwaki (JAP)
1983 K.Tletseri (USSR)
1985 S.Hosokawa (JAP)
1987 J.Kim (SKO)

Most Titles:
4 Yasuhiro Yamashita, Shozo Fujii

OLYMPIC GAMES

Judo was introduced into the Olympic programme in 1964 but was not included four years later. It was reintroduced in 1972. Women had a judo competition in 1988 but only as a demonstration sport. The weight divisions were changed for the 1980 Games to make eight categories. The Open category was dropped in 1988.

Winners:

Open
1964 A.Geesink (HOL)
1972 W.Ruska (HOL)
1976 H.Uemura (JAP)
1980 D.Lorenz (GDR)
1984 Y.Yamashita (JAP)

Over 95kg
1964 I.Inokuma (JAP)
1972 W.Ruska (HOL)
1976 S.Novikov (USSR)
1980 A.Parisi (FRA)
1984 H.Saito (JAP)
1988 H.Saito (JAP)

Under 95kg
1972 S.Chochoshvili (USSR)
1976 K.Ninomiya (JAP)
1980 R.Van de Walle (BEL)
1984 Hyung-Zoo (SKO)
1988 A.Miguel (BRA)

Under 86kg
1964 I.Okano (JAP)
1972 S.Sekine (JAP)
1976 I.Sonoda (JAP)
1980 J.Rothlisberger (SWI)
1984 P.Seisnenbacher (AUT)
1988 P.Seisenbacher (AUT)

Under 78kg
1972 T.Nomura (JAP)
1976 V.Nevzorov (USSR)
1980 S.Khabareli (USSR)
1984 S.Weineke (FRG)
1988 W.Legien (POL)

Under 71kg
1964 T.Nakatani (JAP)
1972 T.Kawaguchi (JAP)
1976 H.Rodriguez Torres (CUB)
1980 E.Gamba (ITA)
1984 B.Yeong Kuen Ahn (SKO)
1988 M.Alexandre (FRA)

Under 65kg
1980 N.Solodukhin (USSR)
1984 Y.Matsuoka (JAP)
1988 K -K.Lee (SKO)

Under 60kg
1980 T.Rey (FRA)
1984 S.Hosokawa (JAP)
1988 J -Y.Kim (SKO)

Most Titles:
2 Wim Ruska, Hitoshi Saito,
Peter Seisenbacher

WOMENS' WORLD CHAMPIONSHIPS

Open
1980 I.Berghmans (BEL)
1982 I.Berghmans (BEL)
1984 I.Berghmans (BEL)
1986 I.Berghmans (BEL)
1987 F.Gao (CHN)

Over 72kg
1980 M.de Cal (ITA)
1982 N.Lupino (FRA)
1984 M -T.Motta (ITA)
1986 F.Gao (CHN)
1987 F.Gao (CHN)

Under 72kg
1980 J.Triadou (FRA)
1982 B.Classen (FRG)
1984 I.Berghmans (BEL)
1986 I.de Kok (HOL)
1987 I.de Kok (HOL)

Under 66kg
1980 E.Simon (AUT)
1982 B.Deydier (FRA)
1984 B.Deydier (FRA)
1986 B.Deydier (FRA)
1987 A.Schreiber (FRG)

Most Titles:
5 Ingrid Berghmans

Under 61kg
1980 A.Staps (HOL)
1982 M.Rothier (FRA)
1984 N.Hernandez (VEN)
1986 D.Bell (GB)
1987 D.Bell (GB)

Under 56kg
1980 G.Winklbauer (AUT)
1982 B.Rodriguez (FRA)
1984 A -M. Burns (USA)
1986 A.Hughes (GB)
1987 C.Arnaud (FRA)

Under 52kg
1980 E.Hovrat (AUT)
1982 L.Doyle (GB)
1984 K.Yamaguchi (JAP)
1986 D.Brun (FRA)
1987 S.Rendle (GB)

Under 48kg
1980 J.Bridge (GB)
1982 K.Briggs (GB)
1984 K.Briggs (GB)
1986 K.Briggs (GB)
1987 Z.Li (CHN)

Lacrosse was first played by the Iroquois Indians in Canada towards the end of the 15th century. The winners of the English Championship are presented with the Iroquois Cup, named after the famous Indians. The sport spread to Britain in the 18th century and the International Federation of Amateur Lacrosse was formed in 1928.

WORLD CHAMPIONSHIPS

The first World Championships for men were held in Toronto, Canada in 1967. They are now held every four years. The first women's championships were in 1969.

Winners

Men	Women
1967 United States	1969 Great Britain
1974 United States	1974 United States
1978 Canada	1978 Canada
1982 United States	1982 United States
1986 United States	1986 Australia

Most Wins:	**Most Wins:**
4 United States	2 United States

OLYMPIC GAMES

Lacrosse was included in the Olympics in 1904 and 1908 and has since appeared as a demonstration sport in 1928, 1932 and 1948.

Winners:
1904 Canada
1908 Canada

Highest Scores:

Men's International: 32-8 United States v England, 1988

Women's international: 40-0 Great Britain v Long Island (USA), 1967

A popular sport amongst Indians, the Iroquois and Algonquin Indians were early exponents, and the Chaughnawage Indians were responsible for introducing the sport to Britain in 1867.

Lawn Tennis evolved from Real Tennis and, while accounts of various forms of 'Field Tennis' were recorded in the 18th century, the real 'father' of Lawn Tennis is regarded as Major Wingfield who showed off his new game, which he called Sphairistike, at a Christmas Party at a country house at Nantclwyd, Wales, in 1873. The Marylebone Cricket Club were responsible in revising Wingfield's initial rules and in 1877 the All England Croquet Club added the name Lawn Tennis to its title.

The following is a list of Women champions who won titles under both maiden and married names.

Married name	Maiden name	Married Name	Maiden Name
N.Bolton	N.Wynne	L.W.King	B.J.Moffitt
R.A.Cawley	E. Goolagong	D.Lambert-Chambers	D.K.Douglass
B.M.Court	M.Smith	T.D.Long	T.Coyne
D.E.Dalton	J.A.M.Tegart	L.R.C.Michel	P.Saunders
M.DuPont	M.E.Osborne	F.S.Moody	H.N.Wills
C.Evert-Lloyd	C.Evert	G.E.Reid	K.Melville
S.Fabyan	S.Palfrey	M.Reitano	M.Carter
L.A.Godfree	K.McKane	A.Sterry	C.Cooper
G.W.Hillyard	B.Bingley	J.R.Susman	K.Hantze

WIMBLEDON CHAMPIONSHIPS

The All England Championships at Wimbledon are regarded as the most prestigious championships in the world. They were first held in 1877 and until 1922 were organised on a challenge round basis.

Winners:
Men's Singles

1877 S.W.Gore (GB)	1905 H.L.Doherty (GB)
1878 P.F.Hadow (GB)	1906 H.L.Doherty (GB)
1879 J.T.Hartley (GB)	1907 N.E.Brookes (AUS)
1880 J.T.Hartley (GB)	1908 A.W.Gore (GB)
1881 W.Renshaw (GB)	1909 A.W.Gore (GB)
1882 W.Renshaw (GB)	1910 A.F.Wilding (NZ)
1883 W.Renshaw (GB)	1911 A.F.Wilding (NZ)
1884 W.Renshaw (GB)	1912 A.F.Wilding (NZ)
1885 W.Renshaw (GB)	1913 A.F.Wilding (NZ)
1886 W.Renshaw (GB)	1914 N.E.Brookes (AUS)
1887 H.F.Lawford (GB)	1915–18 Not held
1888 E.Renshaw (GB)	1919 G.L.Patterson (AUS)
1889 W.Renshaw (GB)	1920 W.T.Tilden (USA)
1890 W.J.Hamilton (GB)	1921 W.T.Tilden (USA)
1891 W.Baddeley (GB)	1922 G.L.Patterson (AUS)
1892 W.Baddeley (GB)	1923 W.M.Johnston (USA)
1893 J.Pim (GB)	1924 J.Borotra (FRA)
1894 J.Pim (GB)	1925 R.Lacoste (FRA)
1895 W.Baddeley (GB)	1926 J.Borotra (FRA)
1896 H.S.Mahoney (GB)	1927 H.Cochet (FRA)
1897 R.F.Doherty (GB)	1928 R.Lacoste (FRA)
1898 R.F.Doherty (GB)	1929 H.Cochet (FRA)
1899 R.F.Doherty (GB)	1930 W.T.Tilden (USA)
1900 R.F.Doherty (GB)	1931 S.B.Wood (USA)
1901 A.W.Gore (GB)	1932 H.E.Vines (USA)
1902 H.L.Doherty (GB)	1933 J.H.Crawford (AUS)
1903 H.L.Doherty (GB)	1934 F.J.Perry (GB)
1904 H.L.Doherty (GB)	1935 F.J.Perry (GB)

1936 F.J.Perry (GB)
1937 J.D.Budge (USA)
1938 J.D.Budge (USA)
1939 R.L.Riggs (USA)
1940–45 Not held
1946 Y.Petra (FRA)
1947 J.A.Kramer (USA)
1948 R.Falkenburg (USA)
1949 F.R.Schroeder (USA)
1950 J.E.Patty (USA)
1951 R.Savitt (USA)
1952 F.A.Sedgman (AUS)
1953 E.V.Seixas (USA)
1954 J.Drobny (TCH)
1955 M.A.Trabert (USA)
1956 L.A.Hoad (AUS)
1957 L.A.Hoad (AUS)
1958 A.J.Cooper (AUS)
1959 A.Olmedo (USA)
1960 N.A.Fraser (AUS)
1961 R.G.Laver (AUS)
1962 R.G.Laver (AUS)
1963 C.R.McKinley (USA)
1964 R.S.Emerson (AUS)

1965 R.S.Emerson (AUS)
1966 M.Santana (SPA)
1967 J.D.Newcombe (AUS)
1968 R.G.Laver (AUS)
1969 R.G.Laver (AUS)
1970 J.D.Newcombe (AUS)
1971 J.D.Newcombe (AUS)
1972 S.R.Smith (USA)
1973 J.Kodes (TCH)
1974 J.S.Connors (USA)
1975 A.R.Ashe (USA)
1976 B.Borg (SWE)
1977 B.Borg (SWE)
1978 B.Borg (SWE)
1979 B.Borg (SWE)
1980 B.Borg (SWE)
1981 J.P.McEnroe (USA)
1982 J.S.Connors (USA)
1983 J.P.McEnroe (USA)
1984 J.P.McEnroe (USA)
1985 B.Becker (FRG)
1986 B.Becker (FRG)
1987 P. Cash (AUS)
1988 S.Edberg (SWE)
1989 B.Becker (FRG)

Most Wins: 7 William Renshaw

Women's Singles
1884 M.Watson (GB)
1885 M.Watson (GB)
1886 B.Bingley (GB)
1887 C.Dod (GB)
1888 C.Dod (GB)
1889 G.W.Hillyard (GB)
1890 H.Rice (GB/IRE)
1891 C.Dod (GB)
1892 C.Dod (GB)
1893 C.Dod (GB)
1894 G.W.Hillyard (GB)
1895 C.Cooper (GB)
1896 C.Cooper (GB)
1897 G.W.Hillyard (GB)
1898 C.Cooper (GB)
1899 G.W.Hillyard (GB)
1900 G.W.HIllyard (GB)
1901 A.Sterry (GB)
1902 A.E.Robb (GB)
1903 D.K.Douglass (GB)
1904 D.K.Douglass (GB)
1905 M.Sutton (USA)
1906 D.K.Douglass (GB)
1907 M.Sutton (USA)
1908 A.Sterry (GB
1909 D.P.Boothby (GB)
1910 D.Lambert-Chambers (GB)
1911 D.Lambert-Chambers (GB)
1912 D.R.Larcombe (GB)
1913 D.Lambert-Chambers (GB)
1914 D.Lambert-Chambers (GB)

1915–18 Not held
1919 S.Lenglen (FRA)
1920 S.Lenglen (FRA)
1921 S.Lenglen (FRA)
1922 S.Lenglen (FRA)
1923 S.Lenglen (FRA)
1924 K.McKane (GB)
1925 S.Lenglen (FRA)
1926 L.A.Godfree (GB)
1927 H.N.Wills (USA)
1928 H.N.Wills (USA)
1929 H.N.Wills (USA)
1930 F.S.Moody (USA)
1931 C.Aussem (GER)
1932 F.S.Moody (USA)
1933 F.S.Moody (USA)
1934 D.E.Round (GB)
1935 F.S.Moody (USA)
1936 H.H.Jacobs (USA)
1937 D.E.Round (GB)
1938 F.S.Moody (USA)
1939 A.Marble (USA)
1940–45 Not held
1946 P.M.Betz (USA)
1947 M.E.Osborne (USA)
1948 A.L.Brough (USA)
1949 A.L.Brough (USA)
1950 A.L.Brough (USA)
1951 D.J.Hart (USA)
1952 M.Connolly (USA)
1953 M.Connolly (USA)

1954 M.Connolly (USA)
1955 A.L.Brough (USA)
1956 S.J.Fry (USA)
1957 A.Gibson (USA)
1958 A.Gibson (USA)
1959 M.E.Bueno (BRA)
1960 M.E.Bueno (BRA)
1961 A.Mortimer (GB)
1962 J.R.Susman (USA)
1963 M.Smith (AUS)
1964 M.E.Bueno (BRA)
1965 M.Smith (AUS)
1966 L.W.King (USA)
1967 L.W.King (USA)
1968 L.W.King (USA)
1969 P.F.Jones (GB)
1970 B.M.Court (AUS)

1971 E.Goolagong (AUS)
1972 L.W.King (USA)
1973 L.W.King (USA)
1974 C.M.Evert (USA)
1975 L.W.King (USA)
1976 C.M.Evert (USA)
1977 S.V.Wade (GB)
1978 M.Navratilova (TCH)
1979 M.Navratilova (TCH)
1980 R.A.Cawley (AUS)
1981 C.Evert-Lloyd (USA)
1982 M.Navratilova (USA)
1983 M.Navratilova (USA)
1984 M.Navratilova (USA)
1985 M.Navratilova (USA)
1986 M.Navratilova (USA)
1987 M.Navratilova (USA)
1988 S.Graf (FRG)
1989 S.Graf (FRG)

Most Wins: 8 Helen Wills-Moody, M.Navratilova

Men's Doubles
1879 L.R.Erskine (GB) H.F.Lawford (GB)
1880 E.Renshaw (GB) W.Renshaw (GB)
1881 E.Renshaw (GB) W.Renshaw (GB)
1882 J.T.Hartley (GB) R.T.Richardson (GB)
1883 C.W.Grinstead (GB) C.E.Welldon (GB)
1884 E.Renshaw (GB) W.Renshaw (GB)
1885 E.Renshaw (GB) W.Renshaw (GB)
1886 E.Renshaw (GB) W.Renshaw (GB)
1887 P.Bowes-Lyon (GB) H.W.W.Wilberforce (GB)
1888 E.Renshaw (GB) W.Renshaw (GB)
1889 E.Renshaw (GB) W.Renshaw (GB)
1890 J.Pim (GB) F.O.Stoker (GB)
1891 H.Baddeley (GB) W.Baddeley (GB)
1892 H.S.Barlow (GB) E.W.Lewis (GB)
1893 J.Pim (GB) F.O.Stoker (GB)
1894 H.Baddeley (GB) W.Baddeley (GB)
1895 H.Baddeley (GB) W.Baddeley (GB)
1896 H.Baddeley (GB) W.Baddeley (GB)
1897 H.L.Doherty (GB) R.F.Doherty (GB)
1898 H.L.Doherty (GB) R.F.Doherty (GB)
1899 H.L.Doherty (GB) R.F.Doherty (GB)
1900 H.L.Doherty (GB) R.F.Doherty (GB)
1901 H.L.Doherty (GB) R.F.Doherty (GB)
1902 F.L.Riseley (GB) S.H.Smith (GB)
1903 H.L.Doherty (GB) R.F.Doherty (GB)
1904 H.L.Doherty (GB) R.F.Doherty (GB)
1905 H.L.Doherty (GB) R.F.Doherty (GB)
1906 F.L.Riseley (GB) S.H.Smith (GB)
1907 N.E.Brookes (AUS) A.F.Wilding (NZ)
1908 M.J.G.Ritchie (GB) A.F.Wilding (NZ)
1909 A.W.Gore (GB) H.Roper Barrett (GB)
1910 M.J.G.Ritchie (GB) A.F.Wilding (NZ)
1911 M.Decugis (FRA) A.H.Gobert (FRA)
1912 C.P.Dixon (GB) H.Roper Barrett (GB)
1913 C.P.Dixon (GB) H.Roper Barrett (GB)

1914 N.E.Brookes (AUS) A.F.Wilding (NZ)
1915–18 Not held
1919 P.O'Hara-Wood (AUS) R.V.Thomas (AUS)
1920 C.S.Garland (USA) R.S.Williams (USA)
1921 R.Lycett (GB) M.Woosnam (GB)
1922 J.O.Anderson (AUS) R.Lycett (GB)
1923 L.A.Godfree (GB) R.Lycett (GB)
1924 F.T.Hunter (USA) V.Richards (USA)
1925 J.Borotra (FRA) R.Lacoste (FRA)
1926 J.Brugnon (FRA) H.Cochet (FRA)
1927 F.T.Hunter (USA) W.T.Tilden (USA)
1928 J.Brugnon (FRA) H.Cochet (FRA)
1929 W.L.Allison (USA) J.Van Ryn (USA)
1930 W.L.Allison (USA) J.Van Ryn (USA)
1931 G.M.Lott (USA) J.Van Ryn (USA)
1932 J.Borotra (FRA) J.Brugnon (FRA)
1933 J.Borotra (FRA) J.Brugnon (FRA)
1934 G.M.Lott (USA) L.R.Stoefen (USA)
1935 J.H.Crawford (USA) A.K.Quist (AUS)
1936 G.P Hughes (GB) C.R.D.Tuckey (GB)
1937 J.D.Budge (USA) G.Mako (USA)
1938 J.D.Budge (USA) G.Mako (USA)
1939 E.T.Cooke (USA) R.L.Riggs (USA)
1940–45 Not held
1946 T.Brown (USA) J.A.Kramer (USA)
1947 R.Falkenburg (USA) J.A.Kramer (USA)
1948 J.E.Bromwich (AUS) F.A.Sedgman (AUS)
1949 R.A.Gonzales (USA) F.A.Parker (USA)
1950 J.E.Bromwich (AUS) A.K.Quist (AUS)
1951 K.McGregor (AUS) F.A.Sedgman (AUS)
1952 K.McGregor (AUS) F.A.Sedgman (AUS)
1953 L.A.Hoad (AUS) K.R.Rosewall (AUS)
1954 R.N.Hartwig (AUS) M.G.Rose (AUS)
1955 R.N.Hartwig (AUS) L.A.Hoad (AUS)
1956 L.A.Hoad (AUS) K.R.Rosewall (AUS)
1957 G.Mulloy (USA) B.Patty (USA)
1958 S.Davidson (SWE) U.Schmidt (SWE)
1959 R.Emerson (AUS) N.A.Fraser (AUS)
1960 R.H.Osuna (MEX) R.D.Ralston (USA)
1961 R.Emerson (AUS) N.A.Fraser (AUS)
1962 R.A.J.Hewitt (AUS) F.S.Stolle (AUS)
1963 R.H.Osuna (MEX) A.Palafox (MEX)
1964 R.A.J.Hewitt (AUS) F.S.Stolle (AUS)
1965 J.D.Newcombe (AUS) A.D.Roche (AUS)
1966 K.N.Fletcher (AUS) J.D.Newcombe (AUS)
1967 R.A.J.Hewitt (SAF) F.D.McMillan (SAF)
1968 J.D.Newcombe (AUS) A.D.Roche (AUS)
1969 J.D.Newcombe (AUS) A.D.Roche (AUS)
1970 J.D.Newcombe (AUS) A.D.Roche (AUS)
1971 R.Emerson (AUS) R.G.Laver (AUS)
1972 R.A.J.Hewitt (SAF) F.D.McMillan (SAF)
1973 J.S.Connors (USA) I.Nastase (ROM)
1974 J.D.Newcombe (AUS) A.D.Roche (AUS)
1975 V.Gerulaitis (USA) A.Mayer (USA)
1976 B.E.Gottfried (USA) R.Ramirez (MEX)
1977 R.L.Case (AUS) G.Masters (AUS)

1978 R.A.J.Hewitt (SAF) F.D.McMillan (SAF)
1979 P.Fleming (USA) J.P.McEnroe (USA)
1980 P.McNamara (AUS) P.McNamee (AUS)
1981 P.Fleming (USA) J.P.McEnroe (USA)
1982 P.McNamara (AUS) P.McNamee (AUS)
1983 P.Fleming (USA) J.P.McEnroe (USA)
1984 P.Fleming (USA) J.P.McEnroe (USA)
1985 H.P.Gunthardt (SWI) B.Taroczy (HUN)
1986 J.Nystrom (SWE) M.Wilander (SWE)
1987 K. Flach (USA) R. Seguso (USA)
1988 K.Flach (USA) R.Seguso (USA)
1989 J.B.Fitzgerald (AUS) A.Jarryd (SWE)

Most Wins: 8 Lawrence and Reginald Doherty

Women's Doubles
1913 R.J.McNair (GB) D.P.Boothby (GB)
1914 A.M.Morton (GB) E.Ryan (USA)
1915–18 Not held
1919 S.Lenglen (FRA) E.Ryan (USA)
1920 S.Lenglen (FRA) E.Ryan (USA)
1921 S.Lenglen (FRA) E.Ryan (USA)
1922 S.Lenglen (FRA) E.Ryan (USA)
1923 S.Lenglen (FRA) E.Ryan (USA)
1924 H.Wightman (USA) H.N.Wills (USA)
1925 S.Lenglen (FRA) E.Ryan (USA)
1926 M.K.Browne (USA) E.Ryan (USA)
1927 H.N.Wills (USA) E.Ryan (USA)
1928 P.Saunders (GB) M.Watson (GB)
1929 L.R.C.Mitchell (GB) M.Watson (GB)
1930 F.S.Moody (USA) E.Ryan (USA)
1931 D.C.Shepherd-Barron (GB) P.E.Mudford (GB)
1932 D.Metaxa (FRA) J.Sigart (BEL)
1933 S.Mathieu (FRA) E.Ryan (USA)
1934 S.Mathieu (FRA) E.Ryan (USA)
1935 F.James (GB) K.E.Stammers (GB)
1936 F.James (GB) K.E.Stammers (GB)
1937 S.Mathieu (FRA) A.M.Yorke (GB)
1938 S.Fabyan (USA) A.Marble (USA)
1939 S.Fabyan (USA) A.Marble (USA)
1940–45 Not held
1946 A.L.Brough (USA) M.E.Osborne (USA)
1947 D.J.Hart (USA) P.C.Todd (USA)
1948 A.L.Brough (USA) M.Osborne-Du Pont (USA)
1949 A.L.Brough (USA) M.Osborne-Du Pont (USA)
1950 A.L.Brough (USA) M.Osborne-Du Pont (USA)
1951 S.J.Fry (USA) D.J.Hart (USA)
1952 S.J.Fry (USA) D.J.Hart (USA)
1953 S.J.Fry (USA) D.J.Hart (USA)
1954 A.L.Brough (USA) M.Osborne-Du Pont (USA)
1955 A.Mortimer (GB) J.A.Shilcock (GB)
1956 A.Buxton (GB) A.Gibson (USA)
1957 A.Gibson (USA) D.R.Hard (USA)
1958 M.E.Bueno (BRA) A.Gibson (USA)
1959 J.Arth (USA) D.R.Hard (USA)
1960 M.E.Bueno (BRA) D.R.Hard (USA)
1961 K.Hantz (USA) B.J.Moffitt (USA)
1962 B.J.Moffitt (USA) J.R.Susman (USA)

1963 M.E.Bueno (BRA) D.R.Hard (USA)
1964 M.Smith (AUS) L.R.Turner (AUS)
1965 M.E.Bueno (BRA) B.J.Moffitt (USA)
1966 M.E.Bueno (BRA) N.Richey (USA)
1967 R.Casals (USA) L.W.King (USA)
1968 R.Casals (USA) L.W.King (USA)
1969 B.M.Court (AUS) J.A.M.Tegart (AUS)
1970 R.Casals (USA) L.W.King (USA)
1971 R.Casals (USA) L.W.King (USA)
1972 L.W.King (USA) B.Stove (HOL)
1973 R.Casals (USA) L.W.King (USA)
1974 E.Goolagong (AUS) M.Michel (USA)
1975 A.Kiyomura (USA) K.Sawamatsu (JAP)
1976 C.Evert (USA) M.Navratilova (TCH)
1977 H.Cawley (AUS) J.C.Russell (USA)
1978 G.E.Reid (AUS) W.Turnbull (AUS)
1979 L.W.King (USA) M.Navratilova (TCH)
1980 K.Jordan (USA) A.E.Smith (USA)
1981 M.Navratilova (TCH) P.H.Shriver (USA)
1982 M.Navratilova (USA) P.H.Shriver (USA)
1983 M.Navratilova (USA) P.H.Shriver (USA)
1984 M.Navratilova (USA) P.H.Shriver (USA)
1985 K.Jordan (USA) E.Smylie (AUS)
1986 M.Navratilova (USA) P.H.Shriver (USA)
1987 C. Kohde-Kilsch (FRG) H. Sukova (TCH)
1988 S.Graf (FRG) G.Sabatini (ARG)
1989 J.Novotna (TCH) H.Sukova (TCH)

Most Wins:
12 Elizabeth Ryan

Mixed Doubles
1913 H.Crisp (GB) C.O.Tuckey (GB)
1914 J.C.Parke (GB) D.R.Larcombe (GB)
1915–18 Not held
1919 R.Lycett (GB) E.Ryan (USA)
1920 G.L.Patterson (AUS) S.Lenglen (FRA)
1921 R.Lycett (GB) E.Ryan (USA)
1922 P.O'Hara-Wood (USA) S.Lenglen (FRA)
1923 R.Lycett (GB) E.Ryan (USA)
1924 J.B.Gilbert (GB) K.McKane (GB)
1925 J.Borotra (FRA) S.Lenglen (FRA)
1926 L.Godfree (GB) K.Godfree (GB)
1927 F.T.Hunter (USA) E.Ryan (USA)
1928 P.D.B.Spence (SAF) E.Ryan (USA)
1929 F.T.Hunter (USA) H.N.Wills (USA)
1930 J.H.Crawford (AUS) E.Ryan (USA)
1931 G.M.Lott (USA) L.A.Harper (USA)
1932 E.Maier (SPA) E.Ryan (USA)
1933 G. von Cramm (GER) H.Krahwinkel (GER)
1934 R.Miki (JAP) D.E.Round (GB)
1935 F.J.Perry (GB) D.E.Round (GB)
1936 F.J.Perry (GB) D.E.Round (GB)

1937 J.D.Budge (USA) A.Marble (USA)
1938 J.D.Budge (USA) A.Marble (USA)
1939 R.L.Riggs (USA) A.Marble (USA)
1940–45 Not held
1946 T.Brown (USA) A.L.Brough (USA)
1947 J.E.Bromwich (AUS) A.L.Brough (USA)
1948 J.E.Bromwich (AUS) A.L.Brough (USA)
1949 E.W.Sturgess (SAF) S.P.Summers (SAF)
1950 E.W.Sturgess (SAF) A.L.Brough (USA)
1951 F.A.Sedgman (AUS) D.J.Hart (USA)
1952 F.A.Sedgman (AUS) D.J.Hart (USA)
1953 E.V.Seixas (USA) D.J.Hart (USA)
1954 E.V.Seixas (USA) D.J.Hart (USA)
1955 E.V.Seixas (USA) D.J.Hart (USA)
1956 E.V.Seixas (USA) S.J.Fry (USA)
1957 M.G.Rose (AUS) D.R.Hard (USA)
1958 R.N.Howe (AUS) N.Coghlan (AUS)
1959 R.G.Laver (AUS) D.R.Hard (USA)
1960 R.G.Laver (AUS) D.R.Hard (USA)
1961 F.S.Stolle (AUS) L.R.Turner (AUS)
1962 N.A.Fraser (AUS) M.Osborne-Du Pont (USA)
1963 K.N.Fletcher (AUS) M.Smith (AUS)
1964 F.S.Stolle (AUS) L.R.Turner (AUS)
1965 K.N.Fletcher (AUS) M.Smith (AUS)
1966 K.N.Fletcher (AUS) M.Smith (AUS)
1967 O.K.Davidson (AUS) L.W.King (USA)
1968 K.N.Fletcher (AUS) B.M.Court (AUS)
1969 F.S.Stolle (AUS) P.F.Jones (GB)
1970 I.Nastase (ROM) R.Casals (USA)
1971 O.K.Davidson (AUS) L.W.King (USA)
1972 I.Nastase (ROM) R.Casals (USA)
1973 O.K.Davidson (AUS) L.W.King (USA)
1974 O.K.Davidson (AUS) L.W.King (USA)
1975 M.C.Reissen (USA) B.M.Court (AUS)
1976 A.D.Roche (AUS) F.Durr (FRA)
1977 R.A.J.Hewitt (SAF) G.R.Stevens (SAF)
1978 F.D.McMillan (SAF) B.Stove (HOL)
1979 R.A.J.Hewitt (SAF) G.R.Stevens (SAF)
1980 J.R.Austin (USA) T.Austin (USA)
1981 F.D.McMillan (SAF) B.Stove (HOL)
1982 K.Curren (SAF) A.E.Smith (USA)
1983 J.M.Lloyd (GB) W.M.Turnbull (AUS)
1984 J.M.Lloyd (GB) W.M.Turnbull (AUS)
1985 P.McNamee (AUS) M.Navratilova (USA)
1986 K.Flach (USA) K.Jordan (USA)
1987 J.Bates (GB) J.Durie (GB)
1988 S.Stewart (USA) Z.Garrison (USA)
1989 J.Pugh (USA) J.Novotna (TCH)

Most Wins: 7 Elizabeth Ryan

UNITED STATES CHAMPIONSHIPS

The first official US Championships were in 1881 and remained in existence until 1969. In 1968 and 1969, however, there were two Championships as there was the Amateur and Open events. Since 1970 it has been an Open competition.

Singles Winners
Men

1881 R.D.Sears (USA)	1929 W.T.Tilden (USA)
1882 R.D.Sears (USA)	1930 J.H.Doeg (USA)
1883 R.D.Sears (USA)	1931 H.E.Vines (USA)
1884 R.D.Sears (USA)	1932 H.E.Vines (USA)
1885 R.D.Sears (USA)	1933 F.J.Perry (GB)
1886 R.D.Sears (USA)	1934 F.J.Perry (GB)
1887 R.D.Sears (USA)	1935 W.L.Allison (USA)
1888 H.W.Slocum (USA)	1936 F.J.Perry (GB)
1889 H.W.Slocum (USA)	1937 J.D.Budge (USA)
1890 O.S.Campbell (USA)	1938 J.D.Budge (USA)
1891 O.S.Campbell (USA)	1939 R.L.Riggs (USA)
1892 O.S.Campbell (USA)	1940 W.D.McNeill (USA)
1893 R.D.Wrenn (USA)	1941 R.L.Riggs (USA)
1894 R.D.Wrenn (USA)	1942 F.R.Schroeder (USA)
1895 F.H.Hovey (USA)	1943 J.R.Hunt (USA)
1896 R.D.Wrenn (USA)	1944 F.A.Parker (USA)
1897 R.D.Wrenn (USA)	1945 F.A.Parker (USA)
1898 M.D.Whitman (USA)	1946 J.A.Kramer (USA)
1899 M.D.Whitman (USA)	1947 J.A.Kramer (USA)
1900 M.D.Whitman (USA)	1948 R.A.Gonzales (USA)
1901 W.A.Larned (USA)	1949 R.A.Gonzales (USA)
1902 W.A.Larned (USA)	1950 A.Larsen (USA)
1903 H.L.Doherty (GB)	1951 F.A.Sedgman (USA)
1904 H.Ward (USA)	1952 F.A.Sedgman (USA)
1905 B.C.Wright (USA)	1953 M.A.Trabert (USA)
1906 W.J.Clothier (USA)	1954 E.V.Seixas (USA)
1907 W.A.Larned (USA)	1955 M.A.Trabert (USA)
1908 W.A.Larned (USA)	1956 K.R.Rosewall (AUS)
1909 W.A.Larned (USA)	1957 M.J.Anderson (AUS)
1910 W.A.Larned (USA)	1958 A.J.Cooper (AUS)
1911 W.A.Larned (USA)	1959 N.A.Fraser (AUS)
1912 M.E.McLoughlin (USA)	1960 N.A.Fraser (AUS)
1913 M.E.McLoughlin (USA)	1961 R.S.Emerson (AUS)
1914 R.N.Williams (USA)	1962 R.G.Laver (AUS)
1915 W.M.Johnston (USA)	1963 R.H.Osuna (MEX)
1916 R.N.Williams (USA)	1964 R.S.Emerson (AUS)
1917 Not held	1965 M.Santana (SPA)
1918 R.L.Murray (USA)	1966 F.S.Stolle (AUS)
1919 W.M.Johnston (USA)	1967 J.D.Newcombe (AUS)
1920 W.T.Tilden (USA)	1968 A.R.Ashe (USA)
1921 W.T.Tilden (USA)	1969 S.R.Smith (USA)
1922 W.T.Tilden (USA)	
1923 W.T.Tilden (USA)	
1924 W.T.Tilden (USA)	
1925 W.T.Tilden (USA)	
1926 R.Lacoste (FRA)	
1927 R.Lacoste (FRA)	
1928 H.Cochet (FRA)	

Women

1887 E.Hansell (USA)	1930 B.Nuthall (GB)
1888 B.L.Townsend (USA)	1931 F.S.Moody (USA)
1889 B.L.Townsend (USA)	1932 H.H.Jacobs (USA)
1890 E.C.Roosevelt (USA)	1933 H.H.Jacobs (USA)
1891 M.E.Cahill (USA)	1934 H.H.Jacobs (USA)
1892 M.E.Cahill (USA)	1935 H.H.Jacobs (USA)
1893 A.Terry (USA)	1936 A.Marble (USA)
1894 H.Helwig (USA)	1937 A.Lizana (CHL)
1895 J.Atkinson (USA)	1938 A.Marble (USA)
1896 E.H.Moore (USA)	1939 A.Marble (USA)
1897 J.Atkinson (USA)	1940 A.Marble (USA)
1898 J.Atkinson (USA)	1941 S.P.Cooke (USA)
1899 M.Jones (USA)	1942 P.M.Betz (USA)
1900 M.McAteer (USA)	1943 P.M.Betz (USA)
1901 E.H.Moore (USA)	1944 P.M.Betz (USA)
1902 M.Jones (USA)	1945 S.P.Cooke (USA)
1903 E.H.Moore (USA)	1946 P.M.Betz (USA)
1904 M.G.Sutton (USA)	1947 A.L.Brough (USA)
1905 E.H.Moore (USA)	1948 M. du Pont (USA)
1906 H.Homans (USA)	1949 M. du Pont (USA)
1907 E.Sears (USA)	1950 M. du Pont (USA)
1908 M.Brager-Wallach (USA)	1951 M.Connolly (USA)
1909 H.Hotchkiss (USA)	1952 M.Connolly (USA)
1910 H.Hotchkiss (USA)	1953 M.Connolly (USA)
1911 H.Hotchkiss (USA)	1954 D.J.Hart (USA)
1912 M.K.Browne (USA)	1955 D.J.Hart (USA)
1913 M.K.Browne (USA)	1956 S.J.Fry (USA)
1914 M.K.Browne (USA)	1957 A.Gibson (USA)
1915 M.Bjurstedt (USA)	1958 A.Gibson (USA)
1916 M.Bjurstedt (USA)	1959 M.E.Bueno (BRA)
1917 Not held	1960 D.R.Hard (USA)
1918 M.Bjurstedt (USA)	1961 D.R.Hard (USA)
1919 G.W.Wightman (USA)	1962 M.Smith (AUS)
1920 F.Mallory (USA)	1963 M.E.Bueno (BRA)
1921 F.Mallory (USA)	1964 M.E.Bueno (BRA)
1922 F.Mallory (USA)	1965 M.Smith (AUS)
1923 H.N.Wills (USA)	1966 M.E.Bueno (BRA)
1924 H.N.Wills (USA)	1967 L.W.King (USA)
1925 H.N.Wills (USA)	1968 B.M.Court (AUS)
1926 F.Mallory (USA)	1969 B.M.Court (AUS)
1927 H.N.Wills (USA)	
1928 H.N.Wills (USA)	
1929 H.N.Wills (USA)	

US OPEN   Men

1968 A.R.Ashe (USA)	1978 J.S.Connors (USA)
1969 R.G.Laver (AUS)	1979 J.P.McEnroe (USA)
1970 K.R.Rosewall (AUS)	1980 J.P.McEnroe (USA)
1971 S.R.Smith (USA)	1981 J.P.McEnroe (USA)
1972 I.Nastase (ROM)	1982 J.S.Connors (USA)
1973 J.D.Newcombe (AUS)	1983 J.S.Connors (USA)
1974 J.S.Connors (USA)	1985 I.Lendl (TCH)
1975 M.Orantes (SPA)	1986 I.Lendl (TCH)
1976 J.S.Connors (USA)	1987 I.Lendl (TCH)
1977 G.Vilas (ARG)	1988 M.Wilander (SWE)

Most Wins:
7 Bill Tilden, Richard Sears, Bill Larned

US OPEN Women

1968 S.V.Wade (GB)	1978 C.M.Evert (USA)
1969 B.M.Court (AUS)	1979 T.Austin (USA)
1970 B.M.Court (AUS)	1980 C.M.Evert-Lloyd (USA)
1971 L.W.King (USA)	1981 T.Austin (USA)
1972 L.W.King (USA)	1982 C.M.Evert-Lloyd (USA)
1973 B.M.Court (AUS)	1983 M.Navratilova (USA)
1974 L.W.King (USA)	1984 M.Navratilova (USA)
1975 C.M.Evert (USA)	1985 H.Mandlikova (TCH)
1976 C.M.Evert (USA)	1986 M.Navratilova (USA)
1977 C.M.Evert (USA)	1987 M.Navratilova (USA)
	1988 S.Graf (FRG)

Most Wins:
7 Molla Mallory, Helen Wills-Moody

DAVIS CUP

The Davis Cup was donated by American player Dwight Davis to be contested by national teams. Until 1972 the competition was organised on a challenge basis. Since 1972 it has been a knockout competition with countries seeded, and divided into different groups, with annual promotion and relegation.

Finals

1900	United States	British Isles	3–0
1901 Not held			
1902	United States	British Isles	3–2
1903	British Isles	United States	4–1
1904	British Isles	Belgium	5–0
1905	British Isles	United States	5–0
1906	British Isles	United States	5–0
1907	Australasia	British Isles	3–2
1908	Australasia	United States	3–2
1909	Australasia	United States	5–0
1910 Not held			
1911	Australasia	United States	5–0
1912	British Isles	Australasia	3–2
1913	United States	British Isles	3–2
1914	Australasia	United States	3–2
1915–18 Not held			
1919	Australasia	British Isles	4–1
1920	United States	Australasia	5–0
1921	United States	Japan	5–0
1922	United States	Australasia	4–1
1923	United States	Australia	4–1
1924	United States	Australia	5–0
1925	United States	France	5–0
1926	United States	France	4–1
1927	France	United States	3–2
1928	France	United States	4–1
1929	France	United States	3–2
1930	France	United States	4–1
1931	France	Great Britain	3–2
1932	France	United States	3–2
1933	Great Britain	France	3–2
1934	Great Britain	United States	4–1
1935	Great Britain	United States	5–0
1936	Great Britain	Australia	3–2

1937	United States	Great Britain	4–1
1938	United States	Australia	3–2
1939	Australia	United States	3–2
1940–45 Not held			
1946	United States	Australia	5–0
1947	United States	Australia	4–1
1948	United States	Australia	5–0
1949	United States	Australia	4–1
1950	Australia	United States	4–1
1951	Australia	United States	3–2
1952	Australia	United States	4–1
1953	Australia	United States	3–2
1954	United States	Australia	3–2
1955	Australia	United States	5–0
1956	Australia	United States	5–0
1957	Australia	United States	3–2
1958	United States	Australia	3–2
1959	Australia	United States	3–2
1960	Australia	Italy	4–1
1961	Australia	Italy	5–0
1962	Australia	Mexico	5–0
1963	United States	Australia	3–2
1964	Australia	United States	3–2
1965	Australia	Spain	4–1
1966	Australia	India	4–1
1967	Australia	Spain	4–1
1968	United States	Australia	4–1
1969	United States	Romania	5–0
1970	United States	West Germany	5–0
1971	United States	Romania	3–2
1972	United States	Romania	3–2
1973	Australia	United States	5–0
1974	South Africa	India	WO
1975	Sweden	Czechoslovakia	3–2
1976	Italy	Chile	4–1
1977	Australia	Italy	3–1
1978	United States	Great Britain	4–1
1979	United States	Italy	5–0
1980	Czechoslovakia	Italy	4–1
1981	United States	Argentina	3–1
1982	United States	France	4–1
1983	Australia	Sweden	3–2
1984	Sweden	United States	4–1
1985	Sweden	West Germany	3–2
1986	Australia	Sweden	3–2
1987	Sweden	India	5–0
1988	West Germany	Sweden	4–1

Most Wins: 28 United States

WIGHTMAN CUP
Former American player Hazel Wightman donated the trophy in 1920 to be contested by national female teams. However, none showed any interest until 1923 when the United States and Great Britain played for the trophy. Since then all Wightman Cup matches have been between the two nations.

1923	United States	Great Britain	7–0
1924	Great Britain	United States	6–1
1925	Great Britain	United States	4–3
1926	United States	Great Britain	4–3
1927	United States	Great Britain	5–2
1928	Great Britain	United States	4–3
1929	United States	Great Britain	4–3
1930	Great Britain	United States	4–3
1931	United States	Great Britain	5–2
1932	United States	Great Britain	4–3
1933	United States	Great Britain	4–3
1934	United States	Great Britain	5–2
1935	United States	Great Britain	4–3
1936	United States	Great Britain	4–3
1937	United States	Great Britain	6–1
1938	United States	Great Britain	5–2
1939	United States	Great Britain	5–2
1940–45 Not held			
1946	United States	Great Britain	7–0
1947	United States	Great Britain	7–0
1948	United States	Great Britain	6–1
1949	United States	Great Britain	7–0
1950	United States	Great Britain	7–0
1951	United States	Great Britain	6–1
1952	United States	Great Britain	7–0
1953	United States	Great Britain	7–0
1954	United States	Great Britain	6–0*
1955	United States	Great Britain	6–1
1956	United States	Great Britain	5–2
1957	United States	Great Britain	6–1
1958	Great Britain	United States	4–3
1959	United States	Great Britain	4–3
1960	Great Britain	United States	4–3
1961	United States	Great Britain	6–1
1962	United States	Great Britain	4–3
1963	United States	Great Britain	6–1
1964	United States	Great Britain	5–2
1965	United States	Great Britain	5–2
1966	United States	Great Britain	4–3
1967	United States	Great Britain	6–1
1968	Great Britain	United States	4–3
1969	United States	Great Britain	5–2
1970	United States	Great Britain	4–3
1971	United States	Great Britain	4–3
1972	United States	Great Britain	5–2
1973	United States	Great Britain	5–2
1974	Great Britain	United States	6–1
1975	Great Britain	United States	5–2
1976	United States	Great Britain	5–2
1977	United States	Great Britain	7–0
1978	Great Britain	United States	4–3
1979	United States	Great Britain	7–0

1980	United States	Great Britain	5–2
1981	United States	Great Britain	7–0
1982	United States	Great Britain	6–1
1983	United States	Great Britain	6–1
1984	United States	Great Britain	5–2
1985	United States	Great Britain	7–0
1986	United States	Great Britain	7–0
1987	United States	Great Britain	5–2
1988	United States	Great Britain	7–0

Most Wins:
50 United States

MEN'S GRAND PRIX MASTERS

Throughout the season various tournaments count towards the Masters and points are awarded depending upon performances. At the end of the season the leading 16 players play off for the Masters title.

Winners:

Year	Singles	Doubles
1970	S.Smith (USA)	S.R.Smith & A.Ashe (USA)
1971	I.Nastase (ROM)	Not held
1972	I.Nastase (ROM)	Not held
1973	I.Nastase (ROM)	Not held
1974	G.Vilas (ARG)	Not held
1975	I.Nastase (ROM)	J.Gisbert & M.Orantes (SPA)
1976	M.Orantes (SPA)	F.McNair & S.Stewart (USA)

1977 No tournament because date changed to January, consequently next tournament was in 1978

1978	J.S.Connors (USA)	R.A.J.Hewitt & F.D.McMillan (SAF)
1979	J.P.McEnroe (USA)	P.Fleming & J.P.McEnroe (USA)
1980	B.Borg (SWE)	P.Fleming & J.P.McEnroe (USA)
1981	B.Borg (SWE)	P.Fleming & J.P.McEnroe (USA)
1982	I.Lendl (TCH)	P.Fleming & J.P.McEnroe (USA)
1983	I.Lendl (TCH)	P.Fleming & J.P.McEnroe (USA)
1984	J.P.McEnroe (USA)	P.Fleming & J.P.McEnroe (USA)
1985	J.P.McEnroe (USA)	P.Fleming & J.P.McEnroe (USA)
1986	I.Lendl (TCH)	A.Jarryd & S.Edberg (SWE)
1987	I.Lendl (TCH)	M.Mecir & T.Smid (TCH)
1988	B.Becker (FRG)	R.Leach & J.Pugh (USA)

Most Wins
(Singles):
4 Ilie Nastase, Ivan Lendl
(Doubles):
7 John McEnroe, Peter Fleming

FRENCH CHAMPIONSHIPS

The French Championships were first held in 1891 but it was a 'closed' competition, open only to nationals. It gained full international status in 1925.

Singles Winners

Year	Men	Women
1925	R.Lacoste (FRA)	S.Lenglen (FRA)
1926	H.Cochet (FRA)	S.Lenglen (FRA)
1927	R.Lacoste (FRA)	K.Bouman (HOL)
1928	H.Cochet (FRA)	H.N.Wills (USA)
1929	R.Lacoste (FRA)	H.N.Wills (USA)
1930	H.Cochet (FRA)	F.S.Moody (USA)
1931	J.Borotra (FRA)	C.Aussem (GER)
1932	H.Cochet (FRA)	F.S.Moody (USA)
1933	J.H.Crawford (AUS)	M.C.Scriven (GB)
1934	G.von Cramm (GER)	M.C.Scriven (GB)
1935	F.J.Perry (GB)	S.Sperling (GER)
1936	G.von Cramm (GER)	S.Sperling (GER)
1937	H.Henkel (GER)	S.Sperling (GER)
1938	J.D.Budge (USA)	R.Mathieu (FRA)
1939	W.D.McNeill (USA)	R.Mathieu (FRA)
1940–45 Not held		
1946	M.Bernard (FRA)	M.E.Osborne (USA)
1947	J.Asboth (HUN)	P.C.Todd (USA)
1948	F.A.Parker (USA)	N.Landry (FRA)
1949	F.A.Parker (USA)	M.Osborne-Du Pont (USA)
1950	J.E.Patty (USA)	D.J.Hart (USA)
1951	J.Drobny (EGY)	S.J.Fry (USA)
1952	J.Drobny (EGY)	D.J.Hart (USA)
1953	K.R.Rosewall (AUS)	M.Connolly (USA)
1954	M.A.Trabert (USA)	M.Connolly (USA)
1955	M.A.Trabert (USA)	A.Mortimer (GB)
1956	L.A.Hoad (AUS)	A.Gibson (USA)
1957	S.Davidson (SWE)	S.J.Bloomer (GB)
1958	M.G.Rose (AUS)	S.Kormoczy (HUN)
1959	N.Pietrangeli (ITA)	C.C.Truman (GB)
1960	N.Pietrangeli (ITA)	D.R.Hard (USA)
1961	M.Santana (SPA)	A.S.Haydon (GB)
1962	R.G.Laver (AUS)	M.Smith (AUS)
1963	R.S.Emerson (AUS)	L.R.Turner (AUS)
1964	M.Santana (SPA)	M.Smith (AUS)
1965	F.S.Stolle (AUS)	L.R.Turner (AUS)
1966	A.D.Roche (AUS)	P.F.Jones (GB)
1967	R.S.Emerson (AUS)	F.Durr (FRA)
1968	K.R.Rosewall (AUS)	N.Richey (USA)
1969	R.G.Laver (AUS)	B.M.Court (AUS)
1970	J.Kodes (TCH)	B.M.Court (AUS)
1971	J.Kodes (TCH)	E.F.Goolagong (AUS)
1972	A.Gimeno (SPA)	L.W.King (USA)
1973	I.Nastase (ROM)	B.M.Court (AUS)
1974	B.Borg (SWE)	C.M.Evert (USA)
1975	B.Borg (SWE)	C.M.Evert (USA)
1976	A.Panatta (ITA)	S.Barker (GB)
1977	G.Vilas (ARG)	M.Jausovec (YUG)
1978	B.Borg (SWE)	V.Ruzici (ROM)
1979	B.Borg (SWE)	C.M.Evert-Lloyd (USA)
1980	B.Borg (SWE)	C.M.Evert-Lloyd (USA)

1981	B.Borg (SWE)	H.Mandlikova (TCH)
1982	M.Wilander (SWE)	M.Navratilova (USA)
1983	Y.Noah (FRA)	C.M.Evert-Lloyd (USA)
1984	I.Lendl (TCH)	M.Navratilova (USA)
1985	M.Wilander (SWE)	C.M.Evert-Lloyd (USA)
1986	I.Lendl (TCH)	C.M.Evert-Lloyd (USA)
1987	I.Lendl (TCH)	S.Graf (FRG)
1988	M.Wilander (SWE)	S.Graf (FRG)
1989	M.Chang (USA)	S.Sanchez (SPA)

Most Wins

(Men):	**(Women):**
6 Bjorn Borg	7 Chris Evert-Lloyd

AUSTRALIAN CHAMPIONSHIPS
The first championships in 1905 were known as the Australasian Championships, and it was not until 1925 that the title changed to its present style. New Zealand twice hosted the championship, in 1906 and 1912.

Singles Winners:

Year	Men	Women
1905	R.W.Heath (AUS)	-
1906	A.F.Wilding (NZ)	-
1907	A.F.Wilding (NZ)	-
1908	H.M.Rice (AUS)	-
1909	F.B.Alexander (USA)	-
1910	R.W.Heath (AUS)	
1911	N.E.Brookes (AUS)	-
1912	J.C.Parke (GB)	-
1913	E.F.Parker (AUS)	-
1914	P.O'Hara–Wood (AUS)	-
1915	F.G.Lowe (GB)	-
1916–18 Not held		
1919	A.R.F.Kingscote (GB)	-
1920	P.O'Hara-Wood (AUS)	-
1921	R.H.Gemmell (AUS)	
1922	J.O.Anderson (AUS)	M.Molesworth (AUS)
1923	P.O'Hara-Wood (AUS)	M.Molesworth (AUS)
1924	J.O.Anderson (AUS)	S.Lance (AUS)
1925	J.O.Anderson (AUS)	D.Akhurst (AUS)
1926	J.B.Hawkes (AUS)	D.Akhurst (AUS)
1927	G.L.Patterson (AUS)	E.F.Boyd (AUS)
1928	J.Borotra (FRA)	D.Akhurst (AUS)
1929	J.C.Gregory (GB)	D.Akhurst (AUS)
1930	E.F.Moon (AUS)	D.Akhurst (AUS)
1931	J.H.Crawford (AUS)	C.Buttsworth (AUS)
1932	J.H.Crawford (AUS)	C.Buttsworth (AUS)
1933	J.H.Crawford (AUS)	J.Hartigan (AUS)
1934	F.J.Perry (GB)	J.Hartigan (AUS)
1935	J.H.Crawford (AUS)	D.E.Round (GB)
1936	A.K.Quist (AUS)	J.Hartigan (AUS)
1937	V.B.McGrath (AUS)	N.Wynne (AUS)
1938	J.D.Budge (AUS)	D.M.Bundy (USA)
1939	J.E.Bromwich (AUS)	V.Westacott (AUS)
1940	A.K.Quist (AUS)	N.Bolton (AUS)

Australian Championships Cont.

1941–45 Not held

Year		Men	Women
1946		J.E.Bromwich (AUS)	N.Bolton (AUS)
1947		D.Pails (AUS)	N.Bolton (AUS)
1948		A.K.Quist (AUS)	N.Bolton (AUS)
1949		F.A.Sedgman (AUS)	D.J.Hart (USA)
1950		F.A.Sedgman (AUS)	A.L.Brough (USA)
1951		R.Savitt (USA)	N.Bolton (AUS)
1952		K.McGregor (AUS)	T.D.Long (AUS)
1953		K.R.Rosewall (AUS)	M.Connolly (USA)
1954		M.G.Rose (AUS)	T.D.Long (AUS)
1955		K.R.Rosewall (AUS)	B.Penrose (AUS)
1956		L.A.Hoad (AUS)	M.Carter (AUS)
1957		A.J.Cooper (AUS)	S.J.Fry (USA)
1958		A.J.Cooper (AUS)	A.Mortimer (GB)
1959		A.Olmedo (USA)	M.Reitano (AUS)
1960		R.G.Laver (AUS)	M.Smith (AUS)
1961		R.S.Emerson (AUS)	M.Smith (AUS)
1962		R.G.Laver (AUS)	M.Smith (AUS)
1963		R.S.Emerson (AUS)	M.Smith (AUS)
1964		R.S.Emerson (AUS)	M.Smith (AUS)
1965		R.S.Emerson (AUS)	M.Smith (AUS)
1966		R.S.Emerson (AUS)	M.Smith (AUS)
1967		R.S.Emerson (AUS)	N.Richey (USA)
1968		W.W.Bowrey (AUS)	L.W.King (USA)
1969		R.G.Laver (AUS)	B.M.Court (AUS)
1970		A.R.Ashe (USA)	B.M.Court (AUS)
1971		K.R.Rosewall (AUS)	B.M.Court (AUS)
1972		K.R.Rosewall (AUS)	S.V.Wade (GB)
1973		J.D.Newcombe (AUS)	B.M.Court (AUS)
1974		J.S.Connors (USA)	E.F.Goolagong (AUS)
1975		J.D.Newcombe (AUS)	E.F.Goolagong (AUS)
1976		M.R.Edmondson (AUS)	R.A.Cawley (AUS)
1977	Jan	R.Tanner (USA)	G.E.Reid (AUS)
	Dec	V.Gerulaitis (USA)	R.A.Cawley (AUS)
1978		G.Vilas (ARG)	C.O'Neill (AUS)
1979		G.Vilas (ARG)	B.Jordan (USA)
1980		B.Teacher (USA)	H.Mandlikova (TCH)
1981		J.Kriek (SAF)	M.Navratilova (TCH)
1982		J.Kriek (SAF)	C.M.Evert–Lloyd (USA)
1983		M.Wilander (SWE)	M.Navratilova (USA)
1984		M.Wilander (SWE)	C.M.Evert–Lloyd (USA)
1985		S.Edberg (SWE)	M.Navratilova (USA)
1987		S.Edberg (SWE)	H.Mandlikova (TCH)
1988		M.Wilander (SWE)	S.Graf (FRG)
1989		I.Lendl (TCH)	S.Graf (FRG)

Most Wins:

(Men):
6 Roy Emerson

(Women):
11 Margaret Court

LONGEST MATCHES

In Grand Slam tournaments, the following matches have all lasted 100 games or more:

WIMBLEDON:

112 games R. Gonzales (USA) beat C. Pasarell (USA) 22-24, 1-6, 16-14, 6-3, 11-9 (1969)

US CHAMPIONSHIPS:

105 games: M. Lara & Loyo-Mayo (MEX) beat M. Santana (SPA) & L. Garcia (MEX) 10-12, 24-22, 11-9, 3-6, 6-2 (1966)

105 games: C. Drysdale & R. Moore (SAF) beat R. Emerson (AUS) & R. Barnes (BRA) 29-31, 8-6, 3-6, 8-6, 6-2 (1967)

100 games: F. D. Robbins (USA) beat D. Dell (USA) 22-20, 9-7, 6-8, 8-10, 6-4 (1969)

FEDERATION CUP
The women's equivalent of the Davis Cup, it is an international team tournament played on a
knockout basis. It was first held in 1963.

1963	United States
1964	Australia
1965	Australia
1966	United States
1967	United States
1968	Australia
1969	United States
1970	Australia
1971	Australia
1972	South Africa
1973	Australia
1974	Australia
1975	Czechoslovakia
1976	United States
1977	United States
1978	United States
1979	United States
1980	United States
1981	United States
1982	United States
1983	Czechoslovakia
1984	Czechoslovakia
1985	Czechoslovakia
1986	United States
1987	West Germany
1988	Czechoslovakia

Most Wins:
12 United States

The Modern Pentathlon is a combination of five gruelling and testing sports, with each discipline being held on a separate day. The five events are: Riding, Fencing, Swimming, Shooting and Cross Country Running.

WORLD CHAMPIONSHIPS

Held annually since 1949, the Olympic champion is the automatic World Champion as well.

Winners:

Men Individual

1949 T.Bjurefelt (SWE)	1968 B.Ferm (SWE)
1950 L.Hall (SWE)	1969 A.Balczo (HUN)
1951 L.Hall (SWE)	1970 P.Kelemen (HUN)
1952 L.Hall (SWE)	1971 B.Onischenko (USSR)
1953 G.Benedek (HUN)	1972 A.Balczo (HUN)
1954 B.Thofelt (SWE)	1973 P.Lednev (USSR)
1955 S.Konstantin (USSR)	1974 P.Lednev (USSR)
1956 L.Hall (SWE)	1975 P.Lednev (USSR)
1957 I.Novikov (USSR)	1976 J.Pyciak-Peciak (POL)
1958 I.Novikov (USSR)	1977 J.Pyciak-Peciak (POL)
1959 I.Novikov (USSR)	1978 P.Lednev (USSR)
1960 F.Nemeth (HUN)	1979 R.Neiman (USA)
1961 I.Novikov (USSR)	1980 A.Starostin (USSR)
1962 S.Dobnikov (USSR)	1981 J.Pyciak-Peciak (POL)
1963 A.Balczo (HUN)	1982 D.Masala (ITA)
1964 F.Toerek (HUN)	1983 A.Starostin (USSR)
1965 A.Balczo (HUN)	1984 D.Masala (ITA)
1966 A.Balczo (HUN)	1985 A.Mizser (HUN)
1967 A.Balczo (HUN)	1986 C.Massullo*
	1987 J.Bouzou (FRA)
	1988 J.Martinek (HUN)

Most Wins:
6 Andras Balczo

* declared champion following disqualification of original winner A.Starostin (HUN)

Team

1949 Sweden	1968 Hungary
1950 Sweden	1969 USSR
1951 Sweden	1970 Hungary
1952 Hungary	1971 USSR
1953 Sweden	1972 USSR
1954 Hungary	1973 USSR
1955 Hungary	1974 USSR
1956 USSR	1975 Hungary
1957 USSR	1976 Great Britain
1958 USSR	1977 Poland
1959 USSR	1978 Poland
1960 Hungary	1979 USA
1961 USSR	1980 USSR
1962 USSR	1981 Poland
1963 Hungary	1982 USSR
1964 USSR	1983 USSR
1965 Hungary	1984 Italy
1966 Hungary	1985 USSR
1967 Hungary	1986 Italy
	1987 Hungary
	1988 Hungary

Most Wins:
16 USSR

Women Individual

1981 A.Ahlgren (SWE)	1984 S.Jakovleva (USSR)
1982 W.Norman (GB)	1985 B.Kotowska (POL)
1983 L.Chormobrywy (CAN)	1986 I.Kisseleva (USSR)
	1987 I.Kisseleva (USSR)
	1988 D.Idzi (POL)

Most Wins:
2 Irina Kisseleva

Team

1981 Great Britain	1984 USSR
1982 Great Britain	1985 Poland
1983 Great Britain	1986 USSR
	1987 USSR
	1988 Poland

Most Wins:
3 Great Britain, USSR

OLYMPIC GAMES

Despite the efforts of Modern Olympics founder Baron de Coubertin to have a multi-sport competition included in the Games the Modern Pentathlon had to wait until 1912 before making its debut. There is only a men's competition.

Winners:

Individual

1912 G.Lilliehook (SWE)	1956 L.Hall (SWE)
1920 G.Dyrssen (SWE)	1960 F.Nemeth (HUN)
1924 B.Lindman (SWE)	1964 F.Torok (HUN)
1928 S.Thofelt (SWE)	1968 B.Ferm (SWE)
1932 J.G.Oxenstierna (SWE)	1972 A.Balczo (HUN)
1936 G.Handrick (GER)	1976 J.Pyciak-Peciak (POL)
1948 W.Grut (SWE)	1980 A.Starostin (USSR)
1952 L.Hall (SWE)	1984 D.Masala (ITA)
	1988 J. Martinek (HUN)

Most Wins:
2 Lars Hall

Team

1952 Hungary	1972 USSR
1956 USSR	1976 Great Britain
1960 Hungary	1980 USSR
1964 USSR	1984 Italy
1968 Hungary	1988 Hungary

Most Wins:
4 USSR, Hungary

Following the building of the first motor cycle by Gottlieb Daimler in 1885 it was a natural assumption that it would not be long before a new sport was born and in 1896 the first Motor Cycle race took place. It was organised by the Automobile Club de France and held over a 152 km (94.5 miles) course from Paris to Nantes and back. The winner's average speed was just over 20 mph a far cry from the 150 mph plus of the modern day machines.

WORLD CHAMPIONSHIPS

The first World Championships were organised by the sport's governing body, the FIM (Federation Internationale Motocycliste) in 1949.

Champions: 750cc
1977 S.Baker (USA)
1978 J.Cecotto (VEN)
1979 P.Pons (FRA)
(Discontinued after 1979)

Formula One
1985 J.Dunlop (GB)
1986 J.Dunlop (GB)

500cc
1949 L.Graham (GB)	1968 G.Agostini (ITÅ)
1950 U.Masetti (ITA)	1969 G.Agostini (ITA)
1951 G.Duke (GB)	1970 G.Agostini (ITA)
1952 U.Masetti (ITA)	1971 G.Agostini (ITA)
1953 G.Duke (GB)	1972 G.Agostini (ITA)
1954 G.Duke (GB)	1973 P.Read (GB)
1955 G.Duke (GB)	1974 P.Read (GB)
1956 J.Surtees (GB)	1975 G.Agostini (ITA)
1957 L.Liberati (ITA)	1976 B.Sheene (GB)
1958 J.Surtees (GB)	1977 B.Sheene (GB)
1959 J.Surtees (GB)	1978 K.Roberts (USA)
1960 J.Surtees (GB)	1979 K.Roberts (USA)
1961 G.Hocking (RHO)	1980 K.Roberts (USA)
1962 M.Hailwood (GB)	1981 M.Lucchinelli (ITA)
1963 M.Hailwood (GB)	1982 F.Uncini (ITA)
1964 M.Hailwood (GB)	1983 F.Spencer (USA)
1965 M.Hailwood (GB)	1984 E.Lawson (USA)
1966 G.Agostini (ITA)	1985 F.Spencer (USA)
1967 G.Agostini (ITA)	1986 E.Lawson (USA)
	1987 W.Gardner (AUS)
	1988 E.Lawson (USA)

350cc

1949 F.Frith (GB)	1966 M.Hailwood (GB)
1950 B.Foster (GB)	1967 M.Hailwood (GB)
1951 G.Duke (GB)	1968 G.Agostini (ITA)
1952 G.Duke (GB)	1969 G.Agostini (ITA)
1953 F.Anderson (GB)	1970 G.Agostini (ITA)
1954 F.Anderson (GB)	1971 G.Agostini (ITA)
1955 B.Lomas (GB)	1972 G.Agostini (ITA)
1956 B.Lomas (GB)	1973 G.Agostini (ITA)
1957 K.Campbell (AUS)	1974 G.Agostini (ITA)
1958 J.Surtees (GB)	1975 J.Cecotto (VEN)
1959 J.Surtees (GB)	1976 W.Villa (ITA)
1960 J.Surtees (GB)	1977 T.Katayama (JAP)
1961 G.Hocking (RHO)	1978 K.Ballington (SAF)
1962 J.Redman (RHO)	1979 K.Ballington (SAF)
1963 J.Redman (RHO)	1980 J.Ekerold (SAF)
1964 J.Redman (RHO)	1981 A.Mang (FRG)
1965 J.Redman (RHO)	1982 A.Mang (FRG)

(Discontinued after 1982)

250cc

1949 B.Ruffo (ITA)	1968 P.Read (GB)
1950 D.Ambrosini (ITA)	1969 K.Carruthers (AUS)
1951 B.Ruffo (ITA)	1970 R.Gould (GB)
1952 E.Lorenzetti (ITA)	1971 P.Read (GB)
1953 W.Haas (FRG)	1972 J.Saarinen (FIN)
1954 W.Haas (FRG)	1973 D.Braun (FRG)
1955 H.Muller (FRG)	1974 W.Villa (ITA)
1956 C.Ubbiali (ITA)	1975 W.Villa (ITA)
1957 C.Sandford (GB)	1976 W.Villa (ITA)
1958 T.Provini (ITA)	1977 M.Lega (ITA)
1959 C.Ubbiali (ITA)	1978 K.Ballington (SAF)
1960 C.Ubbiali (ITA)	1979 K.Ballington (SAF)
1961 M.Hailwood (GB)	1980 A.Mang (FRG)
1962 J.Redman (RHO)	1981 A.Mang (FRG)
1963 J.Redman (RHO)	1982 J -L.Tournadre (FRA)
1964 P.Read (GB)	1983 C.Lavado (VEN)
1965 P.Read (GB)	1984 C.Sarron (FRA)
1966 M.Hailwood (GB)	1985 F.Spencer (USA)
1967 M.Hailwood (GB)	1986 C.Lavado (VEN)
	1987 A.Mang (FRG)
	1988 S.Pons (SPA)

125cc

1949 N.Pagani (ITA)	1968 P.Read (GB)
1950 B.Ruffo (ITA)	1969 D.Simmonds (GB)
1951 C.Ubbiali (ITA)	1970 D.Braun (FRG)
1952 C.Sandford (GB)	1971 A.Nieto (SPA)
1953 W.Haas (FRG)	1972 A.Nieto (SPA)
1954 R.Hollaus (AUT)	1973 K.Andersson (SWE)
1955 C.Ubbiali (ITA)	1974 K.Andersson (SWE)
1956 C.Ubbiali (ITA)	1975 P.Pileri (ITA)
1957 T.Provini (ITA)	1976 P -P.Bianchi (ITA)
1958 C.Ubbiali (ITA)	1977 P -P.Bianchi (ITA)
1959 C.Ubbiali (ITA)	1978 E.Lazzarini (ITA)
1960 C.Ubbiali (ITA)	1979 A.Nieto (SPA)
1961 T.Phillis (AUS)	1980 P -P.Bianchi (ITA)
1962 L.Taveri (SWI)	1981 A.Nieto (SPA)
1963 H.Anderson (NZ)	1982 A.Nieto (SPA)
1964 L.Taveri (SWI)	1983 A.Nieto (SPA)
1965 H.Anderson (NZ)	1984 A.Nieto (SPA)
1966 L.Taveri (SWI)	1985 F.Gresini (ITA)
1967 B.Ivy (GB)	1986 L.Cadalora (ITA)
	1987 F.Gresini (ITA)
	1988 J.Martinez (SPA)

80 cc

1984 S.Dorflinger (SWI)
1985 S.Dorflinger (SWI)
1986 J.Martinez (SPA)
1987 J.Martinez (SPA)
1988 J.Martinez (SPA)

50cc

1962 E.Degner (FRG)	1973 J.de Vries (HOL)
1963 H.Anderson (NZ)	1974 H.van Kessel (HOL)
1964 H.Anderson (NZ)	1975 A.Nieto (SPA)
1965 R.Bryans (IRE)	1976 A.Nieto (SPA)
1966 H -G.Anscheidt (FRG)	1977 A.Nieto (SPA)
1967 H -G.Anscheidt (FRG)	1978 R.Tormo (SPA)
1968 H -G.Anscheidt (FRG)	1979 E.Lazzarini (ITA)
1969 A.Nieto (SPA)	1980 E.Lazzarini (ITA)
1970 A.Nieto (SPA)	1981 R.Tormo (SPA)
1971 J.de Vries (HOL)	1982 S.Dorflinger (SWI)
1972 A.Nieto (SPA)	1983 S.Dorflinger (SWI)

(Replaced by 80 cc class)

Sidecar

1949 E.Oliver (GB)	1968 H.Fath (FRG)
1950 E.Oliver (GB)	1969 K.Enders (FRG)
1951 E.Oliver (GB)	1970 K.Enders (FRG)
1952 C.Smith (GB)	1971 H.Owesle (FRG)
1953 E.Oliver (GB)	1972 K.Enders (FRG)
1954 W.Noll (FRG)	1973 K.Enders (FRG)
1955 W.Faust (FRG)	1974 K.Enders (FRG)
1956 W.Noll (FRG)	1975 R.Steinhausen (FRG)
1957 F.Hillebrand (FRG)	1976 R.Steinhausen (FRG)
1958 W.Schneider (FRG)	1977 G.O'Dell (GB)
1959 W.Schneider (FRG)	1978 R.Biland (SWI)
1960 H.Fath (FRG)	1979 R.Biland (SWI)
1961 M.Deubel (FRG)	1980 J.Taylor (GB)
1962 M.Deubel (FRG)	1981 R.Biland (SWI)
1963 M.Deubel (FRG)	1982 W.Schwarzel (FRG)
1964 M.Deubel (FRG)	1983 R.Biland (SWI)
1965 F.Scheidegger (SWI)	1984 E.Streur (HOL)
1966 F.Scheidegger (SWI)	1985 E.Streur (HOL)
1967 K.Enders (FRG)	1986 E.Streur (HOL)
	1987 S.Webster (GB)
	1988 S.Webster (GB)

Most World Titles:
15 Giacomo Agostini

MOTO CROSS

Known as Scrambling in Britain, it was first seen at Camberley, Surrey in 1924. The World Championships were introduced 1957

500cc Champions:

1957 B.Nilsson (SWE)	1972 R.De Coster (BEL)
1958 R.Baeten (BEL)	1973 R.De Coster (BEL)
1959 S.Lundin (SWE)	1974 H.Mikkola (FIN)
1960 B.Nilsson (SWE)	1975 R.De Coster (BEL)
1961 S.Lundin (SWE)	1976 R.De Coster (BEL)
1962 R.Tibblin (SWE)	1977 H.Mikkola (FIN)
1963 R.Tibblin (SWE)	1978 H.Mikkola (FIN)
1964 J.Smith (GB)	1979 G.Noyce (GB)
1965 J.Smith (GB)	1980 A.Malherbe (BEL)
1966 P.Friedrichs (GDR)	1981 A.Malherbe (BEL)
1967 P.Friedrichs (GDR)	1982 B.Lackey (USA)
1968 P.Friedrichs (GDR)	1983 H.Carlqvist (SWE)
1969 B.Aberg (SWE)	1984 A.Malherbe (BEL)
1970 B.Aberg (SWE)	1985 D.Thorpe (GB)
1971 R.De Coster (BEL)	1986 D.Thorpe (GB)
	1987 G.Job (BEL)
	1988 E. Geboers (BEL)

Most Wins:
5 Roger De Coster

ISLE OF MAN TT RACES

The Tourist Trophy races on the Isle of Man each June are the most famous road races in Motor Cycling. The first races were in 1911. The most prestigious race during the week of racing is the Senior TT.

Winners

1911 O.Godfrey	1955 G.Duke
1912 F.Applebee	1956 J.Surtees
1913 T.Wood	1957 R.McIntyre
1914 C.Pullin	1958 J.Surtees
1915–1919 not held	1959 J.Surtees
1920 T.De La Hay	1960 J.Surtees
1921 H.Davies	1961 M.Hailwood
1922 A.Bennett (IRE)	1962 G.Hocking (RHO)
1923 T.Sheard	1963 M.Hailwood
1924 A.Bennett (IRE)	1964 M.Hailwood
1925 H.Davies	1965 M.Hailwood
1926 S.Woods	1966 M.Hailwood
1927 A.Bennett (IRE)	1967 M.Hailwood
1928 C.Dodson	1968 G.Agostini (ITA)
1929 C.Dodson	1969 G.Agostini (ITA)
1930 W.Handley	1970 G.Agostini (ITA)
1931 T.Hunt	1971 G.Agostini (ITA)
1932 S.Woods	1972 G.Agostini (ITA)
1933 S.Woods	1973 J.Findlay (AUS)
1934 J.Guthrie	1974 P.Carpenter
1935 S.Woods	1975 M.Grant
1936 J.Guthrie	1976 T.Herron (IRE)
1937 F.Frith	1977 P.Read
1938 H.Daniell	1978 T.Herron (IRE)
1939 G.Meier (FRG)	1979 M.Hailwood
1940–1946 not held	1980 G.Crosby
1947 H.Daniell	1981 M.Grant
1948 A.Bell	1982 N.Brown
1949 H.Daniell	1983 R.McElnea
1950 G.Duke	1984 R.McElnea
1951 G.Duke	1985 J.Dunlop (IRE)
1952 R.Armstrong (IRE)	1986 R.Burnett
1953 R.Amm (RHO)	1987 J. Dunlop (IRE)
1954 R.Amm (RHO)	1988 J.Dunlop (IRE)
	1989 S.Hislop (GB)

Most Wins:

7 Mike Hailwood

JUNIOR TT (250cc)
Between 1922-76 known as the Lightweight 250cc Class Winners all British unless otherwise stated: From 1987, for 350cc machines.

1922 G. Davison	1958 T. Provini (ITA)
1923 J. Porter	1959 T. Provini (ITA)
1924 E. Twemlow	1960 G. Hocking (RHO)
1925 E. Twemlow	1961 M. Hailwood
1926 C. Johnson	1962 D. Minter
1927 W. Handley	1963 J. Redman (RHO)
1928 F. Longman	1964 J. Redman (RHO)
1929 S. Crabtree	1965 J. Redman (RHO)
1930 J. Guthrie	1966 M. Hailwood
1931 G. Walker	1967 M. Hailwood
1932 L. Davenport	1968 W. Ivy
1933 S. Gleave	1969 K. Carruthers (AUS)
1934 J. Simpson	1970 K. Carruthers (AUS)
1935 S. Woods	1971 P. Read
1936 A. Foster	1972 P. Read
1937 D. Tenni (ITA)	1973 C. Williams
1938 E. Kluge (GER)	1974 C. Williams
1939 E. Mellors	1975 C. Mortimer
1940-46 Not held	1976 T. Herron (IRE)
1947 M. Barrington (IRE)	1977 C. Williams
1948 M. Cann	1978 C. Mortimer
1949 M. Barrington (IRE)	1979 C. Williams
1950 D. Amrosini (ITA)	1980 C. Williams
1951 T. Wood	1981 S. Tonkin
1952 F. Anderson	1982 C. Law
1953 F. Anderson	1983 C. Law
1954 W. Haas (FRG)	1984 G. McGregor (AUS)
1955 W. Lomas	1985 J. Dunlop (IRE)
1956 C. Ubbiali (ITA)	1986 S. Cull (IRE)
1957 C. Sandford	1987 E.Laycock
	1988 J.Dunlop (IRE)
	1989 J.Ray (GB)

MOST WINS:
5 Charlie Williams

Bob McIntyre, in 1957, became the first man to lap the Isle of Man TT course at 100 mph but Geoff Duke, two years earlier, thought he was the first man past the landmark...During the senior race, it was announced over the loudspeakers that his third lap average speed was 100mph, but this was then corrected to 99.97mph.

Top British motor cyclist Ron Haslam was fined £130 by local magistrates in 1983 for riding at 5mph... he had no insurance, was not wearing a crash helmet and was not displaying L plates because he did not have a licence!

Although motor car races had been held in the United States in 1878 and in France nine years later the first real race was from Paris to Bordeaux, and back, in 1895. The great road races using Paris as a starting point soon followed, as did the Gordon Bennett series of races. Eventually road racing was banned and this lead to purpose-built circuits being constructed. The first Grand Prix was the French GP in 1906.

FORMULA ONE WORLD CHAMPIONSHIP

A World Championship for Formula One drivers was established in 1950 with seven races counting towards the championship. A championship for contructors was introduced in 1958.

Winners: World Drivers' Championship

1950 G. Farina (ITA)
1951 J. M. Fangio (ARG)
1952 A. Ascari (ITA)
1953 A. Ascari (ITA)
1954 J. M. Fangio (ARG)
1955 J. M. Fangio (ARG)
1956 J. M. Fangio (ARG)
1957 J. M. Fangio (ARG)
1958 M. Hawthorn (GB)
1959 J. Brabham (AUS)
1960 J. Brabham (AUS)
1961 P. Hill (USA)
1962 G. Hill (GB)
1963 J. Clark (GB)
1964 J. Surtees (GB)
1965 J. Clark (GB)
1966 J. Brabham (AUS)
1967 D. Hulme (NZ)
1968 G. Hill (GB)

1969 J. Stewart (GB)
1970 J. Rindt (AUT)
1971 J. Stewart (GB)
1972 E. Fittipaldi (BRA)
1973 J. Stewart (GB)
1974 E. Fittipaldi (BRA)
1975 N. Lauda (AUT)
1976 J. Hunt (GB)
1977 N. Lauda (AUT)
1978 M. Andretti (USA)
1979 J. Scheckter (SAF)
1980 A. Jones (AUS)
1981 N. Piquet (BRA)
1982 K. Rosberg (FIN)
1983 N. Piquet (BRA)
1984 N. Lauda (AUT)
1985 A. Prost (FRA)
1986 A. Prost (FRA)
1987 N. Piquet (BRA)
1988 A. Senna (BRA)

Most Wins:
5 Juan Manuel Fangio

Constructors' Championship

1958 Vanwall
1959 Cooper-Climax
1960 Cooper-Climax
1961 Ferrari
1962 BRM
1963 Lotus-Climax
1964 Ferrari
1965 Lotus-Climax
1966 Repco-Brabham
1967 Repco-Brabham
1968 Lotus-Ford
1969 Matra-Ford
1970 Lotus-Ford
1971 Tyrrell-Ford
1972 Lotus

1973 Lotus
1974 McLaren
1975 Ferrari
1976 Ferrari
1977 Ferrari
1978 Lotus
1979 Ferrari
1980 Williams-Ford
1981 Williams-Ford
1982 Ferrari
1983 Ferrari
1984 McLaren-Porsche
1985 McLaren-Porsche
1986 Williams-Honda
1987 Williams-Honda
1988 McLaren-Honda

Most Wins:
8 Ferrari

GRAND PRIX WINNERS

Since the introduction of the world driver's championship in 1950 there have been more than 30 Grands Prix. The following were on the 1988 calendar, and all results of those Grands Prix follow:

AUSTRALIAN GP
1985 K. Rosberg (FIN)
1986 A. Prost (FRA)
1987 G. Berger (AUT)
1988 A. Prost (FRA)

BELGIAN GP
1950 J. M. Fangio (ARG)
1951 G. Farina (ITA)
1952 A. Ascari (ITA)
1953 A. Ascari (ITA)
1954 J. M. Fangio (ARG)
1955 J. M. Fangio (ARG)
1956 P. Collins (GB)
1957 Not held
1958 T. Brooks (GB)
1959 Not held
1960 J. Brabham (AUS)
1961 P. Hill (USA)
1962 J. Clark (GB)
1963 J. Clark (GB)
1964 J. Clark (GB)
1965 J. Clark (GB)
1966 J. Surtees (GB)
1967 D. Gurney (USA)
1968 B. McLaren (NZ)

1969 Not held
1970 P. Rodriguez (MEX)
1971 Not held
1972 E. Fittipaldi (BRA)
1973 J. Stewart (GB)
1974 E. Fittipaldi (BRA)
1975 N. Lauda (AUT)
1976 N. Lauda (AUT)
1977 G. Nilsson (SWE)
1978 M. Andretti (USA)
1979 J. Scheckter (SAF)
1980 D. Pironi (FRA)
1981 C. Reutemann (ARG)
1982 J. Watson (GB)
1983 A. Prost (FRA)
1984 M. Albereto (ITA)
1985 A. Senna (BRA)
1986 N. Mansell (GB)
1987 A. Prost (FRA)
1988 A. Senna (BRA)

BRAZILIAN GP
1973 E. Fittipaldi (BRA)
1974 E. Fittipaldi (BRA)
1975 C. Pace (BRA)
1976 N. Lauda (AUT)
1977 C. Reutemann (ARG)
1978 C. Reutemann (ARG)
1979 J. Laffite (FRA)
1980 R. Arnoux (FRA)

1981 C. Reutemann (ARG)
1982 A. Prost (FRA)
1983 N. Piquet (BRA)
1984 A. Prost (FRA)
1985 A. Prost (FRA)
1986 N. Piquet (BRA)
1987 A. Prost (FRA)
1988 A. Prost (FRA)
1989 N. Mansell (GB)

BRITISH GP

1950 G. Farina (ITA)	1969 J. Stewart (GB)
1951 J. F. Gonzalez (ARG)	1970 J. Rindt (AUT)
1952 A. Ascari (ITA)	1971 J. Stewart (GB)
1953 A. Ascari (ITA)	1972 E. Fittipaldi (BRA)
1954 J. F. Gonzalez (ARG)	1973 P. Revson (USA)
1955 S. Moss (GB)	1974 J. Scheckter (SAF)
1956 J. M. Fangio (ARG)	1975 E. Fittipaldi (BRA)
1957 T. Brooks/S. Moss (GB)	1976 N. Lauda (AUT)
1958 P. Collins (GB)	1977 J. Hunt (GB)
1959 J. Brabham (AUS)	1978 C. Reutemann (ARG)
1960 J. Brabham (AUS)	1979 C. Regazzoni (SWI)
1961 W. von Trips (FRG)	1980 A. Jones (AUS)
1962 J. Clark (GB)	1981 J. Watson (GB)
1963 J. Clark (GB)	1982 N. Lauda (AUT)
1964 J. Clark (GB)	1983 A. Prost (FRA)
1965 J. Clark (GB)	1984 N. Lauda (AUT)
1966 J. Brabham (AUS)	1985 A. Prost (FRA)
1967 J. Clark (GB)	1986 N. Mansell (GB)
1968 J. Siffert (SWI)	1987 N. Mansell (GB)
	1988 A. Senna (BRA)

CANADIAN GP

1967 J. Brabham (AUS)	1977 J. Scheckter (SAF)
1968 D. Hulme (NZ)	1978 G. Villeneuve (CAN)
1969 J. Ickx (BEL)	1979 A. Jones (AUS)
1970 J. Ickx (BEL)	1980 A. Jones (AUS)
1971 J. Stewart (GB)	1981 J. Laffite (FRA)
1972 J. Stewart (GB)	1982 N. Piquet (BRA)
1973 P. Revson (USA)	1983 R. Arnoux (FRA)
1974 E. Fittipaldi (BRA)	1984 N. Piquet (BRA)
1975 Not held	1985 M. Albereto (ITA)
1976 J. Hunt (GB)	1986 N. Mansell (GB)
	1987 Not held
	1988 A. Senna (BRA)

DETROIT GP

1982 J. Watson (GB)	1985 K. Rosberg (FIN)
1983 M. Alboreto (ITA)	1986 A. Senna (BRA)
1984 N. Piquet (BRA)	1987 A. Senna (BRA)

FRENCH GP

1950 J. M. Fangio (ARG)	1962 D. Gurney (USA)
1951 L. Fagioli (ITA)/J.M.Fangio (ARG)	1963 J. Clark (GB)
1952 A. Ascari (ITA)	1964 D. Gurney (USA)
1953 M. Hawthorn (GB)	1965 J. Clark (GB)
1954 J. M. Fangio (ARG)	1966 J. Brabham (AUS)
1955 Not held	1967 J. Brabham (AUS)
1956 P. Collins (GB)	1968 J. Ickx (BEL)
1957 J. M. Fangio (ARG)	1969 J. Stewart (GB)
1958 M. Hawthorn (GB)	1970 J. Rindt (AUT)
1959 T. Brooks (GB)	1971 J. Stewart (GB)
1960 J. Brabham (AUS)	1972 J. Stewart (GB)
1961 G. Baghetti (ITA)	1973 R. Peterson (SWE)

1974 R. Peterson (SWE)
1975 N. Lauda (AUT)
1976 J. Hunt (GB)
1977 M. Andretti (USA)
1978 M. Andretti (USA)
1979 J -P. Jabouille (FRA)
1980 A. Jones (AUS)

1981 A. Prost (FRA)
1982 R. Arnoux (FRA)
1983 A. Prost (FRA)
1984 N. Lauda (AUT)
1985 N. Piquet (BRA)
1986 N. Mansell (GB)
1987 N. Mansell (GB)
1988 A. Prost (FRA)
1989 A. Prost (FRA)

GERMAN GP

1951 A. Ascari (ITA)
1952 A. Ascari (ITA)
1953 G. Farina (ITA)
1954 J. M. Fangio (ARG)
1955 Not held
1956 J. M. Fangio (ARG)
1957 J. M. Fangio (ARG)
1958 T. Brooks (GB)
1959 T. Brooks (GB)
1960 Not held
1961 S. Moss (GB)
1962 G. Hill (GB)
1963 J. Surtees (GB)
1964 J. Surtees (GB)
1965 J. Clark (GB)
1966 J. Brabham (AUS)
1967 D. Hulme (NZ)
1968 J. Stewart (GB)

1969 J. Ickx (BEL)
1970 J. Rindt (AUT)
1971 J. Stewart (GB)
1972 J. Ickx (BEL)
1973 J. Stewart (GB)
1974 C. Regazzoni (SWI)
1975 C. Reutemann (ARG)
1976 J. Hunt (GB)
1977 N. Lauda (AUT)
1978 M. Andretti (USA)
1979 A. Jones (AUS)
1980 J. Laffite (FRA)
1981 N. Piquet (BRA)
1982 P. Tambay (FRA)
1983 R. Arnoux (FRA)
1984 A. Prost (FRA)
1985 M. Albereto (ITA)
1986 N. Piquet (BRA)
1987 N. Piquet (BRA)
1988 A. Senna (BRA)

HUNGARIAN GP

1986 N. Piquet (BRA)
1987 N. Piquet (BRA)
1988 A. Senna (BRA)

ITALIAN GP

1950 G. Farina (ITA)
1951 A. Ascari (ITA)
1952 A. Ascari (ITA)
1953 J. M. Fangio (ARG)
1954 J. M. Fangio (ARG)
1955 J. M. Fangio (ARG)
1956 S. Moss (GB)
1957 S. Moss (GB)
1958 T. Brooks (GB)
1959 S. Moss (GB)
1960 P. Hill (USA)
1961 P. Hill (USA)
1962 G. Hill (GB)
1963 J. Clark (GB)
1964 J. Surtees (GB)
1965 J. Stewart (GB)
1966 L. Scarfiotti (ITA)
1967 J. Surtees (GB)
1968 D. Hulme (NZ)

1969 J. Stewart (GB)
1970 C. Regazzoni (SWI)
1971 P. Gethin (GB)
1972 E. Fittipaldi (BRA)
1973 R. Peterson (SWE)
1974 R. Peterson (SWE)
1975 C. Regazzoni (SWI)
1976 R. Peterson (SWE)
1977 M. Andretti (USA)
1978 N. Lauda (AUT)
1979 J. Scheckter (SAF)
1980 N. Piquet (BRA)
1981 A. Prost (FRA)
1982 R. Arnoux (FRA)
1983 N. Piquet (BRA)
1984 N. Lauda (AUT)
1985 A. Prost (FRA)
1986 N. Piquet (BRA)
1987 N. Piquet (BRA)
1988 G. Berger (AUT)

JAPANESE GP

1976 M. Andretti (USA)
1977 J. Hunt (GB)
1987 G. Berger (AUT)
1988 A. Senna (BRA)

MEXICAN GP

1963 J. Clark (GB)
1964 D. Gurney (USA)
1965 R. Ginther (USA)
1966 J. Surtees (GB)
1967 J. Clark (GB)
1968 G. Hill (GB)

1969 D. Hulme (NZ)
1970 J. Ickx (BEL)
1971-1985 Not held
1986 G. Berger (AUT)
1987 N. Mansell (GB)
1988 A. Prost (FRA)
1989 A. Senna (BRA)

MONACO GP

1950 J. M. Fangio (ARG)
1951–54 not held
1955 M. Trintignant (FRA)
1956 S. Moss (GB)
1957 J. M. Fangio (ARG)
1958 M. Trintignant (FRA)
1959 J. Brabham (AUS)
1960 S. Moss (GB)
1961 S. Moss (GB)
1962 B. McLaren (NZ)
1963 G. Hill (GB)
1964 G. Hill (GB)
1965 G. Hill (GB)
1966 J. Stewart (GB)
1967 D. Hulme (NZ)
1968 G. Hill (GB)
1969 G. Hill (GB)

1970 J. Rindt (AUT)
1971 J. Stewart (GB)
1972 J –P. Beltoise (FRA)
1973 J. Stewart (GB)
1974 R. Peterson (SWE)
1975 N. Lauda (AUT)
1976 N. Lauda (AUT)
1977 J. Scheckter (SAF)
1978 P. Depailler (FRA)
1979 J. Scheckter (SAF)
1980 C. Reutemann (ARG)
1981 G. Villeneuve (CAN)
1982 R. Patrese (ITA)
1983 K. Rosberg (FIN)
1984 A. Prost (FRA)
1985 A. Prost (FRA)
1986 A. Prost (FRA)
1987 A. Senna (BRA)
1988 A. Prost (FRA)
1989 A. Senna (BRA)

PORTUGUESE GP

1958 S. Moss (GB)
1959 S. Moss (GB)
1960 J. Brabham (AUS)
1961-1983 Not held

1984 A. Prost (FRA)
1985 A. Senna (BRA)
1986 N. Mansell (GB)
1987 A. Prost (FRA)
1988 A. Prost (FRA)

SAN MARINO GP

1981 N. Piquet (BRA)
1982 D. Pironi (FRA)
1983 P. Tambay (FRA)
1984 A. Prost (FRA)

1985 E. de Angelis (ITA)
1986 A. Prost (FRA)
1987 N. Mansell (GB)
1988 A. Senna (BRA)
1989 A. Senna (BRA)

SPANISH GP

1951 J. M. Fangio (ARG)	1974 N. Lauda (AUT)
1952-53 Not held	1975 J. Mass (FRG)
1954 M. Hawthorn (GB)	1976 J. Hunt (GB)
1955-1967 Not held	1977 M. Andretti (USA)
1968 G. Hill (GB)	1978 M. Andretti (USA)
1969 J. Stewart (GB)	1979 P. Depailler (FRA)
1970 J. Stewart (GB)	1980 Not held
1971 J. Stewart (GB)	1981 G. Villeneuve (CAN)
1972 E. Fittipaldi (BRA)	1982-1985 Not held
1973 E. Fittipaldi (BRA)	1986 A. Senna (BRA)
	1987 N. Mansell (GB)
	1988 A. Prost (FRA)

INDIANAPOLIS 500

Held over 200 laps of the 2½-mile Indianapolis Raceway, the race is held at the end of May each year. Between 1950-60 the race formed part of the Formula One World Driver's Championship

Winners (all USA unless otherwise stated)

1911 R. Harroun	1937 W. Shaw	1965 J. Clark (GB)
1912 J. Dawson	1938 F. Roberts	1966 G. Hill (GB)
1913 J. Goux	1939 W. Shaw	1967 A. J. Foyt, Jnr
1914 R. Thomas	1940 W. Shaw	1968 B. Unser
1915 R. DePalma	1941 F. Davis/M. Rose	1969 M. Andretti
1916 D. Resta	1942-45 Not held	1970 A. Unser
1917-18 Not held	1946 G. Robson	1971 A. Unser
1919 H. Wilcox	1947 M. Rose	1972 M. Donohue
1920 G. Chevrolet	1948 M. Rose	1973 G. Johncock
1921 T. Milton	1949 B. Holland	1974 J. Rutherford
1922 J. Murphy	1950 J. Parsons	1975 B. Unser
1923 T. Milton	1951 L. Wallard	1976 J. Rutherford
1924 L. Corum/J. Boyer	1952 T. Ruttmann	1977 A. J. Foyt, Jnr
1925 P. DePaolo	1953 W. Vukovich	1978 A. Unser
1926 F. Lockhart	1954 W. Vukovich	1979 R. Mears
1927 G. Souders	1955 B. Sweikert	1980 J. Rutherford
1928 L. Meyer	1956 P. Flaherty	1981 B. Unser
1929 R. Keech	1957 S. Hanks	1982 G. Johncock
1930 B. Arnold	1958 J. Bryan	1983 T. Sneva
1931 L. Schneider	1959 R. Ward	1984 R. Mears
1932 F. Frame	1960 J. Rathmann	1985 D. Sullivan
1933 L. Meyer	1961 A. J. Foyt, Jnr	1986 B. Rahal
1934 B. Cummings	1962 R. Ward	1987 A. Unser
1935 K. Petillo	1963 P. Jones	1988 R. Mears
1936 L. Meyer	1964 A. J. Foyt, Jnr	1989 E. Fittipaldi (BRA)

MOST WINS:

4 A. J. Foyt, Jnr. A. Unser

LE MANS
The most famous of all endurance races, the Le Mans 24-hour race, was first held in May 1923.

1923 A. Lagache/R. Leonard	1963 L. Scarfiotti/L. Bandini
1924 J. Duff/F. Clement	1964 J. Guichet/N. Vaccarella
1925 H. de Courcells/A. Rossignol	1965 J. Rindt/M. Gregory
1926 R. Bloch/A. Rossignol	1966 C. Amon/B. McLaren
1927 J. Benjafield/S. Davis	1967 D. Gurney/A. J. Foyt, Jnr.
1928 W. Barnato/B. Rubin	1968 P. Rodriguez/L. Bianchi
1929 W. Barnato/H. Birkin	1969 J. Ickx/J. Oliver
1930 W. Barnato/G. Kidston	1970 H. Herrmann/R. Attwood
1931 E. Howe/H. Birkin	1971 H. Marko/G. van Lennep
1932 R. Sommer/L. Chinetti	1972 H. Pescarolo/G. Hill
1933 R. Sommer/T. Nuvolari	1973 H. Pescarolo/G. Larrousse
1934 L. Chinetti/P. Etancelin	1974 H. Pescarolo/G. Larrousse
1935 J. Hindmarsh/L. Fontes	1975 J. Ickx/D. Bell
1936 Not held	1976 J. Ickx/G. van Lennep
1937 J-P. Wimille/R. Benoist	1977 J. Ickx/J. Barth/H. Haywood
1938 E. Chaboud/J. Tremoulet	1978 J-P. Jaussaud/D. Pironi
1939 J-P. Wimille/P. Veyron	1979 K. Ludwig/
1940-48 Not Held	W. Whittington/D. Whittington
1949 L. Chinetti/P. Selsdon	1980 J-P. Jaussaud/J. Rondeau
1950 L. Rosier/J-L. Rosier	1981 J. Ickx/D. Bell
1951 P. Walker/P. Whitehead	1982 J. Ickx/D. Bell
1952 H. Lang/K. Riess	1983 V. Schuppan/H. Haywood/A. Holbert
1953 T. Rolt/D. Hamilton	1984 K. Ludwig/H. Pescarolo
1954 F. Gonzalez/M. Trintignant	1985 K. Ludwig/
1955 M. Hawthorn/I. Bueb	P. Barillo/'John Winter'
1956 R. Flockhart/N. Sanderson	1986 H-J. Stuck/D. Bell/A. Holbert
1957 R. Flockhart/I. Bueb	1987 H -J. Stuck/D. Bell/A. Holbert
1958 O. Gendebien/P. Hill	1988 J. Lammers/J. Dumfries/A. Wallace
1959 C. Shelby/R. Salvadori	1989 J. Mass/M. Reuter/S. Dickens
1960 O. Gendebien/P. Frere	
1961 O. Gendebien/P. Hill	
1962 O. Gendebien/P. Hill	

MOST WINS:
6 Jacky Ickx

Former British Formula Three champion Johnny Dumfries was certainly not in motor racing for the money. As the Earl of Dumfries, he was heir to a massive £100 million fortune.

In the 1983 Long Beach Grand Prix, McLaren team-mates John Watson and Niki Lauda started the race from 22nd and 23rd positions on the starting grid. Remarkably they finished first and second...

Most Grand Prix Wins
Drivers
35 Alain Prost (FRA) 1981-88 ●
27 Jackie Stewart (GB) 1965-73 ●
25 Jim Clark (GB) 1962-68 ●
25 Niki Lauda (AUT) 1974-85 ●
24 Juan Manuel Fangio (ARG) 1950-57 ●
20 Nelson Piquet (BRA) 1980-87 ●
16 Stirling Moss (GB) 1955-61
14 Jack Brabham (AUS) 1959-70 ●
14 Graham Hill (GB) 1962-69 ●
14 Emerson Fittipaldi (BRA) 1970-75 ●
14 Ayrton Senna (BRA) 1985-88 ●
13 Alberto Ascari (ITA) 1951-53 ●
13 Nigel Mansell (GB) 1985-87
12 Mario Andretti (USA) 1971-78 ●
12 Carlos Reutemann (ARG) 1974-81
12 Alan Jones (AUS) 1977-81 ●
10 James Hunt (GB) 1975-77 ●
10 Ronnie Peterson (SWE) 1973-78
10 Jody Scheckter (SAF) 1974-79 ●

● Indicates a former world champion

Most Grand Prix Wins
Manufacturers
94 Ferrari 1951-88
79 Lotus 1960-87
70 McLaren 1968-88
40 Williams 1979-87
35 Brabham 1964-85
23 Tyrrell 1971-83
17 BRM 1959-72
16 Cooper 1958-67
15 Renault 1979-83
10 Alfa Romeo 1950-51
 9 Mercedes-Benz 1954-55
 9 Maserati 1953-57
 9 Vanwall 1957-58
 9 Matra 1968-69
 8 Ligier 1977-81

Most Wins in a Season
8 Ayrton Senna (BRA) 1988
7 Jim Clark (GB) 1963
  Alain Prost (FRA) 1984, 1988
6 Alberto Ascari (ITA) 1952
  Juan Manuel Fangio (ARG) 1954
  Jim Clark (GB) 1965
  Jackie Stewart (GB) 1969, 1971
  James Hunt (GB) 1976
  Mario Andretti (USA) 1978
  Nigel Mansell (GB) 1987

Most Successive Wins
9 Alberto Ascari (ITA) 1952-3
5 Jack Brabham (AUS) 1960
  Jim Clark (GB) 1965

Most Pole Positions
33 Jim Clark (GB) 1962-68
29 Juan Manuel Fangio (ARG) 1950-58
29 Ayrton Senna (BRA) 1985-88
24 Niki Lauda (AUT) 1974-78
   Nelson Piquet (BRA) 1980-87

NETBALL
Developed from basketball, it is a seven-a-side women's team game, invented in 1891 in USA. The International Federation of Women's Basketball and Netball Associations was formed in 1960.

WORLD CHAMPIONSHIP
Known as the World Tournament, it was first held in 1963 and every four years since then.

1963 Australia
1967 New Zealand
1971 Australia
1975 Australia
1979 Australia, New Zealand, Trinidad & Tobago
1983 Australia
1987 New Zealand

Most Wins:
5 Australia

Recorded details show that the Ancient Olympic Games were held in 776 BC but some sources believe the Games were held even before that date. The Ancient Games were abolished in 394 AD but revived 1500 years later when Frenchman Baron Pierre de Coubertin initiated the inauguration of the Modern Games in 1896. The first Modern Games were held in Athens and, like its Ancient counterpart, have been held every four years. There was an intercalated Games in 1906 to celebrate ten years of the rebirth of the Games. Most sources ignore performances at these Games for record purposes. Since 1924 a Winter Olympics celebration has been staged.

VENUES

The following is a list of the venues of all Summer and Winter Olympics.

Summer:

Year	Venue	Year	Venue
1896	Athens, Greece	1944	Not held
1900	Paris, France	1948	London, England
1904	St.Louis, United States	1952	Helsinki, Finland
1906	Athens, Greece	1956	Melbourne, Australia*
1908	London, England	1960	Rome, Italy
1912	Stockholm, Sweden	1964	Tokyo, Japan
1916	Not held	1968	Mexico City, Mexico
1920	Antwerp, Belgium	1972	Munich, West Germany
1924	Paris, France	1976	Montreal, Canada
1928	Amsterdam, Holland	1980	Moscow, USSR
1932	Los Angeles, United States	1984	Los Angeles, United States
1936	Berlin, Germany	1988	Seoul, South Korea
1940	Not held	1992	Barcelona, Spain

* Equestrian events at Stockholm, Sweden.

Winter:

Year	Venue	Year	Venue
1924	Chamonix, France	1964	Innsbruck, Austria
1928	St.Moritz, Switzerland	1968	Grenoble, France
1932	Lake Placid, United States	1972	Sapporo, Japan
1936	Garmisch-Partenkirchen, Germany	1976	Innsbruck, Austria
1948	St.Moritz, Switzerland	1980	Lake Placid, USA
1952	Oslo, Norway	1984	Sarajevo, Yugoslavia
1956	Cortina d'Ampezzo, Italy	1988	Calgary, Canada
1960	Squaw Valley, United States	1992	Albertville, France

Sweden's Ingemar Johansson was disqualified from the 1952 Olympic heavyweight boxing final for 'not trying'. Seven years later he won the world heavyweight title. In 1982, however, 30 years after he should have received his Olympic medal, it was eventually presented to him.

ALL-TIME MEDAL WINNERS

Summer Games:	Gold	Silver	Bronze	Total
United States	746	560	475	1781
USSR	395	323	299	1017
Great Britain	173	222	206	601
West Germany (incl. Germany)	157	207	207	571
France	153	167	177	497
Sweden	131	139	169	439
East Germany	153	129	127	409
Italy	147	121	124	392
Hungary	124	112	136	372
Finland	97	75	110	282
Japan	87	75	82	244
Australia	71	67	87	225
Romania	55	64	82	201
Poland	40	56	95	191
Canada	39	62	73	174
Switzerland	40	65	58	163
Holland	43	47	63	153
Bulgaria	37	62	52	151
Denmark	33	58	33	144
Czechoslovakia	45	48	49	142
Belgium	35	48	42	125
Norway	42	33	33	108
Greece	22	39	39	100
Yugoslavia	26	29	28	83
Austria	19	27	33	79
South Korea	19	22	29	70
China	20	19	21	60
Cuba	23	21	15	59
New Zealand	26	6	33	55
South Africa	16	15	21	52
Turkey	24	13	10	47
Argentina	13	19	14	46
Mexico	9	12	18	39
Brazil	7	9	20	36
Kenya	11	9	11	31
Iran	4	11	15	30
Spain	4	12	9	25
Jamaica	4	10	8	22
Estonia	6	6	9	21
Egypt	6	6	6	18
India	8	3	3	14
Ireland	4	4	5	13
Portugal	2	4	7	13
North Korea	2	5	5	12
Mongolia	—	5	6	11
Ethiopia	5	1	4	10
Pakistan	3	3	3	9
Uruguay	2	1	6	9
Venezuela	1	2	5	8
Chile	—	6	2	8
Trinidad	1	2	4	7
Philippines	—	1	6	7
Morocco	3	1	2	6
Uganda	1	3	1	5
Tunisia	1	2	2	5
Colombia	—	2	3	5
Lebanon	—	2	2	4

Nigeria	—	1	3	4
Puerto Rico	—	1	3	4
Peru	1	2	—	3
Latvia	—	2	1	3
Ghana	—	1	2	3
Taiwan	—	1	2	3
Thailand	—	1	2	3
Luxembourg	1	1	—	2
Bahamas	1	—	1	2
Tanzania	—	2	—	2
Cameroun	—	1	1	2
Haiti	—	1	1	2
Iceland	—	1	1	2
Algeria	—	—	2	2
Panama	—	—	2	2
Surinam	1	—	—	1
Zimbabwe	1	—	—	1
Costa Rica	—	1	—	1
Dutch Antiles	—	1	—	1
Indonesia	—	1	—	1
Ivory Coast	—	1	—	1
Senegal	—	1	—	1
Singapore	—	1	—	1
Sri Lanka	—	1	—	1
Syria	—	1	—	1
US Virgin Islands	—	1	—	1
Bermuda	—	—	1	1
Djibouti	—	—	1	1
Dominican Republic	—	—	1	1
Guyana	—	—	1	1
Iraq	—	—	1	1
Niger	—	—	1	1
Zambia	—	—	1	1
Winter Games:	**Gold**	**Silver**	**Bronze**	**Total**
USSR	79	57	59	195
Norway	54	60	54	168
United States	42	47	34	123
East Germany	39	36	35	110
Finland	33	43	34	110
Austria	28	38	32	98
Sweden	36	25	31	92
West Germany (incl. Germany)	26	26	23	75
Switzerland	23	25	25	73
Canada	14	12	18	44
Netherlands	13	17	12	42
France	13	10	16	39
Italy	14	10	9	33
Czechoslovakia	2	8	13	23
Great Britain	7	4	10	21
Liechtenstein	2	2	5	9
Japan	1	4	2	7
Hungary	0	2	4	6
Belgium	1	1	2	4
Poland	1	1	2	4
Yugoslavia	—	3	1	4
Spain	1	—	—	1
North Korea	—	1	—	1
Bulgaria	—	—	1	1
Romania	—	—	1	1

PARALYMPICS

The Olympic belief that 'taking part is the important thing' is most evident at the Paralympics for disabled athletes. There is no finer stimulus for the handicapped person than the ability to compete at a sporting level, and the four-yearly gathering of competitors for a wide variety of sports is now one of the truly great sporting moments.

The idea of competitive sport for the handicapped was devised by Dr. Ludwig Guttmann as part of the medical treatment for paraplegics. On the day the 1948 Olympics opened in London he organised an archery competition at Stoke Mandeville Hospital for 14 men and two women. This was the start of the Stoke Mandeville Games. They soon became an international event with competitors from all corners of the globe taking part. Since then, competition for the disabled has grown dramatically and the Paralympics are held at the same venue as the main Olympic Games and immediately after them. The first time they were held alongside the Summer Olympics was at Rome in 1960 and that pattern has followed ever since, with the exception of Mexico City (1968) and Moscow (1980). The opening ceremonies are as spectacular as those of their 'senior' counterparts, and competition is just as intense.

Orienteering is basically a form of cross-country running but with the aid of a compass. British soldiers were first to organise such races but Orienteering is accredited to Ernst Killander of Sweden who devised the modern-day sport in 1918. The International Orienteering Federation was founded in 1961.

WORLD CHAMPIONSHIPS

The first championships, for both men and women, were inaugurated in 1966. Individual and team competitions are contested.

Individual

Men	Women
1966 A.Hadler (NOR)	U.Lindquist (SWE)
1968 K.Johansson (SWE)	U.Lindquist (SWE)
1970 S.Berge (NOR)	I.Hadler (NOR)
1972 A.Hadler (NOR)	S.Monspart (HUN)
1974 B.Frilen (SWE)	M.Norgaard (DEN)
1976 E.Johansen (NOR)	L.Veijalainen (FIN)
1978 E.Johansen (NOR)	A.Berit Eid (NOR)
1979 O.Thon (NOR)	O.Bergonstrom (FIN)
1981 O.Thon (NOR)	A.Kringstad (SWE)
1983 M.Berglia (NOR)	A.Kringstad-Svensson (SWE)
1985 K.Sallinen (FIN)	A.Kringstad-Svensson (SWE)
1987 K.Olsson (SWE)	A.Hannus (SWE)

Most Wins (Men):
2 Age Hadler, Egil Johansen, Ogvin Thon
(Women):
3 Annichen Kringstad-Svensson

Team

Men	Women
1966 Sweden	Sweden
1968 Norway	Sweden
1970 Sweden	Norway
1972 Finland	Sweden
1974 Sweden	Sweden
1976 Sweden	Sweden
1978 Finland	Norway
1979 Finland	Sweden
1981 Sweden	Norway
1983 Sweden	Sweden
1985 Norway	Sweden
1987 Norway	Norway

Most Wins (Men):
6 Sweden
(Women):
8 Sweden

Polo is said to have been played in Persia around 600 BC when a match between the Persians and the Turkomans is described by a poet of the day. The game eventually spread throughout Asia, and visiting Britons, notably to India, became attached to the sport. The first organised game was in the 1850s and it spread to the United States in the latter part of the 19th century. By the outbreak of the First World War, Polo was an international game.

COWDRAY CUP

The Cowdray Park Gold Cup, for the British Open Championship, is Polo's most famous trophy. It was first contested in 1956.

Winners:

1956 Los Indios	1972 Pimms
1957 Windsor Park	1973 Stowell Park
1958 Cowdray Park	1974 Stowell Park
1959 Casarejo	1975 Greenhill Farm
1960 Casarejo	1976 Stowell Park
1961 Cowdray Park	1977 Foxcote
1962 Cowdray Park	1978 Stowell Park
1963 La Vulchi	1979 Songhai
1964 Jersey Lilies	1980 Stowell Park
1965 Jersey Lilies	1981 Falcons
1966 Windsor Park	1982 Southfield
1967 Woolmers Park	1983 Falcons
1968 Pimms	1984 Southfield
1969 Windsor Park	1985 Maple Leafs
1970 Boca Raton	1986 Tramontona
1971 Pimms	1987 Tramontona
	1988 Tramontona

Most Wins:
5 Stowell Park

OLYMPIC GAMES

Polo was included in the Olympic Games five times between 1900–36.

Winners:

1900 Great Britain	1924 Argentina
1908 Great Britain	1936 Argentina
1920 Great Britain	

Most Wins:
3 Great Britain

Rackets derived itself as a form of handball and became popular in the 17th century. Inmates of the Fleet debtor's prison in London used to play Rackets as a form of exercise and it was one such inmate, Robert McKay, who claimed to be the sport's first World Champion.

WORLD CHAMPIONSHIP

Since Robert McKay claimed the first world title in 1820 it has changed hands, normally, by the defending champion accepting a challenge from a contender.

Winners

(all GB unless otherwise stated):

1820 R.Mackay	1911 C.Williams
1825 T.Pittman	1914 J.Soutar (USA)
1834 J.Pittman	1928 C.Williams
1838 J.Lamb	1937 D.S.Milford
1846 L.C.Mitchell	1947 J.Dear
1860 F.Erwood	1954 G.W.T.Atkins
1862 W.H.Dyke	1972 W.Surtees (USA)
1863 H.Gray	1974 H.Angus
1866 W.Gray	1978 W.Surtees
1876 H.B.Fairs	1981 J.Prenn
1878 J.Gray	1984 W.Boone
1887 P.Latham	1986 J.Prenn
1903 J.Jamsetjhi (IND)	

Longest Reigning Champion:
28 years Geoffrey Atkins

The regular series of Oxford and Cambridge varsity Rackets matches started in 1858. Only the Boat Race and the cricket matches have been going longer

The beaten finalist in the 1952 amateur rackets championship was former England test cricket captain Colin Cowdrey. He lost 3-0 to Geoffrey Atkins, who won the first of his five singles titles.

Rally driving cannot conclusively trace its beginnings because, since the day the motor car was born, rallying, a means of getting from A to B, was the aim of all drivers. The first great long-distance rally was the Peking to Paris race in 1907 and in 1911 the first Monte Carlo Rally was staged.

WORLD CHAMPIONS

Although a World Championship for makes was introduced by the FIA in 1973, a Drivers' World Championship was not introduced until 1979.

Winners:

1979 B.Waldegaard (SWE)		1983 H.Mikkola (FIN)	
1980 W.Rohrl (FRG)		1984 S.Blomqvist (SWE)	
1981 A.Vatanen (FIN)		1985 T.Salonen (FIN)	
1982 W.Rohrl (FRG)		1986 J. Kankkunen (FIN)	
		1987 J.Kankkunen (FIN)	
		1988 M.Biasion (ITA)	

Most Wins:
2 Walter Rohrl, Juha Kankkunen

MONTE CARLO RALLY

The most famous rally in the world, the 'Monte' was first staged in 1911.

Winners:

1911 H.Rougier	Turcat-Mery
1912 J.Beutler	Berliet
1913–23 Not held	
1924 J.Ledure	Bignan
1925 F.Repusseau	Renault
1926 Hon.V.Bruce	A.C.
1927 Lefebvre	Amilcar
1928 J.Bignan	Fiat
1929 Dr.Sprenger van Eijk	Graham-Paige
1930 H.Petit	Licorne
1931 D.M.Healey	Invicta
1932 M.Vasselle	Hotchkiss
1933 M.Vasselle	Hotchkiss
1934 Gas/J.Trevoux	Hotchkiss
1935 C.Lahaye/R.Quatresous	Renault
1936 I.Zamfirescu/J.Quinlin	Ford
1937 R.le Begue/J.Quinlin	Delahaye
1938 G.Bakker Schut/K.Ton	Ford
1939 J.Trevoux/M.Lesurque	Hotchkiss
1940–48 Not held	
1949 J.Trevoux/M.Lesurque	Hotchkiss
1950 M.Becquart/H.Secret	Hotchkiss
1951 J.Trevoux/R.Crovetto	Delahaye
1952 S.H.Allard/G.Warburton	Allard
1953 M.Gatsonides/P.Worledge	Ford
1954 L.Chiron/C.Basadonna	Lancia
1955 P.Malling/G.Fadum	Talbot
1956 R.J.Adams/F.E.A.Bigger	Jaguar
1957 Not held	
1958 G.Monraise/J.Feret	Renault
1959 P.Coltelloni/P.Alexander	Citroen
1960 W.Schock/R.Moll	Mercedes Benz
1961 M.Martin/R.Bateua	Panhard

Monte Carlo Winners Cont.

Year	Driver/Co-driver	Car
1962	E.Carlsson/G.Haggbom	Saab
1963	E.Carlsson/G.Palm	Saab
1964	P.Hopkirk/H.Liddon	Mini-Cooper
1965	T.Makinen/P.Easter	Mini-Cooper
1966	P.Toivonen/E.Mikander	Citroen
1967	R.Aaltonen/H.Liddon	Mini-Cooper
1968	V.Elford/D.Stone	Porsche
1969	B.Waldegaard/L.Helmer	Porsche
1970	B.Waldegaard/L.Helmer	Porsche
1971	O.Andersson/D.Stone	Alpine Renault
1972	S.Munari/M.Manucci	Lancia Fulvia
1973	J -C.Andruet/'Biche'	Alpine Renault
1974	Not held	
1975	S.Munari/M.Manucci	Lancia Stratos
1976	S.Munari/S.Maiga	Lancia Stratos
1977	S.Munari/M.Manucci	Lancia Stratos
1978	J -P.Nicolas/V.Laverne	Porsche Carrera
1979	B.Darniche/A.Mahe	Lancia Stratos
1980	W.Rohrl/C.Geistdorfer	Fiat Abarth
1981	J.Ragnotti/J -M.Andrie	Renault 5
1982	W.Rohrl/C.Geistdorfer	Opel Ascona
1983	W.Rohrl/C.Geistdorfer	Opel Ascona
1984	W.Rohrl/C.Geistdorfer	Audi Quattro
1985	A.Vatanen/T.Harryman	Peugeot 205
1986	H.Toivonen/S.Cresto	Lancia Delta
1987	M.Biasion/T. Siviero	Lancia Delta
1988	B.Saby/J.F.Fauchille	Lancia Delta
1989	M.Biasion/T.Sivieri	Lancia Integrale

Most wins:
4 Sandro Munari, Walter Rohrl, Christian Geistdorfer

RAC INTERNATIONAL RALLY

Although a forerunner of the RAC Rally was held in 1922, using Torquay as its finishing point, the Rally only became recognised as an international event in 1951.

Winners:

Year	Driver	Car	Year	Driver	Car
1951	I.Appleyard	Jaguar	1969	H.Kallstrom	Lancia Fulvia
1952	G.Imhof	Allard	1970	H.Kallstrom	Lancia Fulvia
1953	I.Appleyard	Jaguar	1971	S.Blomqvist	Saab
1954	J.Wallwork	Triumph	1972	R.Clark	Ford Escort
1955	J.Ray	Standard	1973	T.Makinen	Ford Escort
1956	L.Sims	Aston Martin	1974	T.Makinen	Ford Escort
1957	Not held		1975	T.Makinen	Ford Escort
1958	P.Harper	Sunbeam Rapier	1976	R.Clark	Ford Escort
1959	G.Burgess	Ford Zephyr	1977	B.Waldegaard	Ford Escort
1960	E.Carlsson	Saab	1978	H.Mikkola	Ford Escort
1961	E.Carlsson	Saab	1979	H.Mikkola	Ford Escort
1962	E.Carlsson	Saab	1980	H.Toivonen	Talbot Sunbeam
1963	T.Trana	Volvo	1981	H.Mikkola	Audi Quattro
1964	T.Trana	Volvo	1982	H.Mikkola	Audi Quattro
1965	R.Aaltonen	Mini-Cooper	1983	S.Blomqvist	Audio Quattro
1966	B.Soderstrom	Ford Cortina-Lotus	1984	A.Vatanen	Peugeot
1967	Not held		1985	H.Toivonen	Lancia Delta
1968	S.Lampinen	Saab	1986	T.Salonen	Peugeot
			1987	J.Kankkunen	Lancia Delta
			1988	M.Alen	Lancia Delta

Most Wins:
4 Hannu Mikkola (Arne Hertz won 5 times as a co-driver)

Real, Royal, or Court tennis was first mentioned in France in the 12th century, and it was very much the sport of Kings – so much so that two French monarchs, Louis X and Charles VIII, died while playing the sport.

WORLD CHAMPIONSHIPS
The Real Tennis World Championships date back further than those of any other sport, to around 1740 when Monsieur Clerge of France won the first title. The title is claimed by successfully challenging the champion.

Men

1740 Clerge (FRA)	1908 C.Fairs (GB)
1765 R.Masson (FRA)	1912 G.F.Covey (GB)
1785 J.Barcellon (FRA)	1914 J.Gould (USA)
1816 Marchesio (ITA)	1916 G.F.Covey (GB)
1819 P.Cox (GB)	1928 P.Etchebaster (FRA)
1829 E.Barre (FRA)	1955 J.Dear (GB)
1862 E.Tomkins (GB)	1957 A.Johnson (GB)
1871 G.Lambert (GB)	1959 N.R.Knox (USA)
1885 T.Pettitt (USA)	1969 G.H.Bostwick (USA)
1890 C.Saunders (GB)	1972 J.Bostwick (USA)
1895 P.Latham (GB)	1976 H.Angus (GB)
1905 C.Fairs (GB)	1981 C.Ronaldson (GB)
1907 P.Latham (GB)	1987 W.Davies (AUS)

Women
The first women's World Championship was held in 1985:
1985 J.Clarke (AUS)
1987 J. Clarke (AUS)

One of the semi-finalists in the 1987 women's world championship at Hayling Island was Sally Jones, a sports presenter on BBC television. She lost to the defending champion, Judy Clarke of Australia.

Rowing dates back to ancient times but the sport in its present form began in 1715 when Irish comedian Thomas Doggett instituted his famous race for scullers, Doggett's Coat and Badge. The first known regatta was on the Thames, near Walton, in 1768. There are no championships in Olympic years.

WORLD CHAMPIONSHIPS

The first World Championships were held at Lucerne in 1962. The first women's championships were in 1974.

Winners
Men
Single Sculls

1962 V.Ivanov (USSR)	1979 P.Karppinen (FIN)
1966 D.Spero (USA)	1981 P -M.Kolbe (FRG)
1970 A.Demiddi (ARG)	1982 R.Reiche (GDR)
1974 W.Honig (GDR)	1983 P -M.Kolbe (FRG)
1975 P -M.Kolbe (FRG)	1985 P.Karppinen (FIN)
1977 J.Dreifke (GDR)	1986 P -M.Kolbe (FRG)
1978 P -M.Kolbe (FRG)	1987 T.Lange (GDR)

Most Wins:
5 Peter-Michael Kolbe

	Double Sculls	Coxless Pairs	Coxed Pairs
1962	France	West Germany	West Germany
1966	Switzerland	East Germany	Holland
1970	Denmark	West Germany	Romania
1974	East Germany	East Germany	USSR
1975	Norway	East Germany	East Germany
1977	Great Britain	USSR	Bulgaria
1978	Norway	East Germany	East Germany
1979	Norway	East Germany	East Germany
1981	East Germany	USSR	Italy
1982	Norway	Norway	Italy
1983	East Germany	East Germany	East Germany
1985	East Germany	USSR	Italy
1986	Italy	USSR	Great Britain
1987	Bulgaria	Great Britain	Italy

	Coxless Fours	Coxed Fours	Quadruple Sculls
1962	West Germany	West Germany	–
1966	East Germany	East Germany	–
1970	East Germany	West Germany	–
1974	East Germany	East Germany	East Germany
1975	East Germany	USSR	East Germany
1977	East Germany	East Germany	East Germany
1978	USSR	East Germany	East Germany
1979	East Germany	East Germany	East Germany
1981	USSR	East Germany	East Germany
1982	Switzerland	East Germany	East Germany
1983	West Germany	New Zealand	West Germany
1985	West Germany	USSR	Canada
1986	United States	East Germany	USSR
1987	East Germany	East Germany	USSR

Eights

1962 West Germany	1979 East Germany
1966 West Germany	1981 USSR
1970 East Germany	1982 New Zealand
1974 United States	1983 New Zealand
1975 East Germany	1985 USSR
1977 East Germany	1986 Australia
1978 East Germany	1987 United States

Women
Single Sculls

1974 C.Scheiblich (GDR)	1981 S.Toma (ROM)
1975 C.Scheiblich (GDR)	1982 I.Fetisova (USSR)
1977 C.Scheiblich (GDR)	1983 J.Hampe (GDR)
1978 C.Scheiblich-Hahn (GDR)	1985 C.Linse (GDR)
1979 S.Toma (ROM)	1986 J.Hampe (GDR)
	1987 M.Georgieva (BUL)

Most Wins:
4 Christine Scheiblich-Hahn

	Double Sculls	Coxless Pairs	Quadruple Sculls
1974	USSR	Romania	East Germany
1975	USSR	East Germany	East Germany
1977	East Germany	East Germany	East Germany
1978	Bulgaria	East Germany	Bulgaria
1979	East Germany	East Germany	East Germany
1981	USSR	East Germany	USSR
1982	USSR	East Germany	USSR
1983	East Germany	East Germany	USSR
1985	East Germany	Romania	East Germany
1986	East Germany	Romania	East Germany
1987	Bulgaria	Romania	East Germany
	Coxed Fours	**Eights**	
1974	East Germany	East Germany	
1975	East Germany	East Germany	
1977	East Germany	East Germany	
1978	East Germany	USSR	
1979	USSR	USSR	
1981	USSR	USSR	
1982	USSR	USSR	
1983	East Germany	USSR	
1985	East Germany	USSR	
1986	Romania	USSR	
1987	Romania	Romania	

OLYMPIC GAMES

The first Olympic rowing competition was on the River Seine in 1900 but in more recent times rowing courses have been on still waters.

Men

Single Sculls

1900	H.Barrelet (FRA)	1952	Y.Tyukalov (USSR)
1904	F.Greer (USA)	1956	V.Ivanov (USSR)
1908	H.Blackstaffe (GB)	1960	V.Ivanov (USSR)
1912	W.Kinnear (GB)	1964	V.Ivanov (USSR)
1920	J.Kelly snr (USA)	1968	H.J.Wienese (HOL)
1924	J.Beresford (GB)	1972	Y.Malishev (USSR)
1928	H.Pearce (AUS)	1976	P.Karppinen (FIN)
1932	H.Pearce (AUS)	1980	P.Karppinen (FIN)
1936	G.Schafer (GER)	1984	P.Karpinnen (FIN)
1948	M.Wood (AUS)	1988	T.Lange (GDR)

Most Wins:

3 Vyacheslav Ivanov, Pertti Karppinen

	Double Sculls	Coxless Pairs	Coxed Pairs
1900	–	–	Holland
1904	United States	United States	–
1908	–	Great Britain	–
1920	United States	–	Italy
1924	United States	Holland	Switzerland
1928	United States	Germany	Switzerland
1932	United States	Great Britain	United States
1936	Great Britain	Germany	Germany
1948	Great Britain	Great Britain	Denmark
1952	Argentina	United States	France
1956	USSR	United States	United States
1960	Czechoslovakia	USSR	West Germany
1964	USSR	Canada	United States
1968	USSR	East Germany	Italy
1972	USSR	East Germany	East Germany
1976	Norway	East Germany	East Germany
1980	East Germany	East Germany	East Germany
1984	United States	Romania	Italy
1988	Holland	Great Britain	Italy

	Coxless Fours	Coxed Fours	Quadruple Sculls
1900	–	Germany	–
	–	France	–
1904	United States	–	–
1908	Great Britain	–	–
1912	–	Germany	–
1920	–	Switzerland	–
1924	Great Britain	Switzerland	–
1928	Great Britain	Italy	–
1932	Great Britain	Germany	–
1936	Germany	Germany	–
1948	Italy	United States	–
1952	Yugoslavia	Czechoslovakia	–
1956	Canada	Italy	–
1960	United States	West Germany	–
1964	Denmark	West Germany	–
1968	East Germany	New Zealand	–
1972	East Germany	West Germany	–
1976	East Germany	USSR	East Germany
1980	East Germany	East Germany	East Germany
1984	New Zealand	Great Britain	West Germany
1988	East Germany	East Germany	Italy

Eights

1900 United States		1952 United States	
1904 United States		1956 United States	
1908 Great Britain		1960 Germany	
1912 Great Britain		1964 United States	
1920 United States		1968 West Germany	
1924 United States		1972 New Zealand	
1928 United States		1976 East Germany	
1932 United States		1980 East Germany	
1936 United States		1984 Canada	
1948 United States		1988 West Germany	

Women
Single Sculls

1976 C.Scheiblich (GDR)
1980 S.Toma (ROM)
1984 V.Racila (ROM)
1988 J.Behrendt (GDR)

	Double Sculls	Coxless Pairs	Quadruple Sculls
1976	Bulgaria	Bulgaria	East Germany
1980	USSR	East Germany	East Germany
1984	Romania	Romania	Romania
1988	East Germany	Romania	East Germany

	Coxed Fours	Eights
1976	East Germany	East Germany
1980	East Germany	East Germany
1984	Romania	United States
1988	East Germany	East Germany

A member of the United States eights that won the gold medal at the 1924 Olympics was Dr. Benjamin Spock who wrote the best-selling book, *The Common Sense Book of Baby and Child Care.*

Susan Brown made Boat Race history in 1981 when she became the first woman to take part in the race, as cox to the winning Oxford team.

Russian Vyacheslav Ivanov was so delighted at winning the gold medal in the single sculls at the 1956 Melbourne Olympics that he threw his medal in the air . . . it landed in Lake Wendouree behind him. Ivanov dived in to retrieve the medal without success. The lake was even drained, but again, no medal could be found. Fortunately for the 'juggling' sculler the International Olympic Committee arranged for him to be presented with a duplicate medal.

UNIVERSITY BOAT RACE

The most famous of all rowing races the Boat Race, between crews from Oxford and Cambridge Universities, is held on the River Thames each year and covers a distance of 4 miles 374 yards between Putney and Mortlake. The first race in 1829 was from Hambledon Lock to Henley.

Winners:

1829 Oxford	1889 Cambridge	1939 Cambridge
1836 Cambridge	1890 Oxford	1946 Oxford
1839 Cambridge	1891 Oxford	1947 Cambridge
1840 Cambridge	1892 Oxford	1948 Cambridge
1841 Cambridge	1893 Oxford	1949 Cambridge
1842 Oxford	1894 Oxford	1950 Cambridge
1845 Cambridge	1895 Oxford	1951 Cambridge
1846 Cambridge	1896 Oxford	1952 Oxford
1849 Cambridge	1897 Oxford	1953 Cambridge
1849 Oxford	1898 Oxford	1954 Oxford
1852 Oxford	1899 Cambridge	1955 Cambridge
1854 Oxford	1900 Cambridge	1956 Cambridge
1856 Cambridge	1901 Oxford	1957 Cambridge
1857 Oxford	1902 Cambridge	1958 Cambridge
1858 Cambridge	1903 Cambridge	1959 Oxford
1859 Oxford	1904 Cambridge	1960 Oxford
1860 Cambridge	1905 Oxford	1961 Cambridge
1861 Oxford	1906 Cambridge	1962 Cambridge
1862 Oxford	1907 Cambridge	1963 Oxford
1863 Oxford	1908 Cambridge	1964 Cambridge
1864 Oxford	1909 Oxford	1965 Oxford
1865 Oxford	1910 Oxford	1966 Oxford
1866 Oxford	1911 Oxford	1967 Oxford
1867 Oxford	1912 Oxford	1968 Cambridge
1868 Oxford	1913 Oxford	1969 Cambridge
1869 Oxford	1914 Cambridge	1970 Cambridge
1870 Cambridge	1920 Cambridge	1971 Cambridge
1871 Cambridge	1921 Cambridge	1972 Cambridge
1872 Cambridge	1922 Cambridge	1973 Cambridge
1873 Cambridge	1923 Oxford	1974 Oxford
1874 Cambridge	1924 Cambridge	1975 Cambridge
1875 Oxford	1925 Cambridge	1976 Oxford
1876 Cambridge	1926 Cambridge	1977 Oxford
1877 Dead-heat	1927 Cambridge	1978 Oxford
1878 Oxford	1928 Cambridge	1979 Oxford
1879 Cambridge	1929 Cambridge	1980 Oxford
1880 Oxford	1930 Cambridge	1981 Oxford
1881 Oxford	1931 Cambridge	1982 Oxford
1882 Oxford	1932 Cambridge	1983 Oxford
1883 Oxford	1933 Cambridge	1984 Oxford
1884 Cambridge	1934 Cambridge	1985 Oxford
1885 Oxford	1935 Cambridge	1986 Cambridge
1886 Cambridge	1936 Cambridge	1987 Oxford
1887 Cambridge	1937 Oxford	1988 Oxford
1888 Cambridge	1938 Oxford	1989 Oxford

Wins:
69 Cambridge
65 Oxford
1 Dead-heat

DIAMOND SCULLS
Instituted in 1844, the Diamond Challenge Sculls at Henley is regarded as the Blue Riband of amateur sculling

Winners:

1844	T.B.Bumpstead	1889	G.Nickalls	1938	J.W.Burk
1845	S.Wallace	1890	G.Nickalls	1939	J.W.Burk
1846	E.G.Moon	1891	G.Nickalls	1946	J.Sepheriades
1847	W.Maule	1892	J.J.K.Ooms	1947	J.B.Kelly
1848	W.L.Bagshawe	1893	G.Nickalls	1948	M.T.Wood
1849	T.R.Bone	1894	G.Nickalls	1949	J.B.Kelly
1850	T.R.Bone	1895	Hon.R.Guiness	1950	A.D.Rowe
1851	E.G.Peacock	1896	Hon.R.Guiness	1951	T.A.Fox
1852	E.Macnaghten	1897	E.H.Ten Eyck	1952	M.T.Wood
1853	S.R.Rippingall	1898	B.H.Howell	1953	T.A.Fox
1854	H.H.Playford	1899	B.H.Howell	1954	P.Vlasic
1855	A.A.Casamajor	1900	E.G.Hemmerde	1955	T.Kocerka
1856	A.A.Casamajor	1901	C.V.Fox	1956	T.Kocerka
1857	A.A.Casamajor	1902	F.S.Kelly	1957	S.A.Mackenzie
1858	A.A.Casamajor	1903	F.S.Kelly	1958	S.A.Mackenzie
1859	E.D.Brickwood	1904	L.F.Scholes	1959	S.A.Mackenzie
1860	H.H.Playford	1905	F.S.Kelly	1960	S.A.Mackenzie
1861	A.A.Casamajor	1906	H.T.Blackstaffe	1961	S.A.Mackenzie
1862	E.D.Brickwood	1907	Capt.W.H.Darell	1962	S.A.Mackenzie
1863	C.B.Lawes	1908	A.McCulloch	1963	G.Kottman
1864	W.B.Woodgate	1909	A.A.Stuart	1964	S.Cromwell
1865	E.B.Michell	1910	W.D.Kinnear	1965	D.M.Spero
1866	E.B.Michell	1911	W.D.Kinnear	1966	A.Hill
1867	W.C.Crofts	1912	E.W.Powell	1967	M.Studach
1868	W.Stout	1913	C.McVilly	1968	H.Wardell-Yerburgh
1869	W.C.Crofts	1914	S.Sinigagalia	1969	H.-J.Bohmer
1870	J.B.Close	1915–19	Not held	1970	J.Meissner
1871	W.Fawcus	1920	J.Beresford, jnr	1971	A.Demiddi
1872	C.C.Knollys	1921	F.E.Eyken	1972	A.Timoshin
1873	A.C.Dicker	1922	W.M.Hoover	1973	S.Drea
1874	A.C.Dicker	1923	M.K.Morris	1974	S.Drea
1875	A.C.Dicker	1924	J.Beresford, jnr	1975	S.Drea
1876	F.L.Playford	1925	J.Beresford, jnr	1976	E.Hale
1877	T.C.Edwards-Moss	1926	J.Beresford, jnr	1977	T.Crooks
1878	T.C.Edwards-Moss	1927	R.T.Lee	1978	T.Crooks
1879	J.Lowndes	1928	J.Wright	1979	H.Matheson
1880	J.Lowndes	1929	L.H.F.Gunther	1980	R.Ibarra
1881	J.Lowndes	1930	J.S.Guest	1981	C.Bailieu
1882	J.Lowndes	1931	R.Pearce	1982	C.Bailieu
1883	J.Lowndes	1932	H.Buhtz	1983	S.Redgrave
1884	W.S.Unwin	1933	T.G.Askwith	1984	C.Ballieu
1885	W.S.Unwin	1934	H.Buhtz	1985	S.Redgrave
1886	F.I.Pitman	1935	E.Rufli	1986	B.Eltang
1887	J.C.Gardner	1936	E.Rufli	1987	P -M.Kolbe
1888	G.Nickalls	1937	J.Hasenohrl	1988	H.McGlashan

Most Wins:
6 Stuart Mackenzie, Guy Nickalls

DOGGETT'S COAT AND BADGE

First raced from London Bridge to Chelsea in 1715 the race was the idea of Thomas Doggett, and it is the oldest annual event in the British sporting calendar. The name of the first winner is unknown.

Winners:

1715 Not known	1766 Not known	1818 W.Nicholls
1716 E.Bishop	1767 Not known	1819 W.Emery
or E.Guildford	1768 W.Watson	1820 J.Hartley
1717 Not known	1769 Not known	1821 T.Cole, snr
1718 Not known	1770 T.Goddard	1822 W.Noulton
1719 J.Dolby	1771 A.Badmann	1823 G.Butcher
1720 Not known	1772 H.Briggs	1824 G.Fogo
1721 C.Gurney	1773 J.Frovley	1825 G.Staples
1722 W.Morris	1774 Not known	1826 J.Poett
1723 E.Howard	1775 Not known	1827 J.Voss
1724 Not known	1776 W.Price	1828 R.Mallett
1725 Not known	1777 J.Pickering	1829 S.Stubbs
1726 T.Barrow	1778 H.J.B.Pearson	1830 W.Butler
1727 Not known	1779 W.Boddington	1831 R.Oliver
1728 J.Gibbs	1780 J.J.Bradshaw	1832 R.Waight
1729 J.Bean	1781 W.Reeves	1833 G.Maynard
1730 J.Broughton	1782 J.Trucke	1834 W.Tomlinson
1731 J.Aliss	1783 J.Bowler	1835 W.Dryson
1732 R.Adam	1784 J.Davis	1836 J.Morris
1733 W.Swabby	1785 Not known	1837 T.Harrison
1734 J.Bellows	1786 J.Nash	1838 S.Bridge
1735 H.Watford	1787 B.Rawlinson	1839 T.Goodrum
1736 W.Hilliard	1788 T.Radbourne	1840 W.Hawkins
1737 J.Heaver	1789 J.Curtis	1841 R.Moore
1738 J.Oakes	1790 W.Byers	1842 J.Liddey
1739 G.Harrington	1791 T.Easton	1843 J.Fry
1740 J.Wing	1792 J.Kettleby	1844 F.Lett
1741 D.Roberts	1793 A.Haley	1845 F.Cobb
1742 Not known	1794 J.Franklin	1846 J.F.Wing
1743 A.Wood	1795 W.Parry	1847 W.H.Ellis
1744 J.Polton	1796 J.Thompson	1848 J.Ash
1745 J.Blasdale	1797 J.Hill	1849 T.Cole
1746 J.White	1798 T.Williams	1850 W.Campbell
1747 J.Joyner	1799 J.Dixon	1851 G.D.Wigget
1748 T.Wagdon	1800 J.Burgoyne	1852 C.Constable
1749 H.Hilden	1801 J.R.Curtis	1853 J.R.Finnis
1750 J.Duncome	1802 W.Burns	1854 D.J.Hemmings
1751 J.Earle	1803 J.Flower	1855 H.J.White
1752 J.Hogden	1804 C.Gingle	1856 G.W.Everson
1753 N.Sandford	1805 T.Johnson	1857 T.C.White
1754 A.Marshall	1806 J.Goodwin	1858 C.J.Turner
1755 C.Gill	1807 J.A.Evans	1859 C.S.Farrow
1756 Not known	1808 G.Newell	1860 H.J.M.Phelps
1757 J.White	1809 F.Jury	1861 S.Short
1758 J.Danby	1810 J.Smart	1862 J.Messenger
1759 J.Clarke	1811 W.Thornton	1863 T.Young
1760 E.Wood	1812 R.May	1864 D.Coombes
1761 W.Penner	1813 R.Farson	1865 J.W.Wood
1762 W.Wood	1814 R.Harris	1866 A.Iles
1763 S.Eggleton	1815 J.Scott	1867 H.M.Maxwell
1764 J.Morris	1816 T.Tenham	1868 A.Egalton
1765 R.Eggleton	1817 J.Robson	1869 G.Wright

1870 R.Harding	1909 G.R.Luck	1948 H.F.Clark
1871 T.J.MacKinney	1910 R.J.Pocock	1949 A.H.Dymott
1872 T.G.Green	1911 W.J.W.Fisher	1950 G.J.Palmer
1873 H.Messum	1912 L.E.Francis	1951 M.A.J.Martin
1874 R.W.Burwood	1913 G.H.J.Gobbett	1952 G.E.Green
1875 W.Phelps	1914 S.J.Mason jnr	1953 R.A.Bowles
1876 C.T.Bulman	1915 L.P.J.West	1954 K.C.Everest
1877 J.Tarryer	1916 F.W.Pearce	1955 J.T.Goulding
1878 T.E.Taylor	1917 J.H.Blackman	1956 C.Williams
1879 H.Cordery	1918 A.Gibbs	1957 K.C.Collins
1880 W.J.Cobb	1919 H.T.Phelps	1958 R.G.Crouch
1881 G.Claridge	1920 H.Hayes	1959 G.L.Saunders
1882 H.Audsley	1921 A.E.Briggs	1960 R.Easterling
1883 J.Lloyd	1922 T.J.Phelps	1961 K.Usher
1884 C.Phelps	1923 R.W.Phelps	1962 C.A.Dearsley
1885 G.Mackinney	1924 H.C.Green	1963 D.Allen
1886 H.Cole	1925 H.A.Barry	1964 F.F.Walker
1887 W.G.East	1926 T.G.M.Green	1965 A.G.Collins
1888 C.R,Harding	1927 L.B.Barry	1966 D.Stent
1889 G.M.Green	1928 J.L.Phelps	1967 C.Briggs
1890 J.T.G.Sansom	1929 C.F.Taylor	1968 J.E.Lupton
1891 W.A.Barry	1930 E.A.Phelps	1969 L.E.Grieves
1892 G.Webb	1931 T.J.Harding	1970 M.Spencer
1893 J.J.Harding	1932 H.T.Silvester	1971 C.V.Dwan
1894 F.Pearce	1933 E.L.Phelps	1972 P.Wilson
1895 J.H.Gibson	1934 H.J.Smith	1973 R.A.Prentice
1896 R.J.Carter	1935 A.E.Gobbett	1974 B.E.Lupton
1897 T.Bullman	1936 J.A.Taylor	1975 C.Drury
1898 A.j.Carter	1937 W.F.Silvester	1976 P.Prentice
1899 J.Lee	1938 E.H.Phelps	1977 J.C.Dwan
1900 J.J.Turffery	1939 D.E.Thomas	1978 A.McPherson
1901 A.H.Brewer	1940 E.G.Lupton	1979 F.K.Bearwood
1902 R.G.Odell	1941 G.D.Bowles	1980 W.Woodward Fisher
1903 E.Barry	1942 F.Dott	1981 W.Hickman
1904 W.A.Pizzey	1943 E.F.McGuiness	1982 G.Anness
1905 H.Sylvester	1944 F.E.Ambler	1983 P.Hickman
1906 E.L.Brewster	1945 S.Thomas	1984 S.McCarthy
1907 A.T.Cook	1946 J.D.Anson	1985 R.B.Spencer
1908 J.Graham	1947 J.V.Palmer	1986 C.Woodward Fisher
		1987 C.Spencer
		1988 G.Hayes

The Rugby League was formed at Huddersfield in 1895 after several northern Rugby clubs broke away from the Rugby Union who would not allow broken-time payments to players who lost wages as a result of playing on a Saturday. Originally called the Northern Union, it became the Northern Rugby League in 1922.

CHALLENGE CUP

The sport's leading knock-out tournament, it was first held in 1897 with the final at Leeds. The first final at Wembley was in 1929.

Winners:

1897 Batley	1930 Widnes	1960 Wakefield T
1898 Batley	1931 Halifax	1961 St.Helens
1899 Oldham	1932 Leeds	1962 Wakefield T
1900 Swinton	1933 Huddersfield	1963 Wakefield T
1901 Batley	1934 Hunslet	1964 Widnes
1902 Broughton R	1935 Castleford	1965 Wigan
1903 Halifax	1936 Leeds	1966 St.Helens
1904 Halifax	1937 Widnes	1967 Featherstone R
1905 Warrington	1938 Salford	1968 Leeds
1906 Bradford	1939 Halifax	1969 Castleford
1907 Warrington	1940 Not held	1970 Castleford
1908 Hunslet	1941 Leeds	1971 Leigh
1909 Wakefield T	1942 Leeds	1972 St.Helens
1910 Leeds	1943 Dewsbury	1973 Featherstone R
1911 Broughton R	1944 Bradford N	1974 Warrington
1912 Dewsbury	1945 Huddersfield	1975 Widnes
1913 Huddersfield	1946 Wakefield T	1976 St.Helens
1914 Hull	1947 Bradford N	1977 Leeds
1915 Huddersfield	1948 Wigan	1978 Leeds
1916–19 Not held	1949 Bradford N	1979 Widnes
1920 Huddersfield	1950 Warrington	1980 Hull KR
1921 Leigh	1951 Wigan	1981 Widnes
1922 Rochdale R	1952 Workington T	1982 Hull
1923 Leeds	1953 Huddersfield	1983 Featherstone R
1924 Wigan	1954 Warrington	1984 Widnes
1925 Oldham	1955 Barrow	1985 Wigan
1926 Swinton	1956 St.Helens	1986 Castleford
1927 Oldham	1957 Leeds	1987 Halifax
1928 Swinton	1958 Wigan	1988 Wigan
1929 Wigan	1959 Wigan	1989 Wigan
		1990 Wigan

Most Wins:
10 Leeds
11 Wigan

PREMIERSHIP TROPHY

First contested at the end of the 1974–75 season, it replaced the old Championship Play-Off competition. The competition is a knockout one involving the top eight clubs in the first division with the champions playing the eighth club, the second club playing the seventh and so on. A second division Premiership was launched in 1987 involving the top eight teams. The final is played on the same day as The Premiership Trophy at Old Trafford, Manchester United FC.

Winners (1st Division Premiership)

1975 Leeds	1981 Hull KR
1976 St.Helens	1982 Widnes
1977 St.Helens	1983 Widnes
1978 Bradford N	1984 Hull KR
1979 Leeds	1985 St.Helens
1980 Widnes	1986 Warrington
	1987 Wigan

Most Wins:
5 Widnes

1988 Widnes
1989 Widnes

Winners (2nd Division Premiership)
1987 Swinton
1988 Oldham
1989 Sheffield Eagles

JOHN PLAYER SPECIAL TROPHY

This knock-out competition was first held in 1971–72; it was known just as the John Player Trophy until 1983 when it was renamed The John Player Special Trophy.

Winners:

1972 Halifax	1980 Bradford N
1973 Leeds	1981 Warrington
1974 Warrington	1982 Hull KR
1975 Bradford N	1983 Wigan
1976 Widnes	1984 Leeds
1977 Castleford	1985 Hull
1978 Warrington	1986 Wigan
1979 Widnes	1987 Wigan
	1988 St.Helens

Most Wins:
4 Wigan

1989 Wigan

LEADING POINTS SCORERS IN ALL THE MAJOR FINALS:

CHALLENGE CUP
20 N. Fox (Wakefield T) v Hull, 1960

JOHN PLAYER SPECIAL TROPHY
15 D. Whitehead (Warrington) v Rochdale H, 1973-4

PREMIERSHIP TROPHY
17 G. Pimblett (St. Helens) v Warrington, 1977

LANCASHIRE CUP
17 S. Hesford (Warrington) v Wigan, 1980

YORKSHIRE CUP
12 S. Moorhouse (Huddersfield) v Leeds, 1919
12 A. Edwards (Bradford N) v Castleford, 1948
12 N. Fox (Wakefield T) v Leeds, 1964

COUNTY CUPS

The Lancashire and Yorkshire Cups both date back to the 1905–06 season. They are currently early-season knock-out competitions for teams both sides of the Pennines.

Winners

	Lancashire Cup	Yorkshire Cup
1906	Wigan	Hunslet
1907	Broughton R	Bradford
1908	Oldham	Hunslet
1909	Wigan	Halifax
1910	Wigan	Huddersfield
1911	Oldham	Wakefield T
1912	Rochdale H	Huddersfield
1913	Wigan	Batley
1914	Oldham	Huddersfield
1915	Rochdale H	Huddersfield
1916–18	not held	
1919	Rochdale H	Huddersfield
1920	Oldham	Huddersfield
1921	Broughton R	Hull KR
1922	Warrington	Leeds
1923	Wigan	York
1924	St.Helens Recs	Hull
1925	Oldham	Wakefield T
1926	Swinton	Dewsbury
1927	St.Helens	Huddersfield
1928	Swinton	Dewsbury
1929	Wigan	Leeds
1930	Warrington	Hull KR
1931	St.Helens Recs	Leeds
1932	Salford	Huddersfield
1933	Warrington	Leeds
1934	Oldham	York
1935	Salford	Leeds
1936	Salford	Leeds
1937	Salford	York
1938	Warrington	Leeds
1939	Wigan	Huddersfield
1940	Swinton	Featherstone R
1941	Not held	Bradford N
1942	Not held	Bradford N
1943	Not held	Dewsbury
1944	Not held	Bradford N
1945	Not held	Halifax
1946	Widnes	Bradford N
1947	Wigan	Wakefield T
1948	Wigan	Wakefield T
1949	Wigan	Bradford N
1950	Wigan	Bradford N
1951	Wigan	Huddersfield
1952	Wigan	Wakefield T
1953	Leigh	Huddersfield
1954	St.Helens	Bradford N
1955	Barrow	Halifax
1956	Leigh	Halifax
1957	Oldham	Wakefield T
1958	Oldham	Huddersfield

1959 Oldham	Leeds
1960 Warrington	Featherstone R
1960 St.Helens	Wakefield T
1962 St.Helens	Wakefield T
1963 St.Helens	Hunslet
1964 St.Helens	Halifax
1965 St.Helens	Wakefield T
1966 Warrington	Bradford N
1967 Wigan	Hull KR
1968 St.Helens	Hull KR
1969 St.Helens	Leeds
1970 Swinton	Hull
1971 Leigh	Leeds
1972 Wigan	Hull KR
1973 Salford	Leeds
1974 Wigan	Leeds
1975 Widnes	Hull KR
1976 Widnes	Leeds
1977 Widnes	Leeds
1978 Workington T	Castleford
1979 Widnes	Bradford N
1980 Widnes	Leeds
1981 Warrington	Leeds
1982 Leigh	Castleford
1983 Warrington	Hull
1984 Barrow	Hull
1985 St.Helens	Hull
1986 Wigan	Hull KR
1987 Wigan	Castleford
1988 Wigan	Bradford N

Most Wins:

19 Wigan   16 Leeds

HARRY SUNDERLAND TROPHY

Named after former Australian team manager, broadcaster and journalist Harry Sunderland, the award is made to the Man of the Match in the Premiership Final (formerly the Championship Play-Off). It was first awarded in 1965.

Winners:

1965 T.Fogerty	Halifax
1966 A.Halsall	St.Helens
1967 R.Owen	Wakefield T
1968 G.Cooper	Wakefield T
1969 B.Risman	Leeds
1970 F.Myler	St.Helens
1971 B.Ashurst	Wigan
1972 T.Clawson	Leeds
1973 M.Stephenson	Dewsbury
1974 B.Philbin	Warrington
1975 M.Mason	Leeds
1976 G.Nicholls	St. Helens
1977 G.Pimblett	St. Helens
1978 B.Haigh	Bradford N
1979 K.Dick	Leeds
1980 M.Aspey	Widnes
1981 L.Casey	Hull KR
1982 M.Burke	Widnes
1983 T.Myler	Widnes

1984	J.Dorahy	Hull KR
1985	H.Pinner	St. Helens
1986	L.Boyd	Warrington
1987	J.Lydon	Wigan
1988	D.Hulme	Widnes
1989	A Tait	Widnes

LANCE TODD AWARD

The Lance Todd Award goes to the Man of the Match in the Challenge Cup Final at Wembley as decided by a panel of journalists. The trophy is named after former New Zealand international Lance Todd who played for Wigan and later managed Salford. The first award was made in 1946.

Winners:

1946	B.Stott	Wakefield T
1947	W.Davies	Bradford N
1948	F.Whitcombe	Bradford N
1949	E.Ward	Bradford N
1950	G.Helme	Warrington
1951	C.Mountford	Wigan
1952	B.Iveson	Workington T
1953	P.Ramsden	Huddersfield
1954	G.Helme	Warrington
1955	J.Grundy	Barrow
1956	A.Prescott	St.Helens
1957	J.Stevenson	Leeds
1958	R.Thomas	Wigan
1959	B.McTigue	Wigan
1960	T.Harris	Hull
1961	D.Huddart	St.Helens
1962	N.Fox	Wakefield T
1963	H.Poynton	Wakefield T
1964	F.Collier	Widnes
1965	R.Ashby (shared with)	Wigan
	B.Gabbitas	Hunslet
1966	L.Killeen	St.Helens
1967	C.Dooler	Featherstone R
1968	D.Fox	Wakefield T
1969	M.Reilly	Castleford
1970	B.Kirkbride	Castleford
1971	A.Murphy	Leigh
1972	K.Coslett	St.Helens
1973	S.Nash	Featherstone R
1974	D.Whitehead	Warrington
1975	R.Dutton	Widnes
1976	G.Pimblett	St.Helens
1977	S.Pitchford	Leeds
1978	G.Nicholls	St.Helens
1979	D.Topliss	Wakefield T
1980	B.Lockwood	Hull KR
1981	M.Burke	Widnes
1982	E.Cunningham	Widnes
1983	D.Hobbs	Featherstone R

1984	J.Lydon	Widnes
1985	B.Kenny	Wigan
1986	B.Beardmore	Castleford
1987	G.Eadie	Halifax
1988	A.Gregory	Wigan
1989	E.Hanley	Wigan
1990	A Gregory	Wigan

Most Wins:
2 Gerry Helme , A. Gregory .

LEAGUE LEADERS
Twenty two clubs formed the first league in 1895. Since then various league formats have been tried and it was not until 1973-74 that the current two division system was introduced. The following is a list of all league leaders champions. (LSC–Lancashire Senior Competition. YSC–Yorkshire Senior Competition)

1896	Manningham	
1897	Broughton R (LSC)	Brighouse R (YSC)
1898	Oldham (LSC)	Hunslet (YSC)
1899	Broughton R (LSC)	Batley (YSC)
1900	Runcorn (LSC)	Bradford (YSC)
1901	Oldham (LSC)	Bradford (YSC)
1902	Broughton R	
1903	Halifax (Div.1)	Keighley (Div.2)
1904	Bradford (Div.1)	Wakefield T (Div.2)
1905	Oldham (Div.1)	Dewsbury (Div.2)
1906	Leigh	
1907	Halifax	
1908	Oldham	
1909	Wigan	
1910	Oldham	
1911	Wigan	
1912	Huddersfield	
1913	Huddersfield	
1914	Huddersfield	
1915	Huddersfield	
1918	Not held	
1919	Rochdale H (Lancs.Lge.)	Hull (Yorks.Lge.)
1920	Huddersfield	
1921	Hull KR	
1922	Oldham	
1923	Hull	
1924	Wigan	
1925	Swinton	
1926	Wigan	
1927	St.Helens Recs	
1928	Swinton	
1929	Huddersfield	
1930	St.Helens	
1931	Swinton	
1932	Huddersfield	
1933	Salford	
1934	Salford	
1935	Swinton	
1936	Hull	
1937	Salford	
1938	Hunslet	
1939	Salford	
1940	Swinton (Lancs.Lge.)	Bradford N (Yorks.Lge.)
1941	Wigan (Lancs.Lge.)	Bradford N (Yorks.Lge.)

League Leaders Cont.
1942 Dewsbury
1943 Wigan
1944 Wakefield T
1945 Bradford N
1946 Wigan
1947 Wigan
1948 Wigan
1949 Warrington
1950 Wigan
1951 Warrington
1952 Bradford N
1953 St.Helens
1954 Halifax
1955 Warrington
1956 Warrington
1957 Oldham
1958 Oldham
1959 St.Helens
1960 St.Helens
1961 Leeds
1962 Wigan
1963 Swinton (Div.1)   Hunslet (Div.2)
1964 Swinton (Div.1)   Oldham (Div.2)
1965 St.Helens
1966 St.Helens
1967 Leeds
1968 Leeds
1969 Leeds
1970 Leeds
1971 Wigan
1972 Leeds
1973 Warrington

Division 1	Division 2
1974 Salford	Bradford N
1975 St.Helens	Huddersfield
1976 Salford	Barrow
1977 Featherstone R	Hull
1978 Widnes	Leigh
1979 Hull KR	Hull
1980 Bradford N	Featherstone R
1981 Bradford N	York
1982 Leigh	Oldham
1983 Hull	Fulham
1984 Hull KR	Barrow
1985 Hull KR	Swinton
1986 Halifax	Leigh
1987 Wigan	Hunslet
1988 Widnes	Oldham
1989 Widnes	Leigh

WORLD CUP

The first World Cup was played in France in 1954 with Great Britain, France, New Zealand and Australia playing each other on a round-robin basis. In 1975 the Great Britain team was divided into England and Wales. The competition discontinued in 1977 but was revived in 1985 when one match from each test series was designated a World Cup game. In 1988 the top two teams played off for the Cup.

Winners:

1954 Great Britain	1970 Australia
1957 Australia	1972 Great Britain
1960 Great Britain	1975 Australia
1968 Australia	1977 Australia
	1988 Australia

Most Wins:
6 Australia

RUGBY LEAGUE IN AUSTRALIA

The Sydney Premiership is the most senior competition in Australia, and possibly the toughest competition in the world to win. The season culminates in the Grand Final each year. It was first contested in 1908.

1908 South Sydney	1942 Canterbury-Bankstown
1909 South Sydney	1943 Newtown
1910 Newtown	1944 Balmain
1911 Eastern Suburbs	1945 Eastern Suburbs
1912 Eastern Suburbs	1946 Balmain
1913 Eastern Suburbs	1947 Balmain
1914 South Sydney	1948 Western Suburbs
1915 Balmain	1949 St. George
1916 Balmain	1950 South Sydney
1917 Balmain	1951 South Sydney
1918 South Sydney	1952 Western Suburbs
1919 Balmain	1953 South Sydney
1920 Balmain	1954 South Sydney
1921 North Sydney	1955 South Sydney
1922 North Sydney	1956 St. George
1923 Eastern Suburbs	1957 St. George
1924 Balmain	1958 St. George
1925 South Sydney	1959 St. George
1926 South Sydney	1960 St. George
1927 South Sydney	1961 St. George
1928 South Sydney	1962 St. George
1929 South Sydney	1963 St. George
1930 Western Suburbs	1964 St. George
1931 South Sydney	1965 St. George
1932 South Sydney	1966 St. George
1933 Newtown	1967 South Sydney
1934 Western Suburbs	1968 South Sydney
1935 Eastern Suburbs	1969 Balmain
1936 Eastern Suburbs	1970 South Sydney
1937 Eastern Suburbs	1971 South Sydney
1938 Canterbury-Bankstown	1972 Manly-Warringah
1939 Balmain	1973 Manly-Warringah
1940 Eastern Suburbs	
1941 St. George	

1974 Eastern Suburbs
1975 Eastern Suburbs
1976 Manly-Warringah
1977 St. George
1978 Manly-Warringah
1979 St. George
1980 Canterbury-Bankstown

1981 Parramatta
1982 Parramatta
1983 Parramatta
1984 Canterbury-Bankstown
1985 Canterbury-Bankstown
1986 Parramatta
1987 Manly-Warringah
1988 Canterbury-Bankstown

MOST WINS:
20 South Sydney

ALL-TIME RECORDS

Biggest win: 119-2 Huddersfield v Swinton Park R, 1914

Most points	- career:	6220 J. Sullivan (Wigan) 1921-46
	- season:	496 B. L. Jones (Leeds) 1956-7
	- match:	53 G. H. West (Hull KR) v Brookland R, 1905
Most tries	- career:	796 B. Bevan (Warrington & Blackpool B) 1946-64
	- season:	80 A. A. Rosenfeld (Huddersfield) 1913-14
	- match:	11 G. H. West (Hull KR) v Brookland R, 1905
Most goals	- career:	2859 J. Sullivan (Wigan) 1921-46
	- season:	221 D. Watkins (Salford) 1972-3
	- match:	22 J. Sullivan (Wigan) v Flimby & F, 1925

Most appearances - career: 921 J. Sullivan (Wigan) 1921-46

Rugby Union was first played at Rugby School in 1823 when William Webb Ellis picked up the ball and ran with it while the boys were playing football. The first Rugby club was founded at Guy's Hospital 20 years later and the Rugby Football Union was founded in 1871.

THE INTERNATIONAL CHAMPIONSHIP

First played by the four Home Countries in 1883. France joined the championship in 1910 to make it a Five Nations tournament. Each country plays each other once, during each year's championship.

Winners:

1883 England
1884 England
1885 Not completed
1886 England, Scotland
1887 Scotland
1888 Not completed
1889 Not completed
1890 England, Scotland
1891 Scotland
1892 England
1893 Wales
1894 Ireland
1895 Scotland
1896 Ireland
1897 Not completed
1898 Not completed
1899 Ireland
1900 Wales
1901 Scotland
1902 Wales
1903 Scotland
1904 Scotland
1905 Wales
1906 Ireland, Wales
1907 Scotland
1908 Wales
1909 Wales
1910 England
1911 Wales
1912 England, Ireland
1913 England
1914 England
1915–19 Not held
1920 England, Scotland, Wales
1921 England
1922 Wales
1923 England
1924 England
1925 Scotland
1926 Scotland, Ireland
1927 Scotland, Ireland
1928 England
1929 Scotland

1930 England
1931 Wales
1932 England, Ireland, Wales
1933 Scotland
1934 England
1935 Ireland
1936 Wales
1937 England
1938 Scotland
1939 England, Ireland, Wales
1940–46 Not held
1947 England, Wales
1948 Ireland
1949 Ireland
1950 Wales
1951 Ireland
1952 Wales
1953 England
1954 England, Wales, France
1955 France, Wales
1956 Wales
1957 England
1958 England
1959 France
1960 France, England
1961 France
1962 France
1963 England
1964 Scotland, Wales
1965 Wales
1966 Wales
1967 France
1968 France
1969 Wales
1970 France, Wales
1971 Wales
1972 Not completed
1973 England, Ireland, Scotland, Wales, France
1974 Ireland
1975 Wales
1976 Wales
1977 France

1978 Wales
1979 Wales
1980 England
1981 France

Most Outright Wins:
21 Wales

1982 Ireland
1983 France, Ireland
1984 Scotland
1985 Ireland
1986 Scotland, France
1987 France
1988 Wales, France
1989 France

COUNTY CHAMPIONSHIP

The English County Championship was introduced in 1889 and Yorkshire declared the first champions. Several different formats have been used over the years and the Final normally takes place at a ground of one of the counties competing in the final.

Winners:

1889 Yorkshire
1890 Yorkshire
1891 Lancashire
1892 Yorkshire
1893 Yorkshire
1894 Yorkshire
1895 Yorkshire
1896 Yorkshire
1897 Kent
1898 Northumberland
1899 Devon
1900 Durham
1901 Devon
1902 Durham
1903 Durham
1904 Kent
1905 Durham
1906 Devon
1907 Devon and Durham (shared)
1908 Cornwall
1909 Durham
1910 Gloucestershire
1911 Devon
1912 Devon
1913 Gloucestershire
1914 Midlands
1915–19 Not held
1920 Gloucestershire
1921 Gloucestershire
1922 Gloucestershire
1923 Somerset
1924 Cumberland
1925 Leicestershire
1926 Yorkshire
1927 Kent
1928 Yorkshire
1929 Middlesex
1930 Gloucestershire
1931 Gloucestershire
1932 Gloucestershire
1933 Hampshire
1934 East Midlands

1935 Lancashire
1936 Hampshire
1937 Gloucestershire
1938 Lancashire
1939 Warwickshire
1940–46 Not held
1947 Lancashire
1948 Lancashire
1949 Lancashire
1950 Cheshire
1951 East Midlands
1952 Middlesex
1953 Yorkshire
1954 Middlesex
1955 Lancashire
1956 Middlesex
1957 Devon
1958 Warwickshire
1959 Warwickshire
1960 Warwickshire
1961 Cheshire
1962 Warwickshire
1963 Warwickshire
1964 Warwickshire
1965 Warwickshire
1966 Middlesex
1967 Surrey and Durham (shared)
1968 Middlesex
1969 Lancashire
1970 Staffordshire
1971 Surrey
1972 Gloucestershire
1973 Lancashire
1974 Gloucestershire
1975 Gloucestershire
1976 Gloucestershire
1977 Lancashire
1978 North Midlands
1979 Middlesex
1980 Lancashire
1981 Northumberland
1982 Lancashire

1983 Gloucestershire
1984 Gloucestershire

Most Wins:
15 Gloucestershire

1985 Middlesex
1986 Warwickshire
1987 Yorkshire
1988 Lancashire
1989 Durham

PILKINGTON CUP

Instituted in 1971-72 as the John Player Cup, it is a knockout tournament for English club sides. It became known as the Pilkington Cup in 1988.

Winners:
1972 Gloucester
1973 Coventry
1974 Coventry
1975 Bedford
1976 Gosforth
1977 Gosforth
1978 Gloucester
1979 Leicester

1980 Leicester
1981 Leicester
1982 Gloucester and Moseley (shared)
1983 Bristol
1984 Bath
1985 Bath
1986 Bath
1987 Bath
1988 Harlequins
1989 Bath

Most Wins:
5 Bath

SCHWEPPES WELSH CUP

Sponsored by Schweppes, it is the Welsh equivalent of the Pilkington Cup in England.

Winners:
1972 Neath
1973 Llanelli
1974 Llanelli
1975 Llanelli
1976 Llanelli
1977 Newport
1978 Swansea
1979 Bridgend

1980 Bridgend
1981 Cardiff
1982 Cardiff
1983 Pontypool
1984 Cardiff
1985 Llanelli
1986 Cardiff
1987 Cardiff
1988 Llanelli
1989 Neath

Most Wins:
6 Llanelli

MIDDLESEX SEVENS

The leading Sevens tournament was inaugurated in 1926. The final of the knockout tournament is played at Twickenham and often attracts crowds in excess of 50,000.

Winners:
1926 Harlequins
1927 Harlequins
1928 Harlequins
1929 Harlequins
1930 London Welsh

1931 London Welsh
1932 Blackheath
1933 Harlequins
1934 Barbarians
1935 Harlequins

1936 Sale	1962 London Scottish
1937 London Scottish	1963 London Scottish
1938 Metropolitan Police	1964 Loughborough Colleges
1939 Cardiff	1965 London Scottish
1940 St.Mary's Hospital	1966 Loughborough Colleges
1941 Cambridge University	1967 Harlequins
1942 St.Mary's Hospital	1968 London Welsh
1943 St.Mary's Hospital	1969 St.Luke's College
1944 St.Mary's Hospital	1970 Loughborough Colleges
1945 Nottingham	1971 London Welsh
1946 St.Mary's Hospital	1972 London Welsh
1947 Rosslyn Park	1973 London Welsh
1948 Wasps	1974 Richmond
1949 Heriot's FP	1975 Richmond
1950 Rosslyn Park	1976 Loughborough Colleges
1951 Richmond II	1977 Richmond
1952 Wasps	1978 Harlequins
1953 Richmond	1979 Richmond
1954 Rosslyn Park	1980 Richmond
1955 Richmond	1981 Rosslyn Park
1956 London Welsh	1982 Stewart's Melville FP
1957 St.Luke's College	1983 Richmond
1958 Blackheath	1984 London Welsh
1959 Loughborough Colleges	1985 Wasps
1960 London Scottish	1986 Harlequins
1961 London Scottish	1987 Harlequins
Most Wins	1988 Harlequins
12 Harlequins	1989 Harlequins

COURAGE CLUBS CHAMPIONSHIP

From 1985-86 season the Rugby Football Union approved a plan to divide the leading English clubs into two Tables, with the leading clubs in the Merit Table A. Selected matches counted towards the Merit Table and an end-of-season 'League Table' was drawn up. A third Merit Table was added in 1986-87. From 1988 it became known as the Courage Clubs Championship and the League tables were re-named League 1, League 2 etc.

Winners
League 1 (formerly Merit Table A)
1986 Gloucester
1987 Bath   1990 WASPS
1988 Leicester
1989 Bath
League 2 (formerly Merit Table B)
1986 Orell
1987 Waterloo   1990 NORTHAMPTON
1988 Rosslyn Park
1989 Saracens
League 3 (formerly Merit Table C)
1987 Vale of Lune
1988 Wakefield   1990 LONDON SCOTTISH
1989 Plymouth Albion

BRITISH LIONS TOUR RECORDS

The British Lions went on their first Tour in 1888. The following is a record of that, and all subsequent Tours.

Year	Country	P	W	D	L	F	A
1888	Australia	16	14	2	0	210	65
	New Zealand	19	13	4	2	82	33
1891	South Africa	19	19	0	0	224	3
1896	South Africa	21	19	1	1	310	45
1899	Australia	21	18	0	3	333	90
1903	South Africa	22	11	3	8	231	138
1904	Australia	14	14	0	0	265	51
	New Zealand	5	2	1	2	22	33
1908	Australia	9	7	0	2	139	48
	New Zealand	17	9	1	7	184	153
1910	South Africa	24	13	3	8	290	236
1924	South Africa	21	9	3	9	175	155
1930	New Zealand	21	15	0	6	420	205
	Australia	7	5	0	2	204	113
1938	South Africa	23	17	0	6	407	272
1950	New Zealand	23	17	1	5	420	162
	Australia	6	5	0	1	150	52
1955	South Africa	24	18	1	5	418	271
1959	Australia	6	5	0	1	174	70
	New Zealand	25	20	0	5	582	266
1962	South Africa	24	15	4	5	351	208
1966	Australia	8	7	1	0	202	48
	New Zealand	25	15	2	8	300	281
1968	South Africa	20	15	1	4	377	181
1971	Australia	2	1	0	1	25	27
	New Zealand	24	22	1	1	555	204
1974	South Africa	22	21	1	0	729	207
1977	New Zealand	25	21	0	4	596	295
	Fiji	1	0	0	1	21	25
1980	South Africa	18	15	0	3	401	244
1983	New Zealand	18	12	0	6	478	276

GRAND SLAM

When one nation beats all other four in the international championship they are said to have performed the Grand Slam.

Winners:

17 Wales; 8 England; 4 France; 2 Scotland; 1 Ireland.

TRIPLE CROWN

The Triple Crown is performed when one of the four home countries beats the other three in the international championship.

Winners:

16 Wales; 15 England; 9 Scotland; 6 Ireland

Twickenham has been the venue for some memorable 'streaks'. The first at the famous ground was during the England-France game on 23 April 1974 when Michael O'Brien appeared naked at half-time. He was later fined £10...

The reigning Olympic Rugby champions are...the United States. They won the gold medal, and the more fancied France the silver medal, at the 1924 Games. The sport has not been included in the programme since.

The referee of France's first international match, against New Zealand in 1906, was Baron Pierre de Coubertin, founder of the Modern Olympic Games.

WORLD CUP

The inaugural World Cup for the Webb Ellis Trophy was contested in New Zealand and Australia in May/June 1987 with the first final at Auckland. Sixteen countries competed.

Final:

1987 New Zealand 29 France 9

RUGBY IN AUSTRALIA

SYDNEY PREMIERSHIP
The Sydney Premiership is the principal domestic competition in Australia. It was first contested 1900.

Winners:

1900 Glebe	1944 Eastern Suburbs
1901 Glebe & University (shared)	1945 University
	1946 Eastern Suburbs
1902 Western Suburbs	1947 Eastern Suburbs
1903 Eastern Suburbs	1948 Randwick
1904 University	1949 Gordon
1905 South Sydney	1950 Manly
1906 Glebe	1951 University
1907 Glebe	1952 Gordon
1908 Newtown	1953 University
1909 Glebe	1954 University
1910 Newtown	1955 University
1911 Newtown	1956 Gordon
1912 Glebe	1957 St. George
1913 Eastern Suburbs	1958 Gordon
1914 Glebe	1959 Randwick
1915-18 Not held	1960 Northern Suburbs
1919 University	1961 University
1920 University	1962 University
1921 Eastern Suburbs	1963 Northern Suburbs
1922 Manly	1964 Northern Suburbs
1923 University	1965 Randwick
1924 University	1966 Randwick
1925 Balmain & Glebe (shared)	1967 Randwick
	1968 University
1926 University	1969 Eastern Suburbs
1927 University	1970 University
1928 University	1971 Randwick
1929 Western Suburbs	1972 University
1930 Randwick	1973 Randwick
1931 Eastern Suburbs	1974 Randwick
1932 Manly	1975 Northern Suburbs
1933 Northern Suburbs	1976 Gordon
1934 Randwick	1977 Parramatta
1935 Northern Suburbs	1978 Randwick
1936 Drummoyne	1979 Randwick
1937 University	1980 Randwick
1938 Randwick	1981 Randwick
1939 University	1982 Randwick
1940 Randwick	1983 Manly
1941 Eastern Suburbs	1984 Randwick
1942 Manly	1985 Parramatta
1943 Manly	1986 Parramatta
	1987 Randwick
	1988 Randwick

MOST WINS:
21 University

RUGBY IN NEW ZEALAND

RANFURLY SHIELD
An inter-provincial competition, it was first held in 1904. A challenge competition, the defending state accepts challenges from other states.
The following is a list of all holders of the Shield, and the dates indicate when they successfully challenged for the trophy.

1904 Wellington	1953 Canterbury
1905 Auckland	1956 Wellington
1913 Taranki	1957 Otago
1914 Wellington	1957 Taranaki
1920 Southland	1959 Southland
1921 Wellington	1959 Auckland
1922 Hawke's Bay	1960 North Auckland
1927 Wairarapa	1960 Auckland
1927 Manawhenua	1963 Wellington
1927 Canterbury	1963 Taranaki
1928 Wairarapa	1965 Auckland
1929 Southland	1966 Waikato
1930 Wellington	1966 Hawke's Bay
1931 Canterbury	1969 Canterbury
1934 Hawke's Bay	1971 Auckland
1934 Auckland	1971 North Auckland
1935 Canterbury	1972 Auckland
1935 Otago	1972 Canterbury
1937 Southland	1973 Marlborough
1938 Otago	1974 South Canterbury
1938 Southland	1974 Wellington
1947 Otago	1974 Auckland
1950 Canterbury	1976 Manawatu
1950 Wairarapa	1978 North Auckland
1950 South Canterbury	1979 Auckland
1950 North Auckland	1980 Waikato
1951 Waikato	1981 Wellington
1952 Auckland	1982 Canterbury
1952 Waikato	1985 Auckland
1953 Wellington	

**Most Successive
Defences:**
26 Auckland 1985-88

NEW ZEALAND NATIONAL CHAMPIONSHIP
A season-long championship involving eleven States who play each other on a round-robin basis. It was launched in 1976.

Winners:

1976 Bay of Plenty	1983 Canterbury
1977 Canterbury	1984 Auckland
1978 Wellington	1985 Auckland
1979 Counties	1986 Wellington
1980 Manawatu	1987 Auckland
1981 Wellington	1988 Auckland
1982 Auckland	

Most Wins:
5 Auckland

RUGBY IN SOUTH AFRICA

CURRIE CUP
The leading South African tournament is the Currie Cup. An inter-provincial tournament it was first held in 1889 but was not an annual event because it was not played in years of an international tour to South Africa. It has, however, been an annual event since 1968.

1889 Western Province	1954 Western Province
1892 Western Province	1956 Northern Transvaal
1894 Western Province	1959 Western Province
1895 Western Province	1964 Western Province
1897 Western Province	1966 Western Province
1898 Western Province	1968 Northern Transvaal
1899 Griqualand West	1969 Northern Transvaal
1904 Western Province	1970 Griqualand West
1906 Western Province	1971 Northern Transvaal
1908 Western Province	& Transvaal (shared)
1911 Griqualand West	1972 Transvaal
1914 Western Province	1973 Northern Transvaal
1920 Western Province	1974 Northern Transvaal
1922 Transvaal	1975 Northern Transvaal
1925 Western Province	1976 Northern Transvaal
1927 Western Province	1977 Northern Transvaal
1929 Western Province	1978 Northern Transvaal
1932 Border	1979 Northern Transvaal
& Western Province	& Western Province (shared)
1934 Border &	1980 Northern Transvaal
Western Province (shared)	1981 Northern Transvaal
1936 Western Province	1982 Western Province
1939 Transvaal	1983 Western Province
1946 Northern Transvaal	1984 Western Province
1947 Western Province	1985 Western Province
1950 Transvaal	1986 Western Province
1952 Transvaal	1987 Northern Transvaal
	1988 Northern Transvaal

MOST WINS:
28 Western Province

Competitive shooting first took place in Switzerland in the middle of the 15th century. The National Rifle Association of Great Britain was formed in 1860 and the Clay Bird Shooting Association was founded in 1903.

OLYMPIC GAMES

Shooting has been part of the Olympic programme since the first Games in 1896. Many different types of competition have been held over the years, including using live pigeons as targets. The following results are for the present-day events. Women's events were first included at the 1984 Los Angeles Games.

Free Pistol

1896 S.Paine (USA)	1952 H.Benner (USA)
1900 K.Roderer (SWI)	1956 P.Linnosvuo (FIN)
1904 Not held	1960 A.Gushchin (USSR)
1906 G.Orphanidis (GRE)	1964 V.Markkanen (FIN)
1908 Not held	1968 G.Kossykh (USSR)
1912 A.Lane (USA)	1972 R.Skanakar (SWE)
1920 K.Frederick (USA)	1976 U.Potteck (GDR)
1924-1932 Not held	1980 A.Melentyev (USSR)
1936 T.Ullmann (SWE)	1984 H.Xu (CHN)
1948 E.Vazquez Cam (PER)	1988 S.Babii (ROM)

Small Bore Rifle (Three Position)

1952 E.Kongshaug (NOR)	1972 J.Writer (USA)
1956 A.Bogdanov (USSR)	1976 L.Bassham (USA)
1960 V.Shamburkin (USSR)	1980 V.Vlasov (USSR)
1964 L.Wigger (USA)	1984 M.Cooper (GB)
1968 B.Klingner (FRG)	1988 M.Cooper (GB)

Rapid Fire Pistol

1896 J.Phrangoudis (GRE)	1948 K.Takacs (HUN)
1900 M.Larrouy (FRA)	1952 K.Takacs (HUN)
1904 Not held	1956 S.Petrescu (ROM)
1906 M.Lecoq (FRA)	1960 W.McMillan (USA)
1908 P.van Asbroeck (BEL)	1964 P.Linnosvuo (FIN)
1912 A.Lane (USA)	1968 J.Zapedzki (POL)
1920 G.Paraense (BRA)	1972 J.Zapedzki (POL)
1924 P.Bailey (USA)	1976 N.Klaar (GDR)
1928 Not held	1980 C.Ion (ROM)
1932 R.Morigi (ITA)	1984 T.Kamachi (JAP)
1936 C.van Oyen (GER)	1988 A.Kouzmine (USSR)

Skeet Shooting

1968 E.Petrov (USSR)	1980 H.K.Rasmussen (DEN)
1972 K.Wirnhier (FRG)	1984 M.Dryke (USA)
1976 J.Panacek (TCH)	1988 A.Wegner (GDR)

Running Game Target

1900 L.Debray (FRA)	1976 A.Gazov (USSR)
1904-68 Not held	1980 I.Sokolov (USSR)
1972 L.Zhelezniak (USSR)	1984 Y.Li (CHN)
	1988 T.Heiestad (NOR)

Trap Shooting

1900 R.de Barbarin (FRA)	1956 G.Rossini (ITA)
1904 Not held	1960 I.Dumitrescu (ROM)
1906 G.Merlin & S.Merlin (GB)	1964 E.Mattarelli (ITA)
1908 W.Ewing (CAN)	1968 R.Braithwaite (GB)
1912 J.Graham (USA)	1972 A.Scalzone (ITA)
1920 M.Arie (USA)	1976 D.Haldeman (USA)
1924 G.Halasy (HUN)	1980 L.Giovanetti (ITA)
1928-48 Not held	1984 L.Giovanetti (ITA)
1952 G.Genereux (CAN)	1988 D.Monakov (USSR)

Small Bore Rifle (prone)

1908 A.A.Carnell (GB)	1956 G.Oullette (CAN)
1912 F.Hird (USA)	1960 P.Kohnke (GER)
1920 F.Nuesslein (USA)	1964 L.Hammerl (HUN)
1924 P.C.de Lisle (FRA)	1968 J.Kurka (TCH)
1928 Not held	1972 Ho Jun Li (SKO)
1932 B.Ronnmark (SWE)	1976 K.Smieszek (FRG)
1936 W.Rogeberg (NOR)	1980 K.Varga (HUN)
1948 A.Cook (USA)	1984 M.Etzel (USA)
1952 J.Sarbu (ROM)	1988 M.Varga (TCH)

Air Rifle

1984 P.Heberle (FRA)
1988 G.Maksimovic (YUG)

Air Pistol

1988 T.Kiriakov (USSR)

Women:

Sport Pistol

1984 L.Thom (CAN)
1988 N.Saloukvadzke (USSR)

Standard Rifle

1984 X.Wu (CHN)
1988 S.Sperber (FRG)

Air Rifle

1984 P.Spurgin (USA)
1988 I.Chilova (USSR)

Air Pistol

1988 J.Sekaric (YUG)

Prehistoric types of ski have been found in Sweden and dated to c.3000BC when it was used as a means of transport. Popular in Nordic countries, it developed as a sport in Norway around 1860, and the first known race was at Christiania (Oslo) in 1866. The Federation Internationale des Skieurs was formed in 1924. There are two types of Skiing; Alpine and Nordic. The former includes the downhill, slalom, giant and super giant slalom races, while the latter is the cross-country-type military style of competition.

ALPINE WORLD CUP

Instituted in 1967, the World Cup is a season-long event in which points are awarded for performances in the major events. In addition to the overall title, a separate competition for the slalom, giant slalom, super-giant slalom and downhill events is held.

Overall Champions:

	Men	Women
1967	J -C. Killy (FRA)	N. Greene (CAN)
1968	J -C. Killy (FRA)	N. Greene (CAN)
1969	K. Schranz (AUT)	G. Gabl (AUT)
1970	K. Schranz (AUT)	M. Jacot (FRA)
1971	G. Thoeni (ITA)	A. Proll (AUT)
1972	G. Thoeni (ITA)	A. Proll (AUT)
1973	G. Thoeni (ITA)	A. Proll (AUT)
1974	P. Gros (ITA)	A. Proll (AUT)
1975	G. Thoeni (ITA)	A. Moser-Proll (AUT)
1976	I. Stenmark (SWE)	R. Mittermaier (GER)
1977	I. Stenmark (SWE)	L -M. Morerod (SWI)
1978	I. Stenmark (SWE)	H. Wenzel (LIE)
1979	P. Luescher (SWI)	A. Moser-Proll (AUT)
1980	A. Wenzel (LIE)	H. Wenzel (LIE)
1981	P. Mahre (USA)	M -T. Nadig (SWI)
1982	P. Mahre (USA)	E. Hess (SWI)
1983	P. Mahre (USA)	T. McKinney (USA)
1984	P. Zurbriggen (SWI)	E. Hess (SWI)
1985	M. Girardelli (LUX)	M. Figini (SWI)
1986	M. Girardelli (LUX)	M. Walliser (SWI)
1987	P.Zurbriggen (SWI)	M. Walliser (SWI)
1988	P. Zurbriggen (SWI)	M. Figini (SWI)
1989	M. Girardelli (LUX)	N. Schneider (SWI)

Most Wins (Men):
4 Gustavo Thoeni

(Women):
6 Annemarie Moser-Proll

ALPINE WORLD CHAMPIONSHIPS

The first Alpine World Championships were held at Murren, Switzerland, in 1931 with a downhill event for men, and a downhill and slalom competition for women. The combined event was not introduced until 1932.

Overall Combined champions

	Men	Women
1932	O. Furrer (SWI)	R. Streiff (SWI)
1933	A. Seelos (AUT)	I. Wersin-Lantschner (AUT)
1934	D. Zogg (SWI)	C. Cranz (GER)
1935	A. Seelos (AUT)	C. Cranz (GER)
1936	R. Rominger (SWI)	E. Pinching (GB)
1937	E. Allais (FRA)	C. Cranz (GER)
1938	E. Allias (FRA)	C. Cranz (GER)
1939	J. Jennewein (GER)	C. Cranz (GER)
1940–1953	Not held	
1954	S. Eriksen (NOR)	I. Schopfer (SWI)
1956	T. Sailer (AUT)	M. Berthod (SWI)
1958	T. Sailer (AUT)	F. Danzer (SWI)
1960	G. Perillat (FRA)	A. Heggtveit (CAN)
1962	K. Schranz (AUT)	M. Goitschel (FRA)
1964	L. Leitner (GER)	M. Goitschel (FRA)
1966	J -C. Killy (FRA)	M. Goitschel (FRA)
1968	J -C. Killy (FRA)	N. Greene (CAN)
1970	W. Kidd (USA)	M. Jacot (FRA)
1972	G. Thoeni (ITA)	A. Proll (AUT)
1974	F. Klammer (AUT)	F. Serrat (FRA)
1976	G. Thoeni (ITA)	R. Mittermaier (FRG)
1978	A. Wenzel (LIE)	A. Moser-Proll (AUT)
1980	P. Mahre (USA)	H. Wenzel (LIE)
1982	M. Vion (FRA)	E. Hess (SWI)
1985	P. Zurbriggen (SWI)	E. Hess (SWI)
1987	M. Garardelli (LUX)	E. Hess (SWI)
1989	M. Girardelli (LUX)	T. McKinney (USA)

Most Wins (Men):

2 Toni Seelos, Emile Allais, Toni Sailer, Jean-Claude Killy, Gustavo Theoni

(Women):

5 Christel Cranz

OLYMPIC GAMES
Although Nordic Skiing first appeared in the Winter Olympics in 1924, Alpine Skiing did not make its debut until 1936, but has been included in every celebration since.

Giant Slalom

	Men	Women
1952	S. Eriksen (NOR)	A. Mead-Lawrence (USA)
1956	A. Sailer (AUT)	O. Reichert (GER)
1960	R. Staub (SWI)	Y. Ruegg (SWI)
1964	F. Boulieu (FRA)	M. Goitschel (FRA)
1968	J.-C. Killy (FRA)	N. Greene (CAN)
1972	G. Thoeni (ITA)	M.-T. Nadig (SWI)
1976	H. Hemmi (SWI)	K. Kreiner (CAN)
1980	I. Stenmark (SWE)	H. Wenzel (LIE)
1984	M. Julen (SWI)	D. Armstrong (USA)
1988	A. Tomba (ITA)	V. Schneider (SWI)

Slalom

1948	E. Reinalter (SWI)	G. Fraser (USA)
1952	O. Schneider (AUT)	A. Mead-Lawrence (USA)
1956	A. Sailer (AUT)	R. Colliard (SWI)
1960	E. Hinterseer (AUT)	A. Heggtveit (CAN)
1964	J. Stiegler (AUT)	C. Goitschel (FRA)
1968	J.-C. Killy (FRA)	M. Goitschel (FRA)
1972	F. Ochoa (SPA)	B. Cochran (USA)
1976	P. Gros (ITA)	R. Mittermaier (FRG)
1980	I. Stenmark (SWE)	H. Wenzel (LIE)
1984	P. Mahre (USA)	P. Magoni (ITA)
1988	A. Tomba (ITA)	V. Schneider (SWI)

Downhill

1948	H. Oreiller (FRA)	H. Schlunegger (SWI)
1952	Z. Colo (ITA)	T. Jochum-Beiser (AUT)
1956	A. Sailer (AUT)	M. Berthod (SWI)
1960	J. Vuarnet (FRA)	H. Biebl (GER)
1964	E. Zimmermann (AUT)	C. Haas (AUT)
1968	J.-C. Killy (FRA)	O. Pall (AUT)
1972	B. Russi (SWI)	M.-T. Nadig (SWI)
1976	F. Klammer (AUT)	R. Mittermaier (FRG)
1980	L. Stock (AUT)	A. Moser-Proll (AUT)
1984	W. Johnson (USA)	M. Figini (SWI)
1988	P. Zurbriggen (SWI)	M. Kiehl (FRG)

Super-Giant Slalom

1988	F. Piccard (FRA)	S. Wolf (AUT)

Alpine Combination

1936	F. Pfnur (GER)	C. Cranz (GER)
1948	H. Oreiller (FRA)	T. Beiser (AUT)
1988	H. Strolz (AUT)	A. Watchter (AUT)

Most Gold Medals (Men):
3 Toni Sailer, Jean-Claude Killy

(Women)
2 Andrea Mead Lawrence, Mariel Goitschel, Marie-Theresa Nadig, Rosi Mittermaier, Hanni Wenzel, Vreni Schneider

Snooker was born in Jubbulpore, India in 1875 when Neville Chamberlain (not to be confused with the Prime Minister of the same name) called a fellow officer in the Devonshire Regiment a 'Snooker' after missing an easy shot during a game of Russian Pool. A 'Snooker' was the name given to a new recruit at the Woolwich Military Academy. The officers eventually added different coloured balls to their game and it was decided to call the new game snooker.

WORLD PROFESSIONAL CHAMPIONSHIP

First organised in 1926–27 the championship was held continuously (except for the war years) until 1952 when the professional players and the governing body, the Billiards Association & Control Club, fell out. The championship was revived in 1964 but, until reverting to a knockout format in 1969, it was on a challenge basis. The first final at its present home, the Crucible Theatre, Sheffield, was in 1977.

Winners:

1927 J.Davis (ENG)	1952 H.Lindrum (AUS)
1928 J.Davis (ENG)	1953–1963 Not held
1929 J.Davis (ENG)	1964–68 J.Pulman (ENG)
1930 J.Davis (ENG)	1969 J.Spencer (ENG)
1931 J.Davis (ENG)	1970 R.Reardon (WAL)
1932 J.Davis (ENG)	1971 J.Spencer (ENG)
1933 J.Davis (ENG)	1972 A.Higgins (NI)
1934 J.Davis (ENG)	1973 R.Reardon (WAL)
1935 J.Davis (ENG)	1974 R.Reardon (WAL)
1936 J.Davis (ENG)	1975 R.Reardon (WAL)
1937 J.Davis (ENG)	1976 R.Reardon (WAL)
1938 J.Davis (ENG)	1977 J.Spencer (ENG)
1939 J.Davis (ENG)	1978 R.Reardon (WAL)
1940 J.Davis (ENG)	1979 T.Griffiths (WAL)
1941–1945 Not held	1980 C.Thorburn (CAN)
1946 J.Davis (ENG)	1981 S.Davis (ENG)
1947 W.Donaldson (SCO)	1982 A.Higgins (NI)
1948 F.Davis (ENG)	1983 S.Davis (ENG)
1949 F.Davis (ENG)	1984 S.Davis (ENG)
1950 W.Donaldson(SCO)	1985 Dennis Taylor (NI)
1951 F.Davis (ENG)	1986 J.Johnson (ENG)
	1987 S.Davis (ENG)

Most Wins:
15 Joe Davis

1988 S.Davis (ENG)
1989 S.Davis (ENG)
1990 S. HENDRY (SCO)

WORLD AMATEUR CHAMPIONSHIP

First held in Calcutta, India in 1963, it became a biennial event until 1985 when it became an annual competition.

Winners:

1963 G.Owen (ENG)	1978 C.Wilson (WAL)
1966 G.Owen (ENG)	1980 J.White (ENG)
1968 David Taylor (ENG)	1982 T.Parsons (WAL)
1970 J.Barron (ENG)	1984 O.B.Agrawal (IND)
1972 R.Edmonds (ENG)	1985 P.Mifsud (MAL)
1974 R.Edmonds (ENG)	1986 P.Mifsud (MAL)
1976 D.Mountjoy (WAL)	1987 D.Morgan (WAL)
	1988 J.Wattana (THA)

Most Wins:
2 Gary Owen, Ray Edmonds, Paul Mifsud

BENSON & HEDGES MASTERS

One of the most prestigious events after the World Professional Championship, entry to the Benson & Hedges Masters is by invitation only, and is open to just 16 leading players.

Winners:

1975 J.Spencer (ENG)	1982 S.Davis (ENG)
1976 R.Reardon (WAL)	1983 C.Thorburn (CAN)
1977 D.Mountjoy (WAL)	1984 J.White (ENG)
1978 A.Higgins (NI)	1985 C.Thorburn (CAN)
1979 P.Mans (SAF)	1986 C.Thorburn (CAN)
1980 T.Griffiths (WAL)	1987 D.Taylor (NI)
1981 A.Higgins (NI)	1988 S.Davis (ENG)
	1989 S.Hendry (SCO)

Most Wins:
3 Cliff Thorburn

UNITED KINGDOM OPEN

First held at Blackpool in 1977 it was known as the United Kingdom Professional Championship until 1984 when it became open to overseas players. All finals since 1978 have been at the Preston Guildhall.

Winners:

1977 P.Fagan (NI)	1982 T.Griffiths (WAL)
1978 D.Mountjoy (WAL)	1983 A.Higgins (NI)
1979 J.Virgo (ENG)	1984 S.Davis (ENG)
1980 S.Davis (ENG)	1985 S.Davis (ENG)
1981 S.Davis (ENG)	1986 S.Davis (ENG)
	1987 S.Davis (ENG)
	1988 D.Mountjoy (WAL)

Most Wins:
6 Steve Davis

POT BLACK

BBC television's *Pot Black* was undoubtedly responsible for the growth of snooker in the 1970s. Although its single-frame format would not be acceptable in today's tournaments, it nevertheless took the sport to millions via the television screen. Sadly the programme was discontinued in 1986.

Winners:

1969 R.Reardon (WAL)	1978 D.Mountjoy (WAL)
1970 J.Spencer (ENG)	1979 R.Reardon (WAL)
1971 J.Spencer (ENG)	1980 E.Charlton (AUS)
1972 E.Charlton (AUS)	1981 C.Thorburn (CAN)
1973 E.Charlton (AUS)	1982 S.Davis (ENG)
1974 G.Miles (ENG)	1983 S.Davis (ENG)
1975 G.Miles (ENG)	1984 T.Griffiths (WAL)
1976 J.Spencer (ENG)	1985 D.Mountjoy (WAL)
1977 P.Mans (SAF)	1986 J.White (ENG)

Most Wins:

3 John Spencer, Eddie Charlton

WORLD RANKINGS

The World Professional Billiards & Snooker Association published its first set of world rankings in 1976. The following is a list of all players that have topped the rankings since then. A revised list is produced after the World Championship each year.

1976 R.Reardon (WAL)	1982 R.Reardon (WAL)
1977 R.Reardon (WAL)	1983 S.Davis (ENG)
1978 R.Reardon (WAL)	1984 S.Davis (ENG)
1979 R.Reardon (WAL)	1985 S.Davis (ENG)
1980 R.Reardon (WAL)	1986 S.Davis (ENG)
1981 C.Thorburn (CAN)	1987 S.Davis (ENG)
	1988 S.Davis (ENG)
	1989 S.Davis (ENG)

THE RECORD BREAKS

The maximum break is 147; it has been officially performed on just ten occasions:

1955	J. Davis (ENG)
1965	R. Williams (ENG)
1982	S. Davis (ENG)
1983	C. Thorburn (CAN)
1984	K. Stevens (CAN)
1987	W. Thorne (ENG)
1988	A. Meo (ENG)
1988	A. Robidoux (CAN)
1989	J. Rea (SCO)
1989	C. Thorburn (CAN)

THE RECORD BREAKS IN THE LEADING TOURNAMENTS:
World Professional Championship: 147 C. Thorburn (CAN) 1983
Mercantile Credit Classic: 147 S. Davis (ENG) 1982
  (formerly Lada Classic)
Tennents UK Championship: 147 W. Thorne (ENG) 1987
  (formerly Coral UK Championship)
Fidelity Unit Trusts International: 140 N. Foulds (ENG) 1984
                          140 S. Davis (ENG) 1987
  (formerly Jameson International, Goya International, BCE International)
Rothmans Grand Prix: 139 D. Reynolds (ENG) 1988
  (formerly Professional Players' Tournament)
MIM Britannia British Open: 145 D. Martin (ENG) 1986
  (formerly Dulux British Open)
Benson & Hedges Masters: 147 K. Stevens (CAN) 1984
European Open: 147 A. Robidoux (CAN) 1988 (Q)
BCE Canadian Masters: 132 D. Taylor (IRE) 1988

(Q) Set in qualifying competition

WOMEN'S SNOOKER

WORLD OPEN SNOOKER CHAMPIONSHIP
1976 V.Selby (ENG)
1977-79 Not held
1980 L.McIlrath (AUS)
1981 V.Selby (ENG)
1982 Not held
1983 S.Foster (ENG)
1984 Not held
1985 Not held
1986 A.Fisher (ENG)
1987 A -M.Farren (ENG)
1988 A.Fisher (ENG)

Most Wins:
2 Vera Selby; Alison Fisher

UNITED KINGDOM OPEN CHAMPIONSHIP
1986 A.Fisher
1987 A.Fisher
1988 A.Fisher

Most Wins:
3 Alison Fisher

Dirt track racing in the United States dates back to 1902 but the first organised Speedway meeting was in Australia in 1923. The first meeting in Britain was at High Beach, Essex in 1928.

WORLD CHAMPIONSHIPS

The first World Championship, for individual riders, was held at Wembley in 1936. The Team competition was introduced in 1960, and the Pairs in 1968. The Long Track championship was inaugurated in 1971.

Individual

1936 L.Van Praag (AUS)	1967 O.Fundin (SWE)
1937 J.Milne (USA)	1968 I.Mauger (NZ)
1938 B.Wilkinson (AUS)	1969 I.Mauger (NZ)
1949 T.Price (ENG)	1970 I.Mauger (NZ)
1950 F.Williams (WAL)	1971 O.Olsen (DEN)
1951 J.Young (AUS)	1972 I.Mauger (NZ)
1952 J.Young (AUS)	1973 J.Szczakiel (POL)
1953 F.Williams (WAL)	1974 A.Michanek (SWE)
1954 R.Moore (NZ)	1975 O.Olsen (DEN)
1955 P.Craven (ENG)	1976 P.Collins (ENG)
1956 O.Fundin (SWE)	1977 I.Mauger (NZ)
1957 B.Briggs (NZ)	1978 O.Olsen (DEN)
1958 B.Briggs (NZ)	1979 I.Mauger (NZ)
1959 R.Moore (NZ)	1980 M.Lee (ENG)
1960 O.Fundin (SWE)	1981 B.Penhall (USA)
1961 O.Fundin (SWE)	1982 B.Penhall (USA)
1962 P.Craven (ENG)	1983 E.Muller (FRG)
1963 O.Fundin (SWE)	1984 E.Gundersen (DEN)
1964 B.Briggs (NZ)	1985 E.Gundersen (DEN)
1965 B.Knutsson (SWE)	1986 H.Nielsen (DEN)
1966 B.Briggs (NZ)	1987 H.Nielsen (DEN)
	1988 E.Gundersen (DEN)

Most Wins:
6 Ivan Mauger

Pairs

1968 Sweden (O.Fundin/T.Harryson)
1969 New Zealand (I.Mauger/B.Andrews)
1970 New Zealand (R.Moore/I.Mauger)
1971 Poland (J.Szczakiel/A.Wyglenda)
1972 England (R.Wilson/T.Betts)
1973 Sweden (A.Michanek/T.Jansson)
1974 Sweden (A.Michanek/S.Sjosten)
1975 Sweden (A.Michanek/T.Jansson)
1976 England (J.Louis/M.Simmons)
1977 England (P.Collins/M.Simmons)
1978 England (M.Simmons/G.Kennett)
1979 Denmark (O.Olsen/H.Nielsen)
1980 England (D.Jessup/P.Collins)

1981 USA (B.Penhall/B.Schwartz)
1982 USA (D.Sigalos/B.Schwartz)
1983 England (K.Carter/P.Collins)
1984 England (P.Collins/C.Morton)
1985 Denmark (E.Gundersen/T.Knudsen)
1986 Denmark (H.Nielsen/E.Gundersen)
1987 Denmark (H.Nielsen/E.Gundersen)
1988 Denmark (H.Nielsen/E.Gundersen)

Most Wins:
7 England

Team

1960 Sweden	1974 England
1961 Poland	1975 England
1962 Sweden	1976 Australia
1963 Sweden	1977 England
1964 Sweden	1978 Denmark
1965 Poland	1979 New Zealand
1966 Poland	1980 England
1967 Sweden	1981 Denmark
1968 Great Britain	1982 United States
1969 Poland	1983 Denmark
1970 Sweden	1984 Denmark
1971 Great Britain	1985 Denmark
1972 Great Britain	1986 Denmark
1973 Great Britain	1987 Denmark
	1988 Denmark

Most Wins:
8 Great Britain/England,
   Denmark

Long Track

1971 I.Mauger (NZ)	1979 A.Weisbock (FRG)
1972 I.Mauger (NZ)	1980 K.Maier (FRG)
1973 O.Olsen (DEN)	1981 M.Lee (ENG)
1974 E.Muller (FRG)	1982 K.Maier (FRG)
1975 E.Muller (FRG)	1983 S.Moran (USA)
1976 E.Muller (FRG)	1984 E.Gundersen (DEN)
1977 A.Michanek (SWE)	1985 S.Wigg (ENG)
1978 E.Muller (FRG)	1986 E.Gundersen (DEN)
	1987 K.Maier (FRG)
	1988 K.Maier (FRG)

Most Wins:
4 Egon Muller, Karl Maier

BRITISH SPEEDWAY LEAGUE

The British League was founded in 1932 but was then known as the National League. It became the British League in 1965 and in 1968 a Second Division was created. This new division was renamed the New National League in 1975 and since 1976 it has been known as the National League.

National League

1932 Wembley	1952 Wembley
1933 Belle Vue	1953 Wembley
1934 Belle Vue	1954 Wimbledon
1935 Belle Vue	1955 Southampton
1936 Belle Vue	1956 Wimbledon
1937 West Ham	1957 Swindon
1938 New Cross	1958 Wimbledon
1939 Belle Vue	1959 Wimbledon
1940–1945 Not held	1960 Wimbledon
1946 Wembley	1961 Wimbledon
1947 Wembley	1962 Southampton
1948 New Cross	1963 Belle Vue
1949 Wembley	1964 Oxford
1950 Wembley	
1951 Wembley	

British League / Division 2

1965 West Ham	–
1966 Halifax	–
1967 Swindon	–
1968 Coventry	Belle Vue Colts
1969 Poole	Belle Vue Colts
1970 Belle Vue	Canterbury
1971 Belle Vue	Eastbourne
1972 Belle Vue	Crewe
1973 Reading	Boston
1974 Exeter	Birmingham

British League / New National League

1975 Ipswich	Birmingham

British League / National League

1976 Ipswich	Newcastle
1977 White City	Eastbourne
1978 Coventry	Canterbury
1979 Coventry	Mildenhall
1980 Reading	Rye House
1981 Cradley Heath	Middlesbrough
1982 Belle Vue	Newcastle
1983 Cradley Heath	Newcastle
1984 Ipswich	Long Eaton
1985 Oxford	Ellesmere Port
1986 Oxford	Eastbourne
1987 Coventry	Eastbourne
1988 Coventry	Hackney

Most Wins:
10 Belle Vue

Squash is believed to have originated at Harrow School in the middle of the 19th century, but it is only since the formation of the Squash Rackets Association in 1929 that the game has grown in popularity world-wide.

WORLD OPEN CHAMPIONSHIP

The first World Open Championships were held in 1976. It is an annual competition for men, and a biennial one for women.

Winners:

	Men	**Women**
1976	G.Hunt (AUS)	H.McKay (AUS)
1977	G.Hunt (AUS)	–
1978	Not held	
1979	G.Hunt (AUS)	H.McKay (AUS)
1980	G.Hunt (AUS)	–
1981	Jahangir Khan (PAK)	R.Thorne(AUS)
1982	Jahangir Khan (PAK)	–
1983	Jahangir Khan (PAK)	V.Cardwell (AUS)
1984	Jahangir Khan (PAK)	–
1985	Jahangir Khan (PAK)	S. Devoy (NZ)
1986	R.Norman (NZ)	–
1987	Jansher Khan (PAK)	S. Devoy (NZ)
1988	Jahangir Khan (PAK)	–
1989		M. Le Moignan (GB)

Most Wins
(Men):
6 Jahangir Khan
(Women):
2 Heather McKay

WORLD AMATEUR CHAMPIONSHIP

First held in 1967, the championship became known as the I.S.R.F. World Championship in 1979 after the sport went open. From 1987 it has been a team competition only.

Winners:

	Individual	**Team**
1967	G.Hunt (AUS)	Australia
1969	G.Hunt (AUS)	Australia
1971	G.Hunt (AUS)	Australia
1973	C.Nancarrow (AUS)	Australia
1975	K.Shawcross (AUS)	Great Britain
1977	M.Ahmed (PAK)	Pakistan
1979	Jahangir Khan (PAK)	Great Britain
1981	S.Bowditch (AUS)	Pakistan
1983	Jahangir Khan (PAK)	Pakistan
1985	Jahangir Khan (PAK)	Pakistan
1987	–	Pakistan

Most Wins
(Individual):
3 Geoff Hunt, Jahangir Khan

BRITISH OPEN CHAMPIONSHIP

First held in 1922 for women, and in 1930 for men, the British Open was regarded as the unofficial World Championship until the creation of the World Amateur Championship in 1967.

	Men	Women
1922	–	J.Cave (GB)
1922	–	S.Huntsman(GB)
1923	–	N.Cave (GB)
1924	–	J.Cave (GB)
1925	–	C.Fenwick (GB)
1926	–	C.Fenwick (GB)
1927 Not held		
1928	–	J.Cave (GB)
1929	–	N.Cave (GB)
1930	D.Butcher (GB)	N.Cave (GB)
1931	D.Butcher (GB)	C.Fenwick (GB)
1932	Abdel Fattah Amr Bey (EGY)	S.Noel (GB)
1933	–	S.Noel (GB)
1934	Abdel Fattah Amr Bey (EGY)	S.Noel (GB)
1934	–	M.Lumb (GB)
1935	Abdel Fattah Amr Bey (EGY)	M.Lumb (GB)
1936	Abdel Fattah Amr Bey (EGY)	M.Lumb (GB)
1937	Abdel Fattah Amr Bey (EGY)	M.Lumb (GB)
1938	J.Dear (GB)	M.Lumb (GB)
1939	–	M.Lumb (GB)
1940–45 Not held		
1946	Mahmoud el Karim (EGY)	
1947	Mahmoud el Karim (EGY)	J.Curry (GB)
1948	Mahmoud el Karim (EGY)	J.Curry (GB)
1949	Mahmoud el Karim (EGY)	J.Curry (GB)
1950	Hashim Khan (PAK)	J.Morgan (GB)
1951	Hashim Khan (PAK)	J.Morgan (GB)
1952	Hashim Khan (PAK)	J.Morgan (GB)
1953	Hashim Khan (PAK)	J.Morgan (GB)
1954	Hashim Khan (PAK)	J.Morgan (GB)
1955	Hashim Khan (PAK)	J.Morgan (GB)
1956	Roshan Khan (PAK)	J.Morgan (GB)
1957	Hashim Khan (PAK)	J.Morgan (GB)
1958	Azam Khan (PAK)	J.Morgan (GB)
1959	Azam Khan (PAK)	
1960	Azam Khan (PAK)	S.Macintosh (GB)
1961	Azam Khan (PAK)	F.Marshall (GB)
1962	Mohibullah Khan (PAK)	H.McKay (AUS)
1963	Abou Taleb (EGY)	H.McKay (AUS)
1964	Abou Taleb (EGY)	H.McKay (AUS)
1965	Abou Taleb (EGY)	H.McKay (AUS)
1966	Abou Taleb (EGY)	H.McKay (AUS)
1967	J.Barrington (GB)	H.McKay (AUS)
1968	J.Barrington (GB)	H.McKay (AUS)
1969	G.Hunt (AUS)	H.McKay (AUS)
1970	J.Barrington (GB)	H.McKay (AUS)
1971	J.Barrington (GB)	H.McKay (AUS)
1972	J.Barrington (GB)	H.McKay (AUS)
1973	J.Barrington (GB)	H.McKay (AUS)
1974	G.Hunt (AUS)	H.McKay (AUS)
1975	Qamar Zaman (PAK)	H.McKay (AUS)
1976	G.Hunt (AUS)	H.McKay (AUS)
1977	G.Hunt (AUS)	H.McKay (AUS)

1978	G.Hunt (AUS)	S.Newman-King (AUS)
1979	G.Hunt (AUS)	B.Wall (AUS)
1980	G.Hunt (AUS)	V.Hoffman (AUS)
1981	G.Hunt (AUS)	V.Hoffman (AUS)
1982	Jahangir Khan (PAK)	V.Hoffman-Cardwell (AUS)
1983	Jahangir Khan (PAK)	V.Hoffman-Cardwell (AUS)
1984	Jahangir Khan (PAK)	S.Devoy (NZ)
1985	Jahangir Khan (PAK)	S.Devoy (NZ)
1986	Jahangir Khan (PAK)	S.Devoy (NZ)
1987	Jahangir Khan (PAK)	S. Devoy (NZ)
1988	Jahangir Khan (PAK)	S. Devoy (NZ)
1989	Jahangir Khan (PAK)	S. Devoy (NZ)

Most Wins
(Men):
8 Geoff Hunt, Jahangir Khan

(Women)
16 Heather McKay

Jahangir Khan of Pakistan went five and a half years without defeat. After losing to Geoff Hunt in the final of the British Open in April 1981 he did not lose again until November 1986 when New Zealander Ross Norman beat him in the world championship final.

Jahangir Khan is the latest in the long line of members from that notable family to have won the British Open. His father Roshan won the title in 1956. Roshan's cousin Hashim won every Open between 1950–55, and regained the title in 1957. Hashim's brother Azam then succeeded him as champion in 1958 and held the title until 1962.

One of squash's most colourful characters was Jonah Barrington. Born in Cornwall he played squash for Ireland because of his father's birthright. Educated at Dublin University he had a succession of 'unusual' jobs before turning to squash professionally. Amongst his earlier jobs were those of bowling green keeper, milkman and . . . artist's model!

Australia's Heather McKay (nee Blundell) was unbeaten in women's squash from 1962 to 1980.

Swimming started to gain popularity as a competitive sport towards the latter part of the 18th century and grew in popularity, particularly in Britain in the 19th century. The first British Championships were held in 1878.

WORLD CHAMPIONSHIPS

The first World Championships were held in Belgrade in 1973. They are now held every four years.

Winners
50 metres Freestyle

Men	Women
1986 T.Jaeger (USA)	T.Costache (ROM)

100 metres Freestyle

Men	Women
1973 J.Montgomery (USA)	K.Ender (GDR)
1975 A.Coan (USA)	K.Ender (GDR)
1978 D.McCagg (USA)	B.Krause (GDR)
1982 J.Woithe (GDR)	B.Meineke (GDR)
1986 M.Biondi (USA)	K.Otto (GDR)

200 metres Freestyle

Men	Women
1973 J.Montgomery (USA)	K.Rothhammer (USA)
1975 T.Shaw (USA)	S.Babashoff (USA)
1978 W.Forrester (USA)	C.Woodhead (USA)
1982 M.Gross (FRG)	A.Verstappen (HOL)
1986 M.Gross (FRG)	H.Friedrich (GDR)

400 metres Freestyle

Men	Women
1973 R.DeMont (USA)	H.Greenwood (USA)
1975 T.Shaw (USA)	S.Babashoff (USA)
1978 V.Salnikov (USSR)	T.Wickham (AUS)
1982 V.Salnikov (USSR)	C.Schmidt (GDR)
1986 R.Henkel (FRG)	H.Friedrich (GDR)

800 metres Freestyle
Women

1973 N.Calligaris (ITA)
1975 J.Turrall (AUS)
1978 T.Wickham (AUS)
1982 K.Linehan (USA)
1986 A.Strauss (GDR)

1500 metres Freestyle
Men

1973 S.Holland (AUS)
1975 T.Shaw (USA)
1978 V.Salnikov (USSR)
1982 V.Salnikov (USSR)
1986 R.Henkel (FRG)

100 metres Backstroke

Men	Women
1973 R.Matthes (GDR)	U.Richter (GDR)
1975 R.Matthes (GDR)	U.Richter (GDR)
1978 R.Jackson (USA)	L.Jezek (USA)
1982 D.Richter (GDR)	O.Kristin (GDR)
1986 I.Poliansky (USSR)	B.Mitchell (USA)

200 metres Backstroke

Men	Women
1973 R.Matthes (GDR)	M.Belote (USA)
1975 Z.Verraszto (HUN)	B.Treiber (GDR)
1978 J.Vassallo (USA)	L.Jezek (USA)
1982 R.Carey (USA)	C.Sirch (GDR)
1986 I.Poliansky (USSR)	C.Sirch (GDR)

100 metres Breaststroke

Men	Women
1973 J.Hencken (USA)	R.Vogel (GDR)
1975 D.Wilkie (GB)	H.Anke (GDR)
1978 W.Kusch (GDR)	J.Bogdanova (USSR
1982 S.Lundquist (USA)	U.Geweniger (GDR)
1986 V.Davis (CAN)	O.Gerasch (GDR)

200 metres Breaststroke

Men	Women
1973 D.Wilkie (GB)	R.Vogel (GDR)
1975 D.Wilkie (GB)	H.Anke (GDR)
1978 N.Nevid (USA)	L.Kachushite (USSR)
1982 V.Davis (CAN)	S.Varganova (USSR)
1986 J.Szabo (HUN)	S.Hoerner (GDR)

100 metres Butterfly

Men	Women
1973 B.Robertson (CAN)	K.Ender (GDR)
1975 G.Jagenburg (USA)	K.Ender (GDR)
1978 J.Bottom (USA)	M -J.Pennington (USA)
1982 M.Gribble (USA)	M.Meagher (USA)
1986 P.Morales (USA)	K.Gresler (GDR)

200 metres Butterfly

Men	Women
1973 R.Backhaus (USA)	R.Kother (GDR)
1975 W.Forrester (USA)	R.Kother (GDR)
1978 M.Bruner (USA)	T.Caulkins (USA)
1982 M.Gross (FRG)	I.Geissler (GDR)
1986 M.Gross (FRG)	M.Meagher (USA)

200 metres Individual Medley

Men	Women
1973 G.Larsson (SWE)	A.Hubner (GDR)
1975 A.Hargitay (HUN)	K.Heddy (USA)
1978 G.Smith (CAN)	T.Caulkins (USA)
1982 A.Sidorenko (USSR)	P.Schneider (GDR)
1986 T.Darnyi (HUN)	K.Otto (GDR)

400 metres Individual Medley

Men	Women
1973 A.Hargitay (HUN)	G.Wegner (GDR)
1975 A.Hargitay (HUN)	U.Tauber (GDR)
1978 J.Vassallo (USA)	T.Caulkins (USA)
1982 R.Prado (BRA)	P.Schneider (GDR)
1986 T.Darnyi (HUN)	K.Nord (GDR)

4x100 metres Freestyle Relay

Men	Women
1973 United States	East Germany
1975 United States	East Germany
1978 United States	United States
1982 United States	East Germany
1986 United States	East Germany

4x200 metres Freestyle Relay

Men	Women
1973 United States	–
1975 West Germany	–
1978 United States	–
1982 United States	–
1986 East Germany	East Germany

4x100 metres Medley Relay

Men	Women
1973 United States	East Germany
1975 United States	East Germany
1978 United States	United States
1982 United States	East Germany
1986 United States	East Germany

Springboard Diving

Men	Women
1973 P.Boggs (USA)	C.Kohler (GDR)
1975 P.Boggs (USA)	I.Kalinina (USSR)
1978 P.Boggs (USA)	I.Kalinina (USSR)
1982 G.Louganis (USA)	M.Meyer (USA)
1986 G.Louganis (USA)	Gao Min (CHN)

Highboard Diving

Men	Women
1973 K.Dibiasi (ITA)	U.Knape (SWE)
1975 K.Dibiasi (ITA)	J.Ely (USA)
1978 G.Louganis (USA)	I.Kalinina (USSR)
1982 G.Louganis (USA)	W.Wyland (USA)
1986 G.Louganis (USA)	Chen Lin (CHN)

Most Gold Medals

(Men):	(Women):
6 Jim Montgomery	8 Kornelia Ender

Synchronised Swimming
Solo Women

1973 T.Andersen (USA)	1982 T.Ruiz (USA)
1975 G.Buzonas (USA)	1986 C.Waldo (CAN)
1978 H.Vanderburg (CAN)	

Duet

1973 United States	1982 Canada
1975 United States	1986 Canada
1978 Canada	

Team

1973 United States	1982 Canada
1975 United States	1986 Canada
1978 United States	

OLYMPIC GAMES
Swimming has been included in every Olympic Games since 1896. Women's events were included for the first time in 1912.

Winners:
50 metres Freestyle

1988 M.Biondi (USA)	K.Otto (GDR)

100 metres Freestyle

Men	Women
1896 A.Hajos (HUN)	–
1904 Z.Halmay (HUN)	–
1908 C.Daniels (USA)	–
1912 D.Kahanamoku (USA)	F.Durack (AUS)
1920 D.Kahanamoku (USA)	E.Bleibtrey (USA)
1924 J.Weissmuller (USA)	E.Lackie (USA)
1928 J.Weissmuller (USA)	A.Osipowich (USA)
1932 Y.Miyazaki (JAP)	H.Madison (USA)
1936 F.Csik (HUN)	H.Mastenbroek (HOL)
1948 W.Ris (USA)	G.Andersen (DEN)
1952 C.Scholes (USA)	K.Szoke (HUN)
1956 J.Henricks (AUS)	D.Fraser (AUS)
1960 J.Devitt (AUS)	D.Fraser (AUS)
1964 D.Schollander (USA)	D.Fraser (AUS)
1968 M.Wenden (AUS)	J.Henne (USA)
1972 M.Spitz (USA)	S.Neilson (USA)
1976 J.Montgomery (USA)	K.Ender (GDR)
1980 J.Woithe (GDR)	B.Krause (GDR)
1984 A.Gaines (USA)	N.Hogshead (USA) & C.Steinseifer (USA)
1988 M.Biondi (USA)	K.Otto (GDR)

200 metres Freestyle

Men	Women
1900 F.Lane (AUS)	–
1904 C.Daniels (USA)	–
1968 M.Wenden (AUS)	D.Meyer (USA)
1972 M.Spitz (USA)	S.Gould (AUS)
1976 B.Furniss (USA)	K.Ender (GDR)
1980 S.Kopliakov (USSR)	B.Krause (GDR)
1984 M.Gross (FRG)	M.Wayte (USA)
1988 D.Armstrong (AUS)	H.Friedrich (GDR)

400 metres Freestyle

Men	Women
1896 P.Neumann (AUT)	–
1904 C.Daniels (USA)	–
1908 H.Taylor (GB)	–
1912 G.Hodgson (CAN)	–
1920 N.Ross (USA)	E.Bleibtrey (USA)
1924 J.Weissmuller (USA)	M.Norelius (USA)
1928 A.Zorilla (ARG)	M.Norelius (USA)
1932 B.Crabbe (USA)	H.Madison (USA)
1936 J.Medica (USA)	R.Mastenbroek (HOL)
1948 W.Smith (USA)	A.Curtis (USA)
1952 J.Boiteaux (FRA)	V.Gyenge (HUN)
1956 M.Rose (AUS)	L.Crapp (AUS)
1960 M.Rose (AUS)	C.von Saltza (USA)
1964 D.Schollander (USA)	V.Duenkel (USA)
1968 M.Burton (USA)	D.Meyer (USA)
1972 B.Cooper (AUS)	S.Gould (AUS)
1976 B.Goodell (USA)	P.Thuemer (GDR)
1980 V.Salnikov (USSR)	I.Diers (GDR)
1984 G.Dicarlo (USA)	T.Cohen (USA)
1988 U.Dassler (GDR)	J.Evans (USA)

1500 metres Freestyle / 800 metres Freestyle

Men	Women
1896 A.Hajos (HUN)	–
1900 J.Jarvis (GB)	–
1904 E.Rausch (GER)	–
1908 H.Taylor (GB)	–
1912 G.Hodgson (CAN)	–
1920 N.Ross (USA)	–
1924 A.Charlton (AUS)	–
1928 A.Borg (SWE)	–
1932 K.Kitamura (JAP)	–
1936 N.Terada (JAP)	–
1948 J.McLane (USA)	–
1952 F.Konno (USA)	–
1956 M.Rose (AUS)	–
1960 J.Konrads (AUS)	–
1964 R.Windle (AUS)	–
1968 M.Burton (USA)	D.Meyer (USA)
1972 M.Burton (USA)	K.Rothhammer (USA)
1976 B.Goodell (USA)	P.Thuemer (GDR)
1980 V.Salnikov (USSR)	M.Ford (AUS)
1984 M.O'Brien (USA)	T.Cohen (USA)
1988 V.Salnikov (USSR)	J.Evans (USA)

100 metres Backstroke

Men	Women
1904 W.Brack (GER)	–
1908 A.Beiberstein (GER)	–
1912 H.Hebner (USA)	–
1920 W.Kealoha (USA)	–
1924 W.Kealoha (USA)	S.Bauer (USA)
1928 G.Kojac (USA)	M.Braun (HOL)
1932 M.Kiyokawa (JAP)	E.Holm (USA)
1936 A.Kiefer (USA)	D.Senff (HOL)
1948 A.Stack (USA)	K.Harup (DEN)
1952 Y.Oyakawa (USA)	J.Harrison (SAF)

1956 D.Thiele (AUS) J.Grinham (GB)
1960 D.Thiele (AUS) L.Burke (USA)
1964 – C.Ferguson (USA)
1968 R.Matthes (GDR) K.Hall (USA)
1972 R.Matthes (GDR) M.Belote (USA)
1976 J.Naber (USA) U.Richter (GDR)
1980 B.Baron (SWE) R.Reinisch (GDR)
1984 R.Carey (USA) T.Andrews (USA)
1988 D.Suzuki (JAP) K.Otto (GDR)

200 metres Backstroke

Men	Women
1900 E.Hoppenberg (GER)	–
1964 J.Graef (USA)	–
1968 R.Matthes (GDR)	L.Watson (USA)
1972 R.Matthes (GDR)	M.Belote (USA)
1976 J.Naber (USA)	U.Richter (GDR)
1980 S.Wladar (HUN)	R.Reinisch (GDR)
1984 R.Carey (USA)	J.de Rover (HOL)
1988 I.Polianski (USSR)	K.Egerszegi (HUN)

100 metres Breaststroke

Men	Women
1968 D.McKenzie (USA)	D.Bjedov (YUG)
1972 N.Taguchi (JAP)	C.Carr (USA)
1976 J.Hencken (USA)	H.Anke (GDR)
1980 D.Goodhew (GB)	U.Geweniger (GDR)
1984 S.Lundquist (USA)	P.Van Staveren (HOL)
1988 A.Moorhouse (GB)	T.Dangalakova (BUL)

200 metres Breaststroke

Men	Women
1908 F.Holman (GB)	–
1912 W.Bathe (FRG)	–
1920 H.Malmroth (SWE)	–
1924 R.Skelton (USA)	L.Morton (GB)
1928 Y.Tsuruta (JAP)	H.Schrader (GER)
1932 Y.Tsuruta (JAP)	C.Dennis (AUS)
1936 T.Hamuro (JAP)	H.Maehata (JAP)
1948 J.Verdeur (USA)	P.van Vliet (HOL)
1952 J.Davies (AUS)	E.Szekely (HUN)
1956 M.Furukawa (JAP)	U.Happe (GER)
1960 W.Mulliken (USA)	A.Lonsbrough (GB)
1964 I.O'Brien (AUS)	G.Prozumenshchikova (USSR)
1968 F.Munoz (MEX)	S.Wichman (USA)
1972 J.Hencken (USA)	B.Whitfield (AUS)
1976 D.Wilkie (GB)	M.Koshevaia (USSR)
1980 R.Zulpa (USSR)	L.Kachushite (USSR)
1984 V.Davis (CAN)	A.Ottenbrite (CAN)
1988 J.Szabo (HUN)	S.Hoerner (GDR)

100 metres Butterfly

Men	Women
1956 –	S.Mann (USA)
1960 –	C.Schuler (USA)
1964 –	S.Stouder (USA)
1968 D.Russell (USA)	L.McClements (AUS)
1972 M.Spitz (USA)	M.Aoki (JAP)
1976 M.Vogel (USA)	K.Ender (GDR)
1980 P.Arvidsson (SWE)	C.Metschuck (GDR)
1984 M.Gross (FRG)	M.Meagher (USA)
1988 A.Nesty (SUR)	K.Otto (GDR)

200 metres Butterfly

Men	Women
1956 W.Yorzyk (USA)	
1960 M.Troy (USA)	
1964 K.Berry (AUS)	
1968 C.Robie (USA)	A.Kok (HOL)
1972 M.Spitz (USA)	K.Moe (USA)
1976 M.Bruner (USA)	A.Pollack (GDR)
1980 S.Fesenko (USSR)	I.Geissler (GDR)
1984 J.Sieben (FRG)	M.Meagher (USA
1988 M.Gross (FRG)	K.Nord (GDR)

200 metres Individual Medley

Men	Women
1968 C.Hickcox (USA)	C.Kolb (USA)
1972 G.Larsson (SWE)	S.Gould (AUS)
1984 A.Baumann (CAN)	T.Caulkins (USA)
1988 T.Darnyi (HUN)	Y.Dendeberova (USSR)

400 metres Individual Medley

Men	Women
1964 R.Roth (USA)	D.De Varona (USA)
1968 C.Hickcox (USA)	C.Kolb (USA)
1972 G.Larsson (SWE)	G.Neall (AUS)
1976 R.Strachan (USA)	U.Tauber (GDR)
1980 A.Sidorenko (USSR)	P.Schneider (GDR)
1984 A.Baumann (CAN)	T.Caulkins (USA)
1988 T.Darnyi (HUN)	J.Evans (USA)

4 × 100 metres Freestyle Relay

Men	Women
1912 Great Britain	–
1916 –	–
1920 –	United States
1924 –	United States
1928 –	United States
1932 –	United States
1936 –	Holland
1948 –	United States
1952 –	Hungary
1956 –	Australia
1960 –	United States
1964 United States	United States
1968 United States	United States
1972 United States	United States
1976 –	United States
1980 –	East Germany
1984 United States	United States
1988 United States	East Germany

4 × 200 metres Freestyle Relay Men

1908 Great Britain	1956 Australia
1912 Australasia	1960 United States
1920 United States	1964 United States
1924 United States	1968 United States
1928 United States	1972 United States
1932 Japan	1976 United States
1936 Japan	1980 USSR
1948 United States	1984 United States
1952 United States	1988 United States

4x100 metres Medley Relay

Men	Women
1960 United States	United States
1964 United States	United States
1968 United States	United States
1972 United States	United States
1976 United States	East Germany
1980 Australia	East Germany
1984 United States	United States
1988 United States	East Germany

Springboard Diving

Men	Women
1908 A.Zurner (GER)	–
1912 P.Gunther (GER)	–
1920 L.Kuehn (USA)	A.Riggin (USA)
1924 A.White (USA)	E.Becker (USA)
1928 P.Desjardins (USA)	H.Meany (USA)
1932 M.Galitzen (USA)	G.Coleman (USA)
1936 D.Degener (USA)	M.Gestring (USA)
1948 B.Harlan (USA)	V.Draves (USA)
1952 D.Browning (USA)	P.McCormick (USA)
1956 R.Clotworthy (USA)	P.McCormick (USA)
1960 G.Tobian (USA)	I.Kramer (GER)
1964 K.Sitzberger (USA)	I.Kramer-Engel (GER)
1968 B.Wrightson (USA)	S.Gossick (USA)
1972 V.Vasin (USSR)	M.King (USA)
1976 P.Boggs (USA)	J.Chandler (USA)
1980 A.Portnov (USSR)	I.Kalinina (USSR)
1984 G.Louganis (USA)	S.Bernier (CAN)
1988 G.Louganis (USA)	Gao Min (CHN)

Highboard Platform Diving

Men	Women
1904 G.Sheldon (USA)	–
1908 H.Johansson (SWE)	–
1912 E.Adlerz (SWE)	G.Johansson (SWE)
1920 C.Pinkston (USA)	S.Fryland-Clausen (DEN)
1924 A.White (USA)	C.Smith (USA)
1928 P.Desjardins (USA)	E.Pinkston (USA)
1932 H.Smith (USA)	D.Poynton (USA)
1936 M.Wayne (USA)	D.Poynton-Hill (USA)
1948 S.Lee (USA)	V.Draves (USA)
1952 S.Lee (USA)	P.McCormick (USA)
1956 J.Capilla (MEX)	P.McCormick (USA)
1960 R.Webster (USA)	I.Kramer (GER)
1964 R.Webster (USA)	L.Bush (USA)
1968 K.Dibiasi (ITA)	M.Duchkova (TCH)
1972 K.Dibiasi (ITA)	U.Knape (SWE)
1976 K.Dibiasi (ITA)	E.Vaytsekhovskaya (USSR)
1980 F.Hoffman (GDR)	M.Jaschke (GDR)
1984 G.Louganis (USA)	J.Zhou (CHN)
1988 G.Louganis (USA)	X.Yanmei (CHN)

Synchronised Swimming

Solo	Duet
1984 T.Ruiz (USA)	1984 United States
1988 C.Waldo (CAN)	1988 Canada

Most Gold Medals

(Men):
9 Mark Spitz

(Women):
4 Pat McCormick, Dawn Fraser, Kornelia Ender

WORLD RECORDS
(as at 1 January 1989)

FREESTYLE	Men			Women	
50 metres	22.14	M.Biondi (USA)		24.98	Y.Wenyi (CHN)
100 metres	48.74	M.Biondi (USA)		54.73	K.Otto (GDR)
200 metres	1:46.25	D.Armstrong (USA)		1:57.55	H.Friedrich (GDR)
400 metres	3:46.95	U.Dassler (GDR)		4:03.85	J.Evans (USA)
800 metres	—			8:17.12	J.Evans (USA)
1500 metres	14:54.76	V.Salnikov (USSR)		—	
BACKSTROKE					
100 metres	54.51	D.Berkoff (USA)		1:00.59	I.Kleber (GDR)
200 metres	1:58.14	I.Poliansky (USSR)		2:08.60	B.Mitchell (USA)
BREASTROKE					
100 metres	1:01.65	S.Lundquist (USA)		1:07.91	S.Hoerner (GDR)
200 metres	2:13.34	V.Davis (CAN)		2:26.71	S.Hoerner (GDR)
BUTTERFLY					
100 metres	52.84	P.Morales (USA)		57.93	M.Meagher (USA)
200 metres	1:56.24	M.Gross (FRG)		2:05.96	M.Meagher (USA)
MEDLEY					
200 metres	2:00.17	T.Darnyi (HUN)		2:11.73	U.Geweniger (GDR)
400 metres	4:14.75	T.Darnyi (HUN)		4:36.10	P.Schneider (GDR)
RELAY					
4 × 100 Free	3:16.53	United States		3:40.57	East Germany
4 × 100 Free	7:12.51	United States		—	
4 × 100 Medley	3:36.93	United States		4:03.69	East Germany

Steven Nice was an All-England swimming champion at 16 despite spending five years of his life in hospital after contracting polio. He later found fame as a pop singer and, as Steve Harley and Cockney Rebel had a number one hit with Make Me Smile (Come Up and See Me) in 1975.

Australia's Dawn Fraser stands unique in Olympic swimming history; she is the only person, male or female, to win the same individual title at three consecutive Games. She won the 100 metres freestyle in 1956, 1960 and 1964.

Pete Desjardins of the United States was the first diver to be awarded the maximum 10.00 for a dive in the Olympic Games. He received the score for a dive during the springboard competition at the 1928 Games.

Table Tennis was played in Britain in the late 19th century and was devised by James Gibb who called the game Gossima. This was later changed to Ping Pong and the Ping Pong Association was formed in 1902. It later became defunct, but was revived in 1921 and reconstituted as the English Table Tennis Association in 1927.

SWAYTHLING CUP

The Men's World Team Championship, the Swaythling Cup, was first contested in 1927 and was an annual event until 1957 when it became biennial.

Winners:

1927 Hungary	1953 England
1928 Hungary	1954 Japan
1929 Hungary	1955 Japan
1930 Hungary	1956 Japan
1931 Hungary	1957 Japan
1932 Czechoslovakia	1959 Japan
1933 Hungary	1961 China
1934 Hungary	1963 China
1935 Hungary	1965 China
1936 Austria	1967 Japan
1937 United States	1969 Japan
1938 Hungary	1971 China
1939 Czechoslovakia	1973 Sweden
1940–46 Not held	1975 China
1947 Czechoslovakia	1977 China
1948 Czechoslovakia	1979 Hungary
1949 Hungary	1981 China
1950 Czechoslovakia	1983 China
1951 Czechoslovakia	1985 China
1952 Hungary	1987 China
	1989 Sweden

Most Wins:
12 Hungary

CORBILLON CUP

The women's equivalent of the Swaythling Cup, the Marcel Corbillon Cup is contested every two years; it was an annual event until 1958.

Winners:

1934 Germany	1951 Romania
1935 Czechoslovakia	1952 Japan
1936 Czechoslovakia	1953 Romania
1937 United States	1954 Japan
1938 Czechoslovakia	1955 Romania
1939 Germany	1956 Romania
1940–46 Not held	1957 Japan
1947 England	1959 Japan
1948 England	1961 Japan
1949 United States	1963 Japan
1950 Romania	1965 China

1967 Japan	1979 China
1969 USSR	1981 China
1971 Japan	1983 China
1973 South Korea	1985 China
1975 China	1987 China
1977 China	

Most Wins:
8 Japan, China

WORLD CHAMPIONSHIPS
First held in 1927 the Championships were held annually until 1957 when they became a biennial event.

Men	**Women**
1927 R.Jacobi (HUN)	M.Mednyanszky (HUN)
1928 Z.Mechlovits (HUN)	M.Mednyanszky (HUN)
1929 F.Perry (GB)	M.Mednyanszky (HUN)
1930 V.Barna (HUN)	M.Mednyanszky (HUN)
1931 M.Szabados (HUN)	M.Mednyanszky (HUN)
1932 V.Barna (HUN)	A.Sipos (HUN)
1933 V.Barna (HUN)	A.Sipos (HUN)
1934 V.Barna (HUN)	M.Kettnerova (TCH)
1935 V.Barna (HUN)	M.Kettnerova (TCH)
1936 S.Kolar (TCH)	R.Aarons (USA)
1937 R.Bergmann (AUT)	-
1938 B.Vana (TCH)	T.Pritzi (AUT)
1939 R.Bergmann (AUT)	V.Depetrisova (TCH)
1940–46 Not held	
1947 B.Vana (TCH)	G.Farkas (HUN)
1948 R.Bergmann (ENG)	G.Farkas (HUN)
1949 J.Leach (ENG)	G.Farkas (HUN)
1950 R.Bergmann (ENG)	A.Rozeanu (ROM)
1951 J.Leach (ENG)	A.Rozeanu (ROM)
1952 H.Satoh (JAP)	A.Rozeanu (ROM)
1953 F.Sido (HUN)	A.Rozeanu (ROM)
1954 I.Ogimura (JAP)	A.Rozeanu (ROM)
1955 T.Tanaka (JAP)	A.Rozeanu (ROM)
1956 I.Ogimura (JAP)	T.Okawa (JAP)
1957 T.Tanaka (JAP)	F.Eguchi (JAP)
1959 J.Kuo-tuan (CHN)	K.Matsuzaki (JAP)
1961 C.Tse-tung (CHN)	C.Chung-hui (CHN)
1963 C.Tse-tung (CHN)	K.Matsuzaki (JAP)
1965 C.Tse-tung (CHN)	N.Fukazu (JAP)
1967 N.Hasegawa (JAP)	S.Morisawa (JAP)
1969 S.Ito (JAP)	T.Kowada (JAP)
1971 S.Bengtsson (SWE)	L.Hui-Ching (CHN)
1973 H.En-Ting (CHN)	Hu Yu-Lan (CHN)
1975 I.Jonyer (HUN)	P.Yung-Sun (NK)
1977 M.Kohno (JAP)	P.Yung-Sun (NK)
1979 S.Ono (JAP)	K.HsinAi (CHN)
1981 G.Yue-Hua (CHN)	T.Ling (CHN)
1983 G.Yue-Hua (CHN)	C.Yan-Hua (CHN)
1985 J.Jialiang (CHN)	C.Yan-Hua (CHN)
1987 J.Jialiang (CHN)	H.Zhili (CHN)
1989 J.-O. Waldnet (SWE)	Q.Hong (CHN)

Most Titles

(Men):	**(Women):**
5 Viktor Barna	6 Angelica Rozeanu

Men's Doubles
1927 R.Jacobi/D.Pesci (HUN)
1928 A.Liebster/R.Thum (AUT)
1929 V.Barna/M.Szabados (HUN)
1930 V.Barna/M.Szabados (HUN)
1931 V.Barna/M.Szabados (HUN)
1932 V.Barna/M.Szabados (HUN)
1933 V.Barna/S.Glancz (HUN)
1934 V.Barna/M.Szabados (HUN)
1935 V.Barna/M.Szabados (HUN)
1936 R.G.Blattner/J.H.McClure (USA)
1937 R.G.Blattner/J.H.McClure (USA)
1938 S.Schiff/J.H.McClure (USA)
1939 V.Barna (HUN)/R.Bergmann (AUT)
1940–46 Not held
1947 B.Vana/A.Slar (TCH)
1948 B.Vana/L.Stipek (TCH)
1949 F.Tokar/I.Andreadis (TCH)
1950 F.Sido/F.Soos (HUN)
1951 B.Vana/I.Andreadis (TCH)
1952 N.Fujii/T.Hayashi (JAP)
1953 J.Koczian/F.Sido (HUN)
1954 V.Harangozo/Z.Dolinar (YUG)
1955 I.Andreadis/L.Stipek (TCH)
1956 I.Ogimura/Y.Tomita (JAP)
1957 L.Andreadis/L.Stipek (TCH)
1959 I.Ogimura/T.Murakami (JAP)
1961 N.Hoshino/K.Kimura (JAP)
1963 C.Shih-Lin/W.Chih-Liang (CHN)
1965 C.Tsa-Tung/H.Yin-Sheng (CHN)
1967 H.Alser/K.Johansson (SWE)
1969 H.Alser/K.Johansson (SWE)
1971 I.Jonyer/T.Klampar (HUN)
1973 S.Bengtsson/K.Johansson (SWE)
1975 G.Gergely/I.Jonyer (HUN)
1977 Chen-Shih Li/L.Ko-Liang (CHN)
1979 D.Surbek/A.Stipancic (YUG)
1981 C.Zhen-Hua/L.Zhen-Shi (CHN)
1983 D.Surbek/Z.Kalinic (YUG)
1985 M.Appelgren/U.Carlsson (SWE)
1987 C.Longcan/W.Quingguang (CHN)
1989 J.Rosskopf/S.Fetzner (FRG)

Most Wins:
8 Viktor Barna

Mixed Doubles
1927 M.Mednyanszky/Z.Mechlovits (HUN)
1928 M.Mednyanszky/Z.Mechlovits (HUN)
1929 A.Sipos/I.Kelen (HUN)
1930 M.Mednyanszky/M.Szabados (HUN)
1931 M.Mednyanszky/M.Szabados (HUN)
1932 A.Sipos/V.Barna (HUN)
1933 M.Mednyanszky/I.Kelen (HUN)
1934 M.Mednyanszky/M.Szabados (HUN)
1935 A.Sipos/V.Barna (HUN)
1936 G.Kleinova/M.Hamr (TCH)
1937 V.Votrubcova/B.Vana (TCH)
1938 W.Woodhead (ENG)/L.Bellak (HUN)
1939 V.Votrubcova/B.Vana (TCH)
1940–1946 Not held
1947 G.Farkas/F.Soos (HUN)
1948 T.Thall/R.Miles (USA)
1949 G.Farkas/S.Sido (HUN)
1950 G.Farkas/S.Sido (HUN)
1951 A.Rozeanu (ROM)/B.Vana(TCH)
1952 A.Rozeanu (ROM)/F.Sido (HUN)
1953 A.Rozeanu (ROM)/F.Sido (HUN)
1954 G.Farkas (HUN)/I.Andeadis (TCH)
1955 E.Koczian/K.Szepesi (HUN)
1956 L.Neuberger/E.Klein (USA)
1957 F.Eguchi/I.Ogimura (JAP)
1959 F.Eguchi/I.Ogimura (JAP)
1961 K.Matsuzaki/I.Ogimura (JAP)
1963 K.Itoh/K.Kimura (JAP)
1965 M.Seki/K.Kimura (JAP)
1967 N.Yamanaka/N.Hasegawa (JAP)
1969 Y.Konno/N.Hasegawa (JAP)
1971 L.Hui-Ching/C.Shih-Lin (CHN)
1973 Li Li/L.Ko-Liang (CHN)
1975 A.Ferdman/S.Gomozkov (USSR)
1977 C.Bergeret/J.Secretin (FRA)
1979 K.Hsin-Ai/L.Ko-Liang (CHN)
1981 H.Junquin/X.Saike (CHN)
1983 N.Xialin/G.Yue-Hua (CHN)
1985 Cao Yan/Cai Zhenhua (CHN)
1987 H.Jun/G.Lijuan (CHN)
1989 Y.Nam-Kyu/H.Jung-Hwa (SKO)

Most Wins:
6 Maria Mednyanszky

Women's Doubles

1928 M.Mednyanszky (HUN)/F.Flamm (AUT)
1929 E.Metzger/E.Ruester (GER)
1930 M.Mednyanszky/A.Sipos (HUN)
1931 M.Mednyanszky/A.Sipos (HUN)
1932 M.Mednyanszky/A.Sipos (HUN)
1933 M.Mednyanszky/A.Sipos (HUN)
1934 M.Mednyanszky/A.Sipos (HUN)
1935 M.Mednyanszky/A.Sipos (HUN)
1936 M.Kettnerova/M.Smidova (TCH)
1937 V.Depetrisova/V.Votrubcova (TCH)
1938 V.Depetrisova/V.Votrubcova (TCH)
1939 T.Pritzi/H.Bussmann (AUT)
1940–46 Not held
1947 G.Farkas (HUN)/T.Pritzi (AUT)
1948 V.Thomas/M.Franks (ENG)
1949 E.Elliot (SCO)/G.Farkas (HUN)
1950 D.Beregi (ENG)/H.Elliot (SCO)
1951 D.Rowe/R.Rowe (ENG)
1952 S.Narahara/T.Nishimura (JAP)
1953 G.Farkas (HUN)/A.Rozeanu (ROM)
1954 D.Rowe/R.Rowe (ENG)
1955 A.Rozeanu/E.Zeller (ROM)
1956 A.Rozeanu/F.Zeller (ROM)
1957 L.Mosoczy/A.Simon (HUN)
1959 T.Namba/K.Yamaizumi (JAP)
1961 M.Alexandru/G.Pitica (ROM)
1963 K.Matsuzaki/M.Seki (JAP)
1965 C.Min-Chih/L.Hui-Ching (CHN)
1967 S.Hirota/S.Morisawa (JAP)
1969 S.Grinberg/Z.Rudnova (USSR)
1971 C.Min-Chih/L.Hui-Ching (CHN)
1973 M.Alexandru (ROM)/M.Hamada (JAP)
1975 M.Alexandru (ROM)/S.Takashima (JAP)
1977 Y.Ok Pak (NK)/Y.Yang (CHN)
1979 Z.Li/Z.Deijing (CHN)
1981 C.Yan-Hua/Z.Deijing (CHN)
1983 S.Jianping/D.Lili (CHN)
1985 D.Lili/G.Lijuan (CHN)
1987 Y.Young-Ja/H.Jung-Hua (SK)
1989 Q.Hong/D.Yaping (CHN)

Most Wins:

7 Maria Mednyanszky

Jackie Bond, former player and, more recently, manager of the Lancashire County Cricket team, was captain of the Isle of Man table tennis team in the late 1970s.

Three-times Wimbledon lawn tennis champion Fred Perry was the world table tennis champion in 1929.

A game of ninepins was taken to the United States by Dutch settlers in the 17th century. The sport was banned in many states in the 19th century and, in order to get round the ban, a tenth pin was added. The United States National Bowling Association was formed in 1895.

WORLD CHAMPIONSHIPS
The Amateur sport's governing body, the FIQ, has organised World Championships since 1954. Women first took part in 1963 and the championships have been held every four years since then.

Winners — Individual

	Men	Women
1954	G.Algeskog (SWE)	–
1955	N.Backstrom (SWE)	–
1958	K.Asukas (FIN)	–
1960	T.Reynolds (MEX)	–
1963	L.Zikes (USA)	H.Shablis (USA)
1967	D.Pond (UK)	H.Weston (USA)
1971	E.Luther (USA)	A.Gonzales (PR)
1975	B.Staudt (USA)	A.Haefker (FRG)
1979	O.Ongtawco (PHI)	L.de la Rosa (PHI)
1983	A.Marino (COL)	L.Sulkanen (SWE)
1987	R.Patrick (FRA)	E.Piccini (ITA)

Scoring in tenpin bowling is perhaps the most complicated of all sports. Hopefully the following will help you understand how it works.

Firstly, a strike (X) is when all ten pins are knocked down with one ball. A spare (/) is when the ten pins are knocked down with two balls, e.g. the first ball knocks down eight pins, and the second ball the remaining two. A game consists of 10 frames, and no more than ten pins can be knocked down in one frame...except frame 10.

The value of pins knocked down in each frame is added up as you go along, but every spare is worth ten points PLUS the pin value of the next ball rolled. So, if you get a spare in frame one, you cannot enter your score until after the first ball of frame two. A strike is worth ten points PLUS the value of the next TWO balls rolled.

Masters

	Men	Women
1979	G.Bugden (GB)	L.de la Rosa (PHI)
198	T.Cariello (USA)	L.Sulkanen (SWE)
1987	R.Pieters (BEL)	A.Hagre (SWE)

All Events

	Men	Women
198	M.Karlsson (SWE)	B.Coo (PHI)
1987	R.Steelsmith (USA)	S.J.Shiery (USA)

Doubles

	Men	Women
1954	Finland	—
1955	Sweden	—
1958	Sweden	—
1960	Mexico	Mexico
196	United States	United States
1967	Great Britain	—
1971	Puerto Rico	Japan
1975	Great Britain	Sweden
1979	Australia	Philippines
198	Great Britain & Australia	Denmark
1987	Sweden	United States

Trios

	Men	Women
1979	Malaysia	United States
198	Sweden	West Germany
1987	United States	United States

Team (5-man)

	Men	Women
1954	Sweden	—
1955	West Germany	—
1958	Finland	—
1960	Venezuela	—
196	United States	—
1967	Finland	Finland
1971	United States	United States
1975	Finland	Japan
1979	Australia	United States
198	Finland	Sweden
1987	Sweden	United States

Trampolining has formed part of circus acts for many years but it only started to attract interest as a sport after the design of trampolines similar to modern day ones, by George Nissen in the United States in 1936. The first official Trampolining tournament took place in the United States in 1947.

WORLD CHAMPIONSHIPS
Instituted in 1964 they have been a biennial event since 1968.

Winners

	Men	Women
1964	D.Millman (USA)	J.Wills (USA)
1965	G.Irwin (USA)	J.Wills (USA)
1966	W.Miller (USA)	J.Wills (USA)
1967	D.Jacobs (USA)	J.Wills (USA)
1968	D.Jacobs (USA)	J.Wills (USA)
1970	W.Miller (USA)	R.Ransom (USA)
1972	P.Luxon (GB)	A.Nicholson (USA)
1974	R.Tisson (FRA)	A.Nicholson (USA)
1976	R.Tisson (FRA)/ E. Janes (USSR)	S.Levina (USSR)
1978	E.Janes (USSR)	T.Anisimova (USSR)
1980	S.Matthews (GB)	R.Keller (SWI)
1982	C.Furrer (GB)	R.Keller (SWI)
1984	L.Pioline (FRA)	S.Shotton (GB)
1986	L.Pioline (FRA)	T. Lushina (USSR)
1988	V.Crasonshapka (USSR)	K.Roussoudan (USSR)

Most Wins (Men):
2 Dave Jacobs, Wayne Miller, Richard Tisson, Evgeni Janes, Leon Pioline
(Women):
5 Judy Wills

The first trampoline in Great Britain was seen at Loxford School, Ilford, Essex, in 1949.

If ever you are asked where you would perform an Adolph, a Baby Fliffus or a Rudolph, the answer is 'On a Trampoline'...they are all types of movement.

Volleyball was invented in the United States by William Morgan in 1895 and the following year the game was given its name by Dr Holsted.

WORLD CHAMPIONSHIPS

The first World Championships were held in 1949, two years after the formation of the International Volleyball Federation.

Winners:

	Men	Women
1949	USSR	–
1952	USSR	USSR
1956	Czechoslovakia	USSR
1960	USSR	USSR
1962	USSR	Japan
1966	Czechoslovakia	Japan
1970	East Germany	USSR
1974	Poland	Japan
1978	USSR	Cuba
1982	USSR	China
1986	United States	China

Most Wins (Men):   **(Women):**
6 USSR   4 USSR

OLYMPIC GAMES
Volleyball was only introduced into the Olympics in 1964

Winners:

	Men	Women
1964	USSR	Japan
1968	USSR	USSR
1972	Japan	USSR
1976	Poland	Japan
1980	USSR	USSR
1984	United States	China
1988	United States	USSR

Most Wins (Men):   **(Women):**
3 USSR   4 USSR

The Polish men's team went to the 1976 Montreal Olympics well prepared. Part of the training included jumping 392 times over a 4½-foot wall while wearing 20-30lb weights on their legs. The training paid off, they beat the Soviet Union in the final, which lasted a gruelling 2½ hours.

Water Polo was first played in Britain in 1870 and, because of its similarity to soccer, was originally called 'Football in the Water'. It was only after devising its own set of rules in 1885 that the new sport was recognised by the Swimming Association of Great Britain.

OLYMPIC GAMES

Water Polo was included in the 1900 Olympics and the winning Great Britain team was represented by the Osborne Swimming Club. Likewise, when the United States won the title four years later it was with a team from one club, the New York Athletic Club.

Winners:

1900	Great Britain	1952	Hungary
1904	United States	1956	Hungary
1908	Great Britain	1960	Italy
1912	Great Britain	1964	Hungary
1920	Great Britain	1968	Yugoslavia
1924	France	1972	USSR
1928	Germany	1976	Hungary
1932	Hungary	1980	USSR
1936	Hungary	1984	Yugoslavia
1948	Italy	1988	Yugoslavia

Most Wins:
6 Hungary

WORLD CHAMPIONSHIPS

Surprisingly the first World Championships were not held until 1973, more than 70 years after the sport was first included in the Olympics. The event is included as part of the World Swimming Championships, now held every four years.

Winners:

1973	Hungary	1982	USSR
1975	USSR	1986	Yugoslavia
1978	Italy		

Most Wins:
2 USSR

Water Skiing derived from snow skiing as a result of the development of the motor boat at the turn of the century, and the first patent on a pair of water skiis was placed by American Fred Walter. The first Water Skiing tournament was at Long Island, United States, in 1935 and it soon developed rapidly as a participant sport thereafter.

WORLD CHAMPIONSHIPS

The first World Championships were held at Juan Les Pins in France and have been held biennially since 1953.

Overall

Men	Women
1949 G.de Clerq (BEL) C.Jourdan (FRA)	W.Worthington (USA)
1950 D.Pope jnr (USA)	W.Worthington-McGuire (USA)
1953 A.Mendoza (USA)	L.M.Rawls (USA)
1955 A.Mendoza (USA)	W.Worthington-McGuire (USA)
1957 J.Cash (USA)	M.Doria (SWI)
1959 C.Stearns (USA)	V. Van Hook (USA)
1961 B.Zaccardi (ITA)	S.Hulsemann (LUX)
1963 B.Spencer (USA)	J.Brown (USA)
1965 R.Hillier (USA)	L.Allan (USA)
1967 M.Suyderhoud (USA)	J.Stewart-Wood (GB)
1969 M.Suyderhoud (USA)	L.Allan (USA)
1971 G.Athans (CAN)	C.Weir (USA)
1973 G.Athans (CAN)	L.St.John (USA)
1975 C.Suarez (VEN)	L.Allan-Shetter (USA)
1977 M.Hazelwood (GB)	C.Todd (USA)
1979 J.McClintock (CAN)	C.Todd (USA)
1981 S.Duvall (USA)	K.Roberge (USA)
1983 S.Duvall (USA)	A.M.Carrasco (VEN)
1985 S.Duvall (USA)	K.Neville(AUS)
1987 S.Duvall (USA)	D.Brush (USA)

Most Wins

(Men):
4 Sammy Duvall

(Women)
3 Willa Worthington-McGuire, Liz Allan Shetter

Tricks

Men	Women
1949 P.Gouin (FRA)	M.Bouteiller (FRA)
1950 J.Andresen (USA)	W.Worthington-McGuire (USA)
1953 W.Witherall (USA)	L.Rawls (USA)
1955 S.Scott (USA)	M.Doria (SWI)
1957 M.Amsbury (USA)	M.Doria (SWI)
1959 P.Logut (FRA)	P.Castlevetri (ITA)
1961 J.M.Muller (FRA)	S.Hulsemann (LUX)
1963 B.Spencer (USA)	G.Dalle (FRA)
1965 K.White (USA)	D.Duflot (FRA)
1967 A.Kempton (USA)	D.Duflot (FRA)
1969 B.Cockburn (AUS)	L.Allan (USA)
1971 R.McCormick (USA)	W.Stahle (HOL)
1973 W.Grimditch (USA)	M.V.Carrasco (VEN)
1975 W.Grimditch (USA)	M.V.Carrasco (VEN)
1977 C.Suarez (VEN)	M.V.Carrasco (VEN)
1979 P.Martin (FRA)	N.Rumiantseva (USSR)
1981 C.Pickos (USA)	A.M.Carrasco (VEN)
1983 C.Pickos (USA)	N.Ponomareva (USSR)
1985 B.LaPoint (USA)	J.McClintock (USA)
1987 P.Martin (FRA)	N.Rumiantseva (USSR)

Most Wins
(Men):
2 Wayne Grimditch, Cory Pickos, Patrice Martin
(Women):
3 Maria Victoria Carrasco

Slalom

Men	Women
1949 C.Jourdan (FRA)	W.Worthington (USA)
1950 D.Pope jnr (USA)	E.Wolford (USA)
1953 C.Blackwell (CAN)	E.Wolford (USA)
1955 A.Mendoza (USA)	W.Worthington-McGuire (USA)
1957 J.Cash (USA)	M.Doria (SWI)
1959 C.Stearns (USA)	V.Van Hook (USA)
1961 J.Jackson (USA)	J.Kirtley (USA)
1963 B.Spencer (USA)	J.Brown (USA)
1965 R.Hillier (USA)	B.Cooper-Clack (USA)
1967 T.Antunano (MEX)	L.Allan (USA)
1969 V.Palomo (SPA)	L.Allan (USA)
1971 M.Suyderhoud (USA)	C.Freeman (USA)
1973 G.Athans (CAN)	S.Maurial (FRA)
1975 R.Zucchi (ITA)	L.Allan-Shetter (USA)
1977 B.LaPoint (USA)	C.Todd (USA)
1979 B.LaPoint (USA)	P.Messner (CAN)
1981 A.Mapple (GB)	C.Todd (USA)
1983 B.LaPoint (USA)	C.Todd (USA)
1985 P.Martin (FRA)	C.Duvall (USA)
1987 B.LaPoint (USA)	K.Laskoff (USA)

Most Wins
(Men):
4 Bob LaPoint
(Women):
3 Liz Allan-Shetter, Cindy Todd

Jumps

Men	Women
1949 G.de Clercq (BEL)	W.Worthington (USA)
1950 G.de Clercq (BEL)	J.Kirkpatrick (USA)
1953 A.Mendoza (USA)	S.Swaney (USA)
1955 A.Mendoza (USA)	W.Worthington-McGuire (USA)
1957 J.Muller (FRA)	N.Rideout (USA)
1959 B.McCalla (USA)	N.Rideout (USA)
1961 L.Penacho (USA)	R.Hansluvka (AUT)
1963 J.Jackson (USA)	R.Hansluvka (AUT
1965 L.Penacho (USA)	L.Allan (USA)
1967 A.Kempton (USA)	J.Stewart-Wood (GB)
1969 W.Grimditch (USA)	L.Allan (USA)
1971 M.Suyderhoud (USA)	C.Weir (USA)
1973 R.McCormick (USA)	L.Allan-Shetter (USA)
1975 R.McCormick (USA)	L.Allan-Shetter (USA)
1977 M.Suyderhoud (USA)	L.Giddens (USA)
1979 M.Hazelwood (GB)	C.Todd (USA)
1981 M.Hazelwood (GB)	D.Brush (USA)
1983 S.Duval (USA)	C.Todd (USA)
1985 G.Carrington (AUS)	D.Brush (USA)
1987 S.Duvall (USA)	D.Brush (USA)

Most Wins

(Men):
2 Guy de Clercq, Alfredo Mendoza, Larry Penacho, Mike Suyderhoud, Rick McCormick, Mike Hazelwood, Sammy Duvall

(Women):
4 Liz Allan-Shetter

Water ski jumping forms part of the world championships, and contestants can reach distances up to 200 feet. However, when Dick Pope, Snr, made the first jump at Miami Beach in 1928, his jump was measured at...25 feet!

One of the early exponents of water skiing was the late Lord Mountbatten . Great names from the movies, David Niven and Errol Flynn also took to the sport shortly after its introduction.

Most world titles: 8 Liz Allan-Shetter (USA) 1965-75. In 1969 she won all four titles: overall, slalom, tricks and jumping.

Weightlifting, albeit in a different form to today's competition, was held in the Ancient Olympic Games. In the 17th and 18th centuries weightlifting became an attraction at fairgrounds and circuses. It developed into a sport towards the latter part of the 19th century and the first international competition was in London in 1891. The International Weightlifting Federation was established in 1920.

OLYMPIC GAMES

Weightlifting was first included in the Olympics in 1896, but only in the heavyweight division. The other divisions followed as listed below.

Flyweight

1972 Z. Smalcerz (POL)
1976 A. Voronin (USSR)
1980 K. Osmonoliev (USSR)
1984 C. Zeng (CHN)
1988 S. Marinov (BUL)

Bantamweight

1948 J. de Pietro (USA)
1952 I. Udodov (USSR)
1956 C. Vinci (USA)
1960 C. Vinci (USA)
1964 A. Vakhonin (USSR)
1968 M. Nassari (IRN)
1972 I. Foldi (HUN)
1976 N. Nurikyan (BUL)
1980 D. Nunez (CUB)
1984 S. Wu (CHN)
1988 O. Mirzoian (USSR)

Featherweight

1920 F. de Haes (BEL)
1924 P. Gabetti (ITA)
1928 F. Andrysek (AUT)
1932 R. Suvigny (FRA)
1936 A. Terlazzo (USA)
1948 M. Fayad (EGY)
1952 R. Chimishkyan (USSR)
1956 I. Berger (USA)
1960 Y. Minayev (USSR)
1964 Y. Miyake (JAP)
1968 Y. Miyake (JAP)
1972 N. Nurikyan (BUL)
1976 N. Kolesnikov (USSR)
1980 V. Mazin (USSR)
1984 W. Chen (CHN)
1988 N. Suleymanoglu (TUR)

Lightweight

1920 A. Neuland (EST)
1924 E. Decottignies (FRA)
1928 K. Helbig (GER) H.Haas (AUT)
1932 R. Duverger (FRA)
1936 A. M. Mesbah (EGY)
       R. Fein (AUT)
1948 I. Shams (EGY)
1952 T. Kono (USA)
1956 I. Rybak (USSR)
1960 V. Bushuyev (USSR)
1964 W. Baszanowski (POL)
1968 W. Baszanowski (POL)
1972 M. Kirzhinov (USSR)
1976 P. Korol (USSR)
1980 Y. Rusev (BUL)
1984 J. Yao (CHN)
1988 J. Kunz (GDR)

Middleweight

1920 H. Gance (FRA)
1924 C. Galimberti (ITA)
1928 R. Francois (FRA)
1932 R. Ismayr (GER)
1936 K. El Thouni (EGY)
1948 F. Spellman (USA)
1952 P. George (USA)
1956 F. Bogdanovski (USSR)

1960 A. Kurinov (USSR)
1964 H. Zdrazila (TCH)
1968 V. Kurentsov (USSR)
1972 Y. Bikov (BUL)
1976 Y. Mitkov (BUL)
1980 A. Zlatev (BUL)
1984 K -H. Radschinsky (FRG)
1988 B. Guidikov (BUL)

Lightheavyweight

1920 E. Cadine (FRA)
1924 C. Rigoulot (FRA)
1928 S. Nosseir (EGY)
1932 L. Hostin (FRA)
1936 L. Hostin (FRA)
1948 S. Stanczyk (USA)
1952 T. Lomakin (USSR)
1956 T. Kono (USA)

1960 I. Palinski (POL)
1964 R. Plufelder (USSR)
1968 B. Selitsky (USSR)
1972 L. Jenssen (NOR)
1976 V. Shary (USSR)
1980 Y. Vardanyan (USSR)
1984 P. Becheru (ROM)
1988 I. Arsamakov (USSR)

Middleheavyweight

1952 N. Schemansky (USA)
1956 A. Vorobyev (USSR)
1960 A. Vorobyev (USSR)
1964 V. Golovanov (USSR)
1968 K. Kangasniemi (FIN)

1972 A. Nikolov (BUL)
1976 D. Rigert (USSR)
1980 P. Baczako (HUN)
1984 N. Vlad (ROM)
1988 A. Khrapaty (USSR)

Up to 100kg

1980 O. Zaremba (TCH)

1984 R. Milser (FRG)
1988 P. Kouznetsov (USSR)

Heavyweight

1896 L. Eliot (GB) V. Jensen (DEN)
1904 A. Osthoff (USA)
     P. Kakousis (GRE)
1906 J. Steinbach (AUT)
     D. Tofalos (GRE)
1920 F. Bottino (ITA)
1924 G. Tonani (ITA)
1928 J. Strassberger (GER)
1932 J. Skobla (TCH)
1936 J. Manger (AUT)
1948 J. Davis (USA)

1952 J. Davis (USA)
1956 P. Anderson (USA)
1960 Y. Vlasov (USSR)
1964 L. Zhabotinsky (USSR)
1968 L. Zhabotinsky (USSR)
1972 J. Talts (USSR)
1976 Y. Zaitsev (USSR)
1980 L. Taranenko (USSR)
1984 N. Oberburger (ITA)
1988 Y. Zakharevich (USSR)

Superheavyweight

1972 V. Alexeyev (USSR)
1976 V. Alexeyev (USSR)

1980 S. Rakhmanov (USSR)
1984 D. Lukin (AUS)
1988 A. Kourlovitch (USSR)

Wrestling was part of the Ancient Olympics, and wall drawings from nearly 6000 years ago depict it as taking place long before then. Wrestling was included in the first Modern Olympics although the International Amateur Wrestling Association was not formed until 1912. There are two forms of wrestling at international level, Freestyle and Greco-Roman.

OLYMPIC GAMES
Greco Roman wrestling was included in the first Olympics in 1896, while the Freestyle variety did not make its debut until 1904.

Winners Freestyle

Light-flyweight
1904 R.Curry (USA)
1972 R.Dmitriev (USSR)
1976 K.Issaev (BUL)
1980 C.Pollio (ITA)
1984 R.Weaver (USA)
1988 T.Kobayashi (JAP)

Flyweight
1904 G.Mehnert (USA
1948 L.Viitala (FIN)
1952 H.Gemici (TUR)
1956 M.Tsalkalamanidze (USSR)
1960 A.Bilek (TUR)
1964 Y.Yoshida (JAP)
1968 S.Nakata (JAP)
1972 K.Kato (JAP)
1976 Y.Takada (JAP)
1980 A.Beloglazov (USSR)
1984 S.Trstena (YUG)
1988 M.Sato (JAP)

Bantamweight
1904 I.Niflot (USA)
1908 G.Mehnert (USA)
1924 K.Pihlajamaki (FIN)
1928 K.Makinen (FIN)
1932 R.Pearce (USA)
1936 O.Zombori (HUN)
1948 N.Akar (TUR)
1952 S.Ishii (JAP)
1956 M.Dagistanli (TUR)
1960 T.McCann (USA)
1964 Y.Uetake (JAP)
1968 Y.Uetake (JAP)
1972 H.Yanagide (JAP)
1976 V.Yumin (USSR)
1980 S.Beloglazov (USSR)
1984 H.Tomiyama (JAP)
1988 S.Beloglazov (USSR)

Featherweight
1904 B.Bradshaw (USA)
1908 G.Dole (USA)
1920 C.Ackerly (USA)
1924 R.Reed (USA)
1928 A.Morrison (USA)
1932 H.Pihlajamaki (FIN)
1936 K.Pihlajamaki (FIN)
1948 G.Bilge (TUR)
1952 B.Sit (TUR)
1956 S.Sasahara (JAP)
1960 M.Dagistanli (TUR)
1964 O.Watanabe (JAP)
1968 M.Kaneko (JAP)
1972 Z.Abdulbekov (USSR)
1976 Jung-Mo Yang (NKO)
1980 M.Abushev (USSR)
1984 R.Lewis (USA)
1988 J.Smith (USA)

Lightweight
1904 O.Roehm (USA)
1908 G.de Relwyskow (GB)
1920 K.Anttila (FIN)
1924 R.Vis (USA)
1928 O.Kapp (EST)
1932 C.Pacome (FRA)
1936 K.Karpati (HUN)
1948 C.Atik (TUR)
1952 O.Anderberg (SWE)
1956 E.Habibi (IRN)
1960 S.Wilson (USA)
1964 E.Valtschev (BUL)
1968 A.M.Ardabili (IRN)
1972 D.Gable (USA)
1976 P.Pinigin (USSR)
1980 S.Absaidov (USSR)
1984 In-Tak You (SKO)
1988 A.Fadzaev (USSR)

Welterweight
1904 C.Erickson (USA)
1924 H.Gehri (SWI)
1928 A.Haavisto (FIN)
1932 J.van Bebber (USA)
1936 F.Lewis (USA)
1948 Y.Dogu (TUR)
1952 W.Smith (USA)
1956 M.Ikeda (JAP)
1960 D.Blubaugh (USA)
1964 I.Ogan (TUR)
1968 M.Atalay (TUR)
1972 W.Wells (USA)
1976 J.Date (JAP)
1980 V.Raitchev (BUL)
1984 D.Schultz (USA
1988 K.Monday (USA)

Middleweight
1908 S.Bacon (GB)
1920 E.Leino (FIN)
1924 F.Hagmann (SWI)
1928 E.Kyburz (SWI)
1932 I.Johansson (SWE)
1936 E.Poilve (FRA)
1948 G.Brand (USA)
1952 D.Tsinakuridze (USSR)
1956 N.Stanschev (BUL)
1960 H.Gungor (TUR)
1964 P.Gardschev (BUL)
1968 B.Gurevitch (USSR)
1972 L.Tediashvili (USSR)
1976 J.Peterson (USA)
1980 I.Abilov (BUL)
1984 M.Schultz (USA)
1988 H.Myung-Woo (SKO)

Light-heavyweight
1920 A.Larsson (SWE)
1924 J.Spellman (USA)
1928 T.Sjostedt (SWE)
1932 P.Mehringer (USA)
1936 K.Fridell (SWE)
1948 H.Wittenberg (USA)
1952 W.Palm (SWE)
1956 G.R.Tahkti (IRN)
1960 I.Alti (TUR)
1964 A.Medved (USSR)
1968 A.Ayik (TUR)
1972 B.Peterson (USA)
1976 L.Tediashvili (USSR)
1980 S.Oganesyan (USSR)
1984 E.Banach (USA)
1988 M.Khadartsev (USSR)

Heavyweight
1904 B.Hansen (USA)
1908 G.O'Kelly (GB)
1920 R.Roth (SWI)
1924 H.Steele (USA)
1928 J.Richthoff (SWE)
1932 J.Richthoff (SWE)
1936 K.Palusalu (EST)
1948 G.Bobis (HUN)
1952 A.Mekokishvili (USSR)
1956 H.Kaplan (TUR)
1960 W.Dietrich (GER)
1964 A.Ivanitsky (USSR)
1968 A.Medved (USSR)
1972 I.Yarygin (USSR)
1976 I.Yarygin (USSR)
1980 I.Mate (YUG)
1984 L.Banach (USA)
1988 V.Puscascu (ROM)

Super-heavyweight
1972 A.Medved (USSR
1976 S.Andiev (USSR)
1980 S.Andiev (USSR)
1984 B.Baumgartner (USA)
1988 D.Gobedzhishvili (USSR)

Most Gold Medals:
3 Alexsandr Medved

Winners Greco-Roman

Light-flyweight
1972 G.Berceanu (ROM)
1976 A.Sjumakov (USSR)
1980 Z.Ushkempirov (USSR)
1984 V.Maenza (ITA)
1988 V.Maenza (ITA)

Flyweight
1948 P.Lombardi (ITA)
1952 B.Gurevich (USSR)
1956 N.Solovyov (USSR)
1960 D.Pirulescu (ROM)
1964 T.Hanahara (JAP)
1968 P.Kirov (BUL)
1972 P.Kirov (BUL)
1976 V.Konstantinov (USSR)
1980 V.Blagidze (USSR)
1984 A.Miyahara (JAP)
1988 J.Ronningen (NOR)

Bantamweight
1924 E.Putsep (EST)
1928 K.Leucht (GER)
1932 J.Brendel (GER)
1936 M.Lorincz (HUN)
1948 K.Pettersen (SWE)
1952 I.Hodos (HUN)
1956 K.Vyrupayev (USSR)
1960 O.Karavayev (USSR)
1964 M.Ichiguchi (JAP)
1968 J.Varga (HUN)
1972 R.Kazakov (USSR)
1976 P.Ukkola (FIN)
1980 S.Serikov (USSR)
1984 P.Passarelli (FRG)
1988 A.Sike (HUN)

Featherweight
1912 K.Koskelo (FIN)
1920 O.Friman (FIN)
1924 K.Anttila (FIN)
1928 V.Vali (EST)
1932 G.Gozzi (ITA)
1936 Y.Erkan (TUR)
1948 M.Oktav (TUR)
1952 Y.Punkin (USSR)
1956 R.Makinen (FIN)
1960 M.Sille (TUR)
1964 I.Polyak (HUN)
1968 R.Rurua (USSR)
1972 G.Markov (BUL)
1976 K.Lipien (POL)
1980 S.Migiakis (GRE)
1984 Weon-Kee Kim (SKO)
1988 K.Madjidov (USSR)

Lightweight
1906 R.Watzl (AUT)
1908 E.Porro (ITA)
1912 E.Ware (FIN)
1920 E.Ware (FIN)
1924 O.Friman (FIN)
1928 L.Keresztes (HUN)
1932 E.Malmberg (SWE)
1936 L.Koskela (FIN)
1948 G.Freij (SWE)
1952 S.Safin (USSR)
1956 K.Lehtonen (FIN)
1960 A.Koridze (USSR)
1964 K.Ayvaz (TUR)
1968 M.Mumemura (JAP)
1972 S.Khisamutdinov (USSR)
1976 S.Nalbandyan (USSR)
1980 S.Rusu (ROM)
1984 V.Lisjak (YUG)
1988 L.Dzhulfalakyan (USSR)

Welterweight
1932 I.Johansson (SWE)
1936 R.Svedberg (SWE)
1948 G.Andersson (SWE)
1952 M.Szilvasi (HUN)
1956 M.Bayrak (TUR)
1960 M.Bayrak (TUR)
1964 A.Kolesov (USSR)
1968 R.Vesper (GDR)
1970 V.Macha (TCH)
1976 A.Bykov (USSR)
1980 F.Kocsis (HUN)
1984 J.Salomaki (FIN)
1988 K.Young-Nam (SKO)

Middleweight
1906 V.Weckman (FIN)
1908 F.Martensson (FIN)
1912 C.Johansson (SWE)
1920 C.Westergren (SWE)
1924 E.Westerlund (FIN)
1928 V.Kokkinen (FIN)
1932 V.Kokkinen (FIN)
1936 I.Johansson (SWE)
1948 A.Gronberg (SWE)
1952 A.Gronberg (SWE)
1956 G.Kartoziya (USSR)
1960 D.Dobrev (BUL)
1964 B.Simic (YUG)
1968 L.Metz (GDR)
1972 C.Hegedus (HUN)
1976 M.Petkovic (YUG)
1980 G.Korban (USSR)
1984 I.Draica (ROM)
1988 M.Mamiachvili (USSR)

Light-heavyweight
1908 V.Weckman (FIN)
1912 No winner declared
1920 C.Johansson (SWE)
1924 C.Westergren (SWE)
1928 I.Moustafa (EGY)
1932 R.Svensson (SWE)
1936 A.Cadier (SWE)
1948 K -E.Nilsson (SWE)
1952 K.Grondahl (FIN)
1956 V.Nikolayev (USSR)
1960 T.Kis (TUR)
1964 B.Radev (BUL)
1968 B.Radev (BUL)
1972 V.Rezantsev (USSR)
1976 V.Resantsev (USSR)
1980 N.Nottny (HUN)
1984 S.Fraser (USA)
1988 A.Komchev (BUL)

Heavyweight
1896 C.Schuhmann (GER)
1908 R.Weisz (HUN)
1912 Y.Saarela (FIN)
1920 A.Lindfors (FIN)
1924 H.Deglane (FRA)
1928 R.Svensson (SWE)
1932 C.Westergren (SWE)
1936 K.Palusalu (EST)
1948 A.Kirecci (TUR)
1952 J.Kotkas (USSR)
1956 A.Parfenov (USSR)
1960 I.Bogdan (USSR)
1964 I.Kozma (HUN)
1968 I.Kozma (HUN)
1972 N.Martinescu (ROM)
1976 N.Bolboshin (USSR)
1980 G.Raikov (BUL)
1984 V.Andrei (ROM)
1988 A.Wronski (POL)

Super-heavyweight
1972 A.Roschin (USSR)
1976 A.Kolchinsky (USSR)
1980 A.Kolchinsky (USSR)
1984 J.Blatnick (USA)
1988 A.Kareline (USSR)

Most Gold Medals
3 Carl Westergren

There have been many cases of relatives winning Olympic medals in wrestling events but the performance of the Beloglazov twins of Russia at the 1980 Games must rank as one of the great feats in Olympic history. Anatoly won the flyweight freestyle gold medal, just over 24 hours later, his twin Sergey won the bantamweight title.

The first known yacht race was in 1661 when Charles II challenged the Duke of York to a race on the River Thames. The sport became popular towards the end of the 18th century, 150 years after the formation of the world's first yacht club, at Cork, Ireland.

AMERICA'S CUP

One of the most famous of all sporting trophies, the Cup was donated by the Royal Yacht Squadron for a race around the Isle of Wight in 1851. The American schooner America won the race and took the trophy to the United States. The New York Yacht club then offered it as a challenge trophy but, despite many efforts, the Cup stayed in American hands until 1983 when it became Australian property, until the United States won it back in 1987.

Winners:

1870 Magic	1930 Enterprise
1871 Columbia	1934 Rainbow
1871 Sappho	1937 Ranger
1876 Madeleine	1958 Columbia
1881 Mischief	1962 Weatherly
1885 Puritan	1964 Constellation
1886 Mayflower	1967 Intrepid
1887 Volunteer	1970 Intrepid
1893 Vigilant	1974 Courageous
1895 Defender	1977 Courageous
1899 Columbia	1980 Freedom
1901 Columbia	1983 Australia II
1903 Reliance	1987 Stars & Stripes
1920 Resolutet	1988 Stars & Stripes

ADMIRAL'S CUP

The Royal Ocean Racing Club donated the trophy in 1957 to encourage yachtsmen from abroad to race in English waters. A series of races in the English Channel, at Cowes, and around Fastnet constitute the competition for the coveted trophy.

Winners:

1957 Great Britain	1973 West Germany
1959 Great Britain	1975 Great Britain
1961 United States	1977 Great Britain
1963 Great Britain	1979 Australia
1965 Great Britain	1981 Great Britain
1967 Australia	1983 West Germany
1969 United States	1985 West Germany
1971 Great Britain	1987 New Zealand

Most Wins:
8 Great Britain

OLYMPIC GAMES

Yachting was included in the second Olympics, in 1900, but should have been in the first Games four years earlier bad weather caused the abandonment of the races. Many different classes have been introduced since 1900 and the following results relate to the eight classes that made up the 1988 competition.

Winners:

Soling Class
1972 United States
1976 Denmark
1980 Denmark
1984 United States
1988 East Germany

Flying Dutchman Class
1956 P.Mander/J.Cropp (NZ)
1960 P.Lunde, jnr/B.Bergvall (NOR)
1964 H.Pedersen/E.Wells (NZ)
1968 R.Pattisson/I.Macdonald Smith (GB)
1972 R.Pattisson/C.Davies (GB)
1976 J.Diesch/E.Diesch (FRG)
1980 A.Abascal/M.Noguer (SPA)
1984 J.McKee/C.Buchan (USA)
1988 T.Bojsen-Moeller/C.Gronborg (DEN)

International Star Class
1932 G.Gray/A.Libano, jnr (USA)
1936 P.Bischoff/H -J.Weise (GER)
1948 H.Smart/P.Smart (USA)
1952 A.Straulino/N.Rode (ITA)
1956 H.Williams/L.Lowe (USA)
1960 T.Pinegin/F.Shutkov (USSR)
1964 D.Knowles/C.Cooke (BAH)
1968 L.North/P.Barrett (USA)
1972 D.Forbes/J.Anderson (AUS)
1976 Not held
1980 V.Mankin/A.Muzychenko (USSR)
1984 W.Buchan/S. Erickson (USA)
1988 M.McIntyre/B.Vaile (GB)

Finn Class
1920 F.Hin/J.Hin (HOL)
1920 F.A. Richards/T. Hedburg (GB)
1924 L.Huybrechts (BEL)
1928 S.Thorell (SWE)
1932 J.Lebrun (FRA)
1936 D.Kagchelland (HOL)
1948 P.Elvstrom (DEN)
1952 P.Elvstrom (DEN)
1956 P.Elvstrom (DEN)
1960 P.Elvstrom (DEN)
1964 W.Kuhweide (GER)
1968 V.Mankin (USSR)
1972 S.Maury (FRA)
1976 J.Schumann (GDR)
1980 E.Rechardt (FIN)
1984 R.Coults (NZ)
1988 J -L. Doreste (SPA)

International 470 Class
1976 F.Hubner/H.Bode (FRG)
1980 M.Soares/E.Penido (BRA)
1984 L.Doreste/R.Molina (SPA)
1988 T.Peponnet/L.Pilot (FRA)

International Tornado Class
1976 R.White/J.Osborn (GB)
1980 A.Welter/L.Bjorkstrom (BRA)
1984 R.Sellers/C.Timms (NZ)
1988 J -Y. Le Deroff/N.Henard (FRA)

Windgliding Class
1984 S.Van Den Berg (HOL)
1988 B.Kendall (NZ)

Women's 470
1988 A.Jolley/L.Jewell (USA)

Most Individual Gold Medals:
4 Paul Elvstrom

Legendary Danish yachtsman Paul Elvstrom took part in his seventh Olympic Games at Los Angeles in 1984. Competing in the Tornado class he was crewed by his daughter Trine, who was not even born when Paul won the 6th, and last of his four Olympic gold medals, in 1960.

The longest yacht race is the Whitbread Round-the-World race held every four years since 1973. Its distance is more than 26,000 nautical miles. The race starts and finishes at Portsmouth.

SPORT	EVENT	DATE	WINNER

SPORT	EVENT	DATE	WINNER

SPORT	EVENT	DATE	WINNER
_____	_____	_____	_____
_____	_____	_____	_____
_____	_____	_____	_____
_____	_____	_____	_____
_____	_____	_____	_____
_____	_____	_____	_____
_____	_____	_____	_____
_____	_____	_____	_____
_____	_____	_____	_____
_____	_____	_____	_____
_____	_____	_____	_____
_____	_____	_____	_____
_____	_____	_____	_____
_____	_____	_____	_____
_____	_____	_____	_____
_____	_____	_____	_____
_____	_____	_____	_____

SPORT	EVENT	DATE	WINNER

SPORT	EVENT	DATE	WINNER

SPORT	EVENT	DATE	WINNER

SPORT	EVENT	DATE	WINNER